THE ORIGINS OF
NONLIBERAL
CAPITALISM

A volume in the series

Cornell Studies in Political Economy

EDITED BY PETER J. KATZENSTEIN

A full list of titles in the series appears at the end of the book.

THE ORIGINS OF NONLIBERAL CAPITALISM

Germany and Japan In Comparison

EDITED BY

Wolfgang Streeck

and

Kozo Yamamura

Cornell University Press

ITHACA AND LONDON

First published 2001 by Cornell University Press

Printed in the United States of America

Library of Congress Cataloging-in-Publication Data

The origins of nonliberal capitalism : Germany and Japan in comparison /
edited by Wolfgang Streeck and Kozo Yamamura.
     p. cm. — (Cornell studies in political economy)
   Includes bibliographical references and index.
   ISBN 0-8014-3917-5 (cloth : alk. paper)
    1. Capitalism—Germany. 2. Germany—Economic policy. 3.
Capitalism—Japan. 4. Japan—Economic policy. I. Streeck, Wolfgang.
II. Yamamura, Kozo. III. Series.
  HC286.8 .O76 2002
  330.12'2'0943—dc21 2001003219

Cloth printing   10 9 8 7 6 5 4 3 2 1

Contents

Tables and Figures

Tables

Figures

Contributors

GREGORY JACKSON is research fellow at the Max-Planck-Institut für Gesellschaftsforschung in Köln, Germany. He is author of several publications on comparative corporate governance, including *The Public Interest and the Corporation in Britain and Germany* (coauthor) (Anglo-German Foundation, 2000).

IKUO KUME is a professor on the Faculty of Law at Kobe University. His publications include: *Disparaged Success: Labor Politics in Postwar Japan* (Cornell University Press, 1998); *Nihongata rōshikankei no seikō* (Yūhikaku, 1998); and "Institutionalizing Post-War Japanese Political Economy: Industrial Policy Revisited," in *State Capacity in East Asia: China, Taiwan, Vietnam, and Japan,* ed. Kjeld Erik Brodsgaard and Susan Young (Oxford University Press, 2000).

GERHARD LEHMBRUCH is professor emeritus of political science at the Universität Konstanz, Germany. He has published extensively on German politics (most recently, *Parteienwettbewerb im Bundesstaat: Regelsysteme und Spannungslagen im politischen System der Bundesrepublik Deutschland* [Westdeutscher Verlag, 3d ed. 2000]), comparative politics, and comparative political economy, and has coedited (with Philippe Schmitter) *Trends toward Corporatist Intermediation* (Sage, 1979) and *Patterns of Corporatist Policy-Making* (Sage, 1982).

PHILIP MANOW is a researcher at the Universität Konstanz, Department of Politics and Management. Together with Bernhard Ebbinghaus, he is currently coediting a volume entitled *Comparing Welfare Capitalism: Social Policy and Political Economy in Europe, Japan, and the USA* (Routledge, 2001) and writing a book on the role of the Bismarckian welfare state in the German political economy. Recent publications include: "Adapting the Welfare State: The Case of Health Care Reform in Britain, Germany and the United States," *Comparative Political Studies* (with Susan Giaimo, 2000); "Adjusting Badly: The German Welfare State, Structural Change, and the Open Economy," in *From Vulnerability to Competitiveness: Welfare and Work in the Open Economy,* ed. Fritz W. Scharpf and Vivian Schmidt (with Eric Seils) (Oxford University Press, 2000); and "The Comparative Institutional Advantages of Welfare State Regimes and New Coalitions in Welfare State Reforms," in *The New Politics of the Welfare State,* ed. Paul Pierson (Oxford University Press, 2000).

WOLFGANG STREECK is director of the Max-Planck-Institut für Gesellschafts-forschung in Köln, Germany. From 1988 to 1995 he was professor of sociology and industrial relations at the University of Wisconsin-Madison. His publications include: *The Political Economy of Modern Capitalism: Mapping Convergence and Diversity* (with Colin Crouch) (Sage, 1997); *Governance in the European Union* (with Gary Marks, Fritz W. Scharpf, and Philippe C. Schmitter) (Sage, 1996); *Work Councils: Consultation, Representation, and Cooperation in Industrial Relations* (with Joel Rogers) (University of Chicago Press, 1995); *Governing Capitalist Economies: Performance and Control of Economic Sectors* (with Rogers Hollingsworth and Philippe C. Schmitter) (Oxford University Press, 1994); and *Social Institutions and Economic Performance: Studies in Industrial Relations in Advanced Capitalist Economies* (Sage, 1992).

KATHLEEN THELEN is associate professor of political science at Northwestern University. Her publications include *Union of Parts: Labor Politics in Postwar Germany* (Cornell University Press, 1991) and *Structuring Politics: Historical Institutionalism in Comparative Politics* (coeditor) (Cambridge University Press, 1992), as well as articles in, among others, *World Politics, Comparative Politics, Politics and Society,* and *The Annual Review of Political Science.*

SIGURT VITOLS is research fellow at the Wissenschaftszentrum Berlin für Sozialforschung. Recent publications include: "Are German Banks Different?" *Small Business Economics* (1998) and "German Industrial Policy: An Overview," *Industry and Innovation* (1997).

KOZO YAMAMURA is Job and Gertrud Tamaki Professor of Japanese Studies, Professor of East Asian Studies, and Adjunct Professor of Economics and International Business at the University of Washington. He is author and editor of numerous volumes, including: *A Vision of New Liberalism? Critical Essays on Murakami's Anticlassical Analysis* (coeditor) (Stanford University Press, 1997); *The Economic Emergence of Modern Japan* (editor) (Cambridge University Press, 1997); *Asia in Japan's Embrace: Building a Regional Production Alliance* (with Walter Hatch) (Cambridge University Press, 1996); Yasusuke Murakami, *An Anticlassical Political Economic*

Analysis (Stanford University Press, 1996) (translation, adaption, and introduction); *The Japanese Civil Service and Economic Development* (coeditor) (Oxford University Press, 1995); and *The Political Economy of Japan*, Vol. 1: *The Domestic Transformation* (coeditor) (Stanford University Press, 1987).

Preface

This book is one of two volumes that resulted from a three-year research project that began when we first met at a conference in Hawaii in September 1995. At the conference, which was on land-use regimes in different types of market economies, we presented background papers on the economic institutions of German and Japanese capitalism.[1] In subsequent discussions—mostly over meals and during coffee breaks—we became fascinated with the many similarities between the two capitalisms, the no less intriguing differences between them, and the differences between the two and Anglo-American "standard capitalism." While the research questions and policy problems associated with these seemed frighteningly complex, they also seemed of enormous significance and attraction.

Hawaii is a place that makes the impossible appear feasible. There obviously was no simple way to investigate the social origins, the economic consequences, and the political prospects of German and Japanese capitalism. Any undertaking as daunting as this would require the combined effort of scholars from a variety of disciplines and with very different research experiences. Nevertheless, it was resolved on the last evening of the conference—optimism squelching caution as we watched the sun sink from the pink and blue sky over the North Shore of Oahu into the turquoise ocean beyond Turtle Bay—to try organizing a planning workshop in the spring of the subsequent year. At the time, Streeck had just moved from the University of Wisconsin-Madison to the Max-Planck-Institut für Gesellschaftsforschung in Köln, Germany, and this was where the workshop took place

---

1. The conference proceedings are now published in Cho and Kim 1998.

in June 1996. Participants were Ronald Dore (London School of Economics), Gregory Jackson (then still at Columbia University), Peter Katzenstein (Cornell University), Herbert Kitschelt (Duke University), Stephen Krasner (Stanford University), Gerhard Lehmbruch (Universität Konstanz), Philip Manow (Max-Planck-Institut), and T.J. Pempel (University of Washington Seattle).

The mid-1990s were a time when the economic fortunes of Germany and Japan had radically deteriorated compared to the previous decade and to a newly prosperous United States. The two economies, which had for so long been extremely successful in international competition, seemed to be finding it unexpectedly and increasingly difficult to cope with accelerating internationalization and the "borderlessness" of economies of the post–cold war world order. This was a development few had anticipated. In the 1980s, the obvious question for a comparative study of the German and Japanese political economies would have been the reasons for their apparent superiority over Anglo-American capitalism. In fact, Wolfgang Streeck had for some time talked with Ronald Dore about a joint study on exactly this topic—a project that was preempted not only by Michel Albert's *Capitalism vs. Capitalism* (1993) and other contingent events, but also by the empirical reality of German and Japanese crisis accompanied by a robust return of American economic hegemony. And Kozo Yamamura, who had coauthored a book with Walter Hatch, *Asia in Japan's Embrace: Building a Regional Production Alliance* (1996), was finding many of the book's central arguments, such as Japan "exporting" its efficiency-promoting close interfirm relationships (*keiretsu*) to Asia and the resilience of government-business and management-labor cooperation, less and less persuasive in the second half of the 1990s.

To many, the crisis of the 1990s was the result of a mismatch between the German and Japanese economic institutions and the demands of a changed economic and political environment. Both inside and outside the two countries, there was a growing belief that their socially embedded economic institutions had turned from assets into liabilities for future performance. Pressures were mounting for German and Japanese capitalism to restructure so as to fit better with a much less regulated international political economy. Indeed, there were strong tendencies in both countries for far-reaching institutional change in the direction of a less-regulated, Anglo-American version of capitalist economy—the same sort of institutional arrangement that a short time earlier had appeared hopelessly in decline. Suddenly, the main question was whether Germany and Japan, confronted with the political and economic challenges of economic internationalization, had to give up their distinctive institutions and the specific competitive advantages these seemed to have produced in the past, or whether they would be able to adapt and retain such institutions and restore their economic competitiveness without losing their social cohesion.

The 1996 planning workshop concluded that the future-oriented perspective of the envisaged project required extensive opportunities for discussion among a diverse group of scholars knowledgeable in political economy, as well as detailed new research on a variety of subjects. A first conference was held in April 1997 at the University of Washington in Seattle, where participants presented work-in-progress and research proposals for comparative studies on the German and Japanese political economies. In addition to the editors and the participants in the planning workshop, paper-givers included Robert Boyer, John Haley, Hiroshi Iyori, Fumio Kodama, Ikuo Kume, Mikio Matsui, Yukio Noguchi, Tsutomu Tanaka, Kathleen Thelen, Sigurt Vitols, and Steven Vogel. Two more conferences followed, one in January 1998 at the Japanisch-Deutsches Zentrum Berlin (JDZB), and another in June 1999 in the new building of the Max-Planck-Institut in Köln. On both occasions the group was joined by other authors of comparative research on Germany and Japan who contributed papers, including Heidi Gottfried, Erica Gould, Ulrich Jürgens, the late Frieder Naschold, and Jacqueline O'Reilly. A companion collection to the current edited volume is in preparation that will include project contributions focusing on the future of German and Japanese "nationally embedded" capitalism in a global economy.

During the long collective effort to assess the prospects of German and Japanese capitalism and its nationally distinctive institutions, we became keenly and increasingly aware that the institutional analyses the group relied upon would be greatly improved by a better understanding of the historical background of the German and Japanese "models" of the 1970s. How had these been assembled in the past? What had made their various elements cohere, and what had made for their distinctiveness? How had they changed? What was the role of culture and politics, of path-dependent evolution, and of external shocks? How had markets fit in, and how had the two countries in the past dealt with pressures for liberalization? Early on, the group discovered that some of the conference papers had the potential, if properly elaborated, of contributing new insights on these issues. Moreover, the fledgling historical papers that could be discerned among the many early project manuscripts happened to address the areas of corporate governance, financial markets, training, and social security—issues clearly fundamental to the construction and identification of "models of capitalism." When the editors succeeded in convincing the authors that only a minor effort was required to turn their initial pieces into publishable manuscripts, the idea of an "origins volume" to supplement the "forward-looking" volume took root.

Thus, what was originally believed to be no more than a side activity, mainly if not exclusively to inform and enlighten other project participants, slowly turned into a research project in its own right. As always in such an undertaking, everything took longer than expected. A series of workshops in Köln brought together authors from the present volume for intensive discussions of successive drafts. The reader will have to judge whether the product is worth the effort. But to entice potential readers, we may be allowed to point to the truly interdisciplinary character of a book that undertakes to combine insights from history, economics, sociology, and political science. Indeed, we feel entitled to state that we know of no other study looking in such detail and by major policy sectors at the historical origins of the distinctive German and Japanese institutions of economic governance and their integration into cohesive national "models of capitalism."

While monographs may sometimes be preferable to collected volumes, we think it obvious that a book like the present one could not have been written by any single author, given the high demands it makes on empirical knowledge of the history of economic governance in two countries on which, in spite of many politically and systematically important parallels, very little directly comparative research exists. And finally, while the book will be useful to specialists in, say, corporate governance or the study of the welfare state, it also shows the potential of economic sociology in general, as well as of an approach to economic history that aims at systematic understanding and not just historical description.

In discharging our debt of gratitude to those who have helped us make this volume possible, we feel we should first mention the authors of the five chapters—Gerhard Lehmbruch, Philip Manow, Gregory Jackson, Sigurt Vitols, Kathleen Thelen, and Ikuo Kume—who have contributed to the Germany-Japan project far beyond the call of duty by agreeing to produce yet another chapter in addition to the one they were preparing for the other, "forward-looking" volume. We are also much obliged to those who participated in our various conferences and drew our attention and that of the authors to important questions and answers. This includes a number of participants who for different reasons did not contribute research papers but acted as discussants, thereby enriching our thinking and helping our project broaden its perspective. Among them are Masahiko Aoki, Harald Baum, Angelika Ernst, Susan Hanley, Anke Hassel, Kenji Hirashima, Thierry Ribault, Michael Shalev, Karen Shire, Akira Takenaka, and Hajo Weber.

Of course, had it not been for the generous and sustained support of the Tamaki Foundation in Seattle, nobody could ever have come to any of our conferences as we would not have been able to fund them. And had it not been for Wolfgang Brenn and the Japanisch-Deutsches Zentrum Berlin, we would have had to do without a memorable conference in the new German capital. This conference included a public session on the future of the German and Japanese models. Among those attending were Klaus Murmann, former president of the German Employers' Confederation (BDA), Kazuo Nukazawa (Keidanren), Noriko Hama (Mitsubishi Research Institute, London), Rainer Hank (Frankfurter Allgemeine Zeitung), Hans-Jürgen Krupp (Landeszentralbank Hamburg), Tsutomo Tanaka (Chuo University, Tokyo), and Norbert Walter (Deutsche Bank Research). It also included a visit to a Japanese restaurant which provided conference participants with unexpected insights into the transformation potential of Japanese cuisine abroad.

Our most heartfelt appreciation, however, goes to Martha Walsh in Seattle and Gregory Jackson in Köln. Martha transformed Germanic, Japanese, and bad English into good English while issuing stern administrative guidance to authors reminding them to respect logical consistency, accuracy of facts, and accepted translation and uses of terms. And Greg, in addition to contributing a chapter to each of the two volumes and working on his dissertation, held it all together by keeping track of an unending stream of manuscripts, conference participants, and visitors. We have no doubt that without their help, we would never have been able to bring this project to a good end.

WOLFGANG STREECK
KOZO YAMAMURA

Köln and Seattle, April 2000

THE ORIGINS OF
NONLIBERAL
CAPITALISM

Introduction: Explorations into the Origins of Nonliberal Capitalism in Germany and Japan

Wolfgang Streeck

The ascendancy of the German and Japanese economies in the 1980s and the apparently inexorable decline of Britain and the United States gave rise to renewed interest in institutional differences between capitalist national economies and their potential impact on economic competitiveness. This interest did not abate when in the 1990s the economic fortunes were reversed and the United States in particular came to be held up by many as a model for Germany and Japan to emulate. At the center of the discussion on what came to be known as the diversity of capitalism was, and continues to be, a range of apparent similarities between the political economies of countries such as Germany and Japan that seem to set them apart from Anglo-American "normal capitalism" (Crouch and Streeck 1997). What exactly these differences are, and how they are best conceptualized, is very much part of the debate. There has by and large been agreement that the German and Japanese economies are in a number of respects more socially and politically regulated, and in this sense less liberal, than their Anglo-American counterparts. As long as their superior performance lasted, different theories were offered to explain what in the eyes of most economists was a puzzling paradox: societies that had turned over their economies to free markets seemed less economically successful than more regulated economies. In the latter half of the 1990s, to the contrary, the same or other differences were drawn upon to account for what was seen as a relative decline of the German and Japanese economies and for justifying political programs to rebuild them in the image of, especially, the United States.

Exactly which differences between Japan and Germany on the one hand

and Anglo-America on the other are relevant for capitalist diversity is not easy to say a priori; there seems to be no theory readily mobilized for the purpose. Michel Albert (1993), in his nontechnical but sometimes highly sophisticated treatment, essentially avoids the issue by defining the opposition to Britain and the United States in the battle of "capitalisme contre capitalisme" as "capitalisme Rhénan"—capitalism of the Rhineland—locating not only Stockholm but also Tokyo on the shores of the Rhine. But capitalist diversity is, of course, not a matter of economic geography, or at least not mainly. For Albert and many others writing in the same vein, what sets aside the economic "Rhineland" from the world of the Thames and the Hudson is an apparent capacity to mobilize noneconomic social ties, noncompetitive cooperation, collective obligations, and moral commitments in support of economic efficiency, while in differently organized societies rational individualism causes high transaction costs that in the end make everyone less well off than they might be. Markets, the message is, have costs, and potentially high ones, especially to the extent that they may erode moral and institutional infrastructures that are essential for an efficient economy. It is therefore wise, even from an economic point of view, to limit their reach and keep them under social control, which is exactly what the successful "Rhineland" economies are said to have managed to do.

Conceptually, then, the premise and starting point of the literature on different "models of capitalism" is that national societies differ importantly with respect to how they organize their economies, and indeed the extent to which they do so. Although some societies prefer to leave as many economic outcomes to the free play of market forces as possible, in others markets are more socially or institutionally embedded. Implicitly or explicitly, the concept of embeddedness runs through most or all of the current work on capitalist diversity (Granovetter 1985; Hollingsworth and Boyer 1997; Shonfield 1965). For a definition that a majority of authors would probably accept, an economy is socially embedded insofar as the transactions by which it is made up either are also supposed to serve other than economic purposes (in other words, are constrained by noneconomic objectives, such as social cohesion or national defense) or are supported by noneconomic social ties (that is, are facilitated by particularistic relations such as tribalism or paternalism or by enforceable social obligations that engender trust among economic actors). Social constraints and opportunities in this sense, typically enforced by social institutions, define the legitimate place and the possible range of market transactions and markets in the economy-*cum*-society in which they take place. By circumscribing and thereby limiting the role of markets, they typically "distort" them, for example by shielding desirable social conditions from market fluctuations or ensuring that such conditions result even if free markets would produce different outcomes.

As long as the decline in the competitiveness of Anglo-American capitalism lasted, embeddedness in the German and Japanese economies was seen as providing for an artificial deceleration in the circulation of the two main production factors, capital and labor, producing a pattern of long-term employment as well as patient investment (Aoki 1994). Less "liquidity" in factor markets, less frequent "exit," and thus in an important sense less market, gave rise to long-term commitments, which in turn allowed for extended mutuality between capital and labor and for negotiated relations between identifiable "social partners," as distinguished from spot-market-type relations between anonymous "market forces." It was essentially with respect to both labor and capital that the alleged economic virtues of embedded—i.e., institutionally constrained as well as facilitated—market relations were believed to arise. For example, committed labor and patient capital were seen as guaranteeing the stability of the firm as an organization, together underwriting long-term organization building and helping actors develop a shared capital of loyalty and trust that can serve as a social infrastructure of cooperation. The benefits of this were thought to include not just social stability but also dynamic economic efficiencies deriving from what may be called "economies of cooperation" ("goodwill," "X-efficiency") at company and societal levels (Dore 1987; Leibenstein 1976).

Clearly it was recognized that the ways markets were embedded in the two countries differed, and in some respects considerably. Various conceptual schemes were proposed to highlight the differences between variants of embedded capitalism, for example, the distinction between Japanese developmentalism, geared toward "catching up" with the West to achieve international status and security, and German postwar needs for national reconstruction and unity as driving concerns behind the social control of markets. Similarly, in institutional analyses, the functional equivalence was often emphasized between the Japanese enterprise community on the one hand, with patient capital obliged to accept paternalistic responsibility for workforces in the name of national advance and solidarity, and society-wide corporatist class compromise on the other. Economically, the Japanese pattern of flexible mass production was contrasted to German diversified quality production, which was regarded as the outcome of capital being impelled by institutional constraints to cooperate in industrial upgrading to a "high-road" production pattern (Streeck 1991). Socially and politically, Japanese segmentalism and dualism were opposed to German solidarism and social democracy. Other such distinctions can be added and are encountered throughout the rest of this volume.

By the mid-1990s at the latest, the competitive fortunes of the two nationally embedded capitalisms of Germany and Japan had dramatically declined. A sizable literature describes that decline and discusses its reasons. Regardless of whether the resurgence of the liberal political economy, of the United States in particular, was due to technological, international, or endogenous developments, the debate on Germany and Japan and their special trajectories (*Sonderwege*) of capitalist development turned overwhelmingly toward pressures for convergence on American "best practice," alleging a compelling need for the two deviant capitalisms to liberalize and disembed economic transactions formerly constrained and facilitated by a national institutional framework.

Pressures for liberalization may take many forms, and they may operate differently on different countries due to different locations in the international system or different institutional makeups (see Streeck and Yamamura forthcoming). In part these pressures may originate in the desire of trading partners for countries to "open up" their markets—of the United States in the case of Japan, of the European Union in the case of Germany. Or they may be endogenous, *pace* the current "globalization" rhetoric, for example, when the costs of subsidizing social cohesion or "buffering" markets (through subsidized interest rates, industrial policy, labor market policy, the use of social insurance to retire excess labor) become excessive, or generally when allocative inefficiencies outweigh dynamic efficiencies. But it may also be the case that the patience of capital may erode in the face of growing opportunities for migrating out of the ambit of national regulation and taking advantage of the greener, or at least easier-to-graze, pastures of less obligational economic systems.

At the turn of the century, the survival of nonliberal models of capitalism that attempt to infuse social obligations in economic transactions is seen by many as doubtful, ironically only a very short time after their heyday in the 1980s when everyone urged the Americans and the British to "learn from Japan" and study "Model Germany." This volume does not directly address the question of whether the German and Japanese political economies may have to converge on a less embedded and less institutionally regulated economic regime. Instead it tries to contribute to the debate about the potential disappearance, restructuring, evolution, or reconstitution of nonliberal capitalism in Germany and Japan by looking at its historical origins, especially from three perspectives:

1. how nonliberal capitalism came about in the first place, what exactly were the liberal alternatives that had to be put aside, or suppressed, for it to emerge and survive over time, and how this was achieved;
2. how the differences between nonliberal capitalism in Japan and Germany are to be accounted for, and what this says about the institutional repertoire of nationally embedded capitalism and, by implication, its variability in changing conditions; and

3. what makes for the internal coherence, or consistency, of national models of an embedded capitalist economy, given that institutional change is not normally driven by a societal master plan but proceeds through highly specific, "sectoralized" and partial responses to emergent contingencies?

The next section of this chapter addresses a number of conceptual issues, following which the five essays that make up the body of this volume are briefly introduced, summarized, and related to each other. Finally, an attempt is made to extract from the material a few general observations on the dynamics of change in nonliberal capitalism and what these may imply for the future of German and Japanese versions of a capitalist economy.

Comparing Capitalisms

This book investigates the origin of some of the social institutions that have constrained the spread of free markets within the capitalist economies of Germany and Japan while providing them with alternative mechanisms of economic governance. The vast differences between the two countries are recognized, and indeed are analyzed in some detail, on the principle that each social configuration is a "historical individual" that must ultimately be understood on its own terms. At the same time, important as the differences between Germany and Japan may be, from the perspective of this book they represent differences within a family of capitalist systems we refer to as "nonliberal." Nonliberal capitalism we distinguish from liberal, or standard, capitalism—a construct we use as a backdrop for our analysis of Germany and Japan. Although liberal capitalism is no more than an ideal type, we believe a close empirical representation is Anglo-American, and especially American, capitalism. As a result, although the chapters of the book, with one exception, look at Germany and Japan only, the United Kingdom and the United States are always also present in the background, if only implicitly and represented mostly by stylized facts.

"Nonliberal" as an Alternative to "Liberal Capitalism"

Economic liberalism sets economic transactions free from obligations other than to serve the interests of those immediately involved; it also tends to be suspicious of collective support of economic action as it may breed collusion and monopoly. Obviously, liberalism is a matter of degree and there can be no economies that are completely liberal. If in this volume we refer to the German and Japanese political economies as "nonliberal," we emphasize the fact that in both countries, regimes of economic governance emerged that up to this day place relatively little trust in free-market *laissez-faire*. Instead they rely on various forms of hierarchical and organizational coordination that sometimes require heavy injections of public authority, with vertical control or horizontal collective bargaining often overriding contractual exchanges as entered into by private agents on their own volition, discretion, and calculation.

Nonliberal defines what it denotes with reference to what it is *not,* and we feel that our choice of a negative rather than a positive term requires justification. Concepts such as "embedded," "organized," and "institutionalized" capitalism would have offered themselves for a variety of reasons, and indeed they and others are sometimes used by the authors of the individual chapters. They might, however, have given rise to the objection that all economic systems, including liberal capitalism, are in some way embedded, organized, and institutionalized in a surrounding society, albeit in different ways. They might also have made it seem as though there were only *two* "models" of capitalism, a liberal one and its positively defined alternative. By *not* using a positive concept to describe both Germany and Japan, we hope to convey that although the two countries' economic regimes are in important respects similar—namely, in that they are *not* liberal—they differ in many ways, very importantly including the ways in which they are not liberal.

Moreover, historically the social and political elites that defined and redefined the German and Japanese economic regimes, as pointed out by Gerhard Lehmbruch in his essay, were often moved by opposition to liberalism more than by any positive image of a preferred economic order. Although this would have suggested antiliberal rather than nonliberal capitalism, since the time of the postwar reorganization of the German and Japanese systems, the political edge against liberalism has been much less acute in the two countries than it was at the end of the nineteenth century.[1]

Implications of the Term "Liberal"

Liberal economies are not unregulated or devoid of institutions; indeed, markets themselves are institutions, and sometimes highly sophisticated ones. But although the institution of the market is to make space for free contracts between self-interested individual actors and secure respect for the substance and the consequences of such contracts, whatever these may be, nonliberal institutions rule out some transactions while promoting oth-

---

1. Given the many terminological uncertainties, the editors decided not to impose a common term on the authors of the chapters, as long as the substantive and theoretical issues behind the terms used were clear.

ers, imposing on economic actors specific terms of trade and requiring their exchanges to result in predetermined outcomes. For the purposes of this volume, therefore, institutionally regulated economic transactions are transactions regulated by institutions *other than markets*—in other words, by market-embedding institutions—notwithstanding the fact that markets typically require regulation to function simply as markets.

Similarly, liberal capitalism, as amply demonstrated by the British and, especially, the American cases, is in the real world far from free of state intervention. In fact, it sometimes depends on the support of a strong state, especially when the tree of economic liberalism, to paraphrase Thomas Jefferson, has to be periodically watered with the blood of revolutionaries of all sorts. But the strong state of liberalism, like the British state under Margaret Thatcher, is fundamentally different from the strong state of nonliberalism in that the former serves to liberate markets and contracts from social constraints and collective obligations whereas the latter tries to do the opposite.

National Models of Capitalism

In most of the literature on the diversity of capitalism, the societies that are assumed to produce different—in particular, differently liberal—versions of a capitalist economy are conceived as national societies, that is, as societies organized by nation-states. The "models of capitalism" that the literature discusses therefore tend to be national models, not regional or local ones. Apart from the competitive attractions of national rankings, the main reason for this seems to be that regulating the behavior of economic agents requires institutions with the capacity to impose enforceable sanctions. Building such institutions is vastly facilitated if recourse can be made to legitimate coercion, in the form of legally binding rules and decisions—backed up, ultimately, by a well-trained police force and, if need be, by an effective army. In the modern world, the capacity to employ legitimate coercion of this sort is vested in the nation-state, not in subnational regions or local communities nor in supranational entities like the European Union. Conceptualizing capitalist diversity in terms of national models assumes that such capacity can make a significant difference with respect to the way and extent in which economic transactions in a capitalist economy are and can be socially embedded. Indeed, as becomes apparent, the evolution of the German and Japanese models of nonliberal capitalism is deeply intertwined with war, dictatorship, and conquest, which at least twice in the twentieth century profoundly reconfigured the economic institutions that constrain and support market transactions in the two countries.

Models of Institutional Change

In a number of contexts, the authors of this book find it helpful to explain specific characteristics of the German and Japanese political
economies with reference to the fact that in both societies, economic liberalism preceded liberal democracy, as a result of which liberal economic institutions were sometimes replaced with alternative, market-constraining or
market-replacing institutions by a strong state. But this is not an endorse-
ment of a sort of "modernization theory" that assumes that economic and
political liberalism should "normally" coevolve smoothly. Nor is it to say
that Britain and the United States were examples of something like a "normal" sort of development that Germany and Japan should have followed
but failed to emulate, embarking instead on a special path that has often
been called a *Sonderweg*. To us, every country's *Weg* (path) is a *Sonderweg*
(and nonliberal capitalism is not simply a deviant form of liberal capitalism). The editors and authors of this book broadly share a political, sequential, constructionist model of institutional change. According to this
model, evolution is in part "path dependent," in part affected by unique exogenous shocks, and in any case replete with accumulating internal inconsistencies that make for a permanent need for reorganization and reconstruction—a need that may not be filled at all or only in ways that could not
have been predicted.

Systemic Dimensions

There is no agreement in the literature on the systemic dimensions of a
"national model of capitalism" or how these can be expected to vary together from one model to the next. Due to the selection of the subjects of
the empirical chapters, in this volume we can show that the nonliberal capitalisms of Germany and Japan resemble each other—and differ from liberal Anglo-American "standard capitalism"—in that they have bank-based
financial systems, regimes of corporate governance that support patient
ownership and discourage "markets for control," industrial citizenship for
workers, long-term employment, productivist and fragmented welfare
states, cooperative industrial relations, nonmarket regimes for workplace-
based training, and relatively egalitarian distribution of wages. Whether
there are other dimensions of economic regimes that are equally or even
more important for capitalist diversity, we cannot really say.[2] Nor can we as-

2. An interesting question is whether family structures also belong to the institutions that
vary between different national models of capitalism. We are not aware of historical work on
the political construction of the family as a socioeconomic institution in Japan and Germany
during the nineteenth and twentieth centuries as part of the evolution of nonliberal capitalism in the two countries. While we were unable to fill what clearly is a gap in the literature in

sume a priori that the properties of German and Japanese capitalism whose historical origins are discussed in the chapters of this book are systemically related—in the sense that for one to be present, the others must be as well.

Of course, whether the empirical evidence supports assumptions of systemic interrelatedness is a question of great historical and theoretical significance that runs through the chapters and this introduction. Below, I speculate, on the basis of our evidence, about the significance and potential sources of what might be called the "intersectoral coherence" of national systems of economic governance.

Aspects of the History of Nonliberal Capitalism in Japan and Germany

Discourses of Conservative Reform

Just as any other social configuration, nonliberal capitalism requires a set of cognitive and normative ideas—in the terminology of the first essay of this volume, a "discourse"—from which to draw both practical orientation and social legitimacy. According to Gerhard Lehmbruch, most societies most of the time simultaneously entertain a number of contradictory discourses that compete for hegemony. But once hegemony is achieved, it may become self-perpetuating, its further evolution taking place in a "path-dependent" fashion. This is because a discourse that has achieved hegemonic status supports the formation of institutions that fit its logic, thereby preventing the development of alternative institutions and ensuring that, when crises arise, the societal repertoire of possible responses is limited to those that are cognitively conceivable, normatively legitimate, and instrumentally feasible inside the dominant discourse.

Lehmbruch's chapter traces the parallel, and to some extent interdependent, evolution of an "embedded capitalism" discourse and its historical rise to hegemony in Germany and Japan. This process began in the late nineteenth century and continued well after World War II. In both countries, moral justifications and technical recipes for social control over markets were sought and eagerly absorbed by state bureaucrats and supplied by scholars-*cum*-social reformers in critical moments of industrialization and nation building—moments when, in the perception of political and administrative elites, economic liberalism appeared as a threat, either to the power and independence of the nation or to domestic economic and social stability. In Japan as well as in Germany, state leaders were eager to form

---

general as well as in this volume in particular, we hope others will feel encouraged by this book to do so.

"discourse coalitions" with social reformers and social scientists, who in Japan were often informed by German traditions (Pyle 1974), embracing conservative reform when liberalism seemed unable to guarantee rapid and uninterrupted economic development and socialism represented a rallying point for a radical opposition poised to exploit the social tensions generated by liberal policies for the overthrow of the existing order.

In Germany, and to a lesser extent in Japan, the ascendancy of nonliberal economic ideas took place against a backdrop of early experiments with liberal solutions. Lehmbruch points out that in Germany, the middle of the nineteenth century was a period of economic liberalism in which the state bureaucracies, especially of Prussia, were strongly influenced by Adam Smith and David Ricardo. Economic liberalism, however, had far preceded political liberalism, which goes a long way to explain why at the end of the century it was possible, and indeed necessary from the point of view of state officials, to turn to more conservative policies. This was all the easier not just because democratization had not yet occurred, but also because Hegelian thought, and, later, Catholic social doctrine and even social democracy, were readily available to justify lasting state activism in economic affairs. As Lehmbruch shows in detail, the new discourse of conservative reform adopted in the financial crash (*Gründerkrise*) of the 1870s soon became structurally entrenched as it became associated with an extensive sharing of public responsibility between the state and organized social groups, ultimately giving rise to the specifically corporatist organizational form of German embedded capitalism.

As seen in other chapters in more detail, a similar development did not take place in Japan, where preindustrial associations and corporations had been suppressed in the course of modernization (in line with liberal ideas), and where their reintegration in the institutional makeup of nationally organized capitalism proved impossible or undesirable. Instead, and regardless of the presence of German corporatist ideas in contemporary debates in Japan, Japanese antiliberalism based itself mostly on a segmentalist pattern of social organization in which the large enterprise was reconstituted as a social community, as opposed to German-style solidarism of nationwide bodies of functional representation. Thus already in the late nineteenth century we can see the beginnings of the differences within the general category of nonliberal capitalism that were to become elaborated in the two countries in subsequent years.

Lehmbruch traces the evolution of German and Japanese "embedded capitalism" discourses, together with the institutional arrangements they supported, in the course of the twentieth century. In particular, he shows how the two world wars reinforced, and at the same time modified, the nonliberal patterns of economic governance on which the two countries had settled. Lehmbruch's account suggests that during and after war, there were likely to be strong incentives for political elites to draw on past institutional experience and accumulated intellectual capital, even and precisely when confronting challenges of an unprecedented sort. Lehmbruch also shows that in Germany and Japan, the embedded capitalism discourse happened to be flexible enough—i.e., sufficiently internally differentiated and externally ambiguous—to adjust to ever-changing contingencies without losing its identity, as embodied among other things in an astonishing personal continuity of the respective discourse coalitions. Not only did the two countries manage to develop a "core discourse" capable of integrating the considerably disparate sectoral discourses taking place in different industries, policy communities, academic schools, and religious groups. They also (in Germany even more than in Japan) proved able to absorb over time important liberal as well as socialist traditions, especially in the German "social market economy" after 1945, in which, although it first originated of all places in the planning apparatus of the Nazi government, not only the liberals but also the Social Democrats eventually found a political home.

Welfare State Particularism

The second essay, by Philip Manow, also emphasizes the essential contribution of bureaucratic elites and conservative reform in the decisive period of industrialization and nation building at the end of the nineteenth century. Looking at the rise of the welfare state in the two countries and its institutional structure and socioeconomic consequences, Manow, like Lehmbruch, locates the origin of nonliberal capitalism in a historical configuration in which industrial development was presided over by a powerful state bureaucracy whose status and activities lacked democratic legitimacy. Manow shows that this created a predisposition on the part of state elites for social reform from above as a means of ensuring social cohesion in the absence of political democracy. Rather than the product of democratic political rights, social rights in Germany and Japan thus came to be granted in compensation for a denial of political rights. More or less directly, according to Manow, the peculiar properties of this sort of welfare state in turn and over time supported the evolution of a range of powerful mechanisms of economic coordination that are today regarded as defining elements of the German and Japanese models of embedded capitalism.

As Manow points out, the political agendas of state elites in the two countries at the end of the nineteenth century were not entirely the same. Whereas in Japan the central national objective was economic development—catching up with the advanced nations of the West—in Germany the leading concern was with state and nation building. Still, Manow shows that contrary to received wisdom, the Japanese and German welfare states, reflecting similar social configurations at the time of their historical origins, resemble each other in important respects. Rather than extending to all members of the community universal social rights to a minimum level of subsistence, the nonliberal welfare states of Germany and Japan came into existence by granting specific privileges to groups whose cooperation in economic modernization and nation building was deemed indispensable by political and economic elites. As Manow points out, these were not necessarily the most needy. In fact, it was mainly the employed, the skilled, and the well organized—groups that often had strong roots in preindustrial settings and forms of organization—that were able to get for themselves the sort of particularistic concessions and protections that gradually accumulated to form the complex structure of welfare state provisions typical of German and Japanese socially embedded capitalism. That later these provisions, especially in Germany, proved suitable for gradual democratic-egalitarian expansion—through co-optation of increasing numbers of social groups in similar structures of particularistic privilege—confirms what Lehmbruch points out about the ambiguity and evolutionary potential of conservative reform; like developments are described also in other chapters in this volume.

At the same time, although social protection in both welfare states is, and in principle continues to be, particularistic and status-based, the social organization differs, in ways familiar from Lehmbruch's account of the two national discourses. In Germany, early welfare state development, motivated by elite concerns with nation building and with the creation of nationwide institutions of functional (*ständische*) representation detached from parliamentary democracy, co-opted a wide range of social interest associations into the administration of state social policy. Manow argues that it was above all this emergent pattern of public-private cooperation in the provision of social welfare that laid the foundation for the constitutive inclusion of corporatist political forms in the modern German nation-state— in what Abelshauser (1984) has called "the first post-liberal nation." Manow also believes that the general organizational development of unions and employer associations was greatly advanced by the role they were allowed to play in the governance of the welfare state. Moreover, it was largely that role that gave them the capacity and also the inclination to cooperate with each other and the state in other areas as well, notably in industrial relations and the management of production.

In Japan, by comparison, state social policy promoted the internalization of social protection in the productive communities of large enterprises, thereby contributing to social integration and even closure of the latter, at the expense of collectivities cutting across the boundaries of firms. As the Japanese story is usually told, this was above all an attempt to limit worker turnover during early industrialization, a problem that seems to have been paramount at the time and whose solution required accommodation of the special interests of highly mobile skilled workers. But it may also be the case, as Manow and others in this volume suspect, that unlike in Germany, the preindustrial pattern of associations that existed in Japan did not easily lend itself to be transformed into modern institutions. In addition, anti-feudal liberal ideas held by bureaucratic elites, especially concerning the conditions of rapid economic growth, may have militated against the sort of co-optation of organized interests, especially those representing the artisan economy, that occurred in the same period in Germany (a point forcefully made especially by Lehmbruch).

In any case, Japanese social policy through the twentieth century consciously contributed to the solidification of the large enterprise as a community of fate and as a source of secure status for its workers. This resulted in a particularistic sort of social protection that was concentrated on the securely employed, and in a social and economic dualism that went far beyond what had evolved and, even more so, was allowed to survive in Germany. It seems all the more remarkable that after World War II, the Japanese pattern of status-based social protection proved, to some extent, open to democratic inclusion of organized labor in the form of the more or less secure establishment of enterprise unions inside the community firms that compose the primary sector of the Japanese economy.

Finally, Manow shows that an early welfare state conceived as a project of conservative reform—one designed by state elites to ensure social cohesion and economic cooperation in the absence of political democracy, rather than being extracted from capital and "the market" through "democratic class struggle" (Korpi 1983)—must be seen as a much more active factor than its liberal counterpart in shaping the architecture of the capitalist system of which it is part. In Germany and Japan, it was not the industrial production regime that gave rise to a corresponding pattern of labor relations which then, in turn, produced a welfare state to match it. According to Manow, it was the other way around: predemocratic, conservative, reform-minded welfare state building from above supported the growth of a pattern of labor relations that then facilitated the emergence of the cooperative, trust-based, long-term production regimes distinctive of German and Japanese capitalism.

Nonmarket economic coordination, through and within corporatist associations in Germany and enterprise communities in Japan, did not precede the welfare state but was made possible by it. After the establishment of particularistic status protections, core participants in the production process were willing and able to extend trust beyond otherwise insurmountable interest cleavages, given that they could assume their status to be protected, not just against the volatility of the market, but also against possible opportunism of other parties. In addition to the typical prevalence of high-trust relations in the two economies and the related capacity of economic agents to engage in profitable long-term exchange relations, this also helps explain the institutional fit between production regimes and social policy in the two countries, and thus the systemic quality of their national systems of capitalism, as an outcome of a historical causal sequence that extends from state building through social policy and labor relations to the organization of production.

Patient Capital and Industrial Citizenship

In the chapter that follows Manow's, Gregory Jackson deals with the large corporation, one of the core institutions of modern capitalism and especially of its nonliberal variant. Corporate governance in the nonliberal capitalisms of Germany and Japan, Jackson shows, differs importantly from corporate governance under Anglo-American liberalism and in ways that make for significant similarities between the two nonliberal countries. In Japan and Germany, large firms as organizations are able to command long-term commitments from both capital and labor because their institutions of corporate governance create a strong nexus between the two that ensures stable and cooperative working relations inside the enterprise. Above all, this is achieved by providing both sides with extensive opportunities for voice, as an alternative to exit (Hirschman 1970). Corporate governance as it evolved in the two nonliberal capitalisms makes for and reflects nonmarket relations of capital and labor, both between them and to the organization in which they are combined—relations-based on the one hand, in systems of "closed ownership" and bank-based finance that prevent the emergence of a "market for control," and on the other in regimes of industrial citizenship that allow for organized participation of committed labor in the management of the firm.

Jackson traces the parallel evolution in the two countries of two sets of institutional arrangements at the company level: those providing for stable ownership and for fending off potentially hostile capital markets, and those establishing industrial citizenship and thereby slowing the turnover of labor and promoting the integration of workers into the firm as a productive community. With respect to ownership regimes, Jackson points to the fact that unlike in the United States, family ownership in Germany and Japan did not give way to fragmented ownership by a myriad of shareholders interacting with each other and the firm through an anonymous capital market, but instead evolved into a complex pattern of highly concentrated intercorporate shareholding, which in both countries was at least in part the result of deliberate public policies. Regarding labor and its status in the corporation, industrial citizenship is shown to be the result of a long evolution that began with the paternalism of owner and founder families; with state policies of repression as well as co-optation of workers, including policies of "reform from above" as described by Lehmbruch and Manow; and with the accommodation by firms, the political system, and the legal order of independent organizations of workers once they had materialized. Jackson discusses in detail how these two strands of development, which were basically independent from each other, were combined after World War II to form the arrangements of nonliberal corporate governance that are today taken as core elements of the German and Japanese models of modern capitalism.

When looking for the origins of nonliberal capitalism in the two countries, Jackson (like Lehmbruch and Manow) turns to the unique constellation at the end of the nineteenth century when in both Germany and Japan late industrialization was progressing well before and without political democratization; when economic liberalism had begun to penetrate in the two societies ahead of and unaccompanied by political liberalism; and when the rising nation-states, keen on establishing their domestic and international standing, found it convenient to draw on preindustrial institutions, not least a strong government bureaucracy, in defining an active role for themselves in the management of their national economies and societies. Concerned about economic development and nation building at the same time, the German and Japanese states came to consider good economic performance in general, and the internal organization of the large firm and the conduct of labor relations in particular, as a matter of public interest and responsibility, the regulation of which could not be left to the market or to managerial prerogative alone.

Once this pattern had been set, remarkable parallels emerged in the subsequent evolution of the two corporate governance systems. These include the rise of independent professional management prominently concerned with mediating between the two main stakeholder groups inside the corporation, capital and labor (Aoki 1988). They also include the later transformation, especially in the second postwar settlement, of social rights conceded in lieu of political rights and of nonliberal institutions such as a strong supervisory board (*Aufsichtsrat*) and paternalistic labor-management consultation into channels for democratic participation and "industrial democracy." A paradoxical consequence of this is that today a country like Germany has far more institutional sites for collective participation in industrial relations, corporate governance, or, as pointed out by Manow, the administration of social security than liberal countries with less bureaucratic or authoritarian traditions.

Jackson does not fail to note the important differences between Japanese and German corporate governance, and here too his account closely resembles Manow's. Whereas Japanese corporate governance, according to Jackson, corresponds to a "community" model of the firm, one in which firms are densely integrated and more or less closed subsocieties, corporate governance in Germany is "constitutionalized" in that the internal life of the firm is, much more than in Japan, penetrated by formal rules imposed by the society at large through legislation or collective agreements negotiated, typically, by corporatist collective actors constituted at a level above the individual firm. Such rules relate, of course, in particular to the status of labor as a stakeholder and participant in corporate decision making and thus inevitably to the exercise of managerial prerogative, which must be limited if labor's opportunities for voice are to be more than perfunctory. But it also applies to the company as a whole, where the manifold protections German law offers against the capital market, above all against unfriendly takeovers, can be had only at the price of legal intervention in firms' internal governance—that is, of an intrusion of a politically and legally defined public interest into the private autonomy of large firms.

Throughout his essay, Jackson returns to the crucial question of how it may have been possible that the parallel development of property rights and industrial citizenship that culminated in the formation of the two nonliberal models of corporate governance actually proceeded in a way that ensured their ultimate compatibility. How was it, in other words, that in both countries the evolution of property rights and labor relations regimes, driven apparently by different forces and shaped by different "policy communities" or "sectoral discourses," resulted in a situation in which their outcomes "fit together" to form two distinct models of corporate governance with institutionalized long-term commitments for both capital *and* labor? Here Jackson tries to unpack the complex notion of "coevolution" in an attempt to reconstruct empirically the systemic character of the two models.

A central factor in this seems to be historical sequence—for example, when free markets are inserted in premodern settings in which they cause friction that, in turn, requires treatment, or when economic liberalization precedes political democracy. The tensions and occasional breakdowns caused by this, as a result of the constraints created by new arrangements for existing ones, seem sometimes to stimulate the invention of hybrid institutions that may or may not be stable enough to create new constraints and opportunities for other elements of the system. In this way, as a result of interaction and piecemeal adjustment over a longer period, institutions may begin to fit with one another even though no such fit was ever really "intended," or could have been. Jackson points out, however, that this outcome is far from guaranteed; for example, during the interwar period the various premodern, liberal, and democratic elements of German as well as Japanese capitalism never really matched each other. Indeed, in both countries it was above all the historical synthesis of the "reconstruction" after 1945 which, with the help of external force applied by Allied occupation governments, apparently enabled the two countries to reconcile their traditional, nonliberal, "embedding" institutions with markets and democracy. The result was several decades of unprecedented political and social peace and unmatched economic performance.

Bank-Based Finance

Like Jackson, Sigurt Vitols, in his inquiry into the historical origins of the financial systems of German and Japanese embedded capitalism, is ultimately interested in explaining systemic affinities between different sectoral regimes within a given country, in his case between the regimes governing the two principal production factors of a capitalist economy, capital and labor. Whereas Jackson focuses on the intersection between the two in the large enterprise, Vitols is concerned with the organization of the financial sector at large and its complementarity with the regulation of labor at the societal macro level.

Taking off from the familiar distinction between bank-based and market-based finance, Vitols rejects the view that bank-based financial systems are the product of late industrialization and the associated need for the state to "target" financial investment (e.g., Gerschenkron 1962). Although such a role is clearly found in Japan with its Industrial Bank and postal savings system, the German state, which also supported the rise of a bank-based system of finance, has played a much smaller role in directing financial flows. Although Germany and Japan equally qualify as "late industrializers," Germany was always much less "developmentalist" than Japan. Drawing on historical evidence from the two countries and referring to the United States for comparison, Vitols concludes that in contrast to the orthodox view, the existence in a country of a bank-based system of finance cannot be satisfactorily explained by a presumed need in late-industrializing countries to deploy capital on a larger scale and in a more targeted way. In the rest of his essay, he develops a quite different story from the functionalist one commonly told by late-industrialization theorists—a story that is much more complex and interesting because it attributes greater causal significance for the formation of institutional regimes to political decisions and interinstitutional dynamics.

According to Vitols, the difference between bank-based and market-based financial regimes is much younger than commonly believed. Rather than to the beginning of industrialization in the late nineteenth century, it dates to the formative years of nation building and state formation in the 1930s when capitalist societies had to react to the Great Depression. Both bank-based and market-based financial regimes are equally products of what Karl Polanyi termed the Great Transformation from nineteenth-century international liberalism to the nationally governed capitalist economies that culminated in the decades following World War II (Polanyi 1944). Before the 1930s, national financial systems, Vitols points out, were much more similar than after, because in all countries early liberalism had removed traditional constraints on financial activities, leaving financial sectors to operate under laissez-faire regimes that did not differ much from each other. It was only in the aftermath of World War I, and as a consequence of a peace settlement that disrupted the liberal world economy, eroded essential conditions of the early laissez-faire regime, and eventually led to the financial crises of the late 1920s, that political elites in the major industrialized countries felt called upon to institute new regimes of financial regulation that would be less subject to failure than those they had inherited after 1918. It was as a result of their choices and decisions that the laissez-faire financial systems of early industrialization bifurcated into liberal and nonliberal, or "embedded," systems, with the United States developing in the first and Germany and Japan in the second direction.

That nationally embedded capitalism had to be wrought from nineteenth-century laissez-faire liberalism, and that rather than being a heritage of a preindustrial past it was a product of modern political construction, is a theme similar to Lehmbruch's account of the evolution of nonliberal discourses and Jackson's story of the intensive political intervention required to defend nonliberal corporate governance against market pressures. Vitols adds to this the insight that twentieth-century market liberalism is as much a result of political choice and institutional design as is German- or Japanese-style embedded capitalism. Financial systems are heavily regulated, not just in Japan and Germany, but also in the United States, although of course the mode of regulation differs widely between bank-based systems, where transactions are governed by organizations, and systems where financial flows are controlled by the rules of a "free market." Vitols shows that it was through decisions of political elites, and not through an automatic extension into the twentieth century of differences between preindustrial societies, that the divergence of American, German, and Japanese national systems of finance came about. But this is not to say that the effects of such interventions must be any easier to remove than historical conditions of much longer duration. In fact, as Vitols mentions, German and Japanese bank-based financial regimes soon became so locked into their institutional contexts that American attempts after World War II to reverse the decisions of the 1930s and impose the U.S. system on the two defeated countries failed dismally.

This, of course, begs the question of what accounts for the differences in the way national political elites decided to regulate their financial systems in the 1930s. Vitols emphasizes the historical coincidence of the search for stable post-laissez-faire financial regimes with nationally different needs to provide for economic development, mobilize for war, and settle domestic class conflicts. Decisions on the governance of financial sectors were deeply affected by this coincidence, just as they were shaped by different ideological visions, the recent political histories of the nations involved, and the traditional institutional repertoires of the three societies that offered models for effective institutional design and promised complementarities with other sectors organized with reference to the same repertoire. Driven by path dependency in this sense, American elites were on the whole much less critical of the market than their German and Japanese counterparts, and tendencies among New Deal leaders for a more state-interventionist approach were ultimately pushed aside. Instead, American policy preferred to draw on the recent heritage of progressive reform, with its strong sentiment against monopoly and, in particular, "big finance," relying on regulated market competition to protect social groups such as farmers from financial organizations accumulating excessive power.

In Germany and Japan, by comparison, policymakers informed by a different "core discourse" had much less confidence in markets, and given the situation of their countries in the 1920s and 1930s, they were also much more inclined to treat the financial sector as a national resource, for war mobilization or national recovery, than as just another industry. Although this encouraged a more institutional approach and militated in favor of financial systems based on banks instead of markets, the ways the two bank-based systems were regulated, and the purposes to which they were put, differed considerably, in line with different institutional "blueprints" inherited from the two countries' pasts. In Germany, nonmarket financial governance became entrusted to corporatist self-regulation of the banking industry, which over time made for remarkable stability and solidity of financial institutions but left little space for state targeting of transactions. In Japan we once more observe a close intertwining between large private corporations, or alliances of such corporations, and the state, allowing for a considerable amount of "administrative guidance" of the "private sector" by the national bureaucracy and turning the financial sector largely into an extension of the Ministry of Finance and the Bank of Japan for the purposes of a developmentalist economic policy.

State activism in Japan, Germany, and the United States and political decisions on an appropriate post-laissez-faire organization of the financial sector were constrained by functional interdependence with other, already organized sectors, especially with the labor market and the resulting distribution of income, and with what Vitols calls the national "savings regime." Financial regimes, as Vitols points out, had to fit the functional requirements of other sectors and adjust to the constraints and opportunities offered by them. Just as a society's historical institutional repertoire keeps on store similar "blueprints" for the design of different sectoral regimes, intersectoral pressures for structural complementarity and mutual fit are powerful forces that make for the compatibility of sectoral designs, and perhaps discourses, inside national aggregates—at least as long as the sectors of a national system regard each other as their principal reference points. Vitols shows that the unequal income distribution that resulted from the American system of labor relations early on generated widespread demand among American households for securitized investment opportunities, a demand reinforced by the absence of a meaningful public pension system.

The much more egalitarian distribution patterns of Germany and Japan, by comparison, for a long time created no such need. Household savings could therefore be absorbed in low-interest savings accounts, mostly offered by public or semipublic financial institutions that, with or without government guidance, channeled accumulated funds into industrial investment. Moreover, the private pension systems of large Japanese companies and, even more so, the early development of a solidaristic public pension system in Germany, which culminated in the pension reforms of the 1950s that promised everyone a retirement income at the level of his previous standard of living, made private provision unnecessary. Both bank-based and market-based financial regimes responded to existing patterns of organization in other sectors of the political economy, recognizing their interdependence with their surrounding society and thus providing for more or less internal coherence of different national "models of capitalism."

Vitols's account gives rise to interesting speculations on the future, not just of the German financial system, but also of the German regime of corporate governance. Income inequality among workers has been growing in Germany for some time, although it is still lower than in many other countries. Moreover, confidence in the pay-as-you-go public pension system is evaporating, and there is general recognition that to defend present levels of retirement income, there will have to be a supplementary, funded component, and its significance is bound to increase in coming years. Both developments are highly likely to generate a further expanding demand for securities. If one follows Vitols, this must in turn add to pressures for a transformation of German financial markets, and of the regime governing them, in a less bank-based, "American" direction.

According to Jackson, however, transition to a more market-based financial system must have consequences for corporate governance, and in particular must weaken the role of labor inside the company as it would disorganize the shareholders' side and thus deprive "patient labor" of its required counterpart, "patient capital." If industrial citizenship was not already threatened directly by growing inequality and declining institutionalized solidarity as such, it could be eroded by the latter setting free the capital markets and clearing away the remnants of the paternalistic ownership tradition that, according to Jackson, was the main inroad for industrial democracy in the twentieth-century version of nationally embedded capitalism.

Solidarism and Segmentalism in Skill Formation

Finally, the chapter by Kathleen Thelen and Ikuo Kume examines the origins of the Japanese and German systems of industrial skill formation. Compared especially to the liberal political economies of the United Kingdom and the United States, Germany and Japan are widely regarded as having for a long time benefited in economic competition from a superior supply of broad and high work skills. Prosperity in the two countries, as the authors recount, to a large extent has been based on an economic performance that requires a highly skilled workforce. That such performance was possible is attributed by the literature to a particular ability of the nonliberal, market-embedding institutions that govern skill formation in Germany and Japan to resolve the endemic collective action problems that especially beset workplace-based training in more market-driven societies. Although the differences between skill formation processes and their outcomes in Germany and Japan on the one hand and the Anglo-American world on the other are by and large taken for granted by the authors, their essay focuses on the origins of the characteristically divergent but functionally equivalent solutions developed by the two nonliberal countries to the problems of work-skill formation in a capitalist economy.

German-Japanese differences in skill formation, as described by Thelen and Kume, resemble the broad picture that emerges in the other contributions to this volume. While the German alternative to market liberalism is based on the "solidarism" of occupational groups cross-cutting the boundaries of individual enterprises and organized in a symbiotic, corporatist relationship with the state, the Japanese training system draws on the social integration and cohesion of large firms closely intertwined structurally and functionally with government and the public sphere—a configuration the authors refer to as "segmentalist." Corporatism and segmentalism are shown to represent equivalent answers to the "poaching" problem that undermines workplace-based skill formation in more liberal societies. The segmentalist regime ensures that firms can expect to internalize the benefits of their training investment through long job tenures of committed core workers, and the corporatist solution protects employers' inclination to train by making most or all competing firms contribute their share to training, in spite of what remains an open external labor market.

Why did German embedded capitalism develop a solidaristic and Japanese embedded capitalism a segmentalist pattern of skill formation? Training regimes, as Thelen and Kume point out, come in functionally linked packages with labor market regimes, nationally specific versions of managerial prerogative and industrial relations, social status structures and status politics, etc. The respective evolution of segmentalist and corporatist-solidaristic training systems must therefore be seen in the context of the evolution of general labor market and corporate governance regimes, which both affect these systems and are affected by them. Here again, the picture looks familiar. In both countries, economic liberalization and its destruction of collective organization in the labor market coincided with rising skill deficits in the rapidly expanding industrial sector. Neither in Japan nor in Germany was redress of such deficits left to market forces: the measures that were taken, however, were very different.

Key to understanding these differences, according to Thelen and Kume, is the different treatment by the two societies in their early industrial periods of their artisan sectors. In Japan the artisan economy was regarded as hopelessly backward by Meiji reformers and was actively disorganized in pursuit of liberal ideas. Instead, large government-owned firms served as training centers for the national economy and were originally more than willing to share the results of their skill-formation efforts with the rest of the economy. With occupational, craft-style labor markets still predominant, the high labor mobility inherited from the artisan past diffused modern work skills throughout the developing industrial economy, thereby turning the results of training in the government sector into a public good.

This mechanism, however, became unsustainable as government-owned firms were increasingly privatized and in any case had to observe imperatives of efficiency and profitability. When as a result labor mobility turned into a deterrent against investment in training, the solution that offered itself in a country whose artisan institutions were regarded as impediments to modernization was the closure of internal labor markets, which was part of a process of state-assisted organization building that instituted large firms as economic and social communities of fate. As Thelen and Kume show, the result was the formation of a cross-class coalition within firms between top management and a new corps of company-trained workers with lifelong employment—the future "organization men." This coalition squeezed out the traditional *oyakata* master artisans and replaced their autonomy with strongly established managerial prerogative exercised, however, only after extensive consultation with a committed company workforce.

Early liberalism and its discontents; the emergence of paternalistic large enterprises in private ownership but with quasi-public status as market-embedding social institutions; and later the incorporation of labor in an enterprise-based version of industrial citizenship all add up to a familiar picture. The German story both resembles and differs from the Japanese experience. Like the latter, it is also about successful institutional reconstruction from above and about the evolution of modern institutions, founded on premodern ones, that later proved ready to absorb trade unions in cross-class compromise and cooperation. But the crucial difference was the presence in Germany of a viable artisan sector, one that managed to attract the support of the state and the legal order. As a consequence, it was able to survive into the twentieth century alongside the modern state, with an enduring capacity to sustain skill formation in an open labor market through a self-governing regime of nationally recognized certification. State support for the artisan economy, and most importantly for the status group of free artisans gradually turning into small businessmen, placed the management of artisan training in the hands of vertical national associations running an effective certification system, which were in turn certified by the state. Thus training was taken not just out of market competition, but also out of the class conflict by which it came to be impeded in more liberal societies. Rather than being governed by a voluntaristic-conflictual regime, like under the British and American craft unions, it came under the state-licensed control of a modern chamber system that took the place of the premodern artisan guilds.

That segmentalism and solidarism are true functional alternatives is indicated by the fact, reported by Thelen and Kume, that also in Germany, large firms tried for a while, and not without temporary success, to remedy their skill shortages through the creation of closed internal labor markets. In the end, however, they failed, freeing the way to a functionally equivalent solution much better fitted to the systemic German context than company-centered segmentalism. Suppression of the latter in the German version of embedded capitalism is explained in part by the continued existence of an external market for skilled labor based on portable certificates, which gave workers the possibility to opt against a skill formation regime that threatened to deprive them of their independence as it took away their freedom to quit. But although certification administered by corporatist artisan organizations protected worker mobility and frustrated attempts of employers to arrest workers inside the boundaries of firms, it also enabled both employers and workers to overcome the dysfunctions of external labor markets for skill formation.

Moreover, the reconstituted artisan training regime served as an institutional blueprint for modern German industry on which isomorphically to model a training regime of its own. Especially the small machine builders, for which a segmentalist solution would have been difficult if not impossible to realize, found it only natural to set up a certification system that emulated that of their artisan competitors: as collective skill certification through corporatist associations had already been invented and proven effective, there was no need to reinvent the wheel and think up something fundamentally different. Relations between the two training regimes, artisanal and industrial, remained precarious in the interwar period, and so did the status of organized labor vis-à-vis the corporatist institutions governing skill formation, but this was ended by the postwar settlement of democratic corporatism that effectively resolved the interwar problems of both institutional synthesis and social inclusion.

German-Japanese differences and similarities with respect to the evolution of the two countries' training regimes, then, may be broadly summarized as follows. Early liberalism lasted longer in Japan, or in any case was more successful in clearing away premodern institutions; in Germany, by comparison, these were reorganized and rehabilitated with the assistance of a conservative-reformist state (for German examples, see Dornseifer and Kocka 1993). In Japan large state firms, typically in the armaments industry and quickly to be privatized, offered themselves as early models for a socially embedded organization of economic transactions, in close cooperation with the nation-state. Over time, the large firm sector became the privileged site of social regulation and filled the space that in Germany was increasingly occupied by the associational sector.

Organization building, or hierarchy building, became the Japanese equivalent of German association building. Furthermore, although in both countries cross-class coalitions between capital and labor were established earlier and more easily than in liberal capitalism, in Japan they emerged vertically in the enterprise, in a specifically Japanese version of managerial prerogative exercised over a committed workforce, whereas in Germany they were formed mainly horizontally, between associations representing their members in collective bargaining. Internalization of training investments in large firms was possible in Japan, where a corporatist alternative did not exist, while collective governance of a nationwide training regime was possible in Germany where large firms, precisely because there was a corporatist alternative, were unable to turn themselves into closed communities. Unions were eventually incorporated in both models. But in Japan they had to be the enterprise unions of the postwar era, whereas in Germany they were modernized and depoliticized industrial unions negotiating collective agreements, like craft unions, at the industrial level.

Comparison of the histories of the skill formation regimes of Germany and Japan confirms the significance of national cultural models and intersectoral functional interdependence in accounting for the internal coherence and homogeneity of different versions of embedded capitalism. How these mechanisms work can best be seen in accounts in which formative moments of sectoral problem solving and institution building are placed in historical sequence. Over time, large Japanese firms, modeling themselves on the cultural ideal of the *ie* (Murakami 1984)—which invokes both extended family and samurai hierarchy—accumulated a wide range of functions in the social regulation and suspension of markets, establishing as a "cultural" matter of course that the privileged site for dealing with new problems of social cohesion and collective action was the large public-*cum*-private firm.

In Germany, by comparison, the artisan sector, with the support of the state, had preserved a solidaristic solution that not only fit other German institutions but was available for emulation by other classes and sectors, especially those looking for arrangements that protected them from state regulation without exposing important interests and objectives to the vagaries of the market. Sectoral interdependence, between artisanal and nonartisanal firms operating in the same labor market and between labor market and training regimes, and the continued presence of modernized traditional institutions thus account for systemic cohesion and cross-sectoral isomorphism of national institutional arrangements and helped to suppress the segmentalist alternative that triumphed in Japan.

Functional interdependence and cultural emulation work as long as (and only as long as) national sectors take other national sectors as their main functional and cultural point of reference. Behind Thelen and Kume's story lies the insight that this is the case in particular situations, such as dictatorship, war, or national reconstruction after defeat—when the state can deploy its law-making and enforcement powers to the fullest to generalize preferred solutions; homogenize sectoral arrangements so as to make them more cohesive and rationalize the society's institutional repertoire; and make preferred models of social organization generally binding on sectors that still adhere to less compatible arrangements and thereby create conflicts and friction. The resolution of the tension in the German skill formation system of the 1920s and early 1930s and between its two competing principles of social organization did not come about automatically or on its own. The contest lasted until the strong state of the 1930s and then the democratic reconstruction after 1945 resolved it politically in favor of the more systemically compatible, corporatist alternative.

Parallels and Differences: A Preliminary Summary

What do the essays in the present volume tell us about the evolutionary dynamics of nonliberal capitalism? In Germany as well as Japan, economic liberalism preceded political democracy. Thus, the expanding capitalist economies of the two countries encountered states that had retained enough authority to be capable of effective intervention when social cohesion and the existing social organization were threatened by the disorder of the market. Conservative reform proceeded by granting social rights to select groups whose support was important for political stability, long before, and at first instead of, universal extension of political rights. Defense of political stability and social solidarity by a predemocratic nation-state gave rise to twentieth-century institutions that, although restructured and rationalized to fit in the framework of modern civil and constitutional law, were imbued with premodern traditionalism and paternalism (on "late-comer conservatism," see Murakami 1982). Elsewhere, the emerging welfare state and the national systems of corporate governance, labor relations, property rights, finance, and training were shaped to a considerable degree by territorial electoral democracy and the associated class polarization. In Germany and Japan, by comparison, they came to be rooted instead in particularistic relations within politically privileged social groups as well as between the state on the one hand and the economy and civil society on the other.

The sectoral regimes designed by conservative reform in the two countries had distinct national characteristics. German reforms throughout were inspired by established corporatist-consociational traditions reaching back to the medieval guild system and the settlement between the two Christian confessions in the Holy Roman Empire at the end of the religious wars in the seventeenth century. In Japan, by comparison, it was increasingly the large modern firm that became the institution of choice for policymakers and other elites in their effort to overcome the divisions and uncertainties brought about by capitalist modernization, with organization and hierarchy building taking the place of association building and the political design of arenas for collective bargaining of all sorts (on this and the following, see Figure 1.1). German politics at the end of the nineteenth century centered around the extension of public status to intermediary organizations in the tradition of premodern corporations, both reinforcing particularistic group loyalties and integrating them in the emerging nation-state. Japanese elites, for their part, fully embraced the liberal destruction of traditional groups and progressively relied for the rebuilding of social cohesion on the large enterprises that were first founded as part of the state apparatus and then spun off to a late-developing private sector while remaining deeply immersed in a public-bureaucratic-nationalist ethos.

For a cultural model, the emerging vertical enterprise communities of modern Japan drew on the family-like community of the premodern *ie*, which in the Japanese version of capitalism played the role that in Germany was taken by corporatist associations (Murakami 1984).[3] Both large enter-

---

3. Our argument here touches on the question, hotly debated in the literature, of whether the nonliberal institutions of German and Japanese capitalism are feudal remnants or, rather, modern constructions modeled on an imagined premodern past. That question, we believe, cannot be answered in general. The empirical chapters in this volume suggest that the exact relationship between continuity, construction, and reconstruction may differ—between sectors or otherwise. Even more important, it appears that some of the most crucial German and Japanese economic institutions may be both modern and premodern at the same time, having achieved their present condition as a result of almost continuous remodeling in line with changing functional pressures but in the image of an increasingly constructed tradition.

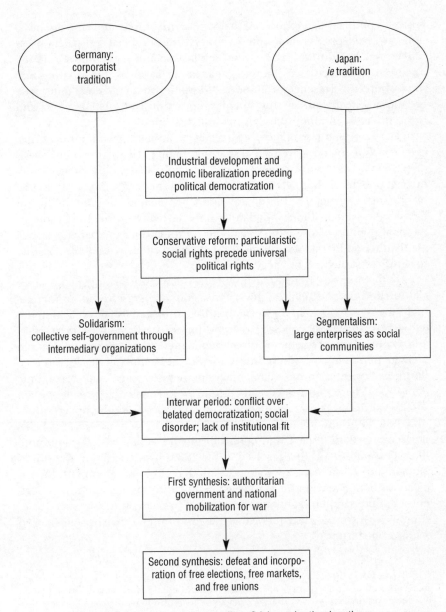

Figure 1.1 Solidarism and segmentalism: Origins and national syntheses

prises and intermediary organizations may be referred to in English as "corporations," reflecting a worldview in which the most fundamental distinction is between individuals and the organizations that comprise and combine them—a cultural "frame" that explains the misleading designation by many Anglo-American authors of both Germany and Japan as "corporatist" political economies. Actually, of course, intermediary organizations and enterprise communities are very different social constructions, as reflected in the differences between solidaristic and segmentalist training regimes or between German and Japanese versions of industrial citizenship, where the presence or absence of loyalties that cut across enterprise boundaries deeply affects the functioning not just of labor markets and firms, but also, and importantly, of national politics.[4]

In Germany and Japan, reconstructed associations and community firms, respectively, early on served as sites of functional participation on the basis of particularistic group membership, although democratic participation through electoral channels and on a universalistic territorial basis was late in coming. During the 1920s, the slow and belated progress of liberal democracy—much slower in Japan than in Germany—brought tensions in national regimes whose elites were bent on defending the benefits associated with nonliberal institutions for national solidarity and the existing structure of status and privilege.

In both countries, functional and liberal-democratic arrangements of social integration and political governance found themselves in an increasingly uneasy relationship. In Germany this manifested itself even within the left, where the division between supporters of parliamentary democracy and a council-based system of "direct democracy" persisted throughout the Weimar Republic, and where inside the Social Democratic Party the relationship between the parliamentary-democratic state and "economic democracy" based on works councils and unions was never really settled. The social disorder that resulted in both countries from the uncertainties over how to accommodate markets, unions, and elections—in Marshall's language, civil, industrial, and political rights (T. Marshall 1964)—in nonliberal capitalism was first resolved in the 1930s by increasingly authoritarian and militaristic states reversing twentieth-century developments toward electoral democracy and a market economy and forcing upon their societies unified national regimes underpinned, in one country, by social associations with strong governing capacities, and in the other by state-backed managerial authority.

---

4. This is not to say that enterprise paternalism did not to some extent survive inside German corporatism, or that Japan's political economy did not develop any corporatist traits at all. "State corporatism" or "corporatism from above" emerged in particular in Japanese agriculture and in several sectors of small firms and large industry. But while some Japanese associations turned into effective interlocutors of the state, bargaining between organized groups as a mode of state-free but quasi-public societal self-regulation did not become nearly as developed as in Germany. In part, this was both effect and cause of the predominant exclusion of organized labor from Japanese politics and society. Similarly, large firms in Germany continued to build loyal company workforces and to some extent succeeded in developing company-specific labor regimes. Still, what they could accomplish was and is more or less narrowly circumscribed by external loyalties and societal organizational ties of workforces and, sometimes, employers.

National mobilization for war in particular made it possible not only to suppress persistent demands for democratization, but also to homogenize each country's divergent sectoral regimes and reorganize them into more or less coherent national patterns of governance and social order. In the late 1930s and early 1940s, both countries thus managed to overcome the friction that had increasingly beset their political economies in the twentieth century, friction between traditionalist particularism and modern universalism on the one hand, and between incompatible sectoral regimes that had evolved without sufficient recognition of national interdependence on the other.

Shortly thereafter, defeat in World War II forever undid the authoritarian synthesis that had attempted to put to rest the tensions of the interwar years, making space for a second synthesis that involved nothing less than the reconciliation of the two countries' national traditions of conservative reform with electoral democracy, free markets, and independent trade unions. This, much more than the rise of Germany and Japan to unprecedented prosperity and to the status of economic superpowers, was the true postwar miracle. The second synthesis, which assigned political parties and labor unions a safe place within or alongside traditional national institutions of functional representation, was initially imposed on the two countries by the Anglo-American victors of the war, especially by the United States, which in Germany and Japan, for a short but highly formative time span, became an occupying power. With the help of national leaders eager to rebuild their countries and reinsert them into international relations inside the emerging Western alliance, the occupation set in motion a process that eventually resulted in two relatively coherent, nationally specific hybridizations of liberal and nonliberal, modern and traditional institutions. In the 1970s and 1980s, these became recognizable as different but similar "models" of capitalism that were distinct from the Anglo-American kind and sufficiently internally integrated to be in crucial respects superior to it.

Although the liberal-democratic reorganization of Germany and Japan after World War II unquestionably turned the two countries into bona fide democracies and capitalist market economies, the results remained noticeably German and Japanese (Smith 1998). In fact, as deeply as the principles of free elections, majority government, private property, and free markets may have penetrated in the two societies, there continues to be a sizable literature that doubts the actual impact of postwar Allied intervention and, for Japan more than for Germany, pretends to uncover behind the "Western" facade an old, unreconstructed reality of authoritarianism, paternalism, particularism, and nationalist collusion against the outside world. Have Allied reforms really stuck, or were they surreptitiously undone in subsequent years by national elites conspiring to resurrect the old order? Are the *keiretsu* really different from the conglomerates of the interwar years? Is *Mitbestimmung* not in reality collusion between management and unions, if not a nationalist alliance between capital and labor against foreign competition and takeovers? Are not second-generation Japanese unions management-run replicas of the patriotic productivity organizations of the war years? And is not the "Japanese model" of the 1980s merely a superficially disguised reincarnation of the "1940 system"?

Leaving aside the studied alarmism of many of these writings, what they do point to is an undoubtable continuity in the development of the two countries' nationally embedded political economies, regardless of their conversion—first imposed and then internalized—to free elections, free markets, and free trade unions. The liberal-traditional synthesis that is now so firmly established in Japan and Germany must appear all the more astonishing since up to the middle of the century its possibility was vehemently denied by conservative elites in each country as well as, from different positions, by many of their domestic and international opponents. With hindsight, one might argue that the institutions left by German and Japanese conservative reform must from the beginning have been less averse to being combined with free markets and parliamentary rule than was widely believed, not least by those who designed them. But it seems more plausible that, like in the first synthesis during the 1930s and early 1940s, it was above all the capacity of the government of the day to apply almost unlimited political power that made it possible to rebuild previously incompatible institutions and make them fit together in more or less organic wholes, turning frictions into synergies and conflict into a source of high requisite variety.

In any case, it was only after total defeat and subsequent foreign occupation that the distinctive institutional configurations came to be assembled that are today identified as the German and Japanese "models of capitalism." Their evolution, as the chapters in this volume show, into the reasonably coherent *Gestalten* they had assumed by the 1970s was anything but the smooth execution of a historical master plan. Unlike what "passive" theories of social change would suggest—theories in which the development of a society is ultimately conceived as the unfolding of an invariable and infallible evolutionary logic—the political economies of Germany and Japan were built by sequences of political decisions, the outcomes of which were far from predetermined and which could have gone in different directions than they eventually did. That the institutional designs independently created by the sectoral politics of the two countries would at some point be structurally compatible and functionally complementary was never a foregone conclusion, even after the establishment of what Lehmbruch calls a hegemonic "core discourse."

The histories of modern Germany and Japan, then, cannot by any stretch of the imagination be read as manifestations of impersonal mechanisms of social reproduction that would somehow have guaranteed that in the second half of the twentieth century the national institutions in Germany and Japan fit together as well as they did and in the way they did. Rather, the structural and functional coherence—the "system integration"—of the two national models of embedded capitalism had to be continuously established, restored, redefined, and defended against all sorts of disorganizing forces, from special sectoral interests to the accidents of local decision making in limited time and with restricted information.

Surveying the five chapters, the historical constitution of German and Japanese capitalism tends to appear in large part as the result of continuous improvisation and experimentation within the limits of changing, and ever newly discovered, institutional constraints and opportunities. In truly dialectical fashion, emerging inconsistencies between sectoral arrangements led to piecemeal adjustment and, sometimes, homogenization of institutional designs, which gave rise to new inconsistencies and required new adjustments, in an apparently never-ending process punctuated only by rare moments of formative political intervention in which divergent sectoral arrangements were forcefully pulled together into a common national pattern. Ex post accommodation of the outcomes of open and unrelated decisions on sectoral institution building seems to have been at least as important for system building as a priori calculations of the advantages of compatibility and complementarity under conditions of interdependence—calculation of which would be excessively demanding on the farsightedness and discipline of sectoral actors. Even public policies at the sectoral level seem to have been frequently driven by concerns different from intersectoral complementarity or their own fit with the core discourse. Coevolution, which is one of the new catchwords in theories of social change, and the resulting "elective affinities" may in fact be mainly the outcome of improvised efforts to mitigate temporarily the frictions caused by uncoordinated developments.

An important lesson to be learned from comparing the histories of German and Japanese capitalism, then, might be that what evolves in the evolution of a society is not just its structural forms and functional relations, but also the direction and the target—the *telos*—of the evolutionary process itself (Aoki 2001; Thelen 1999). To the extent that decisions in one sector constrain decisions in others, they change the set of possible futures for the system and thereby redefine, at every historical stage, the condition toward which the society is developing. Unintended or unconsidered consequences of sectoral policies, or the results of sectoral tests of political strength, permanently create new opportunities and constraints for subsequent decisions and developments in other sectors of society. Such is the case with the German welfare state, which, through its influence on the structure and conduct of industrial relations, helped create an institutional infrastructure of cooperation and coordination in the workplace, which in turn supported the evolution of a specifically German production regime and, perhaps, mode of production (for Japan, see Aoki 1997). Although cultural models, such as medieval guilds or village communities, may inspire isomorphic solutions in different sectors (DiMaggio and Powell 1983), they are less than completely instructive, as they can always be differently interpreted and in any case must be continually reinterpreted as national systems make themselves up and reinvent their traditions.

Neither in Germany nor in Japan, however, did piecemeal adjustment suffice to ensure intersectoral coherence and a shared interpretation of national cultures. But although this is true, it was only after catastrophic social breakdowns, first in a revolution from above that in both countries ended the long impasse and the sustained crisis of the 1920s, and then in total defeat and foreign conquest, that holistic revisions and renewals of national models became possible. That the two national syntheses, which pulled together the political economies of Germany and Japan and homogenized their sectoral arrangements, were of a very different nature is in itself illustrative of the general dynamics of institutional change. It is a moot question whether the Germany and Japan that existed in the early 1940s could have survived had they prevailed in the war, or in what direction they would have developed. What seems highly unlikely, however, is that they would have evolved into the German and Japanese models we know today. And what is also clear is that the sectoral and national politics that over the years defined the German and Japanese models always had to do so in relation to democracy and the market economy—in response to internal and external pressures for universal political and social rights on the one hand and for "free trade," for disembedded and socially not obligated market exchange, on the other. Throughout their contorted national histories, and certainly far earlier than the 1990s, the nonliberal capitalisms of Germany and Japan had to invent and reinvent themselves against a background of liberal ideas and practices—although the ways they did so differed dramatically over time: moving in a relatively short period from a self-definition exclusive of markets and democracy to one blending these into each nation's institutional endowment and making them work inside it.

Long before "globalization," then, liberalism—in the economy even more than in the polity—represented a historical baseline, a default option for nationally embedded capitalism from which it had to be wrought, against which it defined itself, and from which it more or less consciously deviated. This holds also for the second synthesis, the postwar settlement, that was externally constrained to accommodate free markets and parliamentary democracy in historical contexts that had long been regarded as incompatible with them. It is true that in the process both countries developed distinctive versions of the new institutions they had to graft onto their respective institutional endowments. But they also redesigned their own institutions to fit the new ones—for example, in reorganizing artisan associations to enable them to function under a rigorous new competition law, or generally rebuild functional representation into a regime of "liberal corporatism" compatible with parliamentary government. Fairly soon, it appears, participants in the two emerging postwar models of embedded capitalism began to realize that it was possible to combine the advantages of nonliberal institutions for cooperation and collective action in the pursuit of collective goods with the benefits of free markets and democratic constraints on the state. Perhaps the gradual formation in the 1950s and 1960s of the German and Japanese "models" can best be conceived as a process of successful institutional hybridization: one that domesticated markets and economic action, for example by slowing down the turnover of capital and labor, while at the same time exposing the traditional institutions in both countries to political and economic competition, thereby opening them up and making them more inclusive and egalitarian.

In many ways, the capstone of the postwar settlement that, for a time at least, reconciled the legacy of economic embeddedness and conservative reform with markets and democracy was the inclusion of organized labor. After 1945, labor repression in Germany and Japan turned into labor co-optation within institutional structures that had historically been designed to exclude organized labor from the political economy. There are significant differences in this respect between the two countries that one must not overlook. Up to the early 1930s, repression of independent trade unions had been much more severe in Japan than in Germany. In fact, in Germany the labor movement had been able in the 1918 revolution, after another lost war, to establish itself for one-and-a-half decades as a legitimate and powerful political force. Although the Nazis eliminated free trade unions at least as ruthlessly and effectively as the Japanese military government, after 1945 Germany—unlike Japan—could build on a historical legacy of union organization, pluralistic industrial relations, and social-democratic labor law. Japanese unions gained astonishing strength immediately after World War II, but ultimately their position in the postwar settlement was considerably weaker than that of their German counterparts. In particular Japanese unions were, throughout the lifetime of the postwar Japanese model, much less in a position than German unions to pursue a public-policy, state-led agenda of welfare policies and reforms.

Still, in both countries institutional arrangements once designed to create and enshrine particularistic privileges for select groups, and to organize those groups in such a way that their loyalty to the state was assured, proved capable of being extended to independent organizations of labor, for example when German trade unions turned the works-council system into their extended arm at the workplace. In Germany in particular, democratization took the form of progressive inclusion of ever-more-organized groups in traditional systems of fragmented privilege and special public status, on increasingly identical terms equalized as a result of democratic politics and economic competition. Nothing illuminates better than the postwar discovery of the inclusive capacity of the German and Japanese institutional heritage the extent to which nationally embedded capitalism is a modern political construction rather than a passive outgrowth of "tradition," "history," or "path-dependent evolution" (see Thelen 1999).

Speculations on the Prospects for Nonliberal Capitalism in Germany and Japan

The nationally organized, socially embedded, nonliberal variants of modern capitalism that emerged in Japan and Germany at the end of the nineteenth century originated in a unique and unrepeatable historical configuration. As the essays in this volume demonstrate, they owe their existence to a coincidence in the two countries of belated industrialization and delayed nation-state building antedating political democracy and allowing predemocratic state elites wide room for political-economic maneuvering. The basic patterns of political and social embedding of the capitalist economy that were formed in the two countries at this time soon became "locked in" and survived until the present, although with considerable modifications and after several instances, sometimes dramatic, of reconfiguration and renewal.

Today, more than a century after German and Japanese capitalism first took shape as distinctive national models of economic governance, there is a question about how long the organizing principles of nonliberal capitalism in the two countries can continue to be instructive for its evolution—how long, in other words, the supply of path-dependent adjustments conforming to the basic patterns established about a hundred years ago can last. The historical record, as reflected in the chapters of this volume, demonstrates an impressive capacity of the two systems to achieve, defend, and restore internal coherence and impose similarly embedded patterns of organization on their various economic and policy sectors. It also shows an enormous ability of the discourse and practice of nonliberal capitalism in the two countries to incorporate and assimilate new elements, including ones originally derived from liberal and democratic contexts—thereby widening the repertoire of the two systems, broadening their social base, and enabling them to meet new challenges without losing their distinctive character and the functional benefits it entails.

Above all, however, the history of nationally embedded capitalism in Germany and Japan was shaped by a small number of formative political moments of revolution, war, and foreign conquest, when national politics and the nation-state assumed supreme significance. Total mobilization before and in war, and the need to rebuild the nation after total defeat, offered states and politics opportunities to reassert their primacy over economy and society and make decisions that were determinative of future events for a long time to come. The requirements of mobilization and the time pressures imposed by approaching hostilities forced state elites to update and generalize patterns of political-economic governance inherited from earlier periods. Indeed, during the two world wars, more liberal countries tried, often in vain, to learn especially from Germany how best to mobilize their economic resources for the purpose of national survival and victory. And total defeat, as was inflicted twice on Germany and once on Japan, made possible and required a new synthesis between historically inherited institutions and practices that were familiar to the nation and could therefore easily be recreated and novel elements included in response to internal and external demands for democratization and for a retreat from national economic autarky.

What do these experiences tell us when today we wonder about the ability of German and Japanese capitalism, with their characteristic emphases on social protection, egalitarian redistribution, and national solidarity, to withstand mounting international and domestic pressures for liberalization and for convergence on Anglo-American forms of economic governance? What seems clear is that the founding conditions of nonliberal capitalism, as they prevailed at the end of the last century, cannot today be replicated in any sense. Perhaps the lock-in effects that result from the general stickiness of social institutions and that condition the range of possible incremental change can ensure the continuity of the two systems even in the absence of their formative conditions. But then the history of German and Japanese nonliberal capitalism shows that there is little reason to expect its continuity to be safeguarded by passive path dependency alone. Three observations in particular stand out: (1) nonliberal capitalism on balance became increasingly more liberal during the twentieth century and often proved open to liberal amendments to an extent impossible to anticipate; (2) the way liberal and nonliberal institutions were configured and reconfigured and the distinctiveness maintained by German and Japanese capitalism were often unpredictable and surprising; and (3) both continuity and change of nationally embedded capitalism in Germany and Japan depended critically on state elites who were capable, in extraordinary political moments, of strategic, autonomous, and authoritative action. None of this can be particularly reassuring to those who would like to see the German and Japanese models as we know them survive into the future, for the following reasons.

1. Nationally embedded capitalism as it developed in Germany and Japan has throughout its history defined itself on a background of and in response to domestic and international pressures for *free exchange* in disembedded markets and for liberty-protecting *restrictions on state discretion.* Although the former kind of pressure is inherent in any political economy based on private property, the latter is inextricably linked to a modern social structure. Nonliberal capitalism must therefore be seen as inevitably subject to steady erosion, in the sense of creeping liberalization, and can maintain its identity only to the extent that its inherent tendencies toward liberal entropy can be actively halted. In Germany and Japan, the reactionary attempt of the interwar period to repress such tendencies once and for all ended in national disasters. The subsequent "second synthesis" defended the distinctiveness of the German and Japanese political economies at the price of integrating into them more liberal elements than ever and thereby, as a mostly unintended side effect, laying them open to further liberalization in subsequent decades. Today Germany and Japan, their distinctiveness as nationally embedded political economies notwithstanding, are more than ever governed by market exchanges and less than ever by state authority, and no end to this development is in sight. In fact, "globalization" of economic and cultural exchange, in the form of growing cross-border mobility of people, resources, and cultural symbols, has in both countries placed further restrictions on the capacity of governments to enforce social obligations on market participants and has driven the continuous redefinition of the German and Japanese models in a far more liberal direction than could possibly have been envisaged in the original postwar settlement.

2. If it is true that the imaginary end of the evolution of a political-economic system is *permanently redefined* by the (mostly unintended) consequences of contingent political decisions, then even if a system's past can be plausibly reconstructed as a continuous unfolding of, and its present as a coherent manifestation of, a historically defined identity, this does not in itself ensure that the future of the system will appear predictable from the point of view of its present. That the history of nonliberal capitalism in Germany and Japan is to a large extent one of experimentation with liberal-nonliberal institutional hybrids may make it particularly difficult to anticipate how the increasingly liberal historical legacies of the two countries will in the future be revised in response to inevitable endogenous and exogenous pressures for further liberalization. Moreover, arrangements that, as long as they are *future* arrangements, may appear incompatible with a system's historical identity may, once instituted, be convincingly constructed with hindsight as ingenious extensions and creative adjustments of traditional institutions. As documented by the surprising turns in the socioeconomic history of Germany and Japan, there are few if any a priori limits to

the possible liberalization of nationally embedded capitalism, although the result may still lend itself to being interpreted ex post as a further permutation of a national "model" that continues to differ from Anglo-American "standard capitalism."

3. Most important, the sort of *state capacity* that was historically required for the defense of nonliberal capitalism against regime incoherence and liberal erosion may no longer be in supply, for both domestic and international reasons. The establishment and defense of embedded capitalism in Germany and Japan coincided with the general development in modern economic history that has been referred to as the Great Transformation (Polanyi 1944): the increasing regulation by interventionist economic and social policies pursued by nation-states of what had already in the nineteenth century become an international free-market economy. Germany and Japan were not the only countries in which that transformation took place, although they were, for reasons discussed in this volume, better placed than others to resist the attractions of free-market liberalism. However, as the crises of the interwar period amply demonstrated, simultaneous attempts by sovereign nation-states to bring the "self-regulating market" under social control by embedding "their" segments of the world economy in national institutions required an international order supporting and indeed licensing national state intervention in the economy. An order of this sort was created by the postwar settlement after 1945, which enabled economic policy in an international economy to be operated as national policy, sustaining national independence by organizing it into an international context within which it could be exercised without negative external effects on other countries.

Polanyi's Great Transformation may have lasted into the 1970s when country after country, in more or less successful attempts at corporatist coalition building, relied on national institutional resources in trying to combat the inflationary consequences of the first oil shock. But at this point already, the irreversible breakdown of the Bretton Woods system had opened the way for a new ascendancy of international capital markets, which in subsequent years forced a deep redefinition of the nation-state as an economic actor. Since the 1980s, states in developed capitalist countries, and a short time later in what were to become the transition economies of Eastern Europe, learned to extricate themselves from the economic responsibilities they had assumed in the postwar settlement, and in fact from any direct responsibility of managing the economy as such. After the demise of the international institutions that had sustained "the embedded liberalism" of the postwar era, everywhere, and increasingly even in Germany and Japan, the economic policy of choice became the disembedding of national economies: their integration in larger international markets for goods, services, capital, and labor; the fostering of competition and competitiveness inside and across national borders; and the privatization of economic infrastructures and social security provisions. In the process, as sectoral actors in national economies were becoming more responsive to arrangements and discourses in the same sectors in other countries, instead of other sectors in the same country, the capacity of national states to ensure internal compatibility and consistency between sectoral institutional arrangements may have irreversibly declined.

Today's second Great Transformation of the state, which in important respects appears to be a direct reversal of Polanyi's, would seem to amount not just to another wave of economic liberalization, but to a perhaps permanent dismantling of collective capacity to resist liberalization or bind it into and reconcile it with a nonliberal institutional context. States embedded in markets, however important they may continue to be for the well-being of their citizens, are something other than markets embedded in states. The emerging nation-state of the future, in Germany already more visible than in Japan, is much more market-making and market-conforming than market-limiting and market-distorting—an "entrepreneurial state" at best helping its society to exploit its opportunities and find its niche in an inevitably and irreversibly market-driven, internationalized economy.

It is hard to see how, with the redesigning of state capacity that is under way—including the irreversible democratization of the state that rules out recourse to authoritarian means—and in the changed international conditions of state action, there should again be formative political moments of the kind required, as shown by the histories of German and Japanese twentieth-century capitalism, to reconfirm national patterns of nonliberal capitalist governance, reverse the gradual advance of "free trade," or integrate it into a nonliberal master discourse. How long the transforming state apparatuses of Germany and Japan will be capable of pulling together the internationalizing sectors of their economies in an overarching national framework, defending the primacy of their societies over their economies and imposing a national purpose on "their" segments of the world economy, would appear to be an open question. And it seems highly unlikely that nation-states of the future, including those of Germany and Japan, will ever again have the historical leeway to make decisions as momentous as those made by states in the politicized era before and after World War II.

The Institutional Embedding of Market Economies: The German "Model" and Its Impact on Japan

Gerhard Lehmbruch

Production regimes such as those in Germany and Japan emerge from processes of institutionalization. The political economies of these two countries are each distinguished by a particular set of institutions that may be characterized as "embedding" the market economy.[1] Such institutions, however, are supported by a distinct cognitive framework from which they cannot be separated. This chapter explores this interplay of institutions and of collectively held beliefs rooted in "social definitions of reality." The underlying hypothesis is that these beliefs about the political economy and their evolution play an important role in explaining both the eventual persistence of such distinctive institutional patterns and phases of institutional change.

In Germany and Japan, two critical periods in the advance toward an embedded market economy can be identified. The first was the formation of a hegemonic discourse of state-led social reform that was inspired by the specter of the "social question" (i.e., the emergence of an industrial proletariat) and by the fear of social disintegration and revolution. The second accompanied the "Great Transformation" (Polanyi 1944) of the capitalist economies and, in both countries, the crisis of liberal democracy which culminated in the preparation for war. In this period of crisis, major institutional innovations took place, some of which became important building blocks for the "coordinated market economy" (Soskice 1999) of the postwar era. To be sure, democratic reconstruction after World War II went ahead with significant reorientations of the discourse. But this should not

---

1. The metaphor of "embedding" the market refers to Karl Polanyi (1944, 57).

lead us to overlook the continuities uncovered by recent research. Whereas in both countries the defeat of 1945 was long regarded as a radical turning point, it is today increasingly acknowledged that some important elements of the postwar order are rooted in the 1930s and early 1940s. However, the different trajectories of the German and Japanese models in the postwar era are not unrelated to the differences in the reconstitution of "discourse coalitions" in the occupation period and can even be traced further back to variations in the original discourse of state-led social reform of the late nineteenth century.

Institutions and "Discourse Coalitions" in Comparative Capitalism

A familiar pursuit of social scientists has become to describe "models" of capitalism, like *Modell Deutschland* (Markovits 1982), or to distinguish the *modèle rhénan* and the *modèle nippon* from the *modèle néo-américain* (Albert 1991). Such "models" may be conceived as relatively coherent configurations of institutions that constrain market exchange, and a certain congruity can be observed in each between the constraints generated by different institutions. Sociologists and political scientists have been attentive to such typological constructs in research on "comparative political economy" and "production regimes."[2] In this literature, the "path dependence" of models has increasingly been acknowledged.

Some social scientists have stressed the interdependence of institutions within a society and the resulting "pressure to have consistency in the rules and norms across institutional sectors." This, they argue, provides continuity in the sense that institutions only change "with a logic that is system specific" (Hollingsworth 1997, 267). For their part, economic historians have focused on the path-dependent character of microeconomic choices. In this literature, the common denominator is that "history matters," since choices made at some point in time produce "lock-in" effects reducing the scope for later choices (David 1985; North 1990, 100). Research on the development of technology has identified "several key features . . . common to path dependent processes: (1) strong technological interrelatedness, (2) increasing returns, or positive feedback, and (3) irreversibility of investment due to learning and habituation" (Powell 1991, 193).

It is the guiding hypothesis of this essay that such "irreversibility of in-

---

2. See, for example, Zysman (1983), P. Hall (1986), or the literature on the "governance of capitalist economies" (Campbell, Hollingsworth, and Lindberg 1991; Hollingsworth, Schmitter, and Streeck 1994) and on "social systems of production" (Hollingsworth and Boyer 1997) or "production regimes" (Soskice 1999).

vestment," and hence the path-dependent character of production regimes, results from the interplay of institutions that constitute the interface between politics and the economy and of the systems of hegemonic beliefs guiding the actor groups. Both the institutional interface and the hegemonic belief systems result from social compromises that have been reached to regulate the relationship of economic and political actors within a given polity or within a given sector (Jobert 1995, 21). Because under normal circumstances abandoning these institutions and beliefs in favor of different ones would entail considerable costs for the majority of actors, their preferred options will tend to be consistent with the antecedent paths of development so as not to endanger the compromises achieved in the past.

Institutional and policy change presupposes changes in the cognitive, normative, and instrumental beliefs of elite decision makers and thus raises the question of how change in hegemonic belief systems is engendered. A *belief system* has been defined as "a configuration of ideas and attitudes in which the elements are bound together by some form of constraint or functional interdependence" (Converse 1964, 207).[3] By *discourse* I mean a communicative process based on a set of conceptually articulated and logically coherent beliefs which are thus distinguished from belief systems lacking that property. *Policy discourse* refers to sets of basic beliefs and assumptions about the normative values, objectives, and regularities underlying the formation of public policy and serving to define the meaning of collective action and to establish the collective identity of the social actors who share this specific discourse.[4]

Discourses about "embedded capitalism" are hence the cognitions, norms, and rules regarding the economic and social order, held in common by strategically placed political, social, and economic elites. They serve to construct the collective identity of a "policy community" and to develop "recipes" and repertoires of strategies for collective action. These elites do not necessarily have scientific training, and their beliefs do not always exhibit the degree of conceptual articulation characteristic of economic or social theories. Instead they may remain on a pretheoretical level of abstraction. The issue, hence, is not merely the rise of new economic or social theories. The degree to which scientific ideas contribute to the formation of discourses about public policies is an empirical question. As Bruno Jobert (1995, 19–23) points out, the interpretation of social reality is

3. In this definition, "constraint" refers to "the interrelatedness of structure of a system of variables."

4. As employed here, the concept of policy discourse closely resembles the notion of *référentiel*, which Bruno Jobert and Pierre Muller introduced to the language of French political scientists (Jobert and Muller 1987; Muller 1984). A *référentiel*, according to these authors, describes the "references" of a policy.

closely intertwined with processes of negotiation and political exchange, but they take place in different "spaces" where either public policies are debated or where shared definitions of reality are negotiated. "Fora" of scientific debates obey a different logic of action than political "arenas," the latter being places of negotiation and formation of social compromises.[5] And when scientific fora become more internationalized, their potential divergence from (national) policy discourses increases and the feedback between both types of discourses becomes more uncertain (see also Jobert 1994, 12–13).

Thus, Keynesian ideas about demand management or the theory of rational expectations circulate on a different level of communication than the discourses explored here. When Keynesian ideas were introduced in different nations, their precise meaning "was affected by the nature of the prevailing political discourse," as Peter Hall has put it. National political discourses "include shared conceptions about the appropriate role of government, a number of common political ideals, and collective memories of past policy experiences." Their specific structure is "based on the networks of associations that relate common political ideals, familiar concepts, key issues, and collective historical experiences" to each other, as these historical experiences are "interpreted by a succession of political leaders" (P. Hall 1989, 383–84). The structure and institutional embedding of elite communication in such networks is thus an important variable for explaining cross-national variations of discourses.

In a more narrow sense, the interaction of policymakers and scholars in structuring such discourses has been labeled "discourse coalitions" (Wittrock, Wagner, and Wollmann 1991, 76). They "aggregate people from a variety of positions who share a particular belief system and who show a nontrivial degree of coordinated activity over time" (Singer 1990, 440).[6] On closer examination, however, the social composition of hegemonic discourse coalitions varies significantly from one country to another, often

---

5. This distinction is somewhat neglected in the literature on "epistemic communities" (Haas 1992).

6. Other, related conceptualizations are "issue networks" (Heclo 1978), "policy communities" (Dudley and Richardson 1996; Kingdon 1984), "policy subsystems" (Baumgartner and Jones 1991), "epistemic communities" (Haas 1992), and "advocacy coalitions" (Sabatier 1993). Like the original concept of "discourse coalition" developed by Wittrock, Wagner, and Wollmann (1991, 75–79), they focus on the role of knowledge in policymaking. I borrow the discourse coalition concept, relating it not to policy discourses in the narrower technical sense just mentioned, but to "national political discourses" as described by Peter Hall (1989, 383–84), and to the sectoral discourses (developed within their reach). The concept of "discourse coalitions" was taken up by Otto Singer in the context of a project on economic strategy change under my direction (Singer 1990), and I am indebted to some of his unpublished manuscripts and oral communications.

with the state administration as a central corporate actor within the coalition (Jobert and Muller 1987). And in both Germany and Japan their cognitive, normative, and instrumental framework of analysis was strongly shaped by their close interaction with social scientists (Pyle 1974). These alliances of bureaucrats and social scientists constituted powerful discourse coalitions within the institutional framework of the nation-state. Such coalitions often persist in their collectively held beliefs over long periods because it helps them to preserve their internal coherence and their intellectual hegemony, and facilitates their political and economic interaction. However, the notion of discourse coalitions should not be interpreted in a superficial "elitist" sense. Although elite actors play a crucial role in their formulation and reformulation, when such discourses acquire hegemonic status they also serve as the basis for the social interpretation of reality by ordinary people in everyday life.

It is important to keep in mind that path-dependent processes are not deterministic but stochastic (David 1997). Hence the persistence of hegemonic discourse coalitions cannot be posited a priori but must be treated as an empirical question. At times discourse coalitions may be so stable and powerful that no heterodox ideas get transported into politics. But under critical circumstances a dominant discourse may be challenged by a dissenting discourse coalition, and a hegemonic discourse coalition can eventually be displaced from this position by another, formerly minority, coalition, thus opening the way for policy change. The experience of Germany in the late nineteenth century has served as a basis for the influential hypothesis, developed in particular by Hans Rosenberg (1967), that sharp breaks in economic development may be followed by profound political realignments and, eventually, institutional transformations. It is very likely that the replacement of a hegemonic discourse coalition is an important element of such realignments related to "economic vicissitudes" (Abelshauser 1991, 12). Rosenberg developed his hypothesis with reference to the analytical framework of "long waves," which had been introduced by Nikolai Kondratieff, and it is indeed tempting to consider the replacement of discourses about the political economy as a phenomenon of long-term cycles and link it to crucial caesuras in the long-term cyclical movement of modern economies.

Such a view implies that, during the critical junctures of the cycle, old hegemonic discourse coalitions are challenged by new ones. Long periods of slow adaptation to changing circumstances are then punctuated by crises inducing more thorough revisions of basic beliefs and norms. That does not necessarily exclude the resilience of path dependencies in the development of new discourses, and the research problem then is to identify the innovative elements on the one hand, and lasting continuity on the other.

Discourses may evolve by integrating new elements or shedding others, a process often related to political realignments and related changes in the composition of the hegemonic discourse coalition (e.g., by the co-optation of new members from different backgrounds). Processes of transnational diffusion and borrowing may sometimes play an important part, and it is of particular interest to look into the role of specific elite groups who mediate such diffusion processes.

The hegemony of a discourse coalition does not imply that the same beliefs are held by all members of society. Rather, discourses of embedded capitalism are conflicting aggregations of beliefs held by independent actor sets who compete for power and for scarce resources but nevertheless are aware of the existence of strong interdependence in the pursuit of their interests. Such competing actor sets may be found in the form of associations (even of ideological subcultures) and increasingly in differentiated sectoral policy networks. Each of these actor sets may develop a specific partial discourse, and the particular discourses distinguishing specific subcultures, organizations, or sectors may contain many controversial and conflicting elements.

However, when the differentiated sectors and organizations within the political economy become increasingly connected into an encompassing context of collective action, a basic compatibility between them has to be achieved. The differentiation is then counterbalanced by the achievement of the hegemony of a "core discourse." It serves to integrate the competing organizations, subcultures, or sectors. Challenging the hegemonic core discourse would result in making the environment of these actor sets highly turbulent and uncertain. Since most relevant actors want to avoid such uncertainty, it is very likely that changes will be made at the margins and kept within limits that do not upset the existing equilibrium. Thus the hegemony of the core discourse results from processes of bargaining and coalition building between the competing actor sets, and one of its crucial functions is the stabilizing of power relations. For many actors involved it would usually be much too costly to challenge the terms of the compromises found in these bargaining processes.

In the historical process, the discourse of embedded capitalism has sometimes manifested a surprising adaptive quality and integrative power. As will be shown, its origins were characterized by a strong desire to check the rise of socialism, but along the way, the discourse managed to absorb the forces that once upheld the socialist counterdiscourse. This would, however, not have been possible without a differentiation of the discourse into, on the one hand, an increasingly ambiguous core discourse and, on the other hand, sectoral and organizational discourses that guide actual policymaking. Challenges to the hegemonic core discourse might disturb complex societal interdependencies, and therefore it is likely that the actors involved in these relationships will prefer adaptive changes to discontinuous change.[7]

The adoption of a shared cognitive framework cannot be seen in isolation from processes of institutionalization. This can be observed in serious historical crises. Such crises have been important catalysts for the building of market-embedding institutions and have at the same time often induced political realignments resulting in transformations of the hegemonic discourse. As will be shown, the economic crisis that shook Imperial Germany (1871–1918) in the first decade of its existence played such a catalytic role. Later, the two world wars provoked important institutional innovations and at the same time acquired overwhelming importance for the introduction of new elements in the core discourse. The hegemony of a discourse facilitates the adoption of institutions congruent with it, and vice versa. It is obvious that, when beliefs in the self-regulating character of markets are shaken, this may help the adoption of market-embedding institutions. But on the other hand, if business associations or labor unions are powerful and approaching a representational monopoly, this may make them particularly receptive to a discourse that might assign them an important place in regulating a political economy. Thus, learning processes taking place in both dimensions can reinforce each other. The formation and institutional consolidation of sectoral policy networks seems to be particularly fertile ground for such developments.

Discourses about the governance of the economy emerge in intellectual communities kept together by language and culture, but they may then diffuse across such boundaries and adapt to different environments. The adoption of Adam Smith's teachings in the Prussian bureaucracy is an early example, and recent cases can be found everywhere in the transformation processes of the former socialist countries of Eastern Europe. Such diffusion processes have been conspicuous in the relationship of Germany and Japan since the end of the nineteenth century. The literature on foreign influence on Japanese development—particularly in the Meiji era (1868–1912)—has either focused on the borrowing from foreign ideas (as in the pioneering article of Pyle 1974) or on the emulation and adaptation of institutions (Westney 1987 being an outstanding example). Here we con-

---

7. In the following analysis I must neglect the differentiation of policy discourses resulting from the "sectorization" and institutional segmentation of modern political systems. Sectoral policy discourses are distinct from the overarching global discourse, or from the core beliefs about society and political action to which the dominant elites adhere and that underpin the interactions of the relevant players within the political economy of a nation-state. In their research on the sectorization of discourses (*référentiels*) and the cognitive management of the "rapport global-sectoriel," Bruno Jobert and Pierre Muller focus on this relationship and interaction of core and sectoral discourses and the problem of their relative autonomy (Jobert and Muller 1987, 51–63; see also Muller 1995, 166–70).

sider both aspects, the diffusion of discourses about embedded capitalism to Meiji Japan as well as the importance of institutional borrowing.

This implies that, as far as Japan is concerned, this comparative case study will focus on the impact of transcultural borrowing on institutional change and its cognitive framework, instead of systematically exploring the generic and specific elements of each case. The observation of isomorphisms and differences between Germany and Japan and of their changing conditions should help us better understand the interplay of discourses and institutional development. My aim is hence not so much a content analysis of specific discourses. Rather, I focus on the interplay of the institutional framework and of the coalitions that generated the discourses, and on the conditions under which discourses achieved hegemony or were again superseded or eliminated by new beliefs and norms.

The Rise of the Discourse of Embedded Capitalism

Germany: From Developmental Liberalism to Statist Social Reform

Deliberate institutional design played an important role in the emergence and growth of embedded capitalism in Germany and Japan. In both countries, the discourse on embedded capitalism emerged in the second half of the nineteenth century, initiated by hegemonic discourse coalitions of bureaucrats and social scientists. But its further development took place in a highly path-dependent process punctuated by major reorientations and readjustment of some basic beliefs and by major reorganizations of the institutional framework. However, whereas in Japan the design of embedded capitalism was closely linked to basic institutional innovations in the building of the modern state, in Germany the process of state building and the embedding of capitalism were two clearly distinctive stages of development, and to confound them can lead to simplistic misinterpretations (Williams 1994 is a recent example).

In Germany, the second half of the nineteenth century was characterized by the rise, and then the breakdown, of one hegemonic discourse and its displacement by another which later developed remarkable adaptive capabilities. A "liberal developmentalist" core discourse that had dominated economic and social policy formation since the profound political reforms of the early nineteenth century was superseded in its last quarter by the alternative core discourse of "socially embedded capitalism." Although we can observe some basic continuities originating in the seventeenth- and eighteenth-century phase of state building, political realignments induced by major crises were accompanied by the emergence of new hegemonic discourses and discourse coalitions.

Bureaucratic Liberalism and the "Revolution from Above." Parallels between Germany and Japan are not infrequently explained by the "late developer" syndrome. German development has often been described as a *Sonderweg* (exceptional path) quite different from the processes of political and social modernization in Britain and other West European countries, and characterized in particular by the survival of premodern social forces and structures. This *Sonderweg*, which presumably culminated in the authoritarian political and institutional structure of Imperial Germany, appears closely related to the authoritarian modernization practiced by the Meiji elites. However, drawing this parallel between the German and Japanese development paths simplifies the strategic problem of Germany's relative backwardness and overlooks the existence of several sequences of modernization.[8] The issue of catching up with more advanced rival nations first emerged in Germany as a response to the French Revolution and led to reforms that remained basic for the process of state building. Yet there is a considerable time lag between this sequence of reform and the later parallel developments in Bismarck's Germany and Meiji Japan. Moreover, the original answers given in Germany to the problem of catch-up modernization differed remarkably from those found two generations later. The hegemonic discourse of the first sequence of modernization was economic liberalism. The "German model" of socially embedded capitalism can only be traced back to the second sequence of the German modernization process. The first sequence of this development is nevertheless important for its institutional legacy.

When the traumatic defeat of Prussia by Napoleon's armies in 1807 ushered in an era of fundamental institutional reform, its main promoters were the bureaucrats. To some degree, this domination of policy discourses by the bureaucracy continued an older tradition, that of the *gute Polizey*, or "the well-ordered police state" (Raeff 1983), of the seventeenth and eighteenth centuries.[9] *Kameralistik* (cameralism), the administrative science of German enlightened absolutism, and its subdiscipline of *Polizeywissenschaft*,

---

8. Martin (1995) points to some possible fallacies of this alleged parallel.

9. *Gute Polizey* is probably best rendered as "good administration." In the language of the older German administrative science, the purpose of *Polizey* was the welfare of the citizens. Raeff's translation of *Polizey* as "police" is somewhat misleading because since the nineteenth century the connotations of "police" (*Polizei* in the modern sense) have undergone considerable change (H. Maier 1980, 92–164). With the appearance of the liberal idea of the *Rechtsstaat*, the concept of *Polizei* became restricted to the protection of citizens against violations of the law by other citizens and to the protection of the state against any form of sedition (Haußherr 1953, 203–4). The older notion of *Polizeystaat* has hence nothing to do with the modern concept of a (totalitarian or authoritarian) "police state" (*Polizeistaat*). In the language of the eighteenth century, and up to Hegel, *Polizey* is synonymous with the modern concept of "administration," and *Polizeywissenschaft* may also be rendered as "policy science."

or "policy science" (H. Maier 1980, 164–90; Tribe 1988; 1995, 8–31), stressed the role of the state and its officials for economic and social transformation toward a society capable of fully exploiting its resources. Some of this heritage survived even after the breakthrough of liberalism as a new economic paradigm.

The leading power in this process of modernization guided by liberal ideas, when bureaucratic reform was conceived as "revolution from above," was Prussia. To be sure, some medium-sized German states (notably Bavaria, Baden, Württemberg, and Nassau) developed their own versions of bureaucratic modernization. Here too, the Napoleonic era opened the way to important bureaucratic reforms. But although the South German reform bureaucrats had a stronger commitment to constitutional reform and representative government than the Prussians, their economic and social ideas were, by and large, more traditionalist, and they remained often closer to the "statist" model of Napoleonic France (most conspicuously in the Bavaria of Montgelas).

What distinguished the Prussian reform from Southern Germany was the ascent of economic liberalism as the predominant discourse of a bureaucracy eager to catch up. The influence of Adam Smith's writings had progressively superseded the tradition of cameralism and mercantilism in the formation of Prussian civil servants (Hasek 1925, 117–21).[10] Some of the most influential among them had been trained as students of Christian Jacob Kraus, Kant's disciple and successor at the University of Königsberg. Kraus was an ardent Smithian and taught his audience that "since the times of the New Testament no literary work has exercised a more beneficial influence than *The Wealth of Nations*" (Treue 1951).[11] The bureaucratic promoters of the Prussian reform since 1808—led by Karl August Baron von Hardenberg (1750–1822), who from 1810 was the kingdom's prime minister (*Staatskanzler*)—were devoted believers in Smith's ideas (Vogel 1983a).

At the same time, however, the reform bureaucrats had a strong "developmentalist" orientation (as demonstrated, in particular, by Koselleck 1975), and their liberalism was tempered by some surviving notions from the erstwhile cameralism or policy science (Stolleis 1979, 315–98). This heritage was particularly visible in the strong concern of "Smithian" reform bureaucrats for the active promotion of trade and industry.[12] Of course

10. Smithian political economy was first introduced in the late eighteenth century at the University of Göttingen (established in 1736 by the elector of Hanover, who was at the same time king of Great Britain) and spread from there to the Prussian universities (Waszek 1988, 75–77). On the limits of the "Smith reception," see Tribe (1988, 146–48).

11. Ludwig von Vincke, the influential *Oberpräsident* (prefect) of Westphalia in the reform era, regularly began his day with reading a chapter from this book.

12. An interesting example of this "synthesis of reformed mercantilism and moderate liberalism" was the "Smithian" Christian Peter Beuth (1781–1853), for many decades the influential architect of Prussian industrial policy (Brose 1993; Mieck 1965).

competing factions and tendencies confronted each other in the administration (Brose 1993; Vogel 1983b, 1988), and after 1820 conservatism
tended to prevail as the dominant political orientation of bureaucrats
(Beck 1995; Wehler 1995). But economic, if not political, liberalism remained predominant, particularly in the period from 1848 to the founding
years of Bismarck's empire. Encouraged by the opening of markets in the
international environment, from the repeal of the British "corn laws" in
1846 to the French-British trade treaty of 1860, free trade developed into a
core element of the hegemonic bureaucratic belief system from mid-cen-
tury. The outstanding representative of this liberal bureaucracy was
Rudolph Delbrück (1817–1903), who became the chief architect of Prussian economic policy and of the economic integration of Germany from the
later period of the *Zollverein* (German Customs Union) and during the first
phase of Bismarck's leadership in the inaugural, liberal decade of the newly
established Reich.[13]

Although after the late 1870s this bureaucratic liberalism was largely superseded by a new and different discourse, the preceding development sequence remained important for the emergence of certain institutional patterns that came to distinguish the "German model" of embedding the
capitalist economy. One was the ascent, since the period of cameralist studies, of a new type of senior civil servant trained in economic reasoning.
However, their convictions were generally coupled with a pragmatic orientation, often a characteristic-mitigating element of the belief systems of
German economic bureaucrats to the present day.[14] Later, with the rise of
outside expertise in economic policymaking (in particular after the rise of
Keynesian economics), this type of bureaucrat appeared highly qualified to
serve as a sort of filter between the political system and the science system.

Bureaucratic liberalism was certainly instrumental in creating the institutional preconditions for economic growth. However, it would be an exag-
geration to depict the bureaucracy itself as the motor of industrial development. In the long run, the bureaucracy proved too weak for such a decisive
leadership role. It might perhaps be more adequate to characterize the relationship of bureaucrats and the emerging entrepreneurial class as one of

13. To depict the German Customs Union as an instrument of a "protectionist-minded
drive to industrialize Germany" (Williams 1994, citing Tsuruta) strangely misreads historical
facts.

14. This is well exemplified by Rudolph Delbrück. In his memoirs he mentions that, upon
entering his administrative career in 1840, he reread *The Wealth of Nations* but also discovered List's *Das nationale System der politischen Ökonomie*, which, he adds with a significant turn
of phrase, "did not repel me because, more than the works of Smith and Say, it took the existing real conditions into consideration" (Delbrück 1905, 115). The eclectic juxtaposition
of liberal economics with List's developmentalism thus served as the basis for the combination of a liberal free trade policy and early industrial policy, the two main political concerns
of Delbrück's career as they emerge from his memoirs (on Delbrück's career, see Treue
1981).

"reciprocal consent"—to borrow from the literature on contemporary Japan (Samuels 1987).

A significant institutional feature of this reciprocal relationship was the importance of associations as intermediary agents. Already the *Polizeystaat* (a notion approximating the later concept of the "welfare state") of German enlightened absolutism relied on the "cooperation of lower, preexisting associations, solidarities, or institutions" for achieving effectiveness in its "overall purpose of guiding and transforming society" (Raeff 1983, 45–46, 153–55). Important continuities—such as reliance of state action on intermediary associations—became visible and would in the future distinguish the path of German capitalist development from that of England (Abelshauser 1990). The liberal bureaucrats were intent not on eliminating guilds and corporations but rather on reforming them. They even encouraged the formation of new associations because this would compensate for the underdevelopment of grassroots dynamism. In particular, the intermediation of associational interest in agriculture was largely initiated by bureaucratic initiative (Lehmbruch 1999).

Furthermore, it was also in the period after 1848 that the specific German system of industrial finance was developed, including the important role of the *Universalbanken* so often stressed in the literature (Gerschenkron 1962, 11–16; Shonfield 1965; Zysman 1983, 251–66). However, it would be too narrow to focus exclusively on this specific type of bank and to overlook the importance of the savings banks (*Sparkassen*), which were closely linked to local governments, and also of the emerging cooperative banks with their importance for small and medium-sized business and agriculture.

Finally, it is important to keep in mind that this institutional framework developed before the formation of the German national state. Given its federal organization, an important consequence was that policy networks linking the administration and economic actors on the level of the later member states of the federation (the *Länder*) continued to play an important role, and that the role of government in industrial or agrarian policy was often characterized by a strong degree of decentralization.

The Crisis of Market Liberalism and the Emergence of Corporatism. The long deflationary crisis that started with the financial crash of 1873 (the Günderkrise) shook the belief of the ruling German elites in the paradigm of market liberalism.[15] In 1879 Bismarck abandoned the free-trade policy that had characterized the preceding decades (Rosenberg 1967). This funda-

15. Whether this crisis marks the advent of a long cyclical downturn called the Great Depression (Hans Rosenberg) is a controversial issue in recent historical research. But there is no doubt that it caused a profound political realignment.

mental change was accompanied by a broad political realignment. The government previously had largely counted on the National-Liberal Party for its legislative majority. But now it began to rely on a coalition of conservatives and Catholics and on the support of the protectionist alliance of heavy industry and agrarian interests. The introduction of protective tariffs was the most controversial element and the symbolic core of the new policy.

Such a change of trade policy, to be sure, was not a German peculiarity. At that time in other European countries too (France and Italy, in particular), free trade gave way to protectionism. But in Germany this new course, baptized "protection of national labor," was part of a larger package of policies reemphasizing the role of the state for the welfare of its subjects. It included the takeover of means of mass transportation (notably railways) and public utilities by the state and local governments (often called "state socialism" or "municipal socialism") in the name of public purpose; a regional policy for the equalization of living conditions (Abelshauser 1980); and the introduction of social security (Manow 1997). A favorite label given by contemporary writers to this new policy was "neomercantilism" (Schmoller 1911; Tschierschky 1913).[16]

This reversal of policy was accompanied by important institutional changes. One was the emergence and rapid growth of powerful national peak associations, in particular for industry (Centralverband Deutscher Industrieller, 1876) and agriculture (Bund der Landwirte, 1893), which acted as agents for protectionist interests. These associations did not achieve organizational monopolies; their ambitions were contested by smaller rival peak associations representing, among others, the interests of export-oriented business and of parts of the peasantry opposed to the dominance of large landholders. Small business interests remained fragmented, but the government offset their weakness by establishing compulsory chamber organizations for trades (*Handwerkskammern* and *Innungen*)—a move that critical contemporaries regarded as a return to the system of guilds abolished by the liberal reforms of the 1869 industry code. An important concomitant of the strengthening of chamber organizations was the self-regulation of vocational training, in particular in the trades sector. In Prussia, compulsory chambers were also introduced for agriculture. Associational

16. Beginning with Veblen (1915) this period was often considered decisive for the emergence of the so-called German *Sonderweg*, supposedly responsible for the later victory of national-socialism. The *Sonderweg* hypothesis, according to which the power of "preindustrial" elites obstructed the modernization of German society, was increasingly contested by those who consider the "embedded" capitalism of Imperial Germany as specifically modern (e.g., Blackbourn and Eley 1984). In the latter view, Imperial Germany was not "premodern" but "the first postliberal nation" (Abelshauser 1984). For a more recent contribution to the *Sonderweg* controversy, see Wehler (1995, 461–86).

growth was thus not simply a spontaneous process. Indeed, the encouragement of corporatist interest associations and of cartels was deliberate government policy (Abelshauser 1987; Wehler 1995, 662–80; Winkler 1972).

In spite of the growth of strong peak associations, considerable elements of decentralization survived in the system of interest intermediation. To be sure, the central government played the decisive role not only in policies of foreign trade and—in particular since the 1930s—market regulation, but also in regulating labor and social policy. But in the German federal system, implementation was largely left to the member states, and, moreover, social security was by and large highly decentralized. This was particularly the case in the health insurance system where, as will be shown, decentralized self-administration developed into an important institutional point of entry for the access of organized labor to participation in policy formation.

The Discourse Coalition of State-Led Social Reform. The abandonment of the free-trade policy was accompanied by a deliberate assault against the hegemony of the liberal discourse. The elimination from power of the liberal discourse coalition was an important precondition for the rise to hegemony of a discourse coalition committed to the embedding of capitalism. This was achieved by the sweeping purge of liberals from the civil service that accompanied Bismarck's change of strategy (Morsey 1957, 262–70). Rudolph Delbrück, the influential chief official of the Chancellery of the Reich, was removed in 1875, and in the following years the liberal bureaucrats were systematically deprived of their influence. In their place, conservatives came to dominate the civil service until the end of the monarchy. But the conservatives were not a homogeneous group. Since the 1840s, the advocacy of paternalist social reforms had gained ground within the ranks of the higher civil service.[17] And conservative proponents of social reform, such as Theodor Lohmann (1831–1905), were now appointed to key positions in the Prussian Department of Commerce and in the Imperial Department of the Interior (Rothfels 1927).

The discourse coalition for state-led social reform thus came to play a pivotal role in the development of social policy and economic organization (Stolleis 1979, 404–6). The civil servants who were the key actors in this coalition had been influenced, among others, by economic writers such as the conservative Ricardian "state socialist" Carl Rodbertus (1805–75) and by Friedrich List, a liberal journalist whose "post-Smithian" views had been strongly shaped by his acquaintance with early American protectionism (Tribe 1995, 32–65). But the most influential pioneer of the state-led social reform discourse undoubtedly was Lorenz (von) Stein with his program of

---

17. An important role as an adviser to Bismarck was played by Hermann Wagener (1815–89), originally a conservative journalist (Beck 1995, 101–22; Saile 1958).

a "monarchy of social reform," which took its inspiration from Hegel's political philosophy (Blasius and Pankoke 1977; Böckenförde 1976).[18]

It was Georg Wilhelm Friedrich Hegel (1770–1831) who laid the theoretical foundations for the German discourse on the social embedding of the market economy. The once-popular caricature of this philosopher as a supposedly reactionary apologist of the Prussian state has been thoroughly revised in modern research.[19] Hegel was quite early on deeply preoccupied with political and social developments in contemporary Britain. From his frequent reading of English and Scottish newspapers and journals, he acquired detailed knowledge of the Industrial Revolution and its social consequences. At the same time, he familiarized himself with the British political economists, notably with James Steuart's *Principles of Political Economy* and with Adam Smith's *The Wealth of Nations* (Dickey 1987, 186–204; Waszek 1988). And the capitalist market dynamics, as analyzed by Adam Smith, David Ricardo, and Jean Baptiste Say, as well as their social consequences, became a central issue in his political writings and lectures, notably in *Jenenser Realphilosophie* (1803–6) and *Philosophie des Rechts* (1821).

Being sharply opposed to the romantic conservatives, Hegel considered not only the French Revolution and the rule of rational law but also the market economy as irreversible achievements in the history of mankind. A basically liberal persuasion was thus an important component of his thought. But he shared Steuart's doubts about the capacity of markets for self-regulation and believed it necessary to check their disruptive tendencies and to correct market failure. The unequal distribution of wealth was in Hegel's eyes an inevitable outgrowth of the natural inequality of human capacities in civil society. But the example of England demonstrated to him that capitalist industrialization resulted not only in the increasing accumulation of wealth but also in augmenting the dependence and deprivation of the working class and letting many of them—through no fault of their own—sink below the level of subsistence required for the dignity of being a member of civil society. Thus, in spite of its excessive riches, society was unable to control the excess of poverty and the resulting generation of a "rabble" that had lost its human self-respect and lacked the incentives for work.[20]

18. Lorenz von Stein (1815–90, ennobled in 1868) should not be confused with the Reichsfreiherr (Baron) Karl vom Stein (1757–1831), the famous leader of the Prussian reform movement at the time of Napoleon I, to whom Meiji reformers such as Yamagata referred when they drew upon his ideas about local government.

19. This revision began with Marcuse (1941) and Weil (1950). See, in particular, Avineri (1972), Kelly (1978), Riedel (1969), J. Ritter (1957), and Waszek (1988).

20. According to Hegel's *Philosophy of Right*, "a rabble is created . . . when there is joined to poverty a disposition of mind, an inner indignation against the rich, against society, against the government, etc." (Hegel 1833 §244, supplement, 302–3).

Yet as concerned as Hegel was about these dilemmas resulting from capitalist industrialization, he had no adequate solution. His programmatic vision remained limited to the idea of correcting market failure by a mix of administrative regulation (*Polizei*, in the older sense of the term) and self-regulation. For this the social classes ("estates") of agriculture, crafts, and merchants should organize themselves into "corporations," which would provide to the individual the social recognition by members of other classes that he needed for his human dignity.[21] The bureaucracy, as the "universal estate" by virtue of education and universalistic ethos, should assume a central role in mediating social conflict and promoting the public interest.[22] But though Hegel was aware of the social problems associated with the formation of a class of proletarians, the latter was not included in his pluralist system of "estates" and "corporations," and obviously it had not yet occurred to him that the working class might be mobilized for collective action.

It took another generation for the Hegelian Lorenz Stein to interpret contemporary French history as a class conflict in which the ruling class tried to colonize the state in order to subdue the working class but, by its attempt, provoked the revolutionary resistance of the latter. In his famous book on the communist and socialist movements in France (Stein 1850, 1964), he concluded that, to avoid revolution, a strategy of social reform was required. Such a strategy, however, could only be developed and implemented by a power institutionally independent from the conflicting classes—an "administration of social reform" drawing its constitutional legitimacy from a "monarchy of social reform" (*Königtum der sozialen Reform*).[23] Stein thus—in Hegel's footsteps—expected the bureaucracy to serve as the vehicle for a reform integrating the working class into the capitalist society. In later years he remained concerned about the revolutionary danger, but nevertheless strongly disapproved Bismarck's antisocialist repression. As mentioned, Stein's ideas had a considerable influence on the social reform bureaucrats around Bismarck who initiated the German tradition of state-led social policy (notably Hermann Wagener and Theodor Lohmann).

A distinctive trait of the new discourse coalition was the close interaction

21. In Hegel's language, "estates" were not based on ascriptive status but on occupation and constituted interest groups recognized by public authority (cf. also Heiman 1971).

22. In the present context we may pass over Hegel's "communitarian" theory of the state as the realization of ethical freedom (*Sittlichkeit*). This theory—often flagrantly misunderstood because of lack of familiarity with the state of research—was essentially an attempt to overcome the contradictions of a modern market society by appealing to the notion of the *polis* as a political community (Pelczynski 1984), which German idealism inherited from classical Greek philosophy.

23. Stein himself pleaded in particular for the participation of workers in capital ownership.

between the reformist bureaucrats and academic social scientists organized in associations devoted to the promotion of scientific belief systems. The Verein für Socialpolitik (Social Policy Association) became the most influential in propagating state-led social reform. This association was set up in 1873 by the conservative economist Gustav Schmoller (1838–1917) together with eminent scholars such as Adolph Wagner (1835–1917). This school became known by the derogatory term of *Kathedersozialisten* (socialists in the academic chair), a term coined by its liberal critics. Schmoller explicitly referred to Stein's concept of the "monarchy of social reform."[24] Although not all of the *Kathedersozialisten* were conservatives in the traditional sense, many also supported economic nationalism and protectionism.[25]

The Verein für Socialpolitik concentrated its efforts on empirically based social research and on the theory of economic and social policy. Other important academic think tanks with close relationships to the bureaucracy included the Evangelisch-Soziale Kongreß, founded in 1890 by social reformers close to the Protestant churches, and the Gesellschaft für Soziale Reform (Association for Social Reform) established in 1902 by the former Prussian minister of trade, Hans Hermann Baron Berlepsch. This *Gesellschaft für Soziale Reform* attracted a younger, more pragmatic generation of bourgeois social reformers who militated in favor of a reform of industrial relations in a spirit of social partnership that would no longer exclude organized labor. So significant changes were under way. To be sure, the specter of social revolution continued to worry the older cohorts of German social reform bureaucrats and their academic advisers. Notwithstanding the epithet of *Kathedersozialisten* bestowed on the latter, they clearly were enemies of socialism. Although they considered Bismarck's policy of repression potentially counterproductive, they aimed at cutting the ground from under the feet of the workers' movement. It is all the

24. It is misleading to identify the *Kathedersozialisten* with the so-called "Historical School" of German economics and to ascribe theoretical continuity to the currents usually subsumed under this label. To be sure, Gustav Schmoller was a leader of the "Younger Historical School" characterized by its disdain of classical economic theory and its emphasis on empirical historical research (Pyle 1974, 132–37). But some of the most outstanding *Kathedersozialisten* (e.g., Adolf Wagner and Albert Schäffle) were far from that tendency. And this tendency was only superficially related to the "(older) historical school" of early nineteenth-century economists (Adam Müller, Friedrich List). Schmoller and his like-minded contemporaries were outspoken empiricists and rather indifferent to that theoretical legacy. As pointed out above, the social policy programs of the *Kathedersozialisten* were much more indebted to Lorenz von Stein and, hence, to Hegel's heritage. Hegel, however, unlike Müller and List, regarded the abstract theorizing of classical "political economy" as an important contribution to understanding modern society (*Philosophy of Right*, §189), and his contemporaries rightly considered Hegel's "philosophical school" as antithetical to the romantic "historical school."

25. There were some notable exceptions, such as the economist Lujo Brentano, who was one of the social reformers but remained a free-trader.

more remarkable that, as will be shown, in a later stage organized labor was increasingly co-opted into the discourse of embedded capitalism.

Discourses of Social Reform in the Organized Subcultures: Social Catholics and "Reformist" Social Democrats on the Path toward Inclusion. All these ideological currents and organizations represented the dominant "bourgeois" and Protestant culture of Imperial Germany. Still, up to the regime of Hitler (and to some degree even beyond), Germany was conspicuously segmented into ideological subcultures. Religion had constituted a central cleavage since the sixteenth century, and after 1871 the Catholics found themselves in a minority position. In the first decades of Imperial Germany they remained pretty much at the margins of the power structure. As big business, the administration, and the universities were dominated by Protestants, the Catholic segment developed its own "counterculture" based on a cohesive network of organizations cultivating their own political and social discourses. A somewhat parallel development took place with the rise of socialism. Under the strong influence of Marxist ideas, the "workers' movement" cut earlier links to the liberal tradition and developed a comparable subculture, again with a cohesive network of organizations.

Thus Imperial Germany had a "pillarized" structure—culturally and politically segmented—comparable to the pillarization (*verzuiling*) of religious and ideological subcultures in the Netherlands. It is well known that Bismarck considered these minorities enemies of the empire and attempted to subdue both, first in his campaign against the Catholic Church (the Kulturkampf), started in 1872, and then in the repressive legislation of 1878 against the Social Democrats. Both exclusionary bids finally failed, and these minorities were then gradually included—many remaining obstacles notwithstanding. The Catholics made their first inroads into the ranks of the higher civil service around the turn of the century, whereas the Social Democrats had to wait until the Weimar Republic (1918–33) and parliamentary democracy to overcome political discrimination. Although the bourgeois-Protestant forces maintained much of their cultural hegemony until Hitler came to power, a slow process of inclusionary assimilation of the minority subcultures had already begun. One of its consequences was a gradual convergence of other discourses of social reform with the tradition going back to Hegel, Lorenz von Stein, and the *Kathedersozialisten*, until finally—as will be shown—these different currents were integrated into the "social market economy" discourse of the Federal Republic.

Considerable importance was first attained by the Social Catholic movement. It had been pioneered by the famous bishop of Mayence, Wilhelm von Ketteler (1811–77), and represented a distinct discourse coalition that for many years remained politically isolated. But the intellectual leaders and activists of the Catholic minority—for example, the priest Adolf Kolp-ing (1813–65), who launched a strong Catholic workers' organization, and the priest and social scientist Franz Hitze (1851–1921)—were successful in mobilizing the political resources of this subculture. The headquarters of their peak association established in 1890, the Volksverein für das kathol-ische Deutschland, served as an important think tank devoted to social re-form. In the later phase of the empire, they succeeded in slowly cracking their former political isolation, and Catholic civil servants even managed to enter the top social policy offices of the imperial administration. In party politics, the Social Catholic movement was represented by the Center Party, a socially heterogeneous formation in which social reformers and Catholic unionists formed an influential and particularly active wing. During the Weimar Republic, the Center Party participated in all government coali-tions, and one of the bureaucratic strongholds of Social Catholics was the Ministry of Labor (Bähr 1989, 52–54). Given the importance of the Catholic labor unions with which they cooperated, the proponents of the Catholic reform discourse contributed to the inclusion of organized labor in a coalition of social reform.

Although the Catholic social reform discourse was not unrelated to the currents encountered in the Protestant milieu, its emphasis was different in some important respects. In the field of industrial relations, Social Catholics favored state intervention in the form of compulsory arbitration (Bähr 1989, 52–62). In social policy, on the other hand, they were less "sta-tist" and stressed the "principle of subsidiarity" (*Subsidiaritätsprinzip*), ac-cording to which state intervention should be limited to the solution of so-cial problems that could not be solved by autonomous societal action. In an elaborate doctrinal version, this led to the formulation of a corporatist doc-trine, most notably in the papal encyclicals *Rerum Novarum* (1892) and *Quadragesimo Anno* (1932).[26] For Germany, with Catholics forming a minor-ity culture, the practical relevance of these doctrinal ideas remained neces-sarily limited, and hence pragmatic cooperation with the Protestant propo-nents of social reform was a more realistic strategy. After World War II, when Catholics occupied a much stronger political position in the Federal Republic of (West) Germany, the Social Catholic discourse attained new prominence. In particular, it made a significant contribution to the eclectic ideas of a "social market economy," and Social Catholics became an impor-tant element of the discourse coalition of embedded capitalism.

26. These encyclicals resulted from the diffusion of the ideas of Social Catholicism to other countries, in particular to Austria (with the aristocrats Karl Baron Vogelsang and Alois Prince Liechtenstein as intellectual leaders, and with the popular mayor of Vienna, Karl Lueger, as its politically most forceful representative around the turn of the century), to France (with the intellectual aristocrats Albert de Mun and René La Tour du Pin), and to Italy (with Giuseppe Toniolo).

On the other hand, the contribution of the reformist tradition in the Social Democratic movement also cannot be neglected. Although the dominant ideological tradition was long permeated by Marxism, in three different currents the reformist discourse gained importance. The first was found among adherents of the heritage of Ferdinand Lassalle, the founder of the first German workers' party; the second consisted of the "revisionist" Marxists led by Eduard Bernstein; and the third was represented by pragmatic labor union leaders such as Carl Legien. The "Lassallean" tradition emphasized state action for social reform and expected its realization from political democracy, in particular from universal suffrage.[27] Revisionist Marxists, for their part, shared with orthodox Marxists a belief in the importance of the development of productive forces for political and social development, but believed in a transformation of capitalism different from that predicted by Marx, whereby a gradual transition to socialism might become possible. The practitioners from organized labor, finally, regarded ideology with skepticism and believed in reform through democratization and through the progress of collective bargaining. The formal hegemony of Marxist theory was maintained for many years within the Social Democratic Party (it was reaffirmed for the last time as the official party manifesto in the Heidelberger Programm of 1925), but the reformist currents slowly gained ground, in particular in the practice of industrial relations, until after World War II they achieved their victory with the Godesberger Programm of 1959.

Three institutional points of leverage proved of particular importance for the progress toward inclusion. The first was the introduction, by Bismarck, of equal and universal (male) suffrage for the Reichstag. The second element was the right to form "coalitions" (particularly labor unions) and the right to strike, both introduced with the industry code of 1869. Compulsory provision of health insurance for workers ironically became a third important institutional access point, thanks to the introduction of decentralized self-administration in the health insurance system with *paritätische* (on the basis of parity) representation of workers and employers.

Bismarck was of course an uncompromising enemy of working-class organizations, and his advisers, in the footsteps of Lorenz von Stein, considered paternalist social reform an expedient to check the influence of organized socialism. Thus it is a remarkable irony of history that the system of social insurance introduced by Bismarck offered, as an unintended consequence, the opportunity for the organized working class to capture positions of influence within the "self-administration" of the insurance

---

27. Universal male suffrage was introduced by Bismarck in 1867 for the North German Federation and in 1871 for the empire. In 1918, the electoral franchise was extended to women.

schemes.[28] This experience, however, helped prepare the unions for integration into the framework of embedded capitalism (Manow 1997). The variety of the discourse stressed the "parity" of participation of capital and labor, an idea clearly distinct from Marxian socialism. And in spite of the dominance of Marxist ideology in the Social Democratic Party in the early twentieth century, within organized labor the idea of "parity" was slowly extended to demands for worker representation in the enterprise and in industrial relations (Rabenschlag-Kräusslich 1983; Teuteberg 1961). At the same time, a more positive image of labor unions began to emerge in the ranks of bourgeois social reformers.

Thus, in the long run it was not the social "paternalism" of some conservative employers (the most prominent being Friedrich Harkort, Alfred Krupp, and Baron Carl Ferdinand von Stumm) who nurtured the idea of the business firm as a "big family" that distinguished the mainstream of social reform. Instead, the idea of "social partnership," based on the inclusion of organized labor, gradually gained ground. As will be shown, this was one dimension where the German version of embedded capitalism remained distinct from the Japanese.

Statist Social Reform in Meiji Japan

It is well known that the Prussian constitution of 1850 served as a model for the Meiji constitution of 1889 and that German experts played an important role in the making of the Japanese constitution (Beasley 1990, 76–80; Martin 1995, 33–37; Schenck 1997; Siemes 1968, 1975). Closely related is the influence of German concepts of state-led social reform on policy discourses in Japan to which Kenneth Pyle (1974) first drew attention. He emphasized in particular the strong influence of the Younger Historical School of German economics on Japanese paternalist strategies in social policy and industrial relations as they developed from the late nineteenth century. Other historians of social and economic thought in Meiji Japan have followed Pyle's lead (Kinzley 1991, 23; Morris-Suzuki 1989, 59–70). This German influence found its most visible expression in the founding, in 1896, of the Shakai Seisaku Gakkai (Society for Social Policy), a Japanese equivalent of the Verein für Socialpolitik (Pyle 1974, 145–48).

Although the lessons of the *Kathedersozialisten* may have been an important stimulus for the Japanese debate on social policy beginning in the 1890s, the acquaintance with German theories of bureaucratic social re-

28. The representation of workers and employers in the bodies of the health insurance system corresponded to the proportion of their contribution to the system: two-thirds were paid by workers, one-third by employers. Therefore, full-time officials of the health insurance funds were increasingly recruited from the labor unions.

form appears to date farther back, with Lorenz von Stein himself as the central figure (Beasley 1990, 77). Around 1881 he was approached by Japanese officials who aroused his interest in Meiji reforms.[29] When in 1882 Hirobumi Itō traveled to Europe to study German constitutional law, he not only met Bismarck but also visited Stein in Vienna and for six weeks received from him private lectures which covered, besides German constitutional law and practice, "social classes and political parties, social reform and elections" (Martin 1995, 36; see also Zöllner 1992, 31–32).[30] The introduction of a Prussian-style civil service in Japan also owed much to the advice given by Stein to Itō (Spaulding 1967) and was of course a logical corollary of the "monarchy of social reform."

To be sure, Stein's Japanese interlocutors may not have become fully aware of the implications of this theory before the "social question" emerged in the 1890s as a consequence of Japan's industrial takeoff (Westney 1987, 21–22). However, both Stein and Itō were guided by the desire to prevent revolutionary unrest, and it is not surprising that both the Prussian constitutional order and state-led social reform finally became integral parts of an early *Modell Deutschland* able to reconcile two main objectives of the Meiji elite: a policy of accelerated modernization and the preservation of stability and social harmony (on this point, see Pyle 1974). Japanese visitors to late nineteenth-century Europe, similar to Lorenz von Stein when he visited France a half-century earlier, observed the social conflicts accompanying the process of industrialization. And likewise they reflected upon the necessity to check the potentially destabilizing political consequences of catch-up modernization (cf. also Kinzley 1991, 18–25). So it is not surprising that Stein was offered an appointment at the Imperial University in Tokyo,[31] and that Itō later instructed many other Japanese visitors bound

29. This interest was expressed by Stein among others in correspondence with Yukichi Fukuzawa published in 1882 (reprinted in Brauneder and Nishiyama 1992, 227–42; see also Stein 1887; Zöllner 1992, 31).

30. Itō first consulted Rudolf von Gneist (1816–95), a leading authority in German public law who was strongly influenced by Stein himself. Gneist served for many years as chairman of the Centralverein für das Wohl der arbeitenden Klassen (Association for the Welfare of the Working Classes), a welfare organization launched by conservative civil servants in 1844 (Beck 1995, 169–97). Itō also received private lectures by Gneist's student Albert Mosse and became acquainted with arguments of the *Kathedersozialisten* (Schenck 1997, 152). He was disappointed by these encounters in Berlin, but enthusiastic about his following contact with Stein. The seventeen lectures Stein gave to Hirobumi Itō and his secretary, Miyoji Itō, were recorded by the latter; this English version was then checked in detail by Stein, and later translated into Japanese to serve as reference material (according to Zöllner, this Japanese version has been published by Shimizu 1939, 241–335). On Stein's influence on the Meiji constitution, see Nishiyama (1992).

31. Stein declined this offer because of his age but agreed to serve as legal adviser for a high salary. Instead, Hermann Roesler, who had been strongly influenced by Stein's doctrine of the "social monarchy" (Siemes 1968, 36–41), and Gneist's disciple Albert Mosse were appointed to the Imperial University in Tokyo. Roesler drafted the Meiji constitution and Mosse advised on the legislation on local government.

for Europe to call on him there—among them Aritomo Yamagata and Kiyo-taka Kuroda.[32]

Japan's borrowing from the German constitutional model was clearly a process of "selective emulation" (as defined by Westney 1987, 27). Most conspicuous was the deliberate rewriting by Hirobumi Itō of Article 1 of Hermann Roesler's draft constitution. In place of the constitutional monarch specified in the draft, Itō substituted the neo-Confucian concept of the emperor as the head of the *kokutai*, the family-like Japanese ethnic community held together by the values of loyalty and ancestor worship, and references to the Shintō myth of the divine origins of the monarchy (Hoston 1986, 28 ff.; Pittau 1967; Siemes 1968, 14, 16–22). Likewise, when Aritomo Yamagata borrowed from the German theories of communal self-government to develop a system of local administration, the adaptation to Japan took a strongly centralist turn and neglected the (limited) autonomy enjoyed by the local citizenship in the German institutional model (Hackett 1971, 107–15; Staubitz 1973; Totten 1977).

Somewhat different, however, was the "Japanization" of German theories of state-led social reform. Unlike cross-societal borrowing on the level of organizational patterns or institutional arrangements, borrowing on the level of discourses may be subject to a selectivity of interpretation when basic propositions are integrated into a different, historically determined context of meaning. The reinterpretation of these propositions is guided by preconceptions due to culture or history.

In the case of the German discourse of social reform, its basic normative propositions were not spelled out in operative terms, and thus a relatively broad scope existed for their translation into concrete policies. When in 1850 Lorenz von Stein formulated his theory of state-led social reform, his most elaborate policy proposal—the participation of workers in capital formation—obviously did not exhaust the normative potential of the theory. In the 1880s, Bismarck's advisers developed from the same normative propositions a quite different operative institutional conclusion, namely, the introduction of a social security system.

It is well known that German innovations in social security served as a model for other European countries (Heclo 1974, 179–85).[33] Hence, given the strong attention of the Meiji leaders to the German example, one may wonder why they did not also adopt this centerpiece of Bismarck's social

---

32. Among others, Itō arranged private lectures by Stein for the emperor. For this purpose, the Imperial Chamberlain Kototada Fujinami traveled to Vienna, and Stein lectured to him "as if he were talking to the emperor in person" (Nishiyama 1992, 54). Fujinami then in thirty-three evening sessions rendered to the emperor what he had learned. It is significant for the breadth of Stein's Japanese contacts that his legacy (at the Schleswig-Holsteinische Landesarchiv, Kiel) contains letters from 50 Japanese correspondents and a collection of 120 business cards (Nawrocki 1992; Zöllner 1990).

33. See, however, Alber (1982, 142–46) on the limits of this model role.

policy.[34] To be sure, the program of factory reform was embraced by authors such as Noburu Kanai (Morris-Suzuki 1989, 66–67). Also, somewhat similar to Germany, a strong social policy bureaucracy developed. The Bureau of Health and Sanitation in the powerful Home Ministry (Naimushō), later supplemented by the Social Affairs Bureau, was its first nucleus. This bureaucracy was relatively independent from employers and constituted a counterweight to the Ministry of Agriculture and Commerce (Nōshōmushō) (Garon 1987, 73–87, 94–95). But when in 1898 bureau chief Shinpei Gotō, an admirer of Bismarck's social policy, proposed a workers' sickness insurance law, the suggestion failed at an early stage, and even later compulsory social insurance schemes never attained the political importance they had in Germany.

Was this striking departure from the German model another instance of deliberate selective emulation, as observed in Japanese borrowing from the Prussian constitution with Itō's rewriting of Roesler's draft? On closer examination, the case of social policy is less clear-cut. In Westney's framework (Westney 1987, 24–32), it is more like the "unintended departure" from the foreign model due to powerful "implicit models" based on the past experience of the adopters. More precisely, when the Meiji reformers drew specific policy conclusions from a German social policy discourse that they regarded as congenial with their neo-Confucian traditions, they based their approach on a tacit reinterpretation within their own intellectual frame of reference.

As mentioned, the basic tenets of the German social policy discourse can be traced back to Hegel and Lorenz von Stein. It should be remembered, however, that Hegel addressed students and readers whom he expected to be familiar with the thought of Adam Smith and Jean-Jacques Rousseau. So when he started from the basic analytical distinction between civil society (*bürgerliche Gesellschaft*) and the state, his notion of civil society as consisting of individual, free, and equal property owners was easy for an educated German public to comprehend. For both Hegel and Stein, society was constituted by the contradictory unity of the individual pursuit of particular interests and the mutual dependence of all members in this very pursuit, and this immanent contradiction results in conflicts the state must regulate in the search for political order.[35]

This concept of society was obviously alien to the early Meiji elites educated in a neo-Confucian philosophy. When Japanese authors of that time

---

34. Because of lack of space, I am neglecting here the strong impact of the German model on the development of agricultural cooperatives in Japan (Pyle 1974, 156–58)

35. Stein, for whom the central problem of political order was the dependence of a class who owned no property on the class of property owners, dropped the adjective "civil" when speaking of "society."

attempted to render basic ideas of Western political thought, they experienced considerable difficulties in finding an adequate Japanese equivalent for the concept of "society."[36] But this should not be interpreted as an expression of fundamental differences due to some immutable cultural uniqueness of Japan. On closer look, there were some remarkable affinities between the social and political thought of Meiji Japan and that of "ancient Europe" (*Alteuropa*). But whereas this older view of the world had been largely abandoned in modern Germany,[37] Japanese borrowings from contemporary German theory were projected back into an older intellectual framework with different references.

It is frequently stressed that in Japanese social thought at the end of the Tokugawa period, and even in later years, the *ie* (house) was perceived as the basic social entity (Coulmas 1993, 73–75; Hirschmeier 1986, 64, 93–95; Murakami 1984; Najita 1974, 23–24; Nakane 1970, 4–8). The *ie* is said to constitute the key element of "the informal system" of Japanese society which "is a native Japanese brew, steeped in a unique characteristic of Japanese culture" (Nakane 1970, 149). The "Japanization" of the German social policy discourse can thus essentially be described as a reinterpretation linking Stein's ideas to "the *ie*-type organizational principle" which, according to Yasusuke Murakami (1984, 356–62) and other authors (Fruin 1994, 307; Hirschmeier 1986, 51), continued "to operate at the intermediate level of society" (of firms and industries).

However, the importance of this reinterpretation can be better assessed if we question the assumption of cultural uniqueness of the *ie* type of social organization claimed by Nakane and unfolded in Murakami's grandiose theory of "*ie* society."[38] In a comparative perspective, the denotation of *ie* (as described by these authors) bears a close resemblance to that of *oikos* or *Haus* (also literally house) in the "ancient European" social discourse up to the mid-eighteenth century. As Otto Brunner (1980a) has shown in an influential essay, the "ancient European" concept of the house was rooted in

36. Japanese etymological research has devoted particular attention to these efforts (Fukuzawa 1988, n. 4). Coulmas (1993, 13–19) makes the point that Yukichi Fukuzawa, as well as Masanao Nakamura with his translation of John Stuart Mill's *On Liberty*, faced such difficulties because "society" had no counterpart in the reality of contemporary Japan.

37. In German historiography the concept of *Alteuropa* was introduced by the Austrian social historian Otto Brunner (1980) to describe the synthesis of the Greco-Roman and the Christian intellectual heritage that dominated in Europe from the Middle Ages to the seventeenth and eighteenth centuries.

38. Murakami's essay was received with ample reservation by some historians and anthropologists who doubted whether indeed "Japan's group-oriented social behavior today has a tradition that extends over a thousand years" (J. Hall 1985, 55) and intimated a certain affinity of this ambitious "multilinear" evolutionary approach toward a comparative history of civilizations with "the ongoing *Nihonjinron* debates about Japan's cultural identity" (J. Hall 1985, 47; see also Lebra 1985; Rohlen 1985, 68–69).

classical Greco-Roman antiquity. Just as the *ie* was at the same time "a corporate residential group" and "a managing body" (Nakane 1970, 4), so was the *Haus* or *oikos*, and the latter could equally be described as a "vertical" authority relationship, with the *pater familias* (in German, *Hausvater*) at its top (see also Tribe 1988, 23–27). Brunner has even asserted that the *Haus* or *Wirtschaft* (in the sense of "household") was "the basic social structure of all peasant and peasant-nobility cultures" (Brunner 1980, 107).[39] Hence, what "ancient European" thought since the *oikonomia* of Xenophon and Aristotle (the "economics" of the household) had first put into a theoretical framework was, according to Brunner, rooted in a much more widespread way of thinking, and the *ie* of Tokugawa Japan is one example among others that would fit perfectly into this hypothesis.

In Germany, however, toward the end of the eighteenth century, social thought moved in a different direction when, as Brunner points out, with the advent of the modern market economy and modern ("classical") economics, the traditional ("ancient European") meaning of *Haus* or *oikos* was increasingly abandoned. Instead, social discourse now centered around the concepts of "political economy" and "society" as they had been developed by the Scottish moral philosophers. This was particularly true of Hegel and of course also of Lorenz von Stein.[40] The obsolescence of the *Haus* as a basic category of social thought was the intellectual prerequisite for Hegel's view of "civil society" structured in interest groups ("estates") and organized in "corporations," or for Stein's view of society as divided into "classes." These concepts designated social units founded upon horizontal ties (and thus distinct from the vertical structure of the traditional *Haus*). However, remnants of the older discourse of social relations persisted during the nineteenth century. The best-known example was the above-mentioned paternalist model of the socially responsible enterprise advocated by

39. Brunner's influential views have provoked some criticism because of their alleged conservative bias, but at least in part this seems due to misunderstandings (Oexle 1984). His essay focused on the dominant social interpretation of reality (or "discourses") rather than on the underlying reality itself. Authors who denounce his concept of the "whole house" as neglecting the progress of the division of labor and market relationships since the Middle Ages (Groebner 1995; Wehler 1987, 82–83) overlook his explicit acknowledgment that the doctrine of the "house" up to the eighteenth century ignored existing market relationships (Brunner 1980, 123–25). One might add that even some leaders of heavy industry in the late nineteenth century such as Alfred Krupp (1812–87) and Karl Ferdinand Baron Stumm (1836–1902) still understood their position as that of a *pater familias* in the traditional—but now clearly anachronistic—sense.

40. This rupture with an ancient tradition of social thought is manifest in Hegel's *Philosophy of Right* (§180) where he reproves the institution of entailment (or *fideicommissum*) inasmuch as inheritance laws should no longer serve the continuance of the traditional household in the (Aristotelian) sense of *oikos* (*Haus oder Stamm*) but of the nuclear family in the modern sense, based on matrimony and consisting exclusively of spouses and their children (Hegel 1833, 243–44).

Harkort, Krupp, and Stumm—at that time a rational and quite effective strategy for controlling the workforce in big industry (Geary 1991), although it had an increasingly anachronistic resonance (Berghoff 1997; Gall 2000, 115–17, 215–37).

In view of these developments, one may wonder whether the assumption of the uniqueness of the *ie* type of social organization is not based on a synchronic fallacy where Japanese social patterns of the late nineteenth century and the meaning given to them in the prevailing discourse are compared to social patterns and discourses of contemporary Europe. In such a synchronic perspective, the *ie* may indeed be defined as a vertical authority relationship distinguished from civil society or *Gesellschaft* conceived as a horizontal aggregation of autonomous individuals.

When industrialization took off in Japan, a discourse emphasizing vertical authority relationships still prevailed, whereas in Germany at that time a similar discourse had largely been abandoned in favor of a conceptual framework stressing horizontal patterns of social relationships and strongly indebted to the social thought of modern Western Europe. Hence, when the Meiji reformers had to translate Stein's teachings into the categories of their own social discourse, the intellectual background from which they read them was more akin to the "ancient European" view of society which German social theory had largely left behind. This resulted in a quite striking lack of fit between the ideas of the statist social reformers in Germany and their Japanese followers. Describing both Germany and Japan as "late developers" blurs this important difference.

Thus in Japan, Lorenz von Stein's notion of the "monarchy of social reform" was amalgamated with the idea, taken from the *kokutai* ideology, of the emperor as "moral and benevolent ruler with profound concern for the welfare of his subjects" (Hoston 1986, 32). Stein's basic distinction of state and society was plainly absent from this adaptation to Japanese intellectual traditions. Therefore it is not surprising that the trajectory of the Japanese variety of embedded capitalism has significantly departed from the German path. To be sure, the political motives were strikingly similar: the worry about the threat of socialism and the dislike of labor unions were certainly shared by the *Kathedersozialisten* and their Japanese followers, and so was the conviction that social reform was needed to avoid these dangers. But because of the rather broad scope of alternatives in translating basic propositions of a discourse into operative solutions of political problems, the institutional consequences were remarkably different.

Moreover, whereas the Meiji elites liked to emphasize the homogeneity of Japanese society, the elites of Imperial Germany became increasingly mindful of the cultural and political segmentation (or "pillarization") of German society. After the fiasco of Bismarck's repressive policies, his successors slowly began to understand that the integration of the minority subcultures of political Catholicism and the workers' movement was an indispensable condition for constitutional governability. A traditional institutional device for this was the "parity" (*Parität*) of subcultures that had developed since the Westphalian Peace of 1648 (Lehmbruch 1996). In Japan, neither the socialist movement nor labor unions had a similar basis in a distinct subculture, and no comparable strategic repertoire for managing social conflict had been developed. This difference is most palpable if we regard a crucial organizational detail of the German system such as the principle of parity in its self-administration. Whereas in the German insurance system the institutional logic of self-administration and *Parität* fostered the gradual inclusion of organized labor in the reformist discourse coalition, it is unlikely that the Japanese proponents of state-led social reform would have accepted this sort of inclusion at the turn of the century. With the social security system as the (originally unintended) institutional basis, the gradual integration of the organized workers' movement into the discourse of "social partnership" marked a second generation of the German discourse of embedded capitalism, whereas Japan pursued a different trajectory.

The system of industrial relations hence became a crossroads where the German and Japanese discourse coalitions parted and where Japan became distinct from Germany for several decades. This material difference in policy outcomes had obvious roots in the reinterpretation of the German social policy discourse by the Japanese as relating to the *ie* rather than to a *Gesellschaft* structured into corporate groups or classes. This reinterpretation was promoted by a discourse coalition that found its organizational expression in the Shakai Seisaku Gakkai, the aforementioned counterpart of the Verein für Socialpolitik, and the Kyōchōkai (Cooperation and Harmony Society) which—responding to the increase in social tensions during World War I—was launched in 1919 by reformist-conservative bureaucrats and businessmen such as Takejiro Tokonami and Eiichi Shibusawa. The Kyōchōkai (which never included labor representatives) interpreted social reform in strictly neo-Confucian terms (Kinzley 1991), and when its leaders referred to a German model, it was the "socially responsible" enterprise of Krupp—in other words, an anachronistic paternalism still indebted to the "ancient European" notion of the *Haus* (Gall 2000). The development in the interwar years of the Japanese employment system (Dore 1973, 375–403), with its strong focus on stabilizing enterprise-level labor relations, was fully consistent with this orientation.

The Japanese interpretation of the German discourse was determined not only by a different background of understanding. A meaningful fit had to be established with the emerging institutional setting of early Meiji Japan. As pointed out above, a significant institutional feature of the German model since the *Polizeystaat* was the reliance of state action on associations as intermediary agents. Although remarkable parallels may be found in contemporary Japan, in the Meiji period the development of the associational system was uneven, and in large parts of industry it lagged considerably behind the German pattern. To be sure, on a general level of development there are some remarkable similarities. Tokugawa Japan had known a tradition of guilds (*nakama*) whose economic functions "were so similar to those of Europe that little needs to be said" (Hirschmeier and Yui 1981, 37). Under the influence of Anglo-American beliefs, Meiji reformers originally suppressed these guilds because they supposedly inhibited the freedom of trade due to their monopolistic practices.

But beginning in the 1880s, the government adopted a policy closer to that of Germany's neomercantilist period by instituting chambers of commerce in the more important cities, and later licensing specialized trade associations (*dōgyō kumiai*) to replace the former guilds (Lockwood 1968, 561–62; B. Marshall 1967, 24–29). Generally speaking, in the late nineteenth century the associability of business was not highly developed, and so it was the government that institutionalized interest organizations, most often by legislation (Ishida 1968; Pempel and Tsunekawa 1979).[41] In large sectors of industry, however, the *zaibatsu* emerged as an alternative channel for the intermediation of interests directly linked to the government.

The emergence of the *zaibatsu* not only permitted these big diversified business groups—which have been described as "family organizations employing the idea of the 'house' in a modernized fashion" (Hirschmeier 1986, 51; see also Morikawa 1992, 114–18)—to largely dispense with associative action. Their intense competition was apparently a strong deterrent to lateral cooperation in the form of business associations; indeed, the only major sector where a trade association gained importance (and restricted competition like a cartel) was the cotton spinning industry in which the *zaibatsu* played no important role (Lockwood 1968, 230–31).

It was not until the Taisho period (1912–26) that business associations emerged that were not government sponsored. The Kōgyō Kurabu (Industrial Club) set up in 1917 was a loose organization dominated by *zaibatsu* representatives. It was primarily interested in industrial relations and served as a counterweight to the Kyōchōkai (Ishida 1968; B. Marshall 1967). As the mouthpiece of big business, it was later superseded by the Keizai Renmeikai (Economic Federation), originally established in 1922 to represent the interests mainly of banks (Hirschmeier and Yui 1981, 184–86). But neither association could ever claim a representational monopoly. Moreover, because the *zaibatsu* could rely on direct channels to the government until the early Showa period (1926–89), these alliances never

41. Also in the domain of agriculture the government at that time established similar associations (*nōkai*) with compulsory membership.

became effective transmission lines between business and government policy, as had the peak associations when they took shape in Germany. This difference would prove fatal when the Japanese leadership emulated the German mobilization of capitalists for war.

The development of labor unions was also rather slow, with the Yūaikai founded in 1912 as the first fairly consolidated organization. The repression of labor movements by the state, which had been the rule in the Meiji period, slowly gave way to a more permissive policy, but the government and business leaders remained reluctant to accept a system of industrial relations based on collective bargaining. However, since World War I the "social bureaucrats" from the Home Ministry turned to a policy of integrating organized labor, combining a commitment to social reforms with control of union activities, and supported the moderate union leaders from Sōdōmei (Garon 1987, 73–119).

The "Great Transformation" and the Mobilization of Capitalism for War

Institutional Change and Discourse Coalitions in Germany, 1914–45

It is to Karl Polanyi that we owe the notion of the "Great Transformation" of nineteenth-century civilization. The institutional core of that system—its "fount and matrix," in Polanyi's words—had been the self-regulating market, and the secular change that transformed this civilization began in the 1920s. According to Polanyi, "World War I and the postwar revolutions still formed part of the nineteenth century" (Polanyi 1944, 20). This precise date looks plausible if we consider that the most important mutation of the core discourse of socially embedded capitalism took place in the 1930s and 1940s. The impact of the world economic crisis that started in 1929 on discourses about capitalism and on the formation of discourse coalitions may be likened to that of the 1873 economic crisis, and so it could make sense to consider this year as a turning point.

Yet if we focus on the institutional framework of embedded capitalism, the dividing line cannot be drawn as neatly as Polanyi suggested. In the case of Germany, it seems more exact to locate the watershed in World War I. This war gave rise to new forms of economic governance that suspended the self-regulating market. To be sure, the institutions of the war economy were at that time considered by many as a temporary expedient for times of crisis. Some of their intellectual authors, though, already saw them as prefiguring new forms for organizing the national economy. Fifteen years later, when the seizure of power by the Nazi Party led to significant institutional innovations in Germany's political economy, these institutions were in part rooted in the earlier experiences of the war economy of 1914–18. The underlying discourse inherited from these experiences was that of "total war." Although substantial parts of this institutional framework disappeared together with that discourse in the catastrophic defeat of 1945, some critical elements survived and contributed to the formation of the postwar economic governance, and particularly of the system of organized interests. A similar legacy of the war economy can be found in Japan, and in this case too it was the ultimate legacy of a disposition to borrow from German models.

At the outbreak of World War I, some executives from the German electrical industry warned the military leadership that Germany would soon run out of raw materials if efficient forms of military procurement were not set up quickly. This was the beginning of a new organization of the economy. The architects and intellectual leaders of this ambitious organizational effort were a distinguished German industrialist, the chairman of the Allgemeine Elektrizitäts Gesellschaft (AEG) Walther Rathenau, and one of his senior managers, Wichard von Moellendorff. Rathenau, a businessman as well as an intellectual and prolific writer, was convinced that the industrial order was in need of a profound transformation. Moellendorff, an engineer influenced by Frederick Taylor, believed in industrial reorganization as a way to use technology efficiently and later developed a much-noticed theory of *Gemeinwirtschaft* (communalistic economy) in which the quest for private profit should be overcome in favor of the common interest (Bowen 1947; Moellendorff 1916). The concept of *Gemeinwirtschaft*, in which the invisible hand as a regulatory principle would be replaced by the requirements of *Bedarfsdeckung* (supply of essential commodities), took its original justification from the overriding imperatives of a war economy, but it survived for many decades as one component of the German concept of "economic democracy" (Naphtali 1928) or, at least, as a corrective element in a mixed economy. Both Rathenau and Moellendorff were admirers of the Prussian state tradition and considered their efforts indebted to the ethos of state-led reform (Feldman 1966; C. Maier 1987, 38–41).

The army chief of staff, General Erich von Falkenhayn, was immediately persuaded by the recommendations of AEG management and had Rathenau appointed as head of a new administrative unit in the Ministry of War, the War Raw Materials Division (Kriegsrohstoffabteilung). Its duty was to supervise and control the affected industries, and for performing this task, Rathenau recruited a staff from the management of these very industries. He was convinced that national interest would be strong enough to reconcile his ideal of "industrial self-government" with the inevitable use of coercion.

At the outset, industry was by no means unanimous in its support for this approach, and conflicts about the autonomy of private enterprise persisted during the war. However, this effort was helped by the business associations themselves. Soon after the outbreak of the war, the peak associations of industry established the Kriegsausschuß der Deutschen Industrie (War Committee of German Industry) with the double function to more effectively represent industrial interests toward government, parliament, and the military, and at the same time to coordinate the war efforts of industry. The trade associations served as organizational transmission lines between government and the army, on one side, and enterprises on the other, and this induced remarkable processes of organizational learning. In particular, rival associations were encouraged to cooperate, and the two competing peak associations of German industry (the Centralverband deutscher Industrieller and the Bund der Industriellen) finally merged in 1919. Their successor, the Reichsverband der Deutschen Industrie, was from then on vested with a de facto organizational monopoly. The war economy thus had durable institutional consequences by paving the way for the corporatist transformation of formerly pluralist patterns of interest intermediation (in the sense of the familiar distinction going back to Schmitter 1974), and for a "coordinated market economy" (Soskice 1999), and it demonstrated that organized interests could serve as instruments for the political goals of government.

Another institutional outgrowth of the war economy was the gradual transformation of industrial relations. When in 1916 the war went into a critical stage, the military high command proclaimed the need for a "total" mobilization, in particular for arms production. This was the turning point of traditional warfare which later inspired the discourse of the "total war." In the immediate short run, however, this strategic change triggered efforts for political inclusion of organized labor and thus had an impact on institution building not anticipated by its authors. The adoption of a law permitting the mandatory assignment of workers to the armaments industry (Hilfsdienstgesetz) was among the priority demands of the military, but to make the restricted freedom of movement of labor acceptable to the unions, the government had to swallow the participation of labor representatives and the establishment of works councils (Feldman 1966). This meant the integration of organized labor as a political support for the war economy.

These developments prepared the creation, at the end of the war, of the basic institutional framework of social partnership by the agreement of leading representatives of labor and employers (the *Stinnes-Legien Abkommen* of 1918) to form a Zentralarbeitsgemeinschaft (Central Working Group) for coordinating the transition from the war economy to peace (Feldman 1981; Feldman and Steinisch 1985). Labor leaders wanted, above all, an orderly transition to parliamentary democracy and shared with businessmen a profound mistrust of bolshevism and socialist experiments. The agreement also revealed the strong skepticism of both business and labor about the capacity of government to manage the economic and social problems of this transition and prefigured the later option of both sides for institutionalizing labor relations without state intervention. To be sure, strong forces within the employers' camp—notably in heavy industry—considered this no more than a transitory arrangement justified by an emergency situation. Thus, not surprisingly, the pact survived only until the early 1920s and was never strong enough to generate widely shared beliefs about social partnership as a constitutive element of the economic and social order. Not surprisingly, attempts to resuscitate the cooperation of business and labor in the final crisis of the Weimar Republic failed, and social partnership remained far from constituting a dominant discourse.

Parallel to these developments, the founding of the Weimar Republic signified the inclusion of the two former minority subcultures, "political Catholicism" and the workers' movement, into a state organized on a democratic and parliamentary basis. The political incorporation of labor led to the institutionalization of industrial relations, with the law on works councils and the decree on collective bargaining (Tarifordnung). However, the autonomy of the partners at that time was restricted by the introduction of the power of government to settle industrial conflict by compulsory arbitration, a scheme that was strongly favored by the Social Catholics and has been interpreted as an ingredient of "conservative modernization" (Bähr 1989, 347). An important institutional innovation was the creation of the Ministry of Labor which—as mentioned—turned into a stronghold of Catholic bureaucrats from the Christian Social movement sympathetic to organized labor.

Taken together, World War I and the postwar period served as an important catalyst for the institutional transformation of German capitalism. For the first time, a "corporatist" pattern of interest intermediation emerged, and although much of it fell apart again in the postwar period, the invention of this institutional repertoire was not entirely lost from the organizational memory and served as an important point of departure for the further development of the discourse of embedded capitalism. The breakdown of Weimar democracy and the period of the National Socialist dictatorship signified a severe setback, but not a wholesale and enduring rupture of continuity. As the economic policy of the Nazi leadership was dominated by preparations for war, the regime attempted to learn from the experience of the 1914–18 war economy in a path-dependent process. In a sense, among the legacies of the Nazi era is also an unintended strengthening of some of those path-dependent patterns that had become visible in World War I.

In the short run, of course, Hitler's regime had to cope with the impact of the depression that began in 1929. Its importance for the spread of

Keynesian ideas has often been discussed. Although the influence of Keynes on German politics was limited, "proto-Keynesian" ideas emerged at that time (Bombach et al. 1976), most explicitly among the labor unionists with the 1932 "WTB plan" for an anticyclical work creation program (Schneider 1975).[42] Their ideas met with strong resistance from the Marxists in the Social Democratic Party, but with approval from the Nazi Party.[43] Indeed, after Hitler's seizure of power, his economic policy was largely guided by a distinct "proto-Keynesian" approach. Yet this soon degenerated into a "rearmament Keynesianism" which finally gave way to planning for the preparation of the war economy. The culminating point was the proclamation of "total war" in early 1943, a discourse that demonstrated the long-run impact of the military crisis of 1916 mentioned above. Military writers as well as men of letters interpreted the World War I experience of large-scale mobilization of the civilian population with the rhetoric of "total war,"[44] and this formed part of the intellectual background for the militarization of the political economy after Hitler's seizure of power.

To be sure, the stereotypical equation of the economic policies of Nazi Germany with economic planning and a command economy (*Zwangswirtschaft*) distorted a more complex historical reality and can no longer be upheld. Hitler supported the principle of economic competition, which he interpreted in Darwinist terms, and was concerned that a planned economy might lead to communism and undermine "the harsh laws of the economic selection of the better and of the destruction of the weak." Yet because of the priority given by him to the preparation for war, he apparently considered the command economy an unavoidable temporary expedient (Herbst 1982, 80–81). Thus the advocates of planning and those of a market economy remained in disagreement until the final years of Hitler's regime. The latter maintained a stronghold in the Ministry of Economics (Boelcke 1983; Herbst 1996, 300–301) and were in frequent conflict with the planners of the total war, notably with the Ministry of Armaments led by Albert Speer.

The transformation of economic governance in the Third Reich did not follow an elaborate, preconceived plan. With the preparation for war as its foremost rationale, it was very much characterized by improvisation. Instead of establishing a completely new order, the Nazi Party opted for the *Gleichschaltung* of the existing system of the intermediation of business in-

42. The authors meant by the acronym were the economists Wladimir Woytinski and Fritz Baade and the union leader Fritz Tarnow.
43. Gregor Strasser, at that time leader of its left wing (and later eliminated by Hitler), even opened discussions with the unions.
44. On the development of these doctrines, see Herbst (1982, 35–44). Their most prominent representatives were the well-known writer Ernst Jünger (1931) and General Ludendorff who from 1916 to 1918 had been chief of staff (Ludendorff 1935).

terests, accompanied by a streamlining of organizational structures. To force organized interests into line, the ruling party had recourse to some central elements of the institutional repertoire developed during World War I. Business associations were transformed into state-controlled organizations with compulsory membership and functional monopolies. Thus, the former Reichsverband der Deutschen Industrie and its constituent trade associations were reorganized as the Reichsgruppe Industrie differentiated into sector groups (*Wirtschaftsgruppen*), branch groups (*Fachgruppen*), and branch subgroups (*Fachuntergruppen*). This was accompanied by a thorough organizational rationalization.

The engineering industry is a good example (Weber 1991, 121–29). In the Weimar Republic, about eighty specialized trade associations had been affiliated with one peak association, the Verein Deutscher Maschinenbau-Anstalten (VDMA; Association of German Engineering Firms), with the exception of the Verein Deutscher Werkzeugmaschinenfabriken (Association of German Machine Tool Manufacturers), which remained autonomous. All these associations were now integrated into one sector group, the Wirtschaftsgruppe Maschinenproduktion (WGM), which was subdivided into seventeen branch groups and seventeen branch subgroups. Among the tasks of the WGM was rationalization by standardizing products and parts and specialization of firms on a limited number of products. State intervention in the sector was expected to be channeled exclusively through the administrative apparatus of the WGM. An important aspect of this reorganization was that most officials of the former associations—except those who were of Jewish descent or had strong links to liberal parties—were kept in their positions, and the Nazi Party refrained from meddling in their business. The introduction of the Nazi *Führerprinzip*, that is, of a strictly hierarchical structure of command, was sufficient to transform these organizations into instruments of the war economy.

The Nazi dictatorship cut much deeper into the organizational fate of labor unions and agricultural interests than into the organization of business. In both cases, hitherto existing associations were subjugated. In the case of agriculture, this meant their transformation into a highly integrated corporatist monopoly with compulsory membership, the Reichsnährstand. The autonomous labor movement, however, was completely suppressed and replaced by the Deutsche Arbeitsfront (DAF), a mass organization under the control of the Nazi Party and including employers as well as workers. The tasks of the DAF were largely restricted to social services at the workplace (including the organization of vacations), whereas wages and working conditions were fixed by a state agency, the Treuhänder der Arbeit (labor trustees). But again the organization was streamlined along industry lines (instead of crafts or profession).

Japan and the Model of the German War Economy:
Discourse Transfer and Institutional Emulation in the 1930s
and 1940s

As noted above, as important as the German contribution to the beginnings of Japan's embedded capitalism in the Meiji period may have been,
the borrowing mainly took place on the level of the core discourse, whereas
the transposition into social and political practice was very much a process
of autochthonous institution building, mediated by the "Japanization" of
the German discourse. It was different with the second wave of borrowing
from the German model which occurred in the early Showa period and culminated in the organization of capitalism for war. Today it is largely acknowledged that Japan's political economy and, in particular, industrial
policy after World War II cannot be fully understood without considering
the lasting impact of patterns established in the war economy (Johnson
1982, 116–56; Murakami 1984, 360; Nakamura 1995, 3–21; Okazaki 1994,
1997), and in this connection the influence of the German model on Japanese leaders between 1935 and 1945 has recently attracted new attention
(Gao 1994, 1997).

The Discourse Coalition of the Managed Economy. The core of the discourse
coalition that came to the forefront in the 1930s consisted of younger civil
servants who were identified by labels such as *kakushin kanryō* (reform bureaucrats) and often came from the social policy tradition (Gao 1997, 93–96;
Johnson 1982, 124–26; Spaulding 1970). Many were familiar with Germany,
and their interest focused increasingly on the institutional framework of German "organized capitalism." In 1930 an aspiring representative of this group,
Nobosuke Kishi, went to Germany to study the industrial rationalization
movement (at that time a fashionable offspring of Taylorism) and concluded
that competition should be replaced by cooperation and control, for which
the German practice of cartels appeared to be a promising instrument
(Johnson 1982, 108). Later the reform bureaucrats cooperated with some
economists who originally had been strongly influenced by Marxism but
later "recanted" (*tenkō*) and turned to nationalism after parliamentary government had been replaced by authoritarian rule (Gao 1994, 1997).

In this group, the sources of the Japanese discourse on the political economy of capitalism were now much more diversified: they included Schum-
peter and Keynes, and the ongoing German influence went beyond the intellectual traditions of state-led social reform and neomercantilism. With
the exhaustion of the Historical School, German economics of the interwar
period had lost its intellectual aura. So Japanese intellectuals such as Hiromi Arisawa during their studies in Germany became interested in new
ideas propagated outside academe, such as Marxism, but also in German

ideas about total war that were also very much in favor with the "German faction" of the Japanese army (Martin 1995, 211–12) and "demanded tight control of the state over the economy" (Gao 1994, 122; 1997, 62). The Showa Research Association was the most important of the think tanks where these intellectuals exchanged ideas with the reform bureaucrats and developed the notion of a "managed economy" (Gao 1997, 103–10). The catchword for this role of the state was "economic general staff." In this period, as Gao has argued, three basic principles of economic policy were developed which—in modified form—survived through the postwar era: (1) a "strategic view of the economy" which aimed at building an optimal industrial structure through government planning and industrial policy; (2) the restraint of excessive competition in view of maintaining order in economic growth; and (3) the rejection of the profit motive in management (Gao 1997, 14).

Emulating the Institutions of the German War Economy. With its references to the German war economy, however, this Japanese discourse coalition not only borrowed from the German discourse of the time. A logical consequence was that it also took German institutions as a model for organizing a capitalist economy. Until the 1920s, close relationships with large enterprises had been the preferred channel for the Japanese state to communicate with business. In the 1930s, economic crisis spurred a policy turn toward cartelization and employing business associations for the control of markets. Then, after 1937, Japan began the authoritarian mobilization for the war economy, and these developments are of considerable importance for our subject because they prepared an institutional framework, much of which survived in the postwar period.

In the economic bureaucracy, a strategic orientation toward encompassing rational planning of the economy took the upper hand (Okazaki 1997, 288–97). After the appointment of Fumimaro Konoe as prime minister, the younger reform bureaucrats propagated a "new economic system" (*keizai shintaisei*) inspired by the German system of economic governance. Kishi, now vice-minister of commerce and industry, was a central figure in these efforts. Among the leading ideas was a restructuring of economic governance—removing business firms from the control of capital and turning them into "an organic unit of capital, management and labor" (Gao 1997, 116). The separation of ownership and management aimed at strengthening the position of managers, and workers were henceforth to be considered "proper members of the firm alongside stockholders and managers" (Okazaki 1997, 297; see also Okazaki 1994, 365–70). The attempted revision of the Commercial Code was, however, prevented by the opposition of business, and the power of this opposition was decisive for the outcome of the reorganization of business associations.

This effort culminated in 1941 with the Jūyō Sangyō Dantei Rei (Important Industries Association Ordinance). It was strongly influenced by the model of the streamlined business organization in Nazi Germany (Hirschmeier and Yui 1981, 249–51) and introduced an organizational architecture of "control associations" (*tōsei-kai*) patterned after the aforementioned Reichsgruppe Industrie with its *Wirtschaftsgruppen* and *Fachgruppen*. As in the German model, the task of the *tōsei-kai* was the rationing of raw materials, the setting of production goals, and the distribution of the output of member firms. However, whereas the German *Wirtschaftsgruppen* were the organizational successors of old and well-functioning trade associations, the Japanese reform bureaucrats could not rely on an established tradition of associational action with experienced managers and with sufficient authority in relation to the member firms. Because of these weaknesses, the efficiency of the Japanese war economy remained limited. Moreover, the anticapitalist overtones of the reform program triggered the strong resistance of big business. To keep the *tōsei-kai* working, the government had to fall back on its traditional strategy privileging big business: the leadership position in the *tōsei-kai* was given to the top manager of the largest member firm.

Hence, the authoritarian reorganization of the economy resulted in the strengthening of the position of the *zaibatsu* as the dominant force in the most important industry associations. This signified, as Murakami put it, that "the *ie* principle again worked against the integration of the whole society" (Murakami 1984, 354). These structural weaknesses of the *tōsei-kai* contributed to the inadequacy of the Japanese war economy (Hirschmeier and Yui 1981, 237–41; Martin 1995, 143–45). Obviously, the "1940 system" was a case of institutional borrowing that only partially achieved its objectives. But it became a point of departure for important institutional developments after World War I.

Of similar lasting importance was the launching, in 1938, of the Sanpō (Sangyō Hōkoku Renmei; Patriotic Industrial Society) as a mass organization for workers, like the Deutsche Arbeitsfront, to replace the labor unions (Gordon 1985, 299–326). Sanpō, and government labor policy, "in a few crucial areas . . . had an observable impact on the aspirations of workers, on management strategy, and on the structure of labor relations," and it provided an organizational experience and an apparatus that could serve as "a point of departure for unions organized after the war" (Gordon 1985, 261–63, 325). One important aspect of this model role was that Sanpō was organized on a workplace or enterprise basis, and this experience discouraged later attempts to constitute effective industrial unions (Tabata 1997, 87). As Masahiko Aoki puts it: "Without the organizational experience of the massive Patriotic Industrial Society, the rapid unionization after World

War II would probably have been unimaginable" (Aoki 1988, 186; cf. Naka-mura 1995, 19).

The Postwar Maturing of Embedded Capitalism

Japan and (West) Germany are not the only countries where major insti-tutional innovations that had been developed during the war economy in-duced processes of organizational learning and thus had a durable impact on important postwar governance patterns. The modern war (and the post-war period) confronted the belligerent nations and even some neutrals with extraordinary problems of scarcity and with the challenge of mobiliz-ing resources that could not be mobilized by the market. Elements of the strategic repertoire as well as of the organizational structures that had been developed under these conditions could then be retained even in the envi-ronment of peace. Which elements of this repertoire were retained and converted to new purposes, often in a fundamentally altered political framework, depended on the continuity of old elites, but also on calcula-tions of new elites who discovered new strategic opportunities in taking up the organizational heritage of the wartime structures—as happened with the relationship of democratic labor unions toward the legacy of the DAF or Sanpō.

Postwar West Germany and the "Social Market Economy"

Institutional Continuity and Changing Elites. The breakdown of the Nazi dictatorship and the Allied occupation of Germany meant of course a sharp rupture with the central elements of Hitler's regime. Nevertheless, some of the path-dependent institutional changes that had been reinforced rather than invented by the Nazi leadership left a lasting imprint at the level of intermediary institutions. As mentioned, the reorganization of or-ganized business in the Nazi era left most officials of the former associa-tions in their positions. This continuity, moreover, extended into the post-World-War-II era, as many officials of these organizations reemerged in the leadership of the business associations that were gradually reestablished in West Germany. Also, Allied intervention into industrial governance and ownership patterns remained limited and transitory,[45] and it is safe to as-

---

45. Although in 1945 many influential business leaders were placed under arrest, and some tried as war criminals, this remained an episode. Also, American efforts at deconcen-trating big corporations had no durable consequences, notwithstanding the divestiture of IG Farben and Vereinigte Stahlwerke (Schulz 1985). The break-up of the three *Großbanken*

sume that by the bias of this basic continuity, the experience of the Reichsgruppe Industrie with its organizational streamlining left durable traces
through organizational learning and transfer into the practice of the new
associations. In the case of engineering, for example, the former autonomous branch associations now became mere branch groups of the new
VDMA (now Verein Deutscher Maschinen-und Anlagenbau; Union of German Engineering and Plant Construction), whereby a considerable degree
of concentration was achieved (Weber 1991, 130–31).

The continuity of leadership across regime changes which we encounter
in the manufacturing industry was less pronounced in the case of organized agriculture, and it was clearly absent for organized labor. But even
the new, democratically recruited leadership of these new interest associations made the conscious decision of retaining the associational monopolies established in the Third Reich instead of returning to the pluralist fragmentation that still had characterized important sectors of the economy in
the Weimar Republic. Thus, although the Reichsnährstand was abolished,
the newly formed Deutscher Bauernverband (German Farmers' Association) kept up its representational monopoly, and the former plurality of
farmers' associations did not reemerge. In a similar vein, the Deutscher
Gewerkschaftsbund (German Confederation of Labor Unions) was organized as a unified union (*Einheitsgewerkschaft*) and included the followers of
the former ideologically divided socialist, Christian, and liberal labor organizations (*Richtungsgewerkschaften*), and functional differentiation on the
basis of industry (instead of craft or profession) was maintained. Thus the
rationalization of the associational system proved a durable legacy of the
Nazi period and resulted in the strengthening of corporatist patterns of organization that became so characteristic of economic governance in post-
1945 West Germany.

Additionally, the political position of organized labor was considerably
bolstered by the sympathies of the occupation authorities (notably in the
British zone), and this in turn led business leaders to seek the support of
the unions in their defense against the dismantling of plants as well as
against eventual threats to their property rights. This was particularly true
for heavy industry in the Ruhr region, which in the Weimar Republic had
been most strongly antilabor, and this signified a decisive change of climate. For its part, labor leadership deliberately opted for cooperation with
organized business, as it had done in 1918, and this time both sides strongly
concurred in rejecting any state intervention in industrial relations. In ret-
rospect, both parties had become wary about the Weimar experiences with
compulsory arbitration and agreed to henceforth defend the autonomy of

---

(Deutsche Bank, Dresdner Bank, and Commerzbank) was reversed within less than a
decade.

collective bargaining (*Tarifautonomie*), a principle that today is even gener-ally considered as being implicitly guaranteed by the constitution. The most important symbol of the new relationship of labor and business after World War II was, however, the institution of codetermination.

One consequence of defeat was thus the modified position of elite groups from which the discourse coalitions were recruited. After a period of insecurity, one observes substantial continuity in the position of business leadership, but its relationship with labor had changed considerably, and labor leaders now enjoyed a much higher standing and political legitimacy. On the other hand, decisive shifts took place in the strategic key positions within the bureaucracy, and in the domain of economic policy this implied that a new discourse coalition got the upper hand and rallied around the motto of the "Soziale Marktwirtschaft" (social market economy).

The Rise of "Ordo-Liberal" Economics. Although the social market economy discourse grew out of the "ordo-liberal" theory, these two variants of ne-oliberalism should not be equated (Ambrosius 1977, 231, n. 110; Lange-von Kulessa and Renner 1998). The social market economy discourse as-sumed its characteristic form in the first years after World War II, whereas "ordo-liberalism" has a longer—and somewhat controversial—history.[46] Be-tween the two world wars, and with the decline of the Historical School, the intellectual profile of German economics had lost its distinctiveness. After Hitler's seizure of power, prominent economists—in particular those of Jewish descent—were driven into exile, but this had only limited impact on the orientation of German economics as an academic profession. In accor-dance with the "polycratic" character of Hitler's dictatorship style (Broszat 1969, 1981), the regime never developed a coherent, let alone monolithic, economic doctrine.[47] For some time the vocal devotees of a state-corporatist order (*Ständestaat*) subsisted in the Nazi movement. But they were soon confined to a marginal role and their views were never significant in the economics of the Third Reich.

It was in this context that the ordo-liberal discourse developed. A long-held view in the literature traces its origins back to a postwar reaction, which had its roots in the resistance to Hitler, against Nazi-era state control of the economy (Blumenberg-Lampe 1973, 1986; E. Müller 1988). But this interpretation is based on the assumption that Hitler and his followers were

46. The "ordo-liberal" school owes its name to the yearbook "ORDO" (order). "Order" is a key term in the economic theory of Walter Eucken discussed below and means a stable sys-tem of rules.

47. This was pointed out quite early by Franz Leopold Neumann (1942) and more re-cently by Turner (1985, 60–83) and Tribe (1995, 247–48). Barkai (1977, 1990), unlike most other authors, has attempted to demonstrate that Nazi economic policy was "a coherent eco-nomic system," but in light of recent research his reasoning has not become convincing.

fundamentally committed to planning and a command economy which, as pointed out above, is now outdated.

Ordo-liberalism originated in the agony of the Weimar Republic as an alternative response to the depression (Abelshauser 1991; Haselbach 1991; Krohn 1981; Nicholls 1994). Its pioneers, notably Alexander Rüstow (at that time a lobbyist of the mechanical engineering industry), Wilhelm Röpke, and Walter Eucken, attributed the crisis to an interventionism achieved by the victory of the "wild beasts of pluralistic economic egoism" over a weak state (Rüstow, cited by Nicholls 1994, 49). Based on this analysis, they pleaded for a strong state committed to the restoration of a competitive economic order. Such an "authoritarian-liberal" program at that time was in basic accordance with the authoritarian platform of chancellor Franz von Papen, who in the final phase of the republic experimented with "presidential dictatorship."[48]

When Hitler came to power, some of the spiritual fathers of the program left Germany (notably Rüstow, who had been linked to Schleicher, and Röpke), but others seized the opportunity to develop these ideas within the Nazi regime. They met in the economics section of the Akademie für Deutsches Recht, an official advisory body established to (as its statutes said) "realize the national-socialist program in the entire field of law and economics, in close and permanent contact with the authorities competent for legislation." The section served as an unofficial substitute for the Verein für Socialpolitik (suppressed by the regime) and formed a sort of counterweight to the supporters of economic planning. Some of its outstanding members were Walter Eucken, Franz Böhm, Leonhard Miksch, and Alfred Müller-Armack, all of whom were to gain prominence in the Adenauer era.

Within the polycratic structure of the Nazi regime, the authoritarian-liberals of the Akademie für Deutsches Recht were a legitimate and reputable school of thought (Abelshauser 1991; Herbst 1982, 147–50; Krohn 1981, 195–98; Tribe 1995, 217–33). As enemies of both classical liberalism and of a planned economy, the later "ordo-liberals" represented an original current in the economic policy discourse of the Third Reich. Their problem, as Tribe has said of Eucken, "was the question of how the programme of Ordoliberalism might be realized under National Socialist rule" (Tribe 1995, 212). They acknowledged that, although Hitler's original commitment to the restoration of the market economy (in his program of government of 23 March 1933) had not been kept, this was not based on principle (Blumenberg-Lampe 1986, 474). Regarding alternatives for the postwar in-

---

48. Krohn (1981, 170, 175) and Tribe (1995, 212) have called attention to the sympathies of the early ordo-liberals for Carl Schmitt's critique of Weimar democracy. The term "authoritarian-liberalism" was coined in 1932 by Hermann Heller, an outstanding Social Democratic constitutional lawyer (Haselbach 1991, 54).

ternational economic order, their research agenda sharply dismissed the goal of autarky (propagated by some Nazi economic spokesmen) but proposed to investigate two alternative options, *Großraumwirtschaft*—the Nazi code term for an economic integration of Europe under the political hegemony of Nazi Germany (Tribe 1995, 241–62)—and *Weltwirtschaft*, that is, an open economy (Blumenberg-Lampe 1986, 42).

Social policy was not among their concerns, but they were strongly interested in the order of the labor market because they expected high unemployment after the war. A draft prepared by Adolf Lampe had no use for an organization such as the Deutsche Arbeitsfront but proposed an alternative with strong state control. Since compulsory organizations were incompatible with a market economy, but competition between rival organizations might lead to mutual outbidding, the appropriate way of organizing the labor market was the readmission of labor unions and employers' organizations with voluntary membership, but with an organizational monopoly to be granted by the state. These licensed organizations should then engage in collective bargaining under the control of the Treuhänder der Arbeit (labor trustees, an institution introduced by the Nazi regime for the regulation of wage and working conditions), who should prevent "abuse of economic power." However, unemployment insurance should no longer be run by the state but by the labor unions, because this might foster their insight in the interdependence of wage policy and employment and might help them to voluntarily accept wage reductions in case of rising unemployment (Blumenberg-Lampe 1986, 387–400).[49]

It is obvious that these ideas had a considerable affinity to the statist tradition of German economics, and this tradition was quite compatible with the credo of the regime. From the Kathedersozialisten, the authoritarian-liberals inherited both their program of reconciling a capitalist economic order with social reform and their emphasis on strong government.[50] But this primacy of the state should no longer be employed to correct market forces, as had often happened in the past. Instead, it was deemed necessary for a sort of "market-conforming interventionism," in particular to guarantee competition as a condition for economic efficiency. And, as Lampe's

49. At that time, the failure of attempts to lower wages in some sectors with scarce labor supply because of the successful resistance of regional party leaders had caused concern among economic policymakers (Mason 1977).

50. This has been well documented by Abelshauser (1991). Alfred Müller-Armack, an early admirer of Italian fascism, wrote in the first year of the regime (in which he also joined the Nazi Party) that a "new form of an active economic policy" was needed to "take the economy into the direction of the will of the state, and at the same time to integrate broad strata of the working estates into the state" (Müller-Armack 1933, 56). The political leadership should be "master of the *Gesamtwirtschaft* as a whole and in its parts"; and "private economic freedom" could be granted "only insofar as competition leads to order" (Böhm 1937, 10, 108).

contribution made clear, corporatist control of the labor market under strong guidance of the state was one important facet of this program.

In the final phase of the Nazi regime, some of the ordo-liberals made contact with the conservative opposition against Hitler, and this gave birth to the claim that the social market economy grew out of the resistance movement. To be sure, the strong authoritarian state that Carl-Friedrich Goerdeler and like-minded leaders of this opposition had in mind, with restoration of the rule of law and of basic humanitarian principles, certainly conformed more to the ordo-liberal conceptions developed in the early years of the regime than to the chaotic and perverse arbitrariness that characterized Hitler's rule.[51] But at the same time, the ideas of the ordo-liberals aroused the interest of influential Nazi officials, such as Otto Ohlendorf, a trained economist, who led the economics section of the intelligence agency of the SS (Reichssicherheitshauptamt). Beginning in 1943, Ohlendorf served also as under secretary of state in the Ministry of the Economy and bolstered its position vis-à-vis the war planners in the Ministry of Armament (Boelcke 1983, 300).[52] Indeed, from 1940, in the postwar economic designs discussed in the ranks of the regime, the restoration of private enterprise and a competitive order were seriously considered, and the program of a return to the market found its supporters even among the ranks of the SS. So it is not surprising that the ordo-liberals were among the experts from academe and industry who contributed to these discussions (Herbst 1982, 128–29).[53]

The Discourse Coalition of the Social Market Economy. In 1945, unconditional surrender and the ensuing elimination of the German central administrative authorities interrupted bureaucratic continuities and eliminated the war planners altogether from the political stage. This constitutes a crucial difference between Germany and Japan. To be sure, in West Germany bureaucratic continuities reemerged when the civil servants who had been ousted because of their Nazi membership were readmitted in the

---

51. Many authors who mention the links of the Freiburg economists to the conservative opposition against Hitler (for example, Nicholls 1994) neglect that the majority of its political leaders were critical of parliamentary democracy and often close to the authoritarian conceptions of the Papen and Schleicher cabinets in the late Weimar Republic. After all, among the reasons for which Goerdeler originally supported the Nazi regime was his approval of the suppression of organized labor.

52. On Ohlendorf, see Herbst (notably 1982, 182–88) and Brackmann (1993, 135–43).

53. Ohlendorf was a central figure in these efforts (Boelcke 1983, 333). On his behalf, Ludwig Erhard drafted a memorandum on the postwar economy (Brackmann 1993, 172). But even Albert Speer—the planner and organizer of the total war effort—has pretended that he one day convinced Hitler to promise to the business community a return to free enterprise (Speer 1969, 368–70).

early 1950s (G. Ritter 1998, 29–32). But these continuities on the aggregate
level masked important shifts in several key sectors of the elite and of the
administration. Among others, when in 1947–48 the American and British
occupation authorities began the gradual reorganization of a West German
economic administration (first limited to the zones of these two powers,
the "Bizone," without the French zone of occupation), this served as a
strategic opportunity for the rise of a new hegemonic core discourse coalition around the early protagonists of an Ordnung der Wirtschaft. Although
the rank and file personnel of the bizonal economic administration were
largely recruited from the former Reich administration (Ambrosius 1977,
76–77), the top positions were filled by newcomers.

   Their ascendancy was the outcome of a struggle for hegemony with a
rival discourse coalition that was fought out in the party system and was
therefore highly visible. Indeed, the reconstruction of an economic administration for the Bizone was from its very beginning highly contested between the political parties (Ambrosius 1977, 61–70). One of the competing
discourse coalitions, which in the beginning looked quite influential, was
committed to the idea of "democratic socialism" and indebted to notions of
"democratic planning" as they had been developed in the 1930s in different West European countries. Such ideas not only dominated in the Social
Democratic Party but found a considerable echo also in the left wing of the
Christian Democrats. But in 1948, after the Economic Council for the
British-American Bizone was constituted, the Social Democrats under the
leadership of Kurt Schumacher opted for a vigorous opposition role
(which in a fatal miscalculation they expected to last only for a short inter-
lude). This set the course for an unstoppable decline of the discourse of
"democratic planning" and opened the way for the rise of the ordo-liberals
to the key positions in economic policy. Though many middle-rank and
also some senior civil servants of the former Reich Ministry of the Economy
were recruited for the new West German authorities, this did not mean simple bureaucratic continuity. The election of Ludwig Erhard as director of
the Bizone economic administration (1948) and then, after the establishment of the Federal Republic in 1949, his appointment as minister of the
economy, opened the way for the placement in key positions of outsiders
recruited from the ordo-liberal school.

   This nucleus of a new ascendant discourse coalition was thus characterized by the important role played by economists with an academic background—a feature familiar from the erstwhile Verein für Socialpolitik.
Their most prominent representative was Alfred Müller-Armack, who in
1952 began to develop and direct the economic policy section (Grundsatz-
abteilung) of the federal Ministry of the Economy. This was an important
institutional achievement because this section became a highly influential

governmental brain trust and guardian of neoliberal beliefs within the machinery of government. And insofar as it was also Müller-Armack who introduced the catchword of the "social market economy" and defined its main tenets, he took a leading role in the new hegemonic discourse coalition. Although he had been associated with the ordo-liberals since his affiliation with the Akademie für Deutsches Recht, Müller-Armack developed a somewhat more eclectic version of the neoliberal creed which was open to state interventionism (Lange-von Kulessa and Renner 1998).

For the purposes of political integration, this eclecticism proved clearly superior to the doctrinal rigidity of the original ordo-liberal beliefs. After all, in the first postwar years, there were many among the Social Catholics (most of whom had already joined the new Christian Democratic Union, CDU) and also in the Protestant camp who were sympathetic to the idea of "Christian Socialism" (Ambrosius 1977, 14–24). Christlicher Sozialismus was at that time a rather vague program, but it made these groups receptive to the ideas of "democratic planning" which then were in vogue in West Germany, as in most West European countries. Whereas the Social Catholics and Christian Socialists strongly supported the goal of full employment, this was anathema to most ordo-liberals, who were also skeptical in regard to other "interventionist" elements of the traditional welfare state. So when the advocates of a "bourgeois" coalition led by Konrad Adenauer prevailed within the CDU, the problem was how to maintain the unity of the party and to reconcile the left wing with the neoliberal restoration of a capitalist market economy. Essentially this was achieved by a pragmatic and eclectic combination of ordo-liberal concepts with social policy postulates from the Social Catholic tradition (Ambrosius 1977, 184–89, 223).

Alfred Müller-Armack played the key intellectual role in this pragmatic reinterpretation of the ordo-liberal approach (Nicholls 1994, 139–45; Tribe 1995, 236). He considered the redistributive welfare state as justified under the (sufficiently vague) proviso that this redistribution did not distort the functioning of markets (Müller-Armack 1956),[54] and he explicitly defended government regulation of utilities, transport, agriculture, and the credit system (Müller-Armack 1976, 120–26). Whereas the ordo-liberal Walter Eucken was highly skeptical of a policy of full employment, Müller-Armack resolutely supported it. The new doctrine thus legitimized regulating the economy as long as regulation could be presented as being nondiscretionary and hence "in conformity with the market" (Lange-von Kulessa and Renner 1998). The distinction between state interventions according to their degree of "market conformity" became the magic formula for this

---

54. The discourse of the social market economy regarded "secondary" redistribution of incomes through social policy as perfectly legitimate as long as government did not interfere with the ("primary") allocative functions of the market economy.

accommodation of the ordo-liberal creed to social policy and helped to reconcile it with the heritage of state-led social reform.[55] Müller-Armack's integration of ordo-liberal concepts into a highly flexible and integrative economic policy discourse was thus an important accomplishment of a scholar turned administrator. The broad success of the notion of the social market economy, to be sure, must to a large degree be credited to the charisma of the "big communicator," Ludwig Erhard, who soon became the dominant idol of this discourse.

The style of reasoning preferred by most postwar neoliberals facilitated this eclectic accommodation. Although scholars such as Walter Eucken distanced themselves from the Younger Historical School of German economics and its lack of theoretical rigor, with their "morphological" approach in terms of economic "systems" they were still indebted to the thought of economists from this tradition (in particular, Werner Sombart). They distinguished themselves from their predecessors by their preference for highly stylized conceptualizations (such as the antithesis of the "market economy" on one hand and the "centrally administered economy" on the other), but when the advocates of the social market economy borrowed this typological approach from the Freiburg ordo-liberal school, it permitted them—notwithstanding its emphasis on rule-bound economic policy—a broad range of political interpretations and reinterpretations. Strict market liberals as well as the *Sozialausschüsse* (the "social committees" of Christian labor unionists) of the CDU left wing could likewise refer to this flexible discourse. It was hence peculiarly suitable for the purpose of integrating a political party with a socially heterogeneous clientele, such as the CDU.

In Imperial Germany and the Weimar Republic, the religious foundation of the Center Party in the Catholic minority had fulfilled similar integrative functions. But since in the early postwar years the mass of Center followers had opted for fusion with the conservative Protestants, an extra-religious substitute was needed, and it was found in the discourse of the "social market economy." This new myth was a rather simplified description of the much more complex institutional reality of the political economy of West Germany. But this very simplification proved helpful because—under the favorable economic conditions of postwar reconstruction—most citizens could interpret their personal experience of rising living standards in these

55. The notion of "market conformity" was originally introduced by Röpke (1942, 259). Herbert Giersch, long-time and extremely influential chairman of the Council of Economic Experts, defined as market-conforming "all measures that do not essentially cripple [*wesentlich lähmen*] neither the price mechanism as instrument for the coordination of decentralized decisions, nor competition as the instrument for the control of selfish endeavors, nor the achievement motivation, nor the preparedness to take risks" (Giersch 1977, 110). But other neoliberal authors have criticized that these criteria are open to divergent interpretations.

terms.[56] To what degree its eclecticism made the doctrine of the social market economy suitable to serve as a hegemonic discourse became particularly clear when its integrative capacity was no longer confined to the CDU and the "bourgeois" coalition. Beginning in the late 1950s, the Social Democrats gradually abandoned the doctrines of democratic planning and came to accept the market economy (Nicholls 1994, 367–89),[57] and this prepared the way for Karl Schiller, Social Democratic minister of the economy from 1967 to 1971, to proclaim the synthesis of the "Keynesian message" and the Freiburger Imperativ.[58] After the demise of Keynesian economics, the discourse had become yet more diluted so that by the 1990s the Social Democrats had lost all hesitation to stress their own commitment to the ideas of the social market economy.

In a parallel development, both labor and business gradually moved away from earlier antagonistic positions. The leadership of the employers' peak association (Bundesvereinigung der Deutschen Arbeitgeberverbände) quite early advocated a social partnership approach involving organized labor (Berghahn 1986, 235–47), and when the unions gradually moved toward Keynesian positions, the implicit acknowledgment of macroeconomic interdependence paved the way for corporatist-style policy coordination (Bergmann, Jacobi, and Müller-Jentsch 1975). Closely linked to these changes, even the institutions of codetermination in industry developed in the direction of convergence. They had a long prehistory dating back to the turn of the century (Abelshauser 1999, 231–35), but in the Weimar Republic the discourse of codetermination found its most conspicuous (and fairly radical) expression in blueprints for "economic democracy" as a syndicalist variant of socialism (Naphtali 1928). When after World War II "paritary" codetermination was first introduced in the iron and steel industry, business resistance was strong and forthright (Berghahn 1986, 207–30). Gradually, however, the institutions of codetermination at the firm and shop levels became closely linked with the collective bargaining system (Thelen 1991) and evolved into a pattern of corporate governance which, although it put some constraints on managerial autonomy, was increasingly regarded as complementing the German tradition of embedded capitalism. This, in turn, contributed decisively to the inclusion of organized labor in the core discourse coalition of the "social market economy."[59]

56. This has already been emphasized by Shonfield (1965).
57. This was accomplished with the Godesberger Programm of 1959, after the Aktionsprogramm of 1952 had prepared this shifting of positions by introducing the formula "competition as far as possible, planning as far as necessary."
58. This refers to the University of Freiburg im Breisgau, the best-known academic stronghold of the ordo-liberals.
59. To discuss the origins and transformation of industrial codetermination is beyond the scope of this article. For a recent synthesis, see the report of the Kommission Mitbestimmung (Bertelsmann Stiftung and Hans-Böckler-Stiftung 1998) and Streeck and Kluge 1999.

Economic Strategies and Managerial Capitalism in Postwar Japan

The German influence on the Japanese discourse, which had been so important from the Meiji era to the authoritarian regime in the 1930s and early 1940s, was brought to an end with the Japanese defeat in 1945. Since the American occupation authority attempted to—more or less successfully—remodel Japanese institutions, the United States succeeded Germany as the most important foreign source of intellectual inspiration. To be sure, the generation of Japanese economists and lawyers trained in German universities remained in key positions in the first postwar decades, but younger intellectuals now preferred to attend American universities and business schools. It is remarkable that both Japanese and German institutions retained many of the characteristics that distinguished them from the American model. This is due, on the one hand, to the path-dependent persistence of important elements of the hegemonic discourse. But we also observe some significant patterns of institutional convergence, for example, between the German and the Japanese system of industrial relations.

The Continuity of Bureaucratic Elites. In Japan, unlike in Germany, the close relationship of government and industry and the active role of the administration in industrial policy survived in the postwar era as a legacy of the war economy (Gao 1997; Johnson 1982; Okazaki 1997). A good example is the "priority production" system started in 1946 to expand production in some key sectors (coal, steel, and chemical fertilizer) as a precondition for the recovery of manufacturing industries (Kosai 1988, 31–35). Its rationale was similar to that of the first French plan launched by Jean Monnet in 1946 with its emphasis on the "basic sectors" (*secteurs de base*) (Cohen 1969, 83–90), and in both countries its implementation relied largely on direct controls of the economy by the bureaucracy. The difference from West Germany is quite interesting: there, a similar investment program focused on industrial bottlenecks (*Investitionshilfegesetz*) was launched much later (in January 1952), when the impact of the Korean crisis and pressure from the Allied High Commission forced a revision of the market liberal strategies pursued by Ludwig Erhard (Abelshauser 1983, 63–70). This law, which established a mandatory levy of one billion Deutsche marks from consumer industries in favor of investment in selected basic industry sectors, was much more modest in scope than the Japanese and French parallels. But its inception was a significant example for the "corporative market economy" progressively superseding the ordo-liberal orthodoxy; it was originally developed—on Adenauer's demand—by the peak associations of business (Abelshauser 1983, 75; Hentschel 1996, 154–59).

To be sure, in Japan too the defeat of 1945 and the Allied postwar reforms had a profound impact on the institutions and on the structure of the former hegemonic discourse coalitions. But this worked differently for its different components. In Germany unconditional surrender led to the complete removal of the central administration, and this resulted in major discontinuities at the top of the bureaucracy. In Japan, on the other hand, the occupation power chose indirect rule through the Japanese government apparatus. Although it practiced a selective reorganization of the bureaucratic structure that hit several core departments and culminated in the dissolution of the Home Ministry (Naimushō), it left the central economic and financial administration largely intact.[60] Hence in these policy domains Japan differed from Germany in its much greater bureaucratic continuity (Pempel 1987). One aspect of this continuity was that, alongside the bureaucracy, economists played an important role in policy formation. Many of these had already taken part in the debates about the "new economic system" of the war years (Gao 1994; 1997, 135–39, 241–45), and this contributed to the survival and the metamorphosis of the three basic principles developed in the wartime managed economy: the "strategic view of the economy," the maintenance of order and the restraint of excessive competition, and the rejection of the profit motive (Gao 1997, 277–79).

However, the ascendancy of a coherent hegemonic discourse took longer in Japan than in Germany. Although economic reconstruction was the uncontested first priority, the bureaucrats and their economic advisers were divided over strategies, not least about the importance of international trade for Japan's future orientation. Moreover, although the party system became a central arena for translating choices into decisions, the mechanism was different. In Germany the initial contest between the advocates of some sort of planning, on the one hand, and those of a market economy, on the other, was fought out between political parties in the electoral and parliamentary arena and finally settled in favor of the market economy with the victory of the CDU-led coalition in 1949.

In Japan, on the other hand, a similar controversy was linked to the rivalry of factions within the ruling Liberal Democratic Party (Kume 1997b). In one of the contending coalitions were the advocates of the resolutely interventionist "priority production" program, who put strong emphasis on the domestic market. Indeed, a closed economy was a basic premise for implementing such an interventionist policy (Gao 1997, 139–40, 164–67, 189–92; Kosai 1988). Among the intellectual leaders of this camp were prominent economists, some of whom—such as Hiromi Arisawa, the architect of "priority production" who was strongly indebted to a Marxist legacy—had already been influential in the planning efforts of the war

---

60. Also, the influential bureaucracy of the Social Affairs Division of Naimushō was by and large transferred to the new Ministry of Labor and remained an important political factor (Garon 1987, 230–42).

economy. The brief hegemony of this "neomercantilist" discourse ended with the deflationary policy of Joseph Dodge (the "Dodge line") imposed by the occupation authorities. This policy change strengthened those who advocated industrial development based on exports of goods processed from imported materials, and the export-led strategy of a "trading nation" became dominant in the 1950s. But, unlike in Germany, the corresponding discourse did not emphasize the primacy of the market but a strategic role of government in industrial policy, with the Ministry of International Trade and Industry (MITI) as a central institution. A further decisive stage was reached in 1960 when the government of Hayato Ikeda—strongly Keynesian in orientation—turned toward the high-growth policy symbolized by the "income-doubling plan" and toward trade liberalization.[61] These developments finally opened the way for the hegemony of a discourse that could serve integrative functions comparable to those of West Germany's "social market economy."

The Discourse Coalition of Managerial Capitalism and the Emergence of the "J-Firm." The two most important changes in the governance of industry due to the occupation reforms had been the rise of managerial capitalism and the political legitimation of organized labor. In Japan as well as in Germany, original Allied interventions in industrial governance were discontinued when, after some years, American beliefs in private enterprise led to the restoration of the social position of business. However, in Japan the early dissolution of the *zaibatsu* had a considerable and lasting impact on the governance of Japanese business (Gao 1997, 127–28). The elimination of important instruments of stockholder control and the separation of ownership from management considerably reinforced the powers of managers and thus amounted to a "managerial revolution from above" (Aoki 1988, 185; Nakamura 1995, 68–69). The family capitalism of the prewar era was thus supplanted by a new type of managerial capitalism. Different from the prewar managers, who had close links to the former owner-families, the new managers felt more loyalty to their employees (Hirschmeier 1976; see also Iwata 1992). Many had acquired their professional experience in the war economy and had become accustomed to associative action. Not surprisingly, the postwar trade associations have been characterized as the successors of the *tōsei-kai* (Murakami 1984, 360). This included, of course, a close cooperative relationship between the trade (as well as peak) associations and government.

These changes explain the emergence of a new reform discourse among

61. "Ikeda will be remembered as the man who pulled together a national consensus for economic growth" (Nakamura 1995, 88).

younger managers who had their organizational foothold in the Keizai Dōyūkai (Japan Committee for Economic Development). Their discourse aimed at a "democratization of the enterprise" (for the following, see Hirschmeier 1976; Hirschmeier and Yui 1981, 330–32; Otake 1987) but also had important roots in the ideology of the "new economic system" discussed above which endeavored to restrict the authority of stockholders and to improve the status of managers and workers in the firm (Gao 1997, 133; Okazaki 1994). Basing their argument on the separation of ownership and management, they perceived management as the mediator between workers and capitalists, and demanded an equal distribution of profits between the three parties. This reformist capitalism, which was remarkably reminiscent of the ideas of James Burnham (1942), was "intended as a countermeasure to a socialist nationalization of enterprises," and it presupposed that "labour would not be influenced by political motives that have no direct relationship with the management of a specific enterprise" (Otake 1987, 370–72).

However, in the early postwar years the militancy of the new Japanese union movement left little room for such an enterprise-centered reform discourse. Both in Germany and in Japan the new labor unions had originally been strongly encouraged by the occupation power. But whereas in Germany labor relations from the beginning remained relatively peaceful, and organized labor preferred a "social partnership" line that had strong roots in the past, in Japan the moderate unions that continued the analogous tradition of the prewar Sōdōmei were outflanked by the more militant leftist unions (Garon 1987, 237–42). The onset of the cold war, and then in 1948 the new economic stabilization policy of the occupation led by Joseph Dodge with the cooperation of the Japanese government, resulted in a high degree of polarization. On the employers' side, militant managers organized in Nikkeiren (the Japanese Employers Federation) got the upper hand in their struggle for restoring managerial prerogatives in the firm (Kume 1998, 59–60). The intense conflicts between 1949 and 1953, in which the concerted efforts of employers, the government, and the American occupation authorities resulted in the destruction of the radical labor organizations, and the subsequent restructuring of organized labor then led to a pattern of social partnership that differed from the German one and was closer to the legacy of those prewar social bureaucrats who had aimed at the promotion of a moderate enterprise unionism. Still, in the 1950s labor relations remained confrontational, since a management strategy of rationalization with massive layoffs met resistance that found its expression in large strike actions.

But with the policy turn toward high growth and trade liberalization and the related breakthrough of a new production model, an adversarial labor-relations system became increasingly dysfunctional, and this spurred both management and labor to reconsider their strategies. It became increasingly clear that for competitive advantage in international markets and for economic growth, production technology was more important than cheap labor. Thus cooperation between management and labor acquired a new significance. In consequence the Nikkeiren employers finally reconciled their positions with the discourse introduced by the Keizai Dōyūkai in the early postwar years. And since labor militancy had been superseded by an enterprise-centered unionism, the way was now open for the emergence of the "J-firm," in which management and employees were supposed to have equal claims with shareholders (Aoki 1988).

But, remarkably, this integrative discourse developed an institutional spillover effect that went beyond enterprise unionism and opened the way for coordinated bargaining on the national level (*shuntō*) and participation in public policymaking (Kume 1998)—trends characterized as "corporatism with labor" (Garon 1987, 242–48).[62] In our comparative perspective we thus observe an institutional convergence where finally in both countries, Japan as well as Germany, the institutionalized negotiation of labor and management on the national and company levels are closely linked and thus exhibit greater resilience to erosion than do highly centralized varieties of corporatism (Kume 1997a, 243). This convergence, however, is no longer the result of ongoing processes of diffusion from Germany to Japan. Rather it is due to the path-dependent logic of a hegemonic discourse of embedded capitalism that has become similar to the German discourse by the strong integration of once contending forces.

Conclusion

Since the late nineteenth century, institutions embedding the capitalist market by constraining market exchange emerged both in Germany and Japan. They cluster into institutional configurations (or "models," to borrow familiar jargon) where a high degree of congruity can be observed between the constraints on market exchange generated by different institutions. These embedding institutions have on the one hand undergone significant transformations as a consequence of major political upheavals, but also in response to economic and social change. On the other hand, as they unfolded, their basic characteristics demonstrated a remarkable resilience to external challenges over more than a century. Both the *modèle rhénan* and the *modèle nippon*, as distinguished from the *modèle néo-américain* (Albert 1991), can thus be characterized as "path-dependent" institutional

---

62. This refers to the well-known characterization of Japanese labor relations as "corporatism without labor" (Pempel and Tsunekawa 1979).

configurations. It is the basic hypothesis developed in this essay that such path dependence is due to the fit between the institutions and the hegemonic "discourses" whose development we have investigated.

In Germany, following the inquiry by Hegel and Lorenz von Stein into the social consequences of the dynamics of the capitalist market, a coalition of bureaucrats and social scientists developed a new discourse that in the economic downturn of the 1870s superseded the market-liberal discourse of the older generation of reform bureaucrats and gradually achieved hegemony. The new discourse emphasized social reform to check the socially disruptive consequences of markets for the fabric of society, and it served as a basis for the building of institutions to buffer individuals and social classes against risks they could not master on their own.

The hegemony achieved by this discourse was the origin of a path-dependent process of institution building in which a close fit was achieved between the basic tenets of the discourse and the emerging institutional setting. Although originally the discourse of social reform was intended as an instrument of conservative defense, the progress of political democracy paved the way for the co-option of the reformist discourses of the minority subcultures ("Social Catholicism" and reformist social democracy). This further strengthened the hegemony of the discourse of embedded capitalism and contributed to the dominant perception of market-constraining institutions as a condition of social and industrial peace.

Japan's social conservatives in the Meiji era borrowed some of the central ideas of the German discourse but integrated them into the social model of the (vertical) "*ie* society," whereas in Germany the corresponding "ancient European" social model focusing on the *oikos* (or *ganzes Haus*) had largely become obsolete. Moreover, the institutional legacy of Germany since the religious wars of the sixteenth and seventeenth centuries was characterized by the quest for institutional formulas to cope with fundamental social cleavages cutting across vertical bonds. Hence, the German discourse increasingly emphasized the solidaristic function of (horizontal) associations or class, whereas the Japanese adaptation of the discourse developed a closer fit with the "family model" of the firm.

The crisis of the 1930s and 1940s (Polanyi's "Great Transformation") resulted in several far-reaching mutations of the core discourse of socially embedded capitalism and of the corresponding institutional framework—mutations already prepared by the institutional innovations of the German war economy in 1914–18. Most important were the breakthrough of "corporatist" peak associations disposing of a representational monopoly and the co-option of working-class organizations into the bargaining networks of economic and social policy. To be sure, this co-option was delayed by protracted conflicts that culminated in the repressive regimes established in both countries in 1933 and 1936, respectively. But important elements of the associational infrastructure of the war economy survived the collapse of these regimes in 1945 and then became building blocks of a new order based on stable democratic institutions.

At the beginning of the twenty-first century, the institutions of embedded capitalism and of the "coordinated market economy" (Soskice 1999) in Germany and Japan are under increasing pressure. This pressure nurtures speculation that both countries may finally converge toward a "liberal" (or "uncoordinated") market economy. If we extrapolate from the observations of our longitudinal analysis, such a convergence cannot be excluded categorically. However, in a century or more, a remarkably close fit has developed between these institutions and the discourse, and the cognitive and normative hegemony achieved and maintained by the dominant discourse coalitions was, and continues to be, an essential condition for the further stability of these path-dependent models. Consequently, if we want to assess the future of embedded capitalism in Germany and Japan, our attention should be directed toward those strains that eventually might jeopardize the continuing intellectual hegemony of the core discourse and the discourse coalitions.

Welfare State Building and Coordinated Capitalism in Japan and Germany

Philip Manow

If one distinguishes two types of capitalism, coordinated and uncoordinated (cf. Soskice 1990), Japan and Germany certainly belong to the former. Job tenure is relatively long in both countries, workers' skill levels are comparatively high, the wage spread is low, the managerial style tends to be consensual, workers and their representatives take part in company decisions, and the distinction between external and internal labor markets is rigid while intrafirm job flexibility is relatively high. Union density is moderate, and business associations have broad-based membership. More important, both unions and employers' associations are usually able to commit their members to negotiated agreements.

At the same time, Japan and Germany achieve economic coordination in very different ways. As a consequence, both economies have comparative advantages in different types of economic activity. Although Japan is said to be "an example of a social system [of production] that emphasizes *quality mass production*," the German system is said to "emphasize *diversified quality production*" (Hollingsworth 1997, 279; emphasis added). Economic coordination in Japan is company based or company-group (*keiretsu*) based, but it is based at the industry-sector level in Germany (Soskice 1995).

An important explanation for the strikingly similar tendency of both pro-

This essay was presented at the 94th annual convention of the American Political Science Association, 3–6 September 1998, Boston. Comments by John Campbell, Gregory Jackson, Ikuo Kume, Wolfgang Streeck, Akira Takenaka, Kathleen Thelen, Kozo Yamamura, and the participants of the conference on "Varieties of Welfare Capitalism" at the Max Planck Institute, 11–13 June 1998, are gratefully acknowledged. Many thanks go also to Martha Walsh for her language editing.

duction systems to favor long-term engagements over short-term spot-market exchanges lies in their institutionally different but "functionally similar" forms of social intervention into and regulation of the economic sphere. These welfare state interventions and regulations have made the German and Japanese labor markets less locations of anonymous economic exchange and more highly regulated, embedded institutions that facilitate long-term engagements. Correspondingly, social intervention helped to make German and Japanese firms less places of command and control and more negotiated and to a certain extent "consented" institutions (see the chapter by Gregory Jackson in this volume).

This chapter investigates the historical roots of the Japanese and German welfare states and their contribution to the emergence of a production model based on long-term economic coordination. Given the many differences in the institutional setup of these two systems of social protection, I focus on similarities or functional equivalents in the incentives and constraints that both welfare systems provide for economic actors. In this chapter, functional equivalents are explained with historical parallels: both Japan and Germany were nonliberal societies in the last three decades of the nineteenth century and for many years thereafter. Both societies were industrial latecomers that struggled for and then had to cope with rapid economic growth. The state elite was central to economic modernization and to the societal integration of workers, which did not happen through the extension of political-participatory rights to the working class. Instead, the main routes of integration were, in Germany, the incorporation of organized labor and capital into the welfare state and, in Japan, social integration of workers through and within the firm ("industrial citizenship"; see the chapter by Jackson in this volume). Given the nonliberal, predemocratic character of Japan and Germany during the formative phase of economic modernization, welfare entitlements could be directed at those parts of the workforce that were most crucial for economic growth, best organized, and thus also politically most powerful: that is, skilled industrial workers.

Since voting rights in particular and the political influence of the public in general were still very much restricted, social entitlements could be made group-specific, nonuniversal, granted from above, based on the employment relationship, and linked to workers' income. This "achievement/performance model of social policy" (Titmuss 1974) helped to establish a production regime centrally based on long-term cooperation between employers and employees; it fostered long and stable career paths and allowed for a highly skilled workforce by rendering individual investments into skill acquisition relatively secure and profitable (Estevez-Abe, Soskice, and Iversen 1999).

Similarly, the apparent *difference* in how workers in the two countries were granted the new social rights—via the employment relationship in Japan or via collective industrial relations and the representation of organized capital and labor in the administration of the welfare state in Germany—is explained with divergent historical trajectories. Although the German state after the depression of 1873–78 turned decidedly nonliberal and sought to "organize capitalism" along corporatist lines, the Japanese state elite was convinced that Japan could only catch up with the West if it broke with the feudal practices of the past. Thus, all old or new (union) forms of "market containment" were perceived as standing in the way of rapid economic growth. Yet the scarcity of skilled labor in the wake of rapid economic growth seemed to render social intervention necessary in Japan as well. Welfare regulations were therefore directed at the firm level, not at the level of interest organizations, associations, unions, or at the industrial bargaining system. The Japanese state forced employers to establish company welfare schemes that would meet standards set by the state. By contrast, in Germany the state established a framework of collective governance between the social partners in which German unions found their place.

Economic Coordination and Welfare State Intervention

Peter Hall has remarked that we do not have as yet a "clear understanding of how . . . different kinds of welfare states interact with different models of the economy" and "why some combinations are more common than others" (P. Hall, 1997, 196). Welfare regimes are still by and large neglected as potential factors of variance in economic performance and economic governance of contemporary capitalism (Crouch and Streeck 1996; Hollingsworth and Boyer 1997; Hollingsworth, Schmitter, and Streeck 1994; Kitschelt et al. 1999). It is only very recently that a new literature has begun to address exactly these questions in a broader comparative framework (Ebbinghaus and Manow 2001; Estevez-Abe, Soskice, and Iversen 1999; Huber and Stephens 2000; Mares 1998). Although differences in the institutional setup of financial systems, industrial relations, and the systems of innovation, training, and education have been studied much more extensively, the welfare state is still rarely analyzed in the comparative political economy literature. Despite the claim that the welfare state has been a "fundamental force in the organization and stratification of modern economies" (Esping-Andersen 1990, 159), the potential linkages between the sphere of "social protection" and the sphere of "capitalist production" have seldom been analyzed systematically.

Yet because we are faced with several "worlds of welfare" and with a limited "variety of capitalism," we may ask whether we can relate certain types of (welfare) state intervention in industrial relations, the labor market, or the employment relationship with certain forms of economic coordination and with a specific governance and performance of the economic sector. If there is a striking "elective affinity" between liberal welfare states and liberal market economies, we wonder if there might exist a similar linkage between other welfare and production regimes (Ebbinghaus and Manow 2001). In particular, with respect to economic coordination we are led to ask if and how the welfare state may have been a source for "external economies" and how the welfare state may have supported long-term commitments among employers and employees, or firms and banks—or may have fostered cooperation among firms.

I claim that the extent to which a welfare state can provide economic agents with external economies depends on the degree to which employers and employees have been integrated into the welfare state and, consequently, on the degree to which welfare benefits have been designed to serve the particular interests of the industrial workforce and of employers/firms respectively. I hold that it was especially the systematic integration of capital and labor into compulsory welfare schemes that offered opportunities for long-term cooperation either between unions and employers' associations—in particular within the framework of the German social insurance system—or between workers/enterprise unions and management—in particular in the Japanese model of "compulsory welfare capitalism."[1] With the establishment of employment-based welfare schemes, the state made long-term economic coordination between em-

---

1. The detailed and uniform state regulation of "private" pension plans in Japan and the steady expansion of coverage for an increasing part of the workforce is what critically distinguishes Japan from the United States, where company plans only received state support via preferential tax-treatment. Thus, I disagree with Sanford Jacoby, who holds that Japan's "private welfare corporatism" most closely resembles the U.S. case (Jacoby 1993; 1996, 69, n. 1; similarly Esping-Andersen 1997). While it is certainly true that in both Japan and the United States large firms and mass production developed before the emergence of mass unionism, the striking difference between the two with respect to the form of state intervention and market-regulation should not be overlooked. The different private-public mixes in pensions in the United States, the United Kingdom, Japan, and Germany reveal the important differences between liberal and nonliberal arrangements. Public versus private shares of pension benefits in 1980 were 68 percent (public) to 32 percent (private) in the United States, 58 to 42 percent in the United Kingdom, 80 to 20 percent in Germany, and 82 to 18 percent in Japan (Davis 1995, 44). Here, the Japanese Employee Pension System (EPS, Kosei Nenkin Hoken) and the Employee Pension Funds (EPF, Kosei Nenkin Kikin) apparently are treated—I think correctly—as public in character.

In my view, Lazonick's distinction is problematic as well. Lazonick writes, that "unlike Japanese enterprises . . . US industrial enterprises had never made long-term employment *commitments* (as distinct from implicit promises)" (Lazonick 1995, 102; emphasis in the original). It is hard to see how Japanese firms should have been able to make credible, self-binding employment commitments without the legislative support of the state (which is not explicitly considered in Lazonick's analysis).

ployers and employees possible to an extent that would not have been sustainable on the basis of voluntary "contractual" agreements alone.

The historical evidence presented in the following two sections shows that welfare programs in both nations targeted especially the relatively well-paid, highly skilled workers and that this helped to establish a production model based on shop-floor cooperation, stable career paths, and high skill levels in the workforce. In helping to establish and then later to stabilize occupationally based welfare schemes, both the Japanese and German states institutionalized what Titmuss (1974) has labeled the "industrial achievement-performance model of social policy." This "achievement model" of social policy facilitates economic coordination in at least four ways.

First, the transition from craft unions to either industrial or enterprise unions was made easier in occupation-based welfare states. It was here that state provision of welfare, targeted especially at the elite segments of the workforce, crowded out the workers' voluntary schemes that often were used as instruments of market closure and market stabilization for certain professions or crafts. In this respect it is important to note that both industrial and enterprise unions, which took the place of craft unions, are more inclusive in the sense that they organize workers with different status and different formal skills (Streeck 1993). Solidaristic wage policies reflected the special receptivity of company or industrial unions to general ideas of a "social" or "livelihood" wage. Such policies also narrowed the wage spread within the firm or the industrial sector. A compressed wage structure forces firms to continuously improve worker productivity, especially if labor law or union power makes shedding labor a very costly strategy.

This relates to the second factor: earning-related premiums and benefits of old-age pensions and unemployment insurance can justify high replacement ratios for the high-wage segment[2] and can legitimize the maintenance of relative pay differentials after retirement or during unemployment. Stable income differentials in the very long run relieve unions—at least to some extent—from the pressure to struggle for significant wage differentials in the short run. Wages for groups of workers were relatively less influenced by sudden changes in their market power caused by shifts in demand and supply or by unions' success in mobilizing and organizing workers. Instead, wages can be made dependent on formal qualifications and on the workers' relative position within a fairly formal, regulated promotion system (see the chapter by Kathleen Thelen and Ikuo Kume in this volume).[3]

---

2. The social security replacement rates based on a final salary of $20,000 and $50,000 have been 65 and 40 percent in the United States (1992), in the United Kingdom 50 and 26 percent (including SERPS), in Germany 70 and 59 percent, and in Japan 54 percent for both income levels. Thus, Germany and Japan possess the two most generous pension systems for earners of high income, only surpassed by the Italian system, which guarantees a replacement ratio of 77 and 73 percent(!) respectively (cf. Davis 1995, 43).

3. In Japan, a highly formal, competitive, and age-graded education system, in which suc-

Correspondingly, generous, long-term unemployment benefits relieve unemployed workers from pressures to accept jobs at levels below their formal qualifications, thus prohibiting loss of status and deskilling. A very high degree of job security for the core workforce has the same effect. The importance of "institutional complementarities" in the organization of work and welfare in both countries is underlined by the promise in Japan of lifetime employment, which corresponds to skill formation within the firm, and in Germany by the very generous acceptability criteria in unemployment insurance (Paqué 1998), corresponding to industry-wide vocational training and to transportable skills. These complementarities are particularly important for the long-term return on investments into human capital. Strictly income-related pensions and generous early retirement provisions that account for the higher risk that elderly workers will become unemployed can be interpreted as "deferred payment arrangements" (Aoki 1990) that provide workers in their early careers with an insurance against uncertain future events.

Third, welfare schemes targeted at the upper segment of the labor market often provided unions with critical organizational support. Unions took part in the administration of state welfare schemes or in company welfare schemes backed by state legislation. Involvement in the administration of compulsory programs in contrast to voluntary programs strengthened unions as organizations. Yet it was not only union strength that mattered, but how and to which purpose that strength was used. Since the "industrial achievement-performance" welfare state model already focused on a worker's status, unions were to some extent relieved from bargaining about detailed job descriptions and visible earning differentials for different jobs or occupations. Instead, industrial and enterprise unions became more interested in the economic fate of the sector in which they worked and of the company, respectively. In this regard, the trade-off between the "logic of influence" and the "logic of membership" (Schmitter and Streeck 1981) be-

---

cess is essential in order to get attractive entry-level jobs, combined with developed internal labor markets with on-the-job training, regular promotions, and seniority wages have led to a gendered distribution of investments in human capital, of full-time versus part-time employment and, consequently, to a gendered wage distribution (see on this the work of Brinton 1994). In both Germany and Japan the "family wage" and the welfare entitlements of dependents only take into account the marital status, and in Germany as well success in school is based upon much support from the family. As a consequence, both countries have settled into a "low fertility equilibrium" (Esping-Andersen 1999) with all the resulting problems of rapid population aging, unfavorable dependency ratios, huge pension liabilities, and rising social insurance contributions. Again, these similarities point to a similar matrix of incentives and constraints: the post-World War II settlement in both countries established a burden sharing and division of labor between the market, the state, and the family in which women were by and large excluded from the "standard employment relationship." Yet these long-term effects of the German and Japanese political economy clearly go beyond the scope of this essay.

came manifest at the micro level. If the welfare state partially relieved unions as voluntary organizations from constant pressure to mobilize their members' support, it enabled them at the same time to engage in more long-term, cooperative relations with employers on either the company or sector level. Hence, industrial relations could become less adversarial—maximizing "joined gains" could achieve priority over the goal of maximizing "relative gains."

This closely relates to the fourth point: the integration of workers and employers in the welfare state often meant that regulations concerning benefits, eligibility, coverage, etc., could be tailored to the needs of each group and made to fit the necessities of the production model. This is today most evident in the diverse pathways into early retirement through which unions and firms can externalize the costs of economic adjustment onto the broader risk community of contribution payers (Kohli et al. 1991). Generous unemployment, (early) retirement, and disability benefits can cushion cyclical downswings and can help to avoid the outbreak of conflict within the enterprise, which would endanger especially the highly trust-based and trust-dependent German and Japanese production models. A similar institutional complementarity is evident in the case of Japanese employee pensions that support the stabilization of a core workforce. At the same time, the contracted-out Japanese pension schemes underpin the practice of mutual shareholding which is central for the creation of patient capital (Estevez-Abe 1996; McKenzie 1992). Patient capital, in turn, allows firms to keep the promise of lifetime employment. Here again, the employment-based welfare state regulations are a crucial element within a broader "framework of incentives and constraints" (Soskice 1995), which is especially conducive for long-term economic coordination (Aoki 1990; Osano and Serita 1994).

Developmentalism and the Welfare State: Japan

The development of the Japanese economy, society, and polity since the 1868 Meiji Restoration often has been interpreted as a classic example of the "late capitalist development syndrome" (Dore 1973, 415). Japan's late entry into the class of industrialized nations has explained the enormous speed of economic growth, the scarcity of skilled labor and capital, the heavy emphasis on education as a precondition for catching up with the "advanced nations," the prominent role of the state in economic activity (Gerschenkron 1962) and—as a consequence—the emergence of the state as a role model for other organizations (Westney 1987, 213), and many other features of Japanese economic and societal development.

This is also said to be true for Japanese welfare state development, a fact already noted by contemporary observers. Considering the labor question in Western countries, a Japanese expert stated in 1914 that social policy in the advanced nations "generally had as its purpose the curing of the evils of extreme free competition. In our country today, since we do not have yet these evils, social policy is fundamentally a preventative rather than a cure" (quoted from Pyle 1974, 160). This statement corresponds to scholarly assessments of the history of Japanese modernization which perceive it as proof of the claim that in late-developing countries there is a "greater likelihood that organizational patterns designed in the advanced countries to cope with specific problems will be adopted before those problems actually arise, in order to preempt and contain them" (Westney 1987, 213; see also Dore 1973, 410; 1979).

In line with this argument is the emphasis Japanese reform bureaucrats themselves put on the fact that social legislation had been granted from above rather than politically demanded from below (Dore 1969, 437; Garon 1987, 18). The proactive character of the bureaucracy was based on the conviction that Japan would thus be able "to solve the [labor] problem before it develops and to save . . . [Japan] from the fate of Europe" (quoted from Gordon 1985, 65; Dore 1969, 439). Early Japanese welfare state development might therefore be interpreted as a good example of what Robert Scalapino (1964, 106) has dubbed "teleological insight."

Although Japan's political and economic elite was acutely aware of the political problems caused by the labor question in Britain, Germany, and the United States, social intervention in Japan—much more than in Western nations—was made instrumental for the expansion of the market. Social policy was not so much a response to a labor question which as yet had not presented itself visibly in Japan, but became part of a developmental strategy. Hence, defining social policy as "politics against markets" (Esping-Andersen 1985) may not be wholly appropriate in the Japanese case. Rather, the early Japanese welfare state "developed in the light of its economic rationale" (Takahashi 1974, 473). Bureaucratic "teleological insight," however, faced clear limits, and bureaucrats were far from acting with full autonomy from societal interests. When Japan encountered acute labor shortages and increased worker protest during and shortly after World War I, the social policies of the advanced nations from which the Japanese hoped to learn were still unsystematic, far from settled, and not at all uniform—and their success with respect to securing labor peace was particularly unimpressive. At the same time, the political priority to catch up with the West meant that the interests of business had to figure prominently in all considerations of the bureaucratic elite.

For many years, the chief "business of Meiji Japan was business" (Garon 1987, 19). Industrial growth however was only the means to a much more fundamental aim: namely, to regain full national sovereignty and achieve equal footing with the great Western powers. Economic success was key to the achievement of any of these fundamentals. Thus, the link between welfare and the developmental state (Anderson 1993; Calder 1990) was particularly strong in Japan.[4] But, at the same time, it made the introduction of a universal social insurance or insurance with fairly wide coverage not a pressing issue in Japan's early industrialization. Social insurance did not promise to "enrich the country and strengthen the army" (Dore 1969, 437). However, social policy promised to be a solution for another burning problem that was—like the scarcity of capital—a result of rapid industrialization: the serious shortage of skilled labor.

By the 1890s, high employee turnover posed serious problems for Japanese heavy industry, especially for steel companies and shipyards. The labor shortage worsened after the Sino-Japanese War (1894–95), when industrial growth accelerated rapidly (Dore 1973, 387). Companies poached workers from each other. Wages were steeply increased by firms trying to outbid one another. Job tenure was short. Big companies were used as buffers for ups and downs in the labor market. During booms, well-trained workers left big companies and searched for higher wages in the small-company sector or became self-employed, only to return to the larger enterprises if economic conditions worsened. The labor market was more a seller's than a buyer's market for skilled workers. This is not surprising given that, for instance, demand for engineers increased from 13,000 to 150,000 in only fifteen years, from 1890 to 1905. Thus job scarcity, which had been a critical factor in the building and sustaining of labor movements elsewhere, did not exist in Meiji Japan (Taira 1997, 269). There was no shortage of labor as such, but a severe shortage of *skilled* labor. Hence, scarcity of labor prevailed in exactly that segment of the labor market from which Western labor movements had recruited most of their members and leaders.

The main economic problem was training and holding on to workers (Dore 1973, 387). Initially the state tried to ease labor scarcity not by legally restricting labor mobility but mainly by acting as a role model. In the state-owned shipyards and steel companies, bonus systems, the establishment of clear status differentials between "regular" and "temporary workers," the granting of sick pay, forced saving from workers' wages for retirement, and lump-sum retirement payments linked to the length of the labor contract were first introduced. These diverse measures were supposed to establish a boundary between a stable, internal, skilled workforce and a flexible, untrained, external one (Dore 1973, 383).[5]

---

4. Strong developmental aspects of welfare state building in Germany are shown *inter alia* by Steinmetz (1993) and Weiss (1998).

5. The state-owned dockyards were even able to offer the "exemption from compulsory military service" as an additional incentive (Dore 1973, 383).

Large private companies—such as Mitsubishi in 1897—followed suit and introduced welfare funds as an additional measure designed to help stabilize the workforce (Dore 1973, 388). Resembling the welfare paternalism of German employers such as Krupp, Stumm, or Zeiss (Fischer 1978; Schulz 1991) or the early welfare capitalism of American employers such as Pullman or Standard Oil (Brandes 1976), these welfare funds provided sick pay and retirement benefits, with employers and employees contributing equally.[6] Again the state pioneered in the shift from voluntary to compulsory enrollment in company-based welfare funds. It was in the state-owned firms that mutual aid associations (MAAs) with compulsory membership were first established. Such associations normally covered on-the-job injury and illness and provided lump-sum retirement benefits. The MAA for the Imperial Railway Office Workers was the first compulsory scheme in 1907. Compulsory MAAs for Printing Bureau Workers (1909), Postal Workers (1909), Taiwan Railway Workers (1909), the Navy (1912), Taiwan Postal and Communications Workers (1913), and many more followed. In the 1920s, twenty such mutual aid associations provided workers with retirement benefits and insurance against accidents and sickness. Workers contributed three percent of their wages; the government added another two percent.

A leading figure in this proliferation of MAAs was Baron Shinpei Gotō, who at various times was head of the medical bureau of the Home Ministry, president of the South Manchuria Railway Company, director-general of the Imperial Railway Agency, and communications and home minister. Gotō had studied medicine in Germany and was heavily influenced by Bismarckian social legislation and by the welfare paternalism of German employers such as Friedrich Krupp (Anderson 1993, 44–45; Lewis 1981, 55–58).[7] Though Gotō failed in his more ambitious plan to introduce national health insurance in Japan (Garon 1997, 38–40), he was successful in

---

6. Employers' interest in special incentives designed to reduce high rates of employee turnover was caused also by a change in work organization, namely, the erosion of the *oyakata* system—the old system of subcontracting to craftsmen (Dore 1973; Gordon 1985; Taira 1997; see also the chapter by Kathleen Thelen and Ikuo Kume in this volume).

7. From 1911 to 1914 one of Gotō's advisers was Otto Wiedfeldt, an influential German bureaucrat from the Reich Office of the Interior, who had been prominently involved in the drafting of the Reich social insurance code (Reichsversicherungsordung, RVO; 1911). The RVO had been the most important piece of social legislation since the Bismarckian legislation of the 1880s. Otto Wiedfeldt later went back to the Reich Office of the Interior and became director of the Krupp company after World War I. He eventually became Germany's ambassador to Washington. Wiedfeldt's predecessor in Japan was Karl Thiess from 1908 to 1911 (Schröder 1964, 66–71). Thus, German ideas were influential in this important formative period of Japanese welfare state development, at least to some extent. World War I, however, marked a break. Until 1918 no Japanese commission was given permission to travel to Germany. Subsequently, Britain and the United States became much more closely watched role models for the "new social bureaucrats" in the Home Ministry, who became very influential after 1918 (Garon 1987).

proliferating mutual aid associations in the different policy domains for which he became responsible during his political career. Subsequently, these MAAs became a forerunner for work-based welfare schemes in the private sector (Anderson 1990, 69).

"Decentralized" welfare state building was a feasible strategy within state structures that showed a high degree of factionalism between different departments and ministries. Moreover, the mutual aid associations for public and private workers were not conceived as being necessarily detrimental to dynamic market expansion. At the same time, MAAs promised to be able to address the problem of high worker turnover. MAAs also fulfilled the paramount concern of the different ministries and agencies by allowing them to retain full regulatory and administrative sovereignty over the welfare schemes, especially over the accumulated capital of these schemes. A company or public agency retained full control over fund management and the respective ministries retained their legal oversight (Anderson 1990, 70). Thus, internal fragmentation of the central state, interest of the bureaucratic elite—especially in the Ministry of Agriculture and Commerce—in rapid market expansion, and a lack of interest in, or rather strong resistance against, a unitary scheme run by one central agency or ministry[8] were some of the important factors that supported decentralized and fragmented welfare state building in Japan.[9]

The Factory Law of 1911 (effective 1916), the first major piece of Japanese social legislation that made sick pay and injury compensation obligatory *for individual companies,* reflects this constellation of interests. Particularly notable was a company's obligation to pay 50 percent of wages for three months (33 percent after three months) to ill or injured workers. Compared, for instance, to statutes in the economically much further developed United States, the Japanese Factory Law cannot prove the backwardness of the early Japanese welfare state. This is especially true if one takes into account the fairly broad coverage of accident insurance, which applied to all firms employing fifteen or more workers. The section of the Factory Law that granted sick pay to ill workers potentially strengthened employee bonds to the company, which was in the particular interests of heavy industry and larger employers. In these companies, sick pay had already been introduced on a voluntary basis as part of the provisions offered by the mutual aid associations founded earlier on a company basis.

Workmen's compensation in the United States, in comparison, was introduced at about the same time, but coverage, benefits, and organizational design differed profoundly from state to state. States offered a wide variety

---

8. This is a notable difference with the German case (see below).

9. An argument linking the fragmentation of the Japanese welfare state to sectionalism between different ministries is also made by Campbell (1992, e.g., 55–56).

of insurance arrangements, including in many cases the right of the employer to be privately insured (Skocpol 1992, 296). As a consequence, the "vast majority of the state-level workmen's compensation laws" in the United States "would undercut rather than promote momentum toward additional forms of public social benefits" (ibid.). In this respect, Japan conformed much more to the general pattern of welfare state development observable in the advanced industrial countries (Flora and Alber 1981, 50–52) in which employers' support for—or at least acquiescence to—a further extension of welfare entitlements via the introduction of public disability or health insurance often resulted from the fact that employers were looking for ways to avoid paying health care costs or workmen's compensation (Skocpol 1992, 296). Japan introduced health insurance in 1922 (effective 1927) as the second element of social insurance after workmen's compensation. Again, welfare provisions were mainly directed at manual laborers in large companies. The health care act offered firms the opportunity to contract out of the public scheme and to run their own sickness funds. Most larger firms set up their own health insurance associations since they already had established firm-specific funds and "wanted to preserve their independence" (Garon 1987, 112).

Within a short period, hundreds of health insurance societies were established. Contributions were paid equally by employers and employees, and the new schemes were jointly administered by both groups. State-sponsored company welfare set precedents for later social legislation and also triggered organizational adaptation processes on the side of the unions. Although the so-called horizontal, industrial unions were confronted with substantial political repression, the active political support for "vertical" unions, the state-sponsored establishment of works councils,[10] and the introduction of company-based welfare schemes affected the path for the further development of the Japanese labor movement. This was because company-based welfare schemes seem to have been an important support for the establishment of moderate "second" or "vertical" (enterprise) unions. At the same time, the increasingly statutory, nonvoluntary character of company welfare schemes made them "trustworthy" in the sense that workers indeed could base their long-term expectations and decisions on wel-

10. After a works councils law was voted down in the Diet in 1920, the home minister introduced works councils in the national railways. Later, in public transportation and in army and naval arsenals, "he inspired other governmental employers, as well as several large *zaibatsu* concerns in heavy industry, to set up similar councils or company unions over the next few years" (Garon 1987, 53). State support of works councils contributed to the rise of enterprise unions as well. Since "many of these 'unions' began as company-sponsored mutual aid societies" (ibid., 114) and since unions repeatedly tried to get a hold on company welfare schemes in order to gain influence over finances and benefits, union development and company welfare are closely linked.

fare entitlements. The private firm thus became a holder of "public" social rights. Company pensions or sick pay increasingly lost the character of being merely employers' promises given in times of prosperity or tight labor markets; they became legal entitlements. As a consequence, they were better able than voluntary schemes to induce long-term cooperation between employees and employers.

This is not contradicted by the predominantly private character of the welfare schemes. The opting-out opportunity offered for health insurance and later also in the Employee Pension System (EPS) did not lead to a simple privatization of social policy, since benefits and the organizational form of the welfare schemes continued to be legally regulated by the state.[11] The public regulation, as opposed to the private provision, of welfare became the primary approach, and in this respect the Asian welfare state is not liberal (Goodman and Peng 1996; Goodman, White, and Kwon 1998; Jacobs 1998).[12] In the long run, a dual system evolved in pension and health insurance: lower premiums, lower copayments, and higher benefits in the state-regulated company schemes and even better conditions in the private schemes of health and pension insurance (Employee Pension System and Employee Health Insurance); and residual provisions, lower benefits, and longer qualifying periods in the public programs (National Pension System [NPS, 1959] and National Health Insurance [NHI, 1938/1958]; cf. Estevez-Abe 1996). The tight state regulation of the "private" schemes established company welfare as more than a simple fringe benefit. Although companies could stabilize their workforces by offering more favorable provisions as compared to the public schemes, the state continued to tightly regulate company welfare and forced uniform standards on the larger part of the industry. The state played the role of a "direct structurer and overseer of occupationally-linked pensions" (Shinkawa and Pempel 1996, 170).

Conventionally, worker mobilization is conceived as being one of the most important, if not *the* most important, factor for welfare state development (Korpi 1983; Shalev 1983; Stephens 1979). Following this line of argument, one can claim that with enterprise unions company welfare, not statutory welfare, should have been expected to develop in Japan (Cho 1994, 28). However, this is a problematic distinction. For example, the Japanese Factory Bill and the Health Insurance Act of 1922 do not clearly show how statutory and company welfare can be separated. The Japanese

11. With respect to pensions, a 1965 law allowed firms to opt out of the Employee Pension System if they guaranteed their workers benefits at least 30 percent higher than under the regular EPS and—importantly—if the majority of the employees and the union gave their consent (Shinkawa and Pempel 1996, 169).

12. That there is no reason to label the Japanese welfare state a liberal regime once we take the health care system into the picture is made clear by Ikegami (1996).

system of state-subsidized company welfare represents a specific public/private or "state-enterprise mix" (Shinkawa and Pempel 1996, 167).

This blurring of the boundaries between state and society is also characteristic of the German welfare state, in which unions and employers' associations are involved in the welfare system's administration. In this respect Japan and Germany clearly diverge from the "clarity of state-society boundaries" found in the "classic liberal political economy" (Crouch 1986, 180). Great Britain and—with qualifications—the United States come closest to this liberal ideal type, as is particularly evident in the case of social policy. In these two liberal countries, welfare is provided *either* by the state *or* by the market, whereas Japan and Germany have established hybrid forms of private and public provision of welfare that integrate firms and workers or unions and employers' associations into the welfare state. This "blurring of the boundaries" and the resulting tight coupling between the welfare state and the economy are particularly important for economic governance and performance in these two coordinated market economies.

But apart from the problems that arise in the Japanese case if one wants to employ the conventional distinction between private/company and public/statutory welfare, one can also doubt whether the causal-historical link is rightly identified as running from enterprise unions to company welfare and not the other way around. The above description of the early development of the welfare state in Japan presents substantial evidence for reversing the commonly assumed causal chain. In other words, company-based welfare schemes helped enterprise unions to grow, stabilize, and finally to dominate the Japanese labor movement. If one takes into account the length of the struggle between industrial and enterprise unions in postwar Japan, it indeed seems problematic to force early Japanese welfare state formation into the analytic framework of the "labor mobilization" thesis. At the same time, it will be hard to deny that a system of company-based social rights was an important factor supporting the organization of workers' interests at the enterprise level.

In the comparative welfare state literature, the insight is gaining acceptance that even for Sweden—the presumed classic example for the labor mobilization thesis—unions have not been an independent variable in welfare state formation. Even such a strong proponent of the labor mobilization thesis as Gøsta Esping-Andersen states today that "the labor movement's role cannot have been decisive in the original institutional designs [of welfare states], but only in their subsequent evolution." Thus, one has to "rethink the historical role of labor movements in the development of social policy." Moreover, "welfare states may be influenced by labor, but labor-movement evolution is, itself, affected by the institutions of the welfare state" (Esping-Andersen 1994, 139). Hence, according to Esping-Andersen, union growth and welfare state development should be studied as a "cybernetic phenomenon" (ibid.).[13] This seems to hold true for Japan as well. The specific institutional setup of Japanese accident and sickness insurance set clear *positive* incentives to organize labor along company lines, while political repression provided clear incentives against organization along class or sector lines. Once unions had been established on the company level, worker mobilization for universal and central welfare schemes was less powerful, since "what was in the best organizational interests of the enterprise unions was not always compatible with national welfare programs" (Shinkawa and Pempel 1996, 161).

The 1930s and early 1940s essentially brought an expansion of social insurance following principles established in previous years. The revised Factory Law of 1923 (effective in 1926) already had extended the benefits and coverage of accident insurance. At the same time, it forced companies to give workers fourteen days' notice in case of dismissals or, alternatively, to pay dismissed workers fourteen days' wages as an allowance (Shinkawa and Pempel 1996, 157). The Retirement Fund Law of 1937 is another important example of the growing importance of state regulation of companies' pensions and severance pay. The Retirement Fund Law required all enterprises of more than fifty employees (such firms employed about 60 percent of the nation's workforce in 1937) to set up funds for retirement and severance pay. The law established minimum levels according to years of seniority (Gordon 1985, 258–59). One of the important upshots of the Retirement Fund Law was that an increasing number of firms introduced retirement pensions (mostly as lump-sum payments). Even if the law had only systematized and extended existing practices, many companies were forced to expand existing welfare schemes or to introduce them.

Severance pay, to which workers felt entitled because they interpreted pensions as deferred wages, became more of a state-mandated entitlement and less of an employer's gratuity. Here again the state helped to overcome the precarious status of company welfare programs. What prior to the Retirement Fund Law had been true for voluntary welfare schemes in general had also applied to pensions and severance pay in particular: namely, they "did not simply generate the long-term commitment or the good will often credited to them. They frequently lacked substance, were cut back or abandoned when business needs so dictated" (Gordon 1985, 200). State regula-

---

13. The feedback effects from welfare state building to worker mobilization are increasingly taken into account by students of the welfare state. Heclo remarked as early as 1974 that "pensions helped advance the organization of the British labor movement as much as the reverse" (Heclo 1974, 165). For case studies see Heidenheimer (1980) on Britain and Germany, Rothstein (1992) on Sweden, and Steinmetz (1991, 1993) and Manow (1997) on Germany.

tion of company pensions reduced the risk that "management enthusiasm [for company welfare programs] declined together with profits" (ibid., 201). The state, thus, increasingly blocked the temptation of business to renege on past welfare promises in times of economic hardship.

The Retirement Fund Law was part of the war economy that brought a further push in welfare state development (as was the National Health Insurance Law of 1938). This push had no spectacular immediate effects with respect to social spending, but it had important institutional long-term consequences. In particular, the introduction of a public pension scheme (the Employee Pension System) for blue-collar workers in 1941 (extended to white-collar workers in 1943) has to be mentioned in this context. In many respects the EPS followed the well-known traits of previous social legislation. The main political motive for the introduction of old-age insurance was to accumulate capital for the war effort. The Ministry of Finance was in charge of the administration of the funds and remained responsible after World War II.[14] The EPS required a long qualifying period for an individual worker (twenty years) before the first pension would be paid out. This provision served the aim of capital accumulation as well, since under a fully or partially funded system like the EPS, funds grow with the length of the qualifying period. Thus, as Martin Collick has argued, the pension system was more of a "disguised war loan, rather than a major step forward in the creation of a universal pension system" (Collick 1988, 210).

Yet long qualifying periods were also proof that social policy in Japan was still far from a contentious issue within the "democratic class struggle" (Korpi 1983). What is trivially true for the period of Japanese authoritarianism from 1931 to 1945 also applies—at least partially—for the preceding period. Since the Japanese polity was still poorly democratized, social legislation was less focused on broader segments of the population or on the "really deserving." The welfare state was not introduced with the intention of easing the plight of the most desperate or those most negatively affected by industrialization. Except perhaps for a short time after the significant extension of the franchise in 1925, social policy was not an issue for electoral politics (Garon 1987, chaps. 4 and 5). Social rights were granted from

14. Large companies that wanted to opt out of the EPS also had to give up administrative responsibility in favor of a bank or a life-insurer. This was one of the conditions under which union consent to the EPS reform of 1965 could be achieved. There is, however, evidence that pension fund contracts remain within the main-bank system or the *keiretsu*, thus underpinning the system of cross-shareholding, providing firms of the same group with patient capital, and protecting them against takeovers and volatile stock markets (McKenzie 1992, 85, 90–96; see also Estevez-Abe 1996, 2001). This system is currently under pressure because of the opening of the huge pension fund market to foreign investment firms—one of the results of U.S.-Japanese trade negotiations.

above by a bureaucratic elite to specific groups or were introduced with the aim of stabilizing certain client-like ties between bourgeois parties and specific interest groups, including the business community.

As a result and in contrast to development in the United Kingdom (Heclo 1974), the United States, Australia, and New Zealand (Castles 1986), neither the most destitute nor very broad segments of the population were prime targets of the newly emerging welfare state. Government-funded pensions for soldiers and civil servants and retirement allowances, sick pay, and disability pensions for the worker elite provide ample evidence that the emerging welfare state focused especially on the comparatively better off. The Japanese welfare state became status oriented, very much like the German welfare state. It established its own system of social stratification, with the employment relationship as its central organizing principle. The welfare state integrated and upgraded existing company schemes and mutual aid associations and created new, "artificial" risk communities for small, limited, privileged groups. Although the models of Japanese industrial relations and production were fully established only after World War II, economic and political actors could later draw upon elements established between 1910 and 1940. Although one cannot identify a clear point at which the high-trust/long-term commitments model gained dominance over liberal, market-based alternatives, which of course had permanently been present in debate and practice as well, it is evident that the early developments described above certainly set the course for those that came later.

National Integration and the Welfare State: Germany

A set of diverse political motives stood behind Bismarckian social legislation between 1883 (health insurance) and 1889 (old age insurance, with accident insurance enacted in 1884). Of course, the most often-mentioned purpose was that the German state sought to respond to the challenge allegedly posed to the existing order by the rise of social democracy and socialist unions. Thus, German social legislation is commonly interpreted as being part of a carrot-and-stick strategy, the newly granted social rights representing the *carrot for* and the Antisocialist Law of 1878 representing the repressive *stick against* the labor movement. However, a less-often-mentioned but equally important motive for early German welfare state building was the advancement of the integration of the new Reich.

The welfare state was supposed to advance the internal foundation of the Reich (*innere Reichsgründung*) after the Prussian-French War of 1870–71 had brought "external," territorial consolidation. As a part of this effort, the new social insurance schemes were supposed to be centrally organized and tax-financed, thus granting to the central state a right of taxation it barely possessed before.[15] The German state of the late nineteenth century was less centralized and less hierarchic than Meiji Japan, mainly because the German constitution of 1871 represented a political compromise that centralized legislative powers but at the same time delegated the responsibility for legal enforcement and administration to the *Länder* (state) governments. This established a system in which policies had to be agreed upon jointly by the central state and the *Länder*, granting the states veto power in most political decisions (Lehmbruch 1976, chap. 6; 1997, 45–48; Huber 1988). Although the Meiji reformers had quickly (by 1869) reorganized the feudal domains as prefectures governed by appointees of the central government (Pyle 1978, 90), the German state was essentially federalist in character and remained so until the early 1930s.

Thus, Bismarckian social legislation itself was in essence the result of a compromise between the central government, the *Länder* in the federal chamber (*Bundesrat*), and the political parties in the Diet, making the new system of social security more federalist, more autonomous, and less state-dependent than had been envisioned in early drafts of the legislation. The political compromise modified Bismarck's original plans in important respects. Instead of a central social insurance bureaucracy, staffed by civil servants and financed solely or mainly through payments of the Reich, which was supposed to pay out roughly equal benefits (without regard to "actuarial fairness"), the new social insurance schemes were essentially financed by contributions, and payments and benefits were—albeit still loosely—related to workers' incomes. The organizational structure of the new social insurance built upon existing forms of collective self-help and self-administration, especially integrating workers' "free funds," which mainly provided sick pay in the case of illness, into the health insurance. The financial burden of, as well as the administrative responsibility for, the new social insurance schemes were shared between workers, employers, and the state. Because the Bundesrat and the Imperial Diet voted against an extension of the Reich's right of taxation, Bismarck's plans to finance social insurance through a centrally collected tax on tobacco soon had to be abandoned. This imposed from the very start tight restrictions on the central state's influence on social insurance. Even then the new social insurance did not become much more liberal in nature. In its initial conception, Bismarckian social legislation had been paternalistic, centralist, étatist, and interventionist. The process of political compromise had watered down some of its

15. The German central state of the late nineteenth century was financially almost entirely dependent on the contributions of the *Länder*.

most radical elements, but only to mix state interventionism with older layers of self-governance (*Selbstverwaltung*) and traditions of corporatist self-regulation. This was not a very liberal cocktail, but neither was it reactionary nor conservative in the sense of an attempt to preserve the status quo. Social insurance legislation was part of the forceful state-led modernization with which the German administrative elite attempted to rationalize the societal order and tried to respond to the depression of 1873–78. In the words of Werner Abelshauser (1984), Germany became the "first post-liberal nation." Bismarckian social legislation in particular marked the birth of many "historically durable 'modern' elements in German economic policy" (ibid., 289).

The federalist character of the German Reich had an impact not only on the legislative process, but also on the further development of social insurance schemes. The division of labor between the federal government and *Länder*, according to which the responsibility for the new social insurance was at the federal level while the states and local authorities retained the responsibility for the poor and destitute, helped to free the new social insurance from poor law traditions. Thus, social insurance focused on social risks and vagaries stemming from industrialization. The social programs were therefore mainly targeted at the core industrial workforce. The welfare entitlements introduced with the new social insurance were based on occupational status and not granted as a universal right. The marginal role of private insurance and collective self-help can be explained by the fact that the depression of the 1870s had led to widespread distrust of the free market and had also revealed the shaky financial base of many voluntary, private mutual insurance schemes.

A comparison of Japanese and German accident insurance helps give a sense of the countries' different approaches to the labor question. The Japanese Factory Law made the company responsible for the compensation of industrial accidents, but German accident insurance searched for a "collective" solution, that is, one that involved specialized insurance schemes covering an entire industrial sector via compulsory membership for all employers in that sector. In Germany, minimization of conflict between workers and employers over liability for industrial accidents was sought through the foundation of special liability associations (*Berufs-genossenschaften*). These liability associations pooled the risks of all employers of the same industrial sector, and the single firm was freed from all legal obligations resulting from industrial accidents. Firms in the same industry were perceived as constituting roughly homogeneous "risk communities." The level of social intervention, thus, was not the single firm as in Japan, but the industrial sector, covered by newly created special-purpose institutions (Gitter 1985; Wickenhagen 1980). Liability associations were deliberately designed to be bodies of public law (*Körperschaften öf-*

fentlichen Rechts) that publicly organized private business.[16] *Berufsgenossen-schaften* established a successful form of self-governance by the business community.

This legal framework quickly helped business to overcome certain collective-action problems. Since premium levels were set according to the frequency of industrial accidents, there was a common interest among all firms to reduce health risks caused by the production process, and since the *Berufsgenossenschaften* organized all employers of one sector, the impact on the firms' competitiveness remained limited. Thus, interfirm coordination became less problematic. This effort included the sharing of state-of-the-art safety standards in order to prevent accidents (Wickenhagen 1980). Employers faced clear incentives to agree on common technological and organizational standards of production. This helped quicken the diffusion of best practices and the prevention of "destructive competition" through low security standards and exploitative working practice. *Berufsgenossenschaften* possessed the legal right to inspect factories and to levy fines against firms that were not complying with the safety standards they set.

Although the liability associations were solely financed out of employers' contributions and were exclusively administered by business representatives, their arbitration committees, which had to decide contentious cases, were comprised of equal numbers of workers and employers and were headed by a neutral civil servant. The sickness funds of the newly introduced health insurance (1883), however, were dominated by union representatives (Heidenheimer 1980; Manow 1997; Tennstedt 1983). Workers held a two-thirds majority in the funds' assemblies and the executive boards, since their contributions to the funds were twice as high as the employers' contribution.[17] This dominance gave the labor movement critical influence in the administration of other social insurance branches as well: the arbitration committees for accident insurance and the assemblies of the old-age pensions were staffed equally by employers and by delegates sent from the sickness funds. Thus, unions could use their majority in health insurance institutions for a systematic "infiltration" of all other social insurance branches.[18] In the emerging social insurance system, orga-

16. Bismarck had hoped initially that the liability associations would become the nucleus of a system of functional representation, which would allow for the circumvention or even the replacement of the Diet. Werner Abelshauser (1984) has shown how this idea of a corporatist representation along industry lines stood at the beginning of the emergence of a very modern system of organized interest intermediation in Germany.

17. Accident insurance was financed by employers alone; old age insurance was financed in equal shares by employers and employees plus a state subsidy.

18. Another important instance of parity representation of organized capital and labor outside the social insurance system were the labor or industrial courts (*Gewerbegerichte*), founded in 1886 and reformed in 1890 (Steinmetz 1993).

nized workers and employers were integrated into a multifaceted system of collaboration long before the state (and business) had officially recognized the unions as the legitimate representatives of workers' interests.

Once the labor movement's position in social insurance was well entrenched, the state began to regulate internal relations between employers and unions. The proto-corporatist system of conflict moderation in social insurance figured later as a model for conflict mediation in the realm of labor-capital antagonism. It "laid the groundwork for the full-fledged corporatism of Weimar and adumbrated the main line of West Germany's social partnership" (Steinmetz 1993, 44).

The principle of *Parität* figured most prominently in this respect (Lehmbruch 1996, 1997).[19] *Parität* between the organized interests of capital and labor became a universal mode of "cleavage management" in German capitalism. Parity representation of organized labor and capital and their compulsory cooperation in the domain of social policy established a precedent for the solution of industrial conflicts between unions and employers' associations (Manow 1997). Here again, state intervention was targeted mainly at the associational level. *Parität* in social insurance administration had been relatively unproblematic, since it did not make direct state recognition of unions necessary. That the majority of the elected representatives in the social insurance administration were union activists and that German social insurance therefore had developed into a major organizational support structure for the socialist and Catholic labor movement had not been intended, but could be tolerated—at least for some time. *Parität* seemed to be legitimized by the fact that social insurance was jointly financed by capital and labor.

After equal representation between the organizations of the insured (the workers) and the employers was established in social insurance, barriers were lowered to the introduction of equal representation of *the corporate actors of both sides* (i.e., unions and employers' associations) in other areas as well. Parity between unions and employers' associations in important public or para-public agencies was first officially introduced in the wake of the massive state-interventionism of the war economy (Hilfsdienstgesetz [Auxiliary Service Law] of 1916), which for the first time extended *Parität* to industrial relations (see especially Feldman 1966). After the war, unions and employers both wanted to free themselves from the interventionist "state-socialism" of the war economy and searched for shelter from the early syndicalist and radical-socialist currents in the Weimarer Räterepublik (repub-

19. *Parität* is defined by Lehmbruch (1997, 57) as "an institutionalized system of conflict accommodation among corporate actors with (corporate) equality, as different from a liberal system based on individual autonomy." It comprises the equal representation of all conflict partners in bodies where decisions are reached by consensus.

lic of soviets). Their voluntary collaboration in the Zentralarbeitsgemein-schaft (Central Working Association) again followed the bipartite parity pattern.

Although the interests especially of the employers' side to continue the collaboration with the unions vanished as soon as the danger of massive so-cializations withered away and as general economic developments became much more favorable to capital, the state built crucially upon this voluntary arrangement in its new social and labor policy. In this way, the Labor Min-istry essentially stabilized a system of collective governance from outside through: (1) declaring bargained solutions as generally binding even for firms and workers who were not members of the respective associations of capital and labor (*Allgemeinverbindlichkeitserklärungen;* "erga omnes" rule); (2) declaring state arbitration in labor-capital conflicts as mandatory and binding, even if one of the conflicting parties did not consent to the arbi-tration (*Zwangsschlichtung*); and (3) legally prohibiting private contracts which would undermine minimum standards set by collective agreements (*Unabdingbarkeit*).

Regulations concerning who would be allowed to officially represent workers and employers in the administrative bodies of the social insurance schemes and in collective bargaining gave the state the opportunity to sta-bilize and also to limit the number of peak interest organizations: in other words, to shape the landscape of societal interests. The central bureau-cracy, which initially had few substantial policy responsibilities of its own, sought to expand its domain at the expense of the *Länder*. This is why it was more willing to support national interest organizations and to collaborate with them in the domain of welfare state administration. The interest orga-nizations were supposed to function as consulting bodies and as exclusive addressees for the policies of the Reich (cf. Sachße and Tennstedt 1988). Thus, the German state was less reluctant—in the words of Colin Crouch (1986, 1993)—to "share public space" with organized societal interests. The "liberal" separation between state and society did not become firmly entrenched in Germany. Support for the establishment of national interest groups, their centralization, and the willingness to grant these central in-terest groups domains of representative monopoly and to bestow them with public status (Offe 1981) became a routine strategy of the German state bu-reaucracy in various policy sectors (for welfare see especially Sachße and Tennstedt 1988).

For instance, the legal definition of *tariffähig* (being partner to collective bargaining agreements) was put down by the state in a number of laws and decrees, with the effect of excluding employer-friendly "yellow" unions from participation in arbitration committees and from access to the ad-ministration of social insurance. The law on elections to the social insur-ance organizations officially ascribed a privileged position to independent unions and employers' associations. Only they held the right to propose delegates to the social insurance assemblies. As long as either side proposed only as many delegates as there were positions to fill, the election itself was omitted (so-called *Friedenswahlen*, literally, "peace elections"). Yellow unions and the so-called free lists were excluded from the elections. State intervention in Germany thus effectively forestalled the development of enterprise unions.

During the interwar years this government strategy remained highly contested. Heavy industry in particular sought to preserve its autonomous status. It protested against mandatory arbitration, favored company-based, private welfare schemes, and thus vigorously protested against Weimar's social policy. Heavy industry supported enterprise unions and refused to collaborate with the so-called "free" unions on questions of vocational training. The employers in the coal and steel industries in particular struggled against any kind of interference with their autonomy and sovereignty, and thus fiercely fought against both the unions and the Labor Ministry (Preller 1978; Weisbrod 1978). It was not until the late 1950s and early 1960s that heavy industry made its peace with the Bismarckian welfare state (cf. Manow 2000). Yet insofar as the welfare state had already exerted a decisive, formative impact on the labor movement and had shaped German industrial relations, the range of options in the 1950s was significantly restricted. That something like the Japanese postwar settlement, which combined enterprise unions and "welfare capitalism," could also emerge in Germany as the new equilibrium was hard to imagine in the 1950s.

The Labor Ministry had used the *Parität* between unions and employers in the social insurance system as an instrument to achieve "political closure" on the union side—to establish a stable network of workers' interest representation. The Labor Ministry used subtle techniques of "legal engineering" to help the three leading unions (social-democratic, liberal, and Catholic) achieve "oligopolistic representation." At the same time, the ministry also sheltered the unions from syndicalist developments through the "juridification" of the task-domains of the works councils and through hindering the creation of "free," non-union-based lists in the social insurance administration.

It is important to emphasize that the integration of unions into the self-administration of social insurance schemes not only provided an important organizational stabilizer for union development and offered state bureaucrats a model of conflict accommodation for the labor-capital conflict. It also shaped the unions' further organizational development *beyond* the negative impact it had on the development of enterprise unions. In particular, the transformation from craft unions to modern, highly centralized and bureaucratized industrial unions has been supported through their integration into the welfare state, since this integration offered a broader basis for union organization (Heidenheimer 1980, 9). As Arnold Heidenheimer has shown, the shift from craft to industrial unions in particular "coincided closely with the decision [of the unions] to dissociate from the craft-based *Hilfskassen* [free funds] and to utilize the broadly based Local funds" (ibid.; see also Tennstedt 1976, 389–90). This decision had also weakened the importance of company welfare, which was integrated into and thus absorbed by the Bismarckian welfare state in the case of company sickness funds (*Betriebskrankenkassen*) or slowly crowded out by the new encompassing schemes.[20]

Craft unions often offered special insurance benefits to their members. The new social insurance increasingly prohibited using these union insurance schemes as "selective incentives." Hence, craft unions lost an instrument that was critical for attracting and keeping members, while industrial unions were gaining a new set of selective incentives, including the power to allocate numerous jobs in the insurance administration to loyal followers and to have a say over impressive welfare budgets (for data, see Manow 1997). The important influence of the German social insurance system on the organizational development of the German labor movement thus corresponds to the above-outlined linkage between Japanese welfare state building and union development. But in contrast to the close coevolution of company welfare and enterprise unionism that prevailed in Japan, the German welfare state put a premium on the organization of interests at the industry level and on regulating conflicts through interorganizational bargaining (with and without state involvement).

In summary, Japanese and German early welfare state development differed in two important respects. First, welfare state building took place within central state structures in Japan and within a federal state in Germany. Second, the main goal of the Meiji reformers was "catching up," while the German bureaucratic elite sought to foster national integration and tried to contain the political influence and the alleged threat to the existing order represented by the swelling labor movement and social democracy. Correspondingly, the Japanese state abstained from strong intervention in employment relations, while Bismarckian social legislation—deliberately—redefined the system of interest organization for business and labor (although the result of this redefinition was not exactly what Bismarck initially had in mind). One can trace these different attitudes toward the labor question even back to the different administrative responsibilities for social policies in both countries. In Germany, the Reich Office of the In-

20. The development of enterprise unions was further blocked by the sharp blue-collar/white-collar distinction introduced through the White-Collar Insurance Act of 1911. This law was, in turn, a response of the white-collar movement to the successful integration of the socialist unions in the social insurance system (Kocka 1981; Manow 1997).

terior held the responsibility for social legislation (after 1918, the Reich Labor Ministry), while in Japan the Ministry of Agriculture and Commerce was in charge of social legislation until the early 1920s.

On the other hand, commonalities between German and Japanese development are found especially in the strict status orientation of their welfare states, as well as in the establishment of an "industrial achievement model of social policy" and in the tendency to integrate labor and capital into the welfare state at either the enterprise or sectoral level. Both welfare states either upgraded existing schemes or created new, "artificial" ones for specific societal groups. The core workforce (or what became the core workforce) was especially targeted by welfare provisions. Late industrialization and late democratization seem to have been the two most important factors responsible for the similar leanings of the two welfare states to grant group-specific entitlements, to make the elite worker the main focus of the welfare state, to pay out status-oriented benefits, to link benefits to contributions, and to introduce long qualifying periods. In both countries an independent, Weberian state elite tried to respond to—what were in their eyes—the "functional necessities" of a modern industrial nation.

Conclusion

The comparison of German and Japanese early social policy undertaken in this chapter provides substantial support for the claim that the welfare state is an important and regularly overlooked factor that helps to explain the varied performance of contemporary market economies and their strikingly different institutions. In the case of Japan and Germany, this is in my view most evident with respect to the "ways and means" of economic coordination prevalent in both countries, based in the firm or firm group in Japan and in the industrial sector in Germany (Soskice 1995). These "ways and means" closely correspond to important institutional features of their respective welfare states: namely, to the company-based welfare system in Japan and to the corporatist/associational German welfare state model.

The analysis of early Japanese welfare state building shows that state interventions were supposed to address primarily the problems of high employee turnover and scarcity of skilled labor. At the same time, social intervention had to avoid any interference with market forces. Employers had a strong interest in state intervention that promised to reduce workers' high mobility. However, legal restrictions on labor mobility were not a promising instrument in the middle of a high-growth period and the rapid industrialization process. Employers were internally divided over whether legal constraints on labor mobility were the right response to their problems. Japanese state bureaucrats perceived restrictions on workers' mobility as having detrimental effects on "efficient factor allocation" and, thus, as being detrimental to economic growth. Hence, firm-specific solutions became dominant and were strongly supported by state legislation.

In Germany, Bismarckian social legislation aimed predominantly to contain the worker movement, to reduce strife between workers and employers over industrial accidents, and to further national integration. Bismarck hoped at the same time that employer liability associations would become the nucleus of a system of "functional representation" that eventually would be able to complement or even substitute for the political power of the parliament.

Yet, despite many institutional differences and differing objectives in the early period of welfare state building, both the German and the Japanese welfare states integrated labor and capital and "targeted" welfare entitlements especially at the core industrial workforce. Japan and Germany closely resemble each other in that the formative period of welfare state development happened in both countries while parliamentary democracy was only poorly developed, be it because voting rights were restricted (in Japan), or because the political influence of the parliament was weak (in Germany). This allowed these countries to direct social programs to certain groups and to try to foster social integration via the expansion of social rights, not *political participatory* rights. These social rights were primarily given to the worker elite segments of the labor force. In the middle of a forceful industrialization process, the welfare beneficiaries were clearly not the most destitute and needy.

Both Japan and Germany started with a fragmented and selective welfare state, which over time became more and more unified and universal (Campbell 1992 for Japan; G. Ritter 1983, 1991 for Germany). However, broader coverage was achieved through the gradual extension of the "performance/achievement" model, not via its substitution through a "citizenship" model with universal, tax-financed, flat-rate benefits. Both welfare states still focus mainly on the employment relationship. They reward long working careers, they offer firms and workers multiple opportunities to externalize adjustment costs, they buffer the employment relationship from cyclical economic swings, and they provide economic agents with a stable institutional framework.

Despite different institutional setups and varying overall economic importance, the welfare state in both countries thus has helped to underpin trusting, long-term cooperation between economic agents on the shop floor or in collective bargaining. Welfare programs became a characteristic, central part of the productivity coalition between workers and employers. It was the state with its coercive power that offered economic agents the opportunity to enter long-term coordination—an opportunity they otherwise would not have had to the same extent. The state made highly asset-specific investments possible by establishing a framework for coordination that made commitments credible and long-term economic cooperation feasible.

The Origins of Nonliberal Corporate Governance in Germany and Japan

Gregory Jackson

Germany and Japan are widely considered to have similar "bank-based" or "stakeholder" models of corporate governance (Crouch and Streeck 1998; De Jong 1996). In contrast to market-oriented varieties of capitalism, these nonliberal models suspend market mechanisms for capital and labor. German and Japanese corporate governance accommodates and promotes both the financial commitment of capital and industrial citizenship for labor. Financial commitment involves dependence on the specific enterprise to generate returns as well as on the ability to control appropriation of those returns (Lazonick and O'Sullivan 1996, 11). Industrial citizenship refers to status rights and obligations that are reciprocal between the rights of workers and the obligations of employers and asymmetric in addressing the unequal power of the two parties in exchange (T. Marshall 1964; Streeck 1997a).

This capital-labor nexus proved to have competitive strengths during much of the postwar era (Aoki 1994; Jackson 1997; Kester 1996). Long-term capital and labor have institutional complementarities that enhanced dynamic (X-) efficiency within the firm. Given beneficial constraints on short-term market rationality (Streeck 1997b), managers learned to draw upon a stock of trust and commitment in building long-term organizational capacities for high-skill and high-quality production. Nonliberal cor-

I thank Masahiko Aoki, Nicola Ebert, Andrew Gordon, Susanne Lütz, Philip Manow, Zenichi Shishido, Wolfgang Streeck, Sabrina Tesoka, Kathleen Thelen, Sigurt Vitols, Martha Walsh, Kozo Yamamura, and the two anonymous reviewers for comments. All errors are my own.

porate governance may thus be understood as a specific form of managerialism in which management mediates between shareholder and employee
interests, and stakeholders each exercise a contingent voice in corporate
governance (see Table 4.1).

Despite their "functional similarities" as nonliberal deviants, the capital-
labor nexus rests upon different institutional mechanisms in Germany and
Japan. Drawing on corporatist traditions, German corporate governance
emerged as a constitutional model wherein public authority is used to con-
stitutionalize the rights and obligations of private actors within the firm. In
Japan, an enterprise community model emerged that builds on mutual dependence and functional specialization within segmented organizations
having "household" (or *ie*-type) characteristics (Dore 1997; Murakami
1984, 301–2, 357; Tabata 1998). These differences broadly reflect the binding versus softer character of legal norms, solidaristic versus segmented patterns of association, and corporatist organization of class interests versus
vertical integration according to the *ie* pattern of organization.

Corporate governance is defined here broadly as the institutionalized
patterns of control and decision making within corporations. Although
many theoretical frameworks exist for studying corporate governance,[1] few
explore why corporate governance institutions differ across countries. German and Japanese similarities are often traced to their "late development"
(Gerschenkron 1962; see also the chapter by Sigurt Vitols in this volume).
Late development theories stress functional aspects of institutions in "efficient" adaptation to markets or technology, but alone tell little about the
political and social viability of institutions. Whereas the literature has recently stressed political variables (Gamble et al. 2000; Roe 1994), the political dynamics of corporate governance remain to be explored comparatively.

This chapter examines the origins of nonliberal corporate governance in
Germany and Japan in terms of two sets of institutional arrangements: (1)
those fostering financial commitment and "closed ownership" within intercorporate networks and bank networks (see Table 4.2), and (2) those establishing industrial citizenship and fostering stable employment tenures
and the integration of workers into the corporation (see Table 4.3). How
did capital and labor become committed to the firm, with both exercising
voice in corporate governance? And where did financial commitment and
industrial citizenship historically intersect, coevolve, and result in a relatively coherent "model"?

---

1. These include "efficiency" explanations (minimization of transaction or agency costs),
"cultural" explanations (differences in group values or norms), political explanations (distribution of power, state regulation), or institutional approaches (most taking institutions as
an exogenous variable and examining their impact on organizations).

Table 4.1 Comparison of corporate governance patterns

	Germany and Japan	United States
Management	Entrenched; modest salaries, stock options rare	Unstable; high salaries tied to shareholder returns
Motives of investment	Sustain implicit contracts	Return on equity
Information asymmetries	Low; intensive private information sharing, implicit contracting	High; extensive public disclosure, formalized contracting
Incentives to monitor	High; voice	Low; exit
Employee constraints	Industrial citizenship; legal or bargained rights to information, consultation, and codetermination	Voluntarism; collective bargaining, low legal intervention
Mechanism of corporate control	Internal coalitions	External takeovers

Table 4.2 Ownership of listed corporations, 1995 (percent)

	Germany[a]	Japan[b]	United States[c]
Banks	10.3	22.3	0.2
Insurance firms and pension funds	12.4	15.9	31.3
Investment firms and other	7.6	6.4	13.0
Nonfinancial firms	42.1	23.8	15.0
Individuals	14.6	23.5	36.4
Government	4.3	0.7	0.0
Foreign	8.7	7.4	4.2

Sources: [a] Deutsche Bundesbank Monthly Report, various years; [b] National Conference of Stock Exchanges as quoted in the *Tokyo Stock Exchange Fact Book*, various years; [c] U.S. Federal Reserve Flow of Funds.
Note: Figures do not total 100 percent due to rounding errors.

The central argument is that financial commitment and industrial citizenship in Germany and Japan emerged through two parallel critical junctures where liberal alternatives were historically suppressed and nonliberal patterns were institutionalized (an outline of the argument is presented in Figure 4.1). The argument is organized in three sections, each of which begins by placing Germany and Japan in relation to liberal models and outlining the main explanatory forces before turning to empirical evidence in the country narratives.

Section 1 examines the critical juncture of the transition from family to intercorporate ownership. Corporate ownership in Germany and Japan developed from family ownership into intercorporate and bank ownership rather than ownership fragmentation and a market for corporate control. Corporate networks fostered financial commitment by limiting the ability of capital to exit and by fusing ownership with strategic organizational in-

Table 4.3 Stability of employment

Current Tenure	Germany[a] (1995)	Japan[b] (1995)	United States (1996)
less than 1 year	16.1	7.6	26.0
1 to 5 years	31.4	28.9	28.5
5 to 20 years	35.6	42.2	36.6
20-plus years	17.0	21.4	9.0
Average tenure in years	9.7	11.3	7.4
Median tenure in years	10.7	8.3	4.2
Elasticity of employment, 1960–93	0.09	0.08	0.33

Sources: Tenure Data from OECD 1993, 1997; Employment Elasticity dates from EPA 1993. Refers to the elasticity of changes in employment relative to production output in manufacturing.

Notes: [a] German data from the Socio-Economic Panel refer to German-born citizens employed at the time of the survey, excluding apprentices and others currently in training programs. [b] Japanese data relate to regular employees (persons hired for an indefinite period); temporary workers hired for more than one month; daily workers hired for over 17 days, in private establishments with over 9 employees.

terests. This transition occurred gradually between the 1920s and 1950s and led to cross-shareholding arrangements of *keiretsu* or horizontal groups of enterprises and main banks in Japan and the pyramidal *Konzern* (conglomerate) in Germany that are loosely connected by universal banks.

Section 2 examines how employees gained rights to industrial citizenship when paternalistic and authoritarian forms of labor management were transformed during the late political democratization of Germany and Japan. Industrialization occurred through a program of conservative social reform in which the state and employers attempted to substitute social for political rights of workers before the extension of democratic citizenship (Bendix 1964; Flora and Alber 1981). Given this fusion of state and enterprise authority, postwar political democratization led to contention over authority relations within the firm. This transformation led to noncontractual "status" rights for employees within enterprise hierarchies that later helped support long-term employment and labor-management cooperation. Rights of industrial citizenship were established in the form of codetermination[2] in Germany and lifetime employment[3] and joint consultation in Japan.

2. The law mandates employee representation on the *Aufsichtsrat* and grants rights of information, consultation, and codetermination to employees in plant-level works councils.

3. "Lifetime employment" in Japan refers to institutionalized practices for core corporate employees such as seniority-related wages, firm-specific skill formation, and high employment security. By contrast, in Germany skills are portable due to nationally organized apprenticeship systems, and seniority-wage curves are very flat, as wages increase only around 20 percent over the life cycle compared to 180 percent in Japan (Economic Planning Agency 1993; Schmidt et al. 1997, 213).

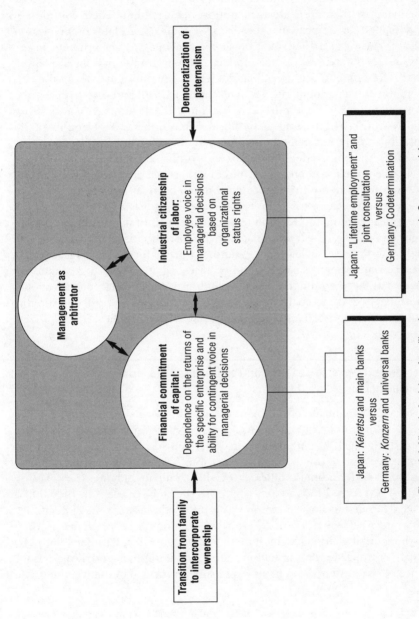

Figure 4.1 Historical origins of nonliberal corporate governance in Germany and Japan

Section 3 returns to the puzzle of the parallel development of nonmarket institutions for both capital and labor. Within the large corporation, the rights of property owners and employees are interdependent but indirectly mediated by their respective relation to management. Their coevolution was shaped by a particular historical sequence[4] of "late-comer conservatism" (Murakami 1982) that presented specific tensions inherent in the prewar corporate governance models: between traditionalism, liberalism, state developmentalism (a public interest in the internal order of the corporation and a national interest in its performance), and social opposition. Postwar political democratization weakened the legitimacy of ownership rights while strengthening the political claims of labor. Past nonliberal institutions were transformed into channels of democratic participation that established labor as a legitimate force in corporate governance.

The economic complementarities or coherence of nonliberal corporate governance were not inevitable and resulted from an unintended fit. Nonliberal models came to "hang together" as institutions were adapted in a piecemeal fashion and took on new functions within new institutional configurations. The constraints placed by industrial citizenship on property rights, and vice versa, led to a new and distinctive form of corporate governance. Management served as the exclusive agents of neither capital nor labor, but faced contingent voice by both groups. Through organizational learning, negotiated coalition building proved able to be crafted in support of successful high-skill and high-quality production regimes.

Corporate Ownership and Control: The Origins of Financial Commitment

How did financial commitment develop in Germany and Japan? Since Adolf Berle and Gardiner Means wrote *The Modern Corporation and Private Property* in 1933, fragmentation of ownership has been viewed as an entropic dynamic of the modern corporation. As firms outgrow the financial resources of founding families, ownership gradually fragments as existing owners are forced to issue new shares in the stock market. In the United States, ownership fragmentation was reinforced by two political decisions. First, antitrust legislation made interfirm relations less cooperative, leading to horizontal mergers that diluted owner control (Chandler 1990). By 1924, "entrepreneurial capitalism" developed into "managerial capitalism," where 40 percent of listed firms were firmly controlled by management (De

---

4. Sequence refers to timing "in relation to and in interaction with other ongoing political processes" (Thelen 1999). For literature stressing the importance of sequence in three different disciplines, see Aoki 2001; Mjøset et al. 1997; and Thelen 1999.

Jong 1992). Second, capital markets underwent political segmentation during the New Deal (1933–41), making financial intermediaries, unlike industrial firms, regionally segmented (Roe 1994). Only in the 1980s was the separation of ownership and control or "strong managers, weak owners" eclipsed by "investor capitalism." Shareholder interests became reasserted through a market for corporate control and the voice of large institutional investors.

In both liberal and nonliberal countries, early corporate ownership was indeed dominated by families with substantial financial commitment to their enterprises (Lazonick and O'Sullivan 1996). Yet corporate ownership in Germany and Japan did not move toward fragmented ownership and market liquidity. Rather, ownership became concentrated among intercorporate networks and banks. Ownership thereby remained concentrated among large blockholders, and stakes were largely motivated by strategic organizational interests rather than maximizing capital-market returns.

Family ownership survived for relatively long periods in Germany and Japan due to the financial and organizational resources of families. Generally, family ownership has strengths when the noneconomic solidarity of family ties supports economic functions such as capital mobilization, organizational trust, and value orientations that subordinate individual interests to a long-term view of business.[5] Family solidarity may be subverted by capitalist rationality or may take on dysfunctional characteristics.[6] How did firms foster the strengths while reducing the weaknesses of family control for so long? Economic historian Hidemasa Morikawa (1992) presents this as a paradox of "exclusive ownership and progressive management."

Family control was supported by corporate law and company statutes that gave disproportionate influence to large shareholders—through the *zaibatsu* holding companies[7] or the *Konzern* structure and the creation of the supervisory board (*Aufsichtsrat*) to oversee management on behalf of shareholders. Furthermore, families had internal mechanisms to prevent mem-

5. Families offer noncapitalist motivation in ownership through patriarchal and personal authority, loyalties, emotion, and traditions (Kocka 1979). Family owners likely take a long-term view and face expectations to subordinate their individual interests to the family—for example, by reinvesting a high proportion of profits into the company. Families have advantages in mobilizing capital through personal loyalties, trust, and the willingness to share risks and endure sacrifices. Such "embeddedness" often gives capital a more "patient" quality and enables transactions in the absence of other formal institutions.

6. Family ownership also has disadvantages: limited access to outside funds, conservative business policies, growing disinterest of family members in strategic decisions, loss of motivation for salaried managers where top positions are monopolized by family members, and conflicts between the private interests of the family and rational management.

7. *Zaibatsu* (literally, financial groups) refers to family-based control (later through holding companies) over interrelated companies organized around specialized financial, sales, and distribution companies. *Zaibatsu* groups were often slow to adopt the legal form of a corporation.

bers from liquidating capital. In Japan, family constitutions constrained family members from liquidating their capital and placed corporations in their collective control. In Germany, family owners could perpetuate disproportional influence relative to other shareholders through board structures and special voting rights. Although they strengthened family control, familialism and corporate law also made owner control less arbitrary, more formalized, and increasingly delegated to professional management recruited from universities. Families were thus able to integrate owner control with professional management and expertise.

Another sociological change that prevented ownership fragmentation in property rights took place through the development of interfirm networks. Salaried managers came to exercise property rights on the basis of their bureaucratic authority—they controlled shares owned by their companies and pursued company interests instead of shareholder interests. Company interests were often multiplex and long-term strategic interests, such as coordinating prices, securing markets, managing technological dependence, or protecting management from outside influence. As corporate structures slowly became "cooperative" and interwoven, the German *Konzern* and the Japanese *zaibatsu* holding companies emerged as instruments of corporate control. "Closed ownership" within interfirm networks depended on a variety of factors: (1) the presence of strong financial intermediaries that channeled assets away from securities markets; (2) market structures and regulations that tolerated interfirm cooperation; and (3) mechanisms available within corporate law that allowed management to shield itself from shareholder influence.

Family control and intercorporate ownership coexisted until after World War II, when family influence was either reduced by Allied policy or gradually waned. Allied policy went further in Japan than in Germany to break up family ownership. Hence, individual share ownership was much higher in Japan—70 percent of total share ownership in 1950, compared to 42 percent in Germany and 90 percent in the United States (Windolf 1994). Quite opposite to developments in the United States, this separation of ownership and control led to the formation by Japanese management of innovative company groups linked horizontally through cross-shareholding. German corporate networks retained their *Konzern* structure and the important role of banks among the largest and most widely held firms. Bank representation in Germany and cross-shareholding in Japan provided effective protection from a takeover market and insulated firms from shareholder pressure. The separation of ownership and control thus occurred very gradually as a slow and incomplete process mediated by the social forms of family relations, the structure of corporate boards, the organization of markets, and the role of financial institutions. The paradox is that ownership by households declined instead of leading to fragmentation as in the United States. In its place, types of shareholders emerged whose interests were primarily organization based and highly committed.

If interfirm networks and banks suppressed the fragmentation of ownership, what accounts for their unique role in Germany and Japan? State policies had important influence on the development of financial commitment in four broad areas: corporate law, financial regulation, market regulation, and welfare state provision.

Corporate Law

Corporate law shapes the nature and purpose of the corporation by institutionalizing rules that channel ownership into the capacity to influence management. Corporate laws in Germany and Japan were initially shareholder-oriented but had different normative conceptions of how to institutionalize shareholder interests. German law constitutionalized shareholder influence within a sharply defined two-tiered board that separated the decision-making power of the management board (*Vorstand*) from the monitoring role of the *Aufsichtsrat*. Legal intervention reflected a view that state intervention into internal governance of the firm was a matter of the public interest (Gamble et al. 2000). Constitutionalism reinforced early patterns of control (such as strong family ownership, bank representation, exclusion of small shareholders) and facilitated interfirm cooperation. Japan, on the other hand, did not develop a two-tiered board model, leaving shareholder interests to the shareholders meeting. However, shareholder rights remained limited in the absence of a common-law tradition. During wartime, authoritarian regimes reshaped legal conceptions of the firm. Notions of the national interest were introduced, opening corporations to direct state intervention. Private shareholder rights were curtailed, while labor was bolstered ideologically as a member of a "classless" national community.

During the postwar era, German and Japanese corporate law gradually returned to a more liberal shareholder orientation, although retaining significant differences from a "private association" model. Despite the strong formal rights of shareholders under Japanese law, few mechanisms assure that shareholders' interests are represented.[8] German corporate law still constitutionalizes interest representation and does not define directors' responsibilities exclusively in terms of fiduciary duties to shareholders. The two-tier board structure and its pluralistic interest representation (e.g., *Aufsichtsrat* representation for employees) defy such definition and imply substantial public-interest obligations in constitutional law. Thus, shareholder interests are not hegemonic under either system.

---

8. In the United States, typical mechanisms include outside directors, managerial incentives, market-oriented disclosure rules, and minority rights.

Financial Regulation

Financial regulation shapes the types of intermediaries in the capital market. Germany and Japan developed "bank-based" financial systems that channeled assets into the hands of banks and away from securities markets (see the chapter by Vitols in this volume). Contrary to the late development thesis, the centrality of banks was reinforced during the regulatory divide of the 1930s rather than resulting from state sponsorship during the nineteenth century. In the 1930s, Germany developed corporatist regulatory patterns, while in Japan direct state intervention helped target investment and monitor banks. The concentration of financial assets in the banking sector meant reduced demand for stocks by small shareholders, made stock markets relatively illiquid, and discouraged the development of Anglo-U.S. style markets for corporate control.

The exact role of banks has been controversial in the academic literature, perhaps because of strong variations depending on the business cycle, industrial sector, and historical period. Long-term credit does not appear to have been the major source of finance for industrialization. Yet banks had other channels of influence (credit, board representation, proxy votes, securities underwriting) with important consequences for corporate governance. First, firms were able to limit the number of liquid shares issued in cases where banks leveraged their retained earnings and protected share prices—thus working against ownership fragmentation. Second, banks took direct stakes in firms, often as a result of a business crisis. Third, banks often took on crucial monitoring functions. In the nineteenth century, German banks exercised proxy votes and were represented in the *Aufsichtsrat*. Early Japanese banks were initially more subordinate to their *zaibatsu* firms and later to the state, although their role as important monitors developed in the postwar period. In sum, as family ownership declined after World War II, banks became the dominant corporate monitors, using a distinct pattern of governance where intervention is contingent upon the long-term financial well-being of the firm and comes in the form of voice.

Market Regulation

Market regulation shaped the environment of interfirm networks. Germany and Japan shared nonliberal notions that the market must be ordered and competition mitigated (see the chapter by Gerhard Lehmbruch in this volume). Market regulation impacted the strategies of growth pursued by firms, in particular the preference for internal growth versus external mergers and the use of trusts and cartels to protect profitability and hence financial autonomy. Cooperation proved to be a flexible alternative to mergers and prevented the dilution of ownership stakes. Interfirm cooperation continued after the war despite the introduction of more liberal competition regimes under U.S. influence. After initial deconcentration efforts, German *Konzern* maintained a pyramidal structure of intercorporate ownership, while Japanese *keiretsu* developed new patterns of horizontal cross-shareholding in the context of new competition rules.

Welfare state arrangements also had unintended consequences for financial commitment, particularly in the postwar era. The relatively strong public component of pension schemes and the organizationally embedded nature of private schemes in Germany and Japan have been supportive of bank-based financial systems (Jackson and Vitols 2000). These welfare state arrangements limited the flow of household savings to the stock market and hindered the rise of large portfolio investors with fiduciary responsibilities, as occurred in Britain and the United States. Conversely, internally held pension savings in German and Japanese firms made important contributions to their capacity for internal finance and hence lessened their dependence on external capital markets.

The next section presents empirical details of the historical development of financial commitment in Germany and Japan, respectively.

Germany

Imperial Germany: Constitutionalism in Corporate Law. The system of state concessions for incorporation with limited liability ended in 1870 and was replaced by a broadly liberal corporate law. However, German corporate law increasingly moved toward a nonliberal organizational constitutionalism in the context of the financial crash of 1873 (*Gründerkrise*)[9] and related political realignments. The efforts to reform corporate law should be appreciated in the context of a more general break with the doctrine of economic liberalism and the rise of a new political discourse coalition among the state bureaucracy in support of "conservative social reform" (see the Lehmbruch chapter in this volume). The 1884 corporate law reform established the modern two-tiered board system that divided decision making between the *Vorstand* and *Aufsichtsrat*.[10] The *Aufsichtsrat* displaced the share-

---

9. The *Gründerkrise* was spurred by the end of the state concession system in 1870 and an influx of speculative capital from war reparation payments from France. The number of corporations quadrupled, with one out of thirteen going bankrupt and one of three being liquidated. Extensive fraud led to public distrust of corporations and culminated in the corporate law reform of 1884 with its stress on corporate organization rather than individual shareholder rights (see Hommelhoff 1985).

10. The *Aufsichtsrat* was influenced by practices in the Netherlands and France as well as by the *Verwaltungsrat* (shareholder committee) often found in German company statutes before 1870 (Hopt 1979).

holders meeting in appointing and controlling management.[11] German lawmakers viewed the shareholders meeting skeptically for several reasons: its uncertain composition might lead to dominance by minority shareholders; it failed to provide continuous monitoring (Hopt 1979, 232); and "democracy" that would give a voice to small shareholders was widely considered undesirable due to their short-term interests and ability to exit (Reich 1979, 269; Passow 1922). Thus, although German law recognized shareholder interests as primary, the role of shareholders was defined dramatically differently than in liberal countries.[12] Rather than a British "private association" approach, German lawmakers constitutionalized shareholder representation through public authority.

Although corporate law reform was the work of a relatively independent bureaucracy, the law altered the balance of power among shareholders in favor of large family owners and banks. Family ownership remained strong in Germany through 1914 (H. Pohl 1982; Brockstedt 1984). Families could control the *Aufsichtsrat* by holding simple majorities, through proxy votes, or by exercising special voting rights. Most small shareholders transferred proxy voting rights to banks, thus having little direct influence on management. Meanwhile, founding families held shares with special voting rights, especially veto rights given to 25 percent minority blocks (Pross 1965). Company statutes requiring *Aufsichtsrat* ratification of specific business decisions were used extensively by family owners, such as Krupp and Siemens, to maintain control over strategic decisions. Given such close control, little notion of "independent" directors emerged to represent small shareholders, and *Aufsichtsrat* seats represented the network of relations to banks, business, and the state. In the largest 1,000 corporations of 1906, two-thirds of *Aufsichtsrat* seats represented interfirm business interests (bank representatives, suppliers, competitors)—banks alone accounted for one-third of all seats, government officials one-third, and other owners only around one-tenth (Eulenburg 1906).

Financial autonomy also slowed the decline of family control. Large corporations financed the rapid growth of capital primarily through retained earnings (H. Pohl 1984; Tilly 1980; Wellhöner 1989). Self-finance de-

11. The shareholders meeting would approve the dividend payout and balance sheets, elect the *Aufsichtsrat*, and approve changes in the capital structure (Horn 1979, 156–62).

12. Liberalism typically relies on strengthening individual shareholders' rights within the shareholders meeting (minority protection, disclosure, etc.), while assuming that shareholders on the whole can solve "agency problems" and monitor management in shareholder interests. Unlike in the United States, German corporate law had no protections for individual minority shareholders or against insider trading. The German position during the reform in 1884 remained, "Every extension of so-called individual rights is a danger for the organization and the entire functioning of the corporation" (Horn 1979, 160).

pended upon low pressure from outside shareholders to pay dividends, low effective taxation, and the stable profitability of cartels. When growth outstripped self-financing, firms mainly turned to capital markets to issue shares. However, the 1884 reform raised the minimum nominal capital of shares to 1,000 marks and thereby discouraged wide investment of household savings in the stock market.[13] Thus, banks were the central actors mediating access to outside capital.

German universal banks combined commercial and investment banking activities, unlike their U.S. counterparts (M. Pohl 1986; Riesser 1910; Tilly 1966, 1986; Vitols chapter in this volume). Universal banks were large relative to industrial firms and linked to large firms through multiple channels: short- and long-term industrial lending, banking services, brokerage of share issues, direct stock ownership, exercise of proxy votes of custodial shares, and *Aufsichtsrat* representation.

Financially, banks were most important in underwriting shares, placing share packages in strategically sound hands, and supporting share prices through direct trading and buybacks. Much literature on the German model overstates the role of bank lending. Available evidence suggests that lending was not a primary source of corporate finance. Loans provided short-term liquidity and gave banks a stable flow of interest payments. Within this multiplex relationship, banks also played a monitoring role. Proxy voting developed around a tax on the transfer of securities, which created a niche for banks to hold shares on deposit and conduct trading between owners internally. Bank directors accounted for over 20 percent of all *Aufsichtsrat* seats in 1914 and individual banks had seats in as many as 186 firms (Kocka 1975, 103; H. Pohl 1982, 164). Bank influence reached its peak around 1900 and was subject to numerous constraints. Private banks competed heavily and rarely had exclusive relations with large firms. Strong family owners fiercely resisted encroachment on their entrepreneurial prerogatives. Thus, bank ties were often involuntary results of failed stock emissions, bad loans, or other bailouts (Wellhöner 1989).

In sum, early corporate governance was dominated by families and banks whose relations were constitutionalized in corporate law. The functions of capital ownership and management were separated within the organization, and owner-managers either occupied the *Aufsichtsrat* or exercised control along with a team of salaried managers. Managerial-controlled firms also emerged (e.g., AEG and Deutsche Bank), but remained uncommon (Pross 1965).

13. Share ownership was perceived as too risky for all but the wealthy classes and asset-rich institutions after the bankruptcies and securities fraud during the *Gründerkrise* (Pross 1965, 64; Reich 1979, 263).

World War I and Weimar Germany (1914–33): Concentration, Cartels, and Interfirm Cooperation. Interwar economic crisis and concentration prompted increases in intercorporate shareholding and cooperation. Interfirm networks involved cartels and new organizational forms, such as the profit-pooling I.G. (*Interessengemeinschaft*, or community of interests) and the vertically integrated conglomerate (*Konzern*).[14] Cooperation proved more flexible than full-scale mergers, which were typical in the United States, in coping with overcapacity and rationalization. Where mergers did occur, such as in the steel and chemical industries after 1924, firms were integrated in the *Konzern* structures rather the American M-form corporations aimed at rational economies of scale (such as purchasing and marketing) for a very large domestic market. The *Konzern* coordinated investment, finance, and rationalization strategies and shared necessary technical expertise for niche production by subsidiary companies (Herrigel 1996, 93–98). The *Konzern* were committed to low-volume production of relatively specialized and high-quality products, while being highly diversified across niche markets (Dornseifer and Kocka 1993).

This "organizational revolution" changed corporate governance in several ways. First, lower levels of merger activity led to slower fragmentation of ownership than in the United States. Family ownership survived through the 1930s and dominated the iron and steel industries (Chandler 1990, 591; Pross 1965, 211). Families and controlling managers relied on special voting shares to secure influence, particularly during the large number of new share issues after World War I. Between 1919 and 1924, over half of listed firms in Germany issued shares with preferential voting rights, often legitimated by the fear of foreign takeovers (Pross 1965, 84). Second, ownership was used to coordinate interfirm strategy, while ultimate ownership became increasingly indirect. The inherent instability of cartels accelerated the diffusion of the I.G. and *Konzern* structures. By 1927, nearly all of the 100 largest corporations were conglomerates organized around holding companies (Siegrist 1980). This shifted the functions of the *Aufsichtsrat*, widening its competence from the representation of shareholder interests to the creation of useful business relations and information.[15]

A third change in corporate governance was the concentration of deci-

---

14. "The I.G. as a profit pool reduced the incentives to cheat on price and output agreements, and by cooperation in functional activities the member firms enhanced their industry's position in foreign markets. The *Konzerne* were more vertically integrated, for they were often established for the defensive purpose of assuring the central enterprise of sources of supply and outlets for its products" (Chandler 1990, 589–90).

15. Mergers and the introduction of labor representatives led the *Aufsichtsrat* in many large firms to grow often to 50–80 persons, decreasing the effectiveness of control (Pross 1965, 80–83). Criticism of the continued exclusion of small shareholders reemerged in some business circles.

sion-making power and the shift to professional managers. No reliable statistical estimates exist, but management-controlled enterprise was likely less widespread in Germany than in the United States, although the proportion of salaried managers grew from one-third to one-half of all German directors between 1914 and the 1930s (Kaelble 1986, 77; Kocka and Siegrist 1979). These managers controlled subsidiary firms through the *Aufsichtsrat*. Managers largely pursued goals similar to those of family owners, guarding against dependence on external capital markets by seeking high profits but keeping dividend payments low and reinvesting in the firm to maximize growth (Kocka 1975, 117–19; H. Pohl 1982).

State policy facilitated interfirm cooperation. Unlike in the United States, cartel contracts were legally enforceable and were already widespread in the late nineteenth century (statistics in Wellhöner 1989; Chandler 1990). In 1890, the Reichsgericht (imperial court) ruled that businesses were allowed to regulate markets by means of "self help on a cooperative basis" in order to prevent ruinous competition (Nörr 1995, 7). Although cartels were supported by nonliberal and nationalist state ideologies, the legal doctrine regarding cartels was justified, particularly by industry itself, by upholding the liberal principle of contractual freedom over the opposing liberal principle of free competition. During the Weimar Republic (1918–33), cartels were also perceived positively by the left as an instrument of a publicly controlled economy (*Gemeinwirtschaft*) anchored in the constitution (see the Lehmbruch chapter in this volume). When the first German cartel law in 1923 instituted a cartel court and supervisory agency, the aim was not to prevent cartels but to protect competitors' interests as well as public and national welfare. Thus, a crucial political difference existed between Germany and the United States, where the use of strong state legal intervention made industrial self-regulation through cartels illegal and protected freedom of competition, thereby unintentionally promoting a merger wave that greatly accelerated the separation of ownership and control (Fligstein 1990, 23, 59).

German banks also underwent concentration and continued their mutual interdependence with industry. Rapid inflation eroded the capital base of private banks, resulting in the state taking ownership stakes. Having a high degree of network centrality, banks could help underpin cartel agreements, arrange mergers, and promote the joint interests of related companies. However, large corporations were less vulnerable to inflationary pressures and came to rely less on banks, further dividing their business between competing banks.

Nazi Germany (1933–45). In the Nazi era, economic policy combined strong state direction and ideological control with capitalist property relations and the profit motive (Neumann 1944). The Nazis favored neither industry nor autonomous private interests; rather, the state used indirect methods of control over industry. During the Nazi period shareholder rights were curtailed, as they were in wartime Japan. Company accounts were approved only by the *Aufsichtsrat*, not the shareholders meeting. And two laws limited dividend payouts to 6 or 8 percent and approved higher payouts only when public bonds of equal value were purchased.[16]

These measures formed part of a policy to control investment and secure war financing by making stocks less attractive than government bonds. Capital investment was directed through mandatory cartels empowered to ban investments in certain industries. These policies did not aim to eliminate the profit motive but to control profit distribution—firms increased their retained earnings rapidly between 1933 and 1938 (Neumann 1944, 318). In conjunction with wage controls that dampened consumption, investment increased and shifted away from consumer-oriented industries toward heavy industry and armaments financed by strong internal reserves and direct state investment. Capitalist property thus came to coexist with strongly circumscribed prerogatives over investment, use of raw materials, choice of products, and discretion over corporate profits.

Unlike the wartime mobilization of the Japanese banking system, the Nazis did not tie banks to industrial governance. Private banks avoided nationalization but were pressed into state finance and gradually decoupled from industry. Ideologically, the Nazis were skeptical of banks and appealed to the "struggle against high finance." Interest rates were held low, banks had small profits, liquidity requirements were increased, and the level of credit stagnated. Banks thus contributed little to net corporate finance, and their funds were forcibly diverted into state bonds.

Although shareholder and bank control declined, the public interest element of corporate law increased. In the 1937 corporate law reform, Paragraph 70 of the Joint Stock Corporation Law (Aktiengesetz) obliged the *Vorstand* to manage the corporation for the good of the enterprise, the employees, and the people and country. The law had Weimar origins reflecting a commitment to the public-interest agenda of the new political coalition and fitting with the idea of a state- or council-run system of economic democracy. Under Nazi rule, the public interest was interpreted in a narrow nationalist fashion that opened management to direct party and state influence—politicizing corporate governance. Although few notable industrialists were open Nazi supporters before 1933 (Turner 1985), big business initially drew advantages from Nazi power: labor unions were destroyed, cartels flourished, and government contracts bolstered growth in particu-

16. These were: (1) the Capital Investment Law, Kapitalanlagengesetz vom 29.März.1934, Reichsgesetzblatt (RGB) 1 I: 295; and (2) the Loan Capital Law, Anleihenstockgesetz vom 4.Dezember 1934, (RGB) 1 I: 1222.

lar sectors. During wartime, many party functionaries became managers, and the state became involved in direct ownership. A state-run enterprise, the Göring-Werke, was established to control plants in the conquered territories. The state also intervened where private interests endangered planning goals. For example, plants of the Vereinigten Stahlwerke were confiscated or forced to be sold in 1937 and 1939. Politicization aimed at eliminating Jews, bankers, and other nonparty members from management (see, for example, the case of Daimler-Benz in Pohl, Habeth, and Brüninghaus 1986).

Federal Republic of Germany: The Social Market Economy. Unlike in Japan, corporate ownership did not change radically after World War II.[17] Although some owners were arrested and tried for war crimes, the Allies' policy aimed to curtail the support of militarism in German industry through deconcentration. The Allies lacked unity on how to restructure firms in different occupied zones, and later firms were returned to their original owners. Deconcentration focused on three complexes: the big private banks (Commerzbank, Deutsche Bank, and Dresdner Bank), the chemical group I.G.-Farben, and coal and steel firms such as Krupp.

The banks were split into regional firms in 1947 and 1948 but were restored to their old form by 1957. Several I.G.-Farben managers were tried for war crimes. However, as share ownership was already fragmented, ownership purges were less important than the deconcentration policy that split I.G.-Farben into twelve firms in 1953 that were similar to the original component firms (G. Plumpe 1990). Coal and steel firms were largely under family ownership. For example, the largest twelve steel firms were split into twenty-eight independent companies. In contrast to the purges of *zaibatsu* families, past owners received shares in each of the new firms in 1951 in equal proportion to their previous shares (Potthoff 1957). Large shareholders were then obligated to sell their shares within five years and reduce their holdings to a single firm. Only a few individuals such as Alfred Krupp and Otto Wolf were ordered to completely divest from coal and steel. Selling large share packets was difficult in Germany's weak capital markets, leading to share swaps between the firms which consolidated ownership, gave renewed influence to large shareholders, and reinforced webs of intercorporate holdings.

Thus, despite deconcentration, corporate ownership remained "closed" among corporate groups and banks. In the largest 110 firms of 1958, 61

17. One can only speculate about why the Allies did not go further in purging owners and fragmenting share ownership in Germany. Disunity among the Allies, the division of Germany, the cold war, and different philosophies of U.S. military governments may have played important roles.

percent were controlled by a single shareholder (20 percent by families, the rest by the state or foreign and domestic corporations), 19 percent by multiple minorities, and only 20 percent manager controlled (Pross 1965, 113–17).[18] Between 1950 and 1995, ownership by banks and insurance firms increased from 3 to 22 percent of total market value and interfirm ownership increased from 22 to 42 percent (Jackson 1997). Conversely, individual and family ownership has declined from 42 to 17 percent. Thus, ownership concentration remains high, often controlled by very large and often more widely held parent firms at the core of the *Konzern*.[19] Even the most widely held parent firms faced very limited threats of hostile takeovers or market-driven shareholder pressures due to the role of banks.

Early channels of bank influence—ownership, credit, proxy voting, and *Aufsichtsrat* representation—have all remained important, although their relative weight has shifted (Schmidt et al. 1997). Rather than corporate finance,[20] banks increasingly performed "contingent" monitoring within a context of relational financing similar to the Japanese main bank system. Proxy voting rights of banks dominate the shareholders meetings of the most widely held firms, where banks in the early 1990s controlled 84 percent of votes cast through direct stakes and proxy voting rights (Baums and Fraune 1995, 104). Finally, banks represent around 10 percent of the total *Aufsichtsrat* seats in the 100 largest firms (Schmidt et al. 1997, 111).

Postwar corporate law remained unchanged until 1965 and since then has increasingly incorporated liberal elements while maintaining its "constitutional" character. For example, the public interest clause established in the 1937 reform was omitted in 1965, when the Bundestag stated that the principle of social responsibility was subsumed under the German Basic Law that specifies that private property entails social obligations.[21] However, constitutional courts reaffirmed this principle, and the "interest of the enterprise" became an important legitimation in debates over codetermination—although divergent interpretations exist that stress public, pluralistic, and procedural ways of defining the company's interest. Thus, although

18. Since the largest firms tended to be widely held, manager control accounted for an estimated 40 percent of turnover.

19. Iber (1985) examined the largest 371 listed firms between 1963 and 1983: majority-owned firms increased from 55.7 to 65.5 percent of firms, and those without blocking minorities decreased from 15.2 to 11.6 percent. Majority-owned and fragmented firms each represented roughly one-third of total market value in both time periods.

20. Following World War II, corporate investment was financed through a roughly equal proportion of depreciation, retained earnings, and external funds. Depreciation and retained earnings increased dramatically over the postwar period, while external finance declined to roughly 10 percent by the 1980s. Bank lending also declined, but still might be considered high compared to other countries.

21. Article 14, Paragraph 2 of the Basic Law states: "Property carries obligations. Its use should simultaneously serve the public good."

the 1965 corporate law reform strove to restore shareholder rights in several areas (disclosure, control over the distribution of profit, shareholder lawsuits, assuring the "collegiality" principle in the *Vorstand*), the basic "constitutional" logic of corporate governance as well as a public interest were maintained into the postwar period (Aktiengesetz 1965).

Japan

The Meiji Period (1868–1912). After more than two decades of legal uncertainty, the Meiji government set up a uniform legal framework for corporations with the Commercial Code in 1893 and its revision in 1899. The Commercial Code was more liberal than in Germany and did not stipulate a formal, constitutionalized pattern of corporate control. Unlike in Germany, the 1899 Commercial Code in Japan gave strong powers to the shareholders meeting to directly elect management and remained very loyal to the principle of mandatory stockholder majorities (Hirata 1996; Shishido 2000).

A variety of nonliberal features was infused into early Japanese corporations through the ideology of state-led "developmentalism." Industrialization was promoted through selective support of entrepreneurs who cultivated close relations with the state bureaucracies of the Meiji government (Yamamura 1997). The Meiji regime promoted the ideal of the businessman as a benefactor of the community and servant of the state (Clark 1979, 29), motivated by group benefits. Developmentalism helped reduce the strong vertical status distinctions and ideological barriers to commerce through nationalism and helped prevent the dominance of liberal notions of the corporation.[22]

Other nonliberal features came through traditions of collective family ownership (Hazama 1992). Although the Commercial Code (1893) and Civil Code (1898) guaranteed the right of individual property, the earliest private joint-stock companies also adapted principles of family property. The Tokugawa merchant house had been conceived as a household entity (*ie*) that extended beyond its members' life spans. The head of the family had a duty to preserve the business for future generations. However, the head of the household was not allowed to make business decisions unilaterally (Matao Miyamoto 1984, 44). Family owners received salaries and their activities were held accountable to the interests of the firm by man-

---

22. As stressed by Hirschmeier (1964), some managerial ideologies were more of a nationalist type ("seek the benefit of the nation"), while others stressed mutual help of the group ("hope to share and enjoy the benefits which it may bring by making our hearts as one and working together"). The examples are respectively taken from the "Abbreviated Rules of Agreement" of the Oji Paper Manufacturing Company in 1872 and "Main Aim of Foundation of Mitsui Bank" in 1876 (found in Hazama 1992, 114).

agers who were entrusted to protect the assets of the house as fictive family members (Iwata 1992, 178).

Family legacy was secured by the existence of "family codes" among the *zaibatsu*[23] firms that typically contained strong restrictions on investment, making it impossible for individuals to voluntarily withdraw portions of investment, take on debts, or become involved in nonfamily businesses (Yasuoka 1984). For example, none of the eleven families of Mitsui could renounce its ownership. Hence property rights were collectively shared rather than individually disposable: "an *ie* was an entity, a name to be honoured by all and protected by all at all costs" (Yamamura 1997, 342; see also Hazama 1997, 12).[24]

Similar to Germany, the financial commitment of family owners allowed early corporations to expand largely through internal reinvestment. Firms with less financial strength also issued new capital to existing owners, who purchased shares on bank credit—creating a cycle of high dividends financing their high interest payments (Georg 1996, 58–59). The state set up a system of postal savings to accumulate savings under government control. From the 1880s onward, private banks began extending short- and long-term credit to industry, yet one must be cautious in estimating its extent comparatively. Although the aggregate data remain mixed, internal reserves and share issues were likely more important sources of capital than bank loans (Yamamura 1997). Most loans took place within groups of related *zaibatsu* companies.

The delegation of management from family members to salaried managers was widespread in emerging *zaibatsu* enterprises. The personal qualities of early entrepreneurs, such as skill in securing political favors and contracts, became rivaled in importance by the necessity of technical and financial skills. Firms looked to the growing system of universities. Up until 1913, although many firms had appointed former bureaucrats or professional managers, less than one-third of the 115 largest firms had more than two salaried managers, and no firm was in managerial control (Morikawa 1993, 12). Some separation of ownership and control occurred, allowing "progressive" management without ownership fragmentation.

23. *Zaibatsu* (literally, financial groups) refers to family-based control (later through holding companies) over interrelated companies organized around specialized financial, sales, and distribution companies. *Zaibatsu* groups were often slow to adopt the legal form of a corporation.

24. Parallels certainly existed in, for example, the notion of *Haus* among German industrial families such as Siemens and Krupp in their efforts to secure the continuity of the family over many generations, and also in similar mechanisms of regulating family behavior such as company ownership through testaments or the establishment of foundations (see Kocka 1975, 1979). It remains an open empirical question as to how strong these parallels were and what systematic differences existed between Germany and Japan, and also vis-à-vis countries such as Britain.

The Concentration of the Zaibatsu, 1911–39. Japanese industry also underwent an interwar "organizational revolution," during which intercorporate ownership increasingly became a source of financial commitment. Japan witnessed rapid industrial concentration, increased bank ownership, and interlocking directorates. *Zaibatsu* firms introduced holding companies to govern their subsidiaries and improve economies of scope and finance strategy (Morikawa 1992).[25]

Holding companies retained majority stakes and absorbed subsidiary profits, reinforcing financial commitment as an "internalized" capital market. Holding companies often paid high dividends but distributed funds were used by families to purchase new shares to maintain control when new capital was issued. *Zaibatsu* banks stabilized this arrangement by leveraging retained earnings (Iwata 1992) and purchasing shares in group companies. Families retained majority control of holding companies, and the holding companies and banks assured a closed system of group control, together owning 90.2 percent of capital at Mitsui, 69.4 percent at Mitsubishi, 79.1 percent at Sumitomo, and 32 percent at Yasuda in 1928 (Teranishi 1994).[26] Given their financial advantages, the *zaibatsu* lessened their dependence on bank loans, while the *zaibatsu* banks themselves increasingly dominated the banking sector in the concentration following the 1920s banking crisis and adopted more features of German universal banks.[27]

This organizational revolution furthered the separation of ownership and control. Organizational size and complexity inevitably outstripped the managerial capacity of *zaibatsu* families. Holding companies provided overall strategic control: after concluding an extensive presubmission discussion with the holding company, subsidiaries submitted strategic decisions for *zaibatsu* holding-company approval, and thus were never vetoed between 1923 and 1932 (Morikawa 1992, 214). Interlocking directorates also emerged but resulted in a growing separation of board functions between supervisory tasks and operational decisions, the latter increasingly made by internally promoted directors. Thus, most corporate boards contained owner-managers and salaried managers. The latter held a majority of board seats in slightly over half of the largest 65 firms in 1930, compared to just 9 percent in 1913 (Morikawa 1986, 1993). Based on a study of the 158 largest firms in 1930, only 17 percent were controlled by salaried managers constituting over two-thirds of the board.

25. Although *zaibatsu* and *Konzern* had similar financial rationales, the two have different organizational structures. *Zaibatsu* groups were more diversified across industries, while *Konzern* controlled producers within the same industry.

26. Holding companies also allowed subsidiaries to raise external funds from the stock market, as long as they maintained a controlling stake.

27. These banks increased their long-term lending relative to their total assets and diversified their loans to other parts of Japanese industry (Yamamura 1997, 333–38).

Despite their market dominance, the four largest *zaibatsu* accounted for only ten of the sixty largest mining and manufacturing firms in 1935. *Zaibatsu* firms differed significantly from other large Japanese firms: they maintained a greater separation of ownership and control (measured by the lower number of owner-directors), a greater concentration of shareholders in families; dividends were lower and less sensitive to profits; and employment adjustment was far lower (see Okazaki 1994, 351–59, for a detailed statistical comparison). Thus, although the *zaibatsu* drew their strength from financial commitment, their features were not yet generalized throughout Japan. A large segment of the Japanese economy had corporate governance patterns similar to those in the United States, as well as the associated problems of establishing effective shareholder control.

The Wartime Planned Economy. The wartime economy began a shift from shareholder-oriented to employee-oriented corporate governance in Japan. State-industry relations changed dramatically beginning in 1936 as the army gained ascendancy over political parties and the wartime economy mobilized to reduce consumption and increase investment for war production. The state adopted a Soviet-inspired system of economic planning. An extensive targeting system gave the state great leverage over capital investment. The Kikakuin (Planning Board), established by the government in 1937, took the position that corporations should be set free from shareholder control and pursuit of profits in order to uphold the national interest. Only reasonable minimum levels of profit and dividends should be guaranteed, and management should be increasingly professionalized.

In 1940, the Planning Board issued its "Outline of the Establishment of a New Economic System" (*Keizai shintaisei kakuritsu yōkō*), which referred to "transforming enterprises to public interest entities," "separating ownership and management," and "restraint of profits" (Aoki 1997, 237). Since 1938, the Ministry of Welfare supported the view that employees imparted more commitment to the firm than did shareholders, who were criticized as being short-term oriented and rent-seeking. Resistance by industry led to a revision in the wording so that the firm appeared as "an organic body composed of capital, management, and labor" (Okazaki 1994, 367). Later, the Munitions Corporation Law (1943) designated a "responsible person" from among the incumbent managers and gave him special powers to act without interference from the shareholders meeting.

These measures helped diffuse some of the distinctive features of the Japanese *zaibatsu*. The number of shareholder-directors declined rapidly. Financial commitment was supported by Article 11 of the National Mobilization Act, which regulated dividends and loans and effectively capped dividend rates at around 10 percent without special permission from the

Ministry of Finance. However, taxes on profits were also imposed on subsidiary firms, holding companies, and individuals so as to weaken *zaibatsu* family control over profits. As in Germany, the reduction of shareholder control did not aim to eliminate the profit motive but to control the distribution of profits and foster investment.

During the 1930s the state rapidly reduced the number of commercial banks. Stock market instability resulting from the laws on dividends led the state to promote saving by workers—whose wages increased and who deposited these savings in banks. The state then helped establish loan consortia to fund war production. Munitions corporations, especially, were coupled with designated banks that provided loans and exclusively mediated payment settlements. The share of loans in corporate finance increased, as did the percentage of shares owned by banks. This pattern is taken to support the "wartime origins" thesis, which argues that the linkages between particular banks and firms foreshadowed the role of main banks in the postwar system. However, state control meant that banks could not enforce criteria of credit-worthiness. Thus, banks during the war lacked true monitoring roles and functioned very differently from the postwar "main banks" (Hashimoto 1996, 18–19).

Postwar Period of High Growth. Following the war, U.S. occupation forces began sweeping institutional reforms: disbanding the *zaibatsu* and beginning a legal reform modeled upon U.S. institutions (an antitrust act, a Securities and Exchange Act that separated banking and securities, and a revision of the Commercial Code). The first measures covered the *zaibatsu* holding companies, although reorganization of *zaibatsu* subsidiaries came later and was less thorough. The Supreme Commander for the Allied Powers sought to preserve private corporate ownership but strip *zaibatsu* families of their power. Their family wealth was reduced by capital levy (de facto confiscation, since this tax on capital was aimed specifically at *zaibatsu*), progressive taxes, and inflation. The purge began by a directive in 1945 that targeted families and executives of the *zaibatsu* parent companies and continued in 1947 with the purge of 1,980 officials at the executive director or full-time auditor level in 238 enterprises (Morikawa 1993, 16). Finally, a law in 1948 widened the scope of the purges by removing 3,625 executives at *zaibatsu* parent and subsidiary companies. Although the purge directives were removed with the signing of the peace treaty in 1951, very few managers returned. The removal of *zaibatsu* family members and top managers radically ushered in a whole new generation of management. These managers were recruited from lower-ranking directors and division and factory management.

The securities of the *zaibatsu* holding companies in 1946 constituted 42 percent of the paid-in book values of Japanese corporations (see Bisson

1954). The Supreme Commander for the Allied Powers took possession and redistributed shares to small individual owners with preference given to employees and local residents, who purchased 47 percent of disposed shares through July 1950. Shares were also offered to brokers in consignment sales, and only a limited number of remaining shares were offered to the general public. By 1949, 69 percent of shares were owned by individuals and families, compared to 16 percent by banks and other industrial firms. By 1951, *zaibatsu* shares had been liquidated, the holding companies reformed into twenty-six new operating companies, and the remaining fifty-seven companies divorced from the *zaibatsu* groups.

Given the high ownership fragmentation, managers enjoyed freedom from shareholder control. Cross-shareholding emerged from this fragmented ownership structure (Kikkawa 1995; Shishido 1994, 672). As individual shareholders quickly sold their stock during the period of high inflation, the Bank of Japan encouraged Japanese banks to purchase shares. Cross-shareholding grew during the 1950s and 1960s, led by the ex-*zaibatsu* companies of Sumitomo, Mitsubishi, and Mitsui, which sought to maintain strong internal control over their shareholdings and mutually reinforce the autonomy of management. Another securities recession in the early 1960s led banks and securities companies to establish cooperative associations for purchasing shares, which were then sold among "stable shareholders." Additional company groups started to take similar shape in the mid-1960s to prevent foreign takeovers as Japan became an Article 8 nation in the International Monetary Fund and could no longer restrict imports and foreign exchange controls. Of these new groups, Sanwa and Daiichi-Kangin had no legacy as *zaibatsu*. The horizontal *keiretsu* links firms by reciprocal small-parcel shareholding that accounted for 10 to 25 percent of the group total (Gerlach 1992). The antimonopoly law limited corporate share ownership in excess of a firm's own capital and banned holding companies until 1998, influencing the horizontal form of cross-shareholding.

Cross-shareholding was organized, in part, around the main banks and increasingly has taken on functions of supporting interfirm cooperation. Today, corporate groups provide a closed ownership structure and foster financial commitment to Japanese firms. Main banks form the center of the network, providing an important share of the bank loans and acting as a "delegated monitor" through the intervention and dispatch of directors in times of distress (Sheard 1994, 313). Given legal limits on bank ownership, usually several group banks are closely linked to companies. As in Germany, banks capture the debt-based and securities-based channels of control. This governance structure ensures that control is only exercised contingent upon company distress and a variety of relational incentives. In addition, groups have developed multiplex ties that commingle ownership with other exchange relationships designed to achieve economies of scope (in banking, insurance, lending, supply, or purchase, or use of a group trading company). Information is shared in monthly meetings of presidents clubs, and firms implicitly guarantee to neither sell shares (coordinated by a lead underwriter) or demand high dividends.

In the absence of main-bank monitoring, shareholder control is very limited within Japanese corporate governance. In part modeled around the U.S. board of directors system, corporate law reform in 1950 limited the powers of the shareholders meeting and more clearly differentiated the powers of the board in determining its representative directors or issuing new shares and share voting rights. The shareholders meeting can recall management only through a qualified majority of two-thirds of votes present at a meeting where over half of the shareholders are represented (unlike German law, where the *Aufsichtsrat* elects and recalls management). The board structure also fails to internalize monitoring, as only around one-third of large Japanese firms have a single outside director, usually dispatched from the main bank (Lincoln, Gerlach, and Ahmadjian 1994). Auditors also have a weak role, being appointed by the management and lacking real independence. In practice, weak shareholder control is reinforced through cross-shareholding, as well as the practice of holding annual shareholders meetings on the same day and keeping them extremely short in order to deter corporate greenmailers. Company directors rise through the ranks internally, and the president is appointed to a long, six-year term and has broad powers. Japan thus has its own particular version of managerialism, but one that, unlike in the United States, has led to an employee-orientation of corporate governance.

Labor Management: The Origins of Industrial Citizenship

Given the absence of industrial citizenship in liberal countries, the corporate governance literature has largely neglected employees. Liberal industrial relations regimes institutionalize adversarial relations between management and labor, who engage in voluntaristic collective bargaining but leave managerial prerogative unquestioned. Within this context, corporate governance is defined in terms of owners and managers—shareholder hegemony is the norm, even when its realization is fraught with agency problems. However, corporate property rights not only give control over material assets but create an authority relationship with employees. Legitimate authority relies on the goodwill of subordinates because employment contracts are fundamentally indeterminate. The social and political limits to such authority can be significant.[28] Industrial citizenship may constrain shareholder control or serve as a counterweight to managerialism, while also providing positive-sum opportunities that complement financial commitment in building long-term organizational capacities. Acknowledging these linkages between property rights, managerial control, and labor management is central to understanding nonliberal corporate governance. As Roe (1994, 214) points out, "While American politics fragmented capital and labor, German politics brought them together in the boardroom."

Industrial citizenship has its origins in the democratization of particular forms of labor rights that had their roots in organizational membership under employer paternalism and state policies of repression and co-optation. Such rights were part of the "conservative social reform" that granted particularistic status rights during industrialization, and they drew upon unique cultural and ideological traditions in each country. These status rights must be understood within their nondemocratic political context as part of a broader political strategy that relied on giving social entitlements to compensate for lack of political rights. These nonliberal institutions were later "democratized" during the process of expanding political citizenship rights. The critical juncture can be found in the simultaneous movements for political and economic democracy. This pathway of "democratized paternalism" was shaped by a configuration of three forces: state labor and social policy, contention between firms and organized labor, and managerial ideologies[29] that legitimate authority within enterprise hierarchies. The changing balance of political power also transformed patterns of authority within enterprises during the interwar period and postwar defeat, occupation, and reconstruction. Democratization led to new institutions but built upon past legacies of contention and institutions of accommodation within the firm.

Early owner-entrepreneurs in Germany and Japan developed managerial ideologies of paternalism aimed at increasing company loyalty and the social integration of employees. As Hiroshi Hazama has noted, "Paternalism is an attitude on the part of the capitalist-manager toward his own employees, a willingness to give them favourable consideration at his own initia-

---

28. In Germany and Japan, employees have formal and informal voice in management selection: through *Aufsichtsrat* representation or through the career patterns of top managers as enterprise union officials in Japan. Likewise, managerial discretion is limited by plant-level codetermination or lifetime employment practices and joint consultation.

29. Managerial ideology is "an ideology that, incorporated in all administrative institutions (the whole system of roles and norms), manifests the aims of the management organization, performs the role of unifying the organization, and at the same time seeks to motivate members of staff and gain legitimacy from people (society) within and without the enterprise" (Hazama 1992, 91).

tive, not in response to any demand from below as a right or as a matter of duty forced upon him from the outside" (Hazama 1997, 34). Such ideologies were partly an instrumental response to the challenges of labor management, but adapted or reinvented broader cultural conceptions to bolster managerial authority and attachment to firms. Paternalism thus reflected and was constrained by cultural values, and it received the support of dominant discourse coalitions in politics. Paternalism implicitly acknowledged employer obligations, even though these did not translate into employee rights. Family ownership was a source of noncapitalist solidarity that imbued management with long-term interests in the enterprise and carried the idea of the firm as something "more" than just property. Nonetheless, family owners undoubtedly viewed early corporations as "their" firms. Hence, employees were not equal members, but "members" nonetheless. Similarly, the recruitment of management from the state bureaucracy and military fused ideologies with state traditions of authority rather than with commercial traditions.

Later, managerial ideologies were transformed by increasing nationalism and growing "public interest" elements of corporate law. The subordination of entrepreneurs to the state reinforced collective orientations of management and the importance of "ultimate values" other than the pursuit of individual profit (Bendix 1956). Labor management was understood to involve the exercise of authority in the service of values rather than a process of individual exchange in the market. War increased state intervention in corporate governance, further breaking with the idea that the corporation was a vehicle of private interests. Authoritarian intervention limited shareholder sovereignty and made employees legitimate members of the firm in state ideology as a microcosm of a national community. In reality, national cohesion was premised on the violent suppression of independent labor organization. Employees only became genuinely legitimate actors in corporate governance with the infusion of the value of "democracy" within the firm. Democratization took hold of the notion of the firm as a "moral community" but redefined and transformed it. Unions directed their activities at ending managerial paternalism, framing their demands in terms of becoming legitimate members of the enterprise.

Industrialization entailed the loss of an unwritten social contract. The old sets of mutual obligations, based upon some claim to protection by one's superiors but strict exclusion from public affairs, broke down with the institutionalization of a free labor market. The formal equality of market processes led to new forms of inequality that became the long-term object of contention in capitalist firms and national politics. Industrialization thus involved a shifting social basis of legitimacy along with the different forms of association in the economy. Although liberal countries fused economic liberalism with a catalog of civil and political rights associated with political liberalism, the sequence of extending rights was very different in Germany and Japan. State-society relations shared two important initial conditions: state bureaucracies were relatively strong compared to emerging industry, and industrialization occurred before the extension of democratic rights to citizens. This led to two important long-term processes.

First, labor had to confront both a strong state *and* industry. In this context, early industrial citizenship can be interpreted as part of elite strategies to substitute social for civil and political rights (Flora and Alber 1981). The use of state power to repress worker mobilization led to the fusion of capitalist authority based on property rights with society-wide patterns of authority relations. This politicized union movements, which sought to defend their rights against both employers and the state (Marks 1989). However, the state attempted to preempt the labor movement through integrative institutions. In gradual and diffuse ways, the idea of the firm as a moral community involving employees was thereby institutionalized before 1945.

In Germany, the development of social insurance made a relatively early contribution through the notion of self-administration and parity representation within firms (see the chapter by Philip Manow in this volume). Likewise, the shadow of state intervention, such as the factory laws in Japan, led to renewed preventive efforts of company paternalism. Wartime mobilization strengthened state intervention in the labor market and production process, as well as the need to develop new integrative institutions for labor within the factory. The experience with works councils during World War I was particularly important in Germany, and the enterprise branches of the Industrial Patriotic Society of World War II were important in Japan. Such interventions in the internal authority structures of enterprises broadly legitimized a role for employees within corporate governance despite employer opposition. However, contrary to the claims of the "wartime origins" thesis, the structural similarities of wartime institutions and postwar institutions is superficial, since no labor independence was protected.

In the second long-term process of state-society relations, the state maintained dominance over industry, subordinating property rights to political prerogatives. Beyond its impact on managerial ideology, the success of mobilizing private corporations for nationalist goals led to a collapse of capitalist authority along with military defeat and political reformation after 1945. Due to their wartime involvement, capitalist owners suffered a crisis of legitimacy in the eyes of the Allies and employees. *Zaibatsu* families were ousted and German owners were subject to (incomplete) denazification programs. The legitimacy of owner authority based on property rights was put into question by its implication in political systems whose legitimacy came to an abrupt end. The political abuse of economic power became an important justification for strengthening the political rights of workers relative to owners. These developments linked the democratization of society closely with the democratization of the firm. The influence of the Allied powers created sufficient political discontinuity to realize changes in the internal structure of the firm.

Political democratization occurred simultaneously through national defeat and foreign occupation, at a time when labor unions were particularly strong relative to capital. Political collapse made possible the recognition and integration of labor. The organization of the labor movement and factors such as skill formation led to important differences in the ways labor was integrated into the firm. For reasons too numerous to detail here, German unions formed along industrial rather than enterprise lines, creating a competitive relationship between class and enterprise loyalties and an institutional separation between collective bargaining and codetermination by works councils (see the chapter by Kathleen Thelen and Ikuo Kume in this volume). By contrast, Japanese unions remained organized around the enterprise, and worker participation at the plant level was less clearly divided from collective bargaining.

Moreover, the labor movement had an earlier impact in Germany. Despite the Nazi period, the German labor movement displayed personal, organizational, and ideological continuities from the Weimar into the postwar period. Postwar works councils were modeled on Weimar legislation, although the political unity of the postwar labor movement was a conscious reaction to past failures. Furthermore, linkages to political parties were strong in Germany, reflecting the strong legal rights for labor (e.g., the codetermination law), whereas Japanese unions became influential in national politics only much later (Kume 1998). Many differences in the form of industrial citizenship relate to these differences in union organization and its linkages to politics.

Germany

Imperial Germany: The Development of Employer Paternalism. The idea of "codetermination" predated modern corporations and labor unions. Its origins have complex roots in Christian, socialist, and romantic philosophies, as well as in the notion of parity (*Parität*) and economic democracy discussed in the 1848 Frankfurt National Assembly (Kotthoff 1994; Teuteberg 1961). At its core, codetermination involves state-sanctioned parity representation of labor in enterprise-based councils. Codetermination represented a socially integrative alternative to revolution or socialism. Analogous to demands of constitutional rights in the political sphere, it recognizes that the freedom of entrepreneurs within a liberal economic order also requires obligations to prevent social ills (Teuteberg 1981). However, few steps toward codetermination were taken during this first era of employer paternalism.

Between 1870 and 1914 the employment share of large industrial enterprises grew rapidly.[30] Most employment in large firms emerged unregulated, rooted in the legal distinctions between craft production and large enterprises and developing in agrarian regions where little craft control was entrenched (Herrigel 1996; Thelen and Kume chapter in this volume). In the absence of strong regulation, management ideologies combined elements of autocratic authority and paternalist ideology—captured by the phrase *Herr im Haus*, or master of the house. Owners stressed their personal authority more than competence-based functional authority. Written work rules often gained the status of "factory laws" enforced by the police (Fischer 1979, 105–6). These managerial ideologies diffused from the German military and state bureaucracy, which unlike in Britain or the United States had developed ahead of industry and from which firms recruited salaried managers (Braun, Eberwein, and Tholen 1992, 193–98).

German unions were first legalized in 1869, but organization rates remained low at around 3 percent until the turn of the century and then grew rapidly to over 20 percent of the industrial labor force, or nearly 3 million members, in 1914 (Marks 1989, 86; Guillen 1994, 95). Unionization was especially low in large firms due to the effectiveness of state repression, antiunion attitudes of employers, and the unskilled makeup of the labor force. Ambiguities in the early trade union laws, the antisocialist law, and renewed efforts of firms to ban strikes gave the state a variety of repressive instruments. Repression politicized unions, which sought to protect their precarious rights vis-à-vis the state and employers (Marks 1989). Political unionism ultimately found its outlet through close organizational linkages to the Social Democratic Party. Worker contention was thus channeled directly toward the state and directly challenged the authority of employers through the symbolic breaking of factory rules (Biernacki 1995, 454).

The German state began to view company-labor relations as a matter of public interest. As the industrial labor force grew and the consequences of strikes became greater, the state adopted a policy of co-optation and repression. The success of self-administration of company welfare, the large coal mining strike of 1889, and the rise of the Social Democrats all prompted the passage of the Industrial Code Amendment (Gewerbeordungsnovelle) in 1891 that legally institutionalized workers committees (*Arbeiterausschüsse*) with limited consultation rights (Teuteberg 1981). The

---

30. In 1870 two-thirds of German industrial labor still worked in small shops with up to five persons. By 1907 less than one-third worked in such small shops and more than 40 percent worked in enterprises with over 50 employees (Fischer 1979, 103).

regulations had little practical influence but established a principle that employment relations were to be regulated in the public interest.[31]

State policy reinforced employer paternalism, as can be seen in company welfare schemes (Fischer 1978; Manow chapter in this volume). Paternalistic company welfare aimed at retaining skilled labor and preventing labor conflict by tying workers to the firm through their contributions. However, unlike those in many other countries, German firms often involved worker representatives in administering funds. These practices had roots in eighteenth- and nineteenth-century traditions of self-administration of welfare funds in the artisan sector and in mining and heavy industries, as well as elements of religiously motivated paternalism. For employers, self-administration through voluntary worker representation was used to enhance the legitimacy of company welfare. An excellent example is the case of Werner Siemens who, in view of impending state legislation, set up company insurance schemes. His rationale was to promote a "stable core of employees" by gaining "their full trust in the schemes and their administration" by allowing "the employees [to] administer the schemes as much as possible" (Werner Siemens, 1 December 1872, cited in Ritter and Kocka 1974, 147).

Some employers also used committees to gain information and suggestions from their labor force and gradually delegated competencies to the councils. Councils voluntarily gained new rights of information, consultation, and codetermination (Decker 1965; Teuteberg 1961, 209). Self-administration shared with codetermination the experience of organizational learning by dealing with questions that could best be solved jointly by employers and labor, creating a framework for cooperative interactions (Teuteberg 1961, 117–18).

Within this context, early employment relations were culturally framed in a nonliberal fashion by all key actors. Employment was understood as an authority relationship oriented toward converting labor power into output, rather than a process of exchange in the "marketplace" for labor (Biernacki 1995, 308). Nonliberal views gave rise to divergent ideals: company loyalty, the firm as family or community, master-servant relations, codetermination, or "organic" relations between firm and employees. Although opponents criticized paternalism as "feudal," many alternatives had equally nonliberal elements of mutual responsibility beyond those implied by freedom of contract.

World War I and Weimar Germany (1914–33): The Challenge to Management. State efforts to mobilize and rationalize the wartime economy transformed

---

31. In 1905, special regulations for the coal industry established mandatory factory councils to reduce labor unrest while circumventing existing unions.

labor management. A wartime "industrial truce" integrated the Social Democrats and labor unions into national politics (Feldman 1966; Marks 1989, 107–11). The end of unilateral employer authority occurred with the passage of the Patrial Auxiliary Service Law (Gesetz über den vaterlandischen Hilfsdienstes) in 1916. As the war effort intensified in anticipation of U.S. intervention, the "Hindenburg Program" obliged all nonmilitary men between the ages of seventeen and sixty to take up employment and forbade leaving jobs in war-related industries without a special permit. The state sought to compensate these restrictions of civil freedom and maintain order in industrial production, fearing a wave of strikes.

The 1916 law mandated workers committees to be elected by secret ballot. Drawing upon the mining reform law of 1905, its controversial paragraph 12 gave councils consultation rights regarding the "demands, wishes and complaints of the work force with regard to the factory, wage and other employment conditions and the social welfare policy of the firm" (Teuteberg 1961, 511). Although councils had no rights to information or codetermination, their power was greater than anticipated. Paragraph 13 provided for mediation by a council with parity composition and chaired by a representative of the War Ministry. The committee subjected the employer to binding decisions, and employers preferred to negotiate and compromise with their councils.

The workers councils thereby fell out of employer control and became increasingly linked with an independent labor movement. Unions were extremely influential in the formation and operations of the councils. Radical labor unions began to see a revolutionary potential, while less-radical labor unions saw Soviet-style councils as a cornerstone in building "economic democracy." Employers resisted implementing the law and emphasized the temporary character of the councils as a wartime institution. Organized labor oriented itself to the retention and development of councils (Teuteberg 1981).

The end of World War I, the collapse of the imperial state, the development of a revolutionary council movement,[32] and the role of Social Democratic politics and unions in the Weimar Republic led to the anchoring of codetermination in the Weimar constitution and the passage of the Works Councils Law (Betriebsrätegesetz) in 1920. The new state sought to limit the impact of the revolutionary council movement by incorporating a less radical notion of works councils into company practice. The law mandated the formation of works councils in all commercial and public establish-

---

32. "Revolutionary" councils were often loyal to their firms and had a generally cooperative orientation. Their demands often included the end of authoritarian management-styles, codetermination in wages and personnel issues, rights to company information, and profit-sharing (Braun, Eberwein, and Tholen 1992).

ments with over twenty employees to be made up of a parity between elected blue-collar and white-collar employees. The supplementary law passed in 1922 allowed the works council to also send a maximum of two employee representatives to the *Aufsichtsrat*. The laws had many features of the contemporary German model: the obligation toward peaceful cooperation of the works council in the interests of the firm, the separation of collective bargaining from the activities of works councils, and codetermination rights in the personnel affairs of the firm. The basic institutional form of the works council was a "dual" role in protecting and representing the independent interests of workers while supporting the business interests of the employer (Fürstenberg 1958). Works councils spread to around half of all plants with over fifty employees from the mid-1920s onward (W. Plumpe 1992).

Although employers opposed the passage of the Works Council Law, their experiences with the councils were mixed (W. Plumpe 1992, 43–55). Political collapse and the rise of social democracy had made unions the only reliable bargaining power. After 1916 labor discipline began to fail due to food shortages, and the piece rate system collapsed in the wake of inflation. The legitimacy of managerial authority suffered and ended in the revolutionary council movement. Particularly in the electrical equipment and chemical industries, employers learned to use the works council as an instrument of constructive communication within the firm and enjoyed renewed legitimacy of managerial decisions (W. Plumpe 1992, 52). For example, in 1931 the social director of an I.G.-Farben plant noted that "there are voices that recognize the works council as a useful entity, even treasure it," since management could use them to communicate with the workforce and gain cooperation in personnel management.

However, both iron and steel firms and employers associations continued to oppose the Works Council Law, particularly *Aufsichtsrat* representation, and sought to discourage cooperative relations between firms and works councils. Labor unions also remained ambivalent toward works councils, which they saw as a possible source of "syndicalism" that would undermine trade union discipline and capacity for multi-employer collective bargaining. Early works councils realized neither all the ambitions nor the worst fears of the major stakeholders. Compromise was necessary, although practices developed unevenly. Pragmatic cooperation developed in some firms, but elsewhere little mutual trust was built. However, the Weimar experiment was interrupted before codetermination could find solid footing.

Nazi Germany: Fascism and Labor Suppression. Upon seizing power, the Nazi Party destroyed all autonomous labor organizations through arrests, confiscation of property, and dissolution of the organizations. Workers were reorganized under the party-run labor front (Neumann 1944). Nazi ideology posited a harmony of interests between capital and labor—work was portrayed as honorable national service. The Law on the Order of National Labor (Gesetz zur Ordnung der nationalen Arbeit) in 1934 codified a plant community ideology, stating that "In the plant, the entrepreneur as the plant leader and the salaried employees and workers as the followers work jointly to further the aims of the plant and for the common benefit of the people and the state." This leadership principle restored managerial prerogatives and the personal authority of managers. Nazi management ideology contained paternalistic elements, and new company rules stressed the obligations of employees to follow the will of their superiors in good faith. For example, work rules at Klöckner-Humboldt-Deutz stated:

> In every human community, be it a state, be it a company, only one force, one mind can determine the direction and path that is to be taken. Where many minds want to determine together, then negotiation takes the place of action. . . . The task of the manual laborer is to willingly obey the well-thought commands and to bring the work to be done to good completion. . . . the plant and its workforce form a community of fate. (Rüther 1988, 91)

The corporate law of 1937 required the *Vorstand* to manage in the interest of the firm, its members, and the general benefit of the people and the Reich. The 1933 Labor Trustee Law (Gesetz über die Treuhänder der Arbeit) transferred codetermination rights to a single state representative (Teuteburg 1981, 41). Works councils were abolished and replaced with new employee councils, now called *Vertrauensrat* or "councils of trust," conceived as plant-level cells of the Nazi Party, whose goals were not the "one-sided interest representation of workers" as with the past works councils. The *Vertrauensrat* were to strengthen trust within the enterprise community under party leadership. The labor market came under state control: changes of employment became illegal without permission of state-run labor exchanges, and wages were set by state trustees. Nazi efforts largely broke down during the war, and the regime increasingly resorted to terror to control labor.

Federal Republic of Germany: Codetermination and the Social Market Economy. Codetermination reemerged as part of postwar democratization and was institutionalized in the coal and steel industry by the 1951 Law on Codetermination in the Mining and Iron and Steel Industries (Montanmitbestimmung). Codetermination was closely related to the project of political democracy and was an attempt to prevent the political abuse of economic power that occurred under the Nazis, particularly in war-related industries. Codetermination enjoyed a wide spectrum of political support, becoming part of the constitutions of many federal states, appearing in platform pa-

pers of the conservative Christian Democratic Union (CDU), and even re-
ceiving support from employers in industries eager to gain the help of
unions to stall Allied plans for socialization.

The Allies sought to incorporate unions into their restructuring plans in
the absence of a functioning German state and given the mistrust of industrialists due to their wartime collaboration. Works councils were encouraged by the Control Council Law (Kontrollratsgesetz), but their rights were
left to plant-level negotiated agreements. Works councils had tremendous
moral authority, and ex-Nazi management feared contradicting them.
Communist party members were also well represented and created personal continuities between the Weimar and postwar works councils.

In the coal and steel industry, unions were able to gain representation in
the *Aufsichtsrat*, develop strong works councils, and elect a labor director to
the *Vorstand*. The specific motives of the British powers for introducing
codetermination remain unclear (G. Müller 1987). The Allies later restored ownership rights in 1948 and disappointed the ambitions of unions
and German political parties to socialize heavy industry. By 1950, under the
new German state, firms fell under German corporate law, which provided
no codetermination rights. The metalworkers' union called for a strike in
1951, leading to the direct involvement of Chancellor Konrad Adenauer regarding codetermination, resulting in the 1951 Montanmitbestimmung
that preserved the parity model of *Aufsichtsrat* representation within the
coal and steel industries.

For other industrial sectors, a weaker model of codetermination developed due to opposition of the liberal party (Freie Demokratische Partei,
FDP) and employers. Unions were unable to apply sufficient pressure to re-
produce the model of the coal and steel industries, and the 1952 Works
Constitution Act (Betriebsverfassungsgesetz) mandated only one-third of
Aufsichtsrat seats for labor, limited rights for works councils, and had no
provisions for a labor director in the *Vorstand*. Sharply contested reforms in
1972 under the Social Democratic Party formalized new rights for works
councils (Thelen 1991), and a 1976 revision widened *Aufsichtsrat* representation, although it remained weaker than the coal and steel model in several regards.

Despite its diverse ideological and institutional origins, codetermination
aimed to "democratize" what had historically been recognized as a relationship of *authority* deriving from the asymmetrical power of firms and employees. The result was a compromise with deeply embedded moral-politi-
cal foundations, despite all that can be said about its economic effects. At
the plant level, works councils prevent management from unilaterally implementing decisions where employees' interests are at stake. At the enterprise level, *Aufsichtsrat* representation introduced accountability of management to employees and thereby altered the constellation of interests in

the firm from a pure shareholders model to a "dual" logic of balancing multiple groups in the interests of the firm as a whole. Codetermination thereby transformed German managerial ideologies, reducing the centralization of power and creating more equality in *Vorstand* and a more consensual character of negotiations. Authority became more functional, managerial accountability toward employees increased, and the role of personnel policy was upgraded. Although related to political democracy, codetermination did not institute pure democratic principles into capitalist enterprises but "constitutionalized" the relations between stakeholders in a regime of participation that implies a sharing of responsibility and mutual obligations (see Kommission Mitbestimmung 1998 for a recent evaluation).

Japan

Paternalism in the Meiji Period. Labor management in the early Meiji era was unregulated by the state or labor unions. A large number of rural females worked in light industries, while male employment in heavy industries was governed by craft-based subcontracting controlled by supervisory workers (*oyakata*) (Hazama 1997; Thelen and Kume chapter in this volume). Because there was a short supply of skilled workers needed by the largest firms adopting Western technology, many of these firms raised wages and/or provided welfare programs to induce loyalty in workers. Employers tended to blame labor turnover on the moral failings of the worker. They opposed labor unions as unnecessary Western imports unsuitable to Japan, where in their view cooperative harmony with labor existed. The first Japanese labor unions nonetheless formed during 1885. Unionism spread during the 1890s, until the expansion was halted by the Public Peace Police Act of 1900 (Evans 1970, 121). Meiji employers responded to labor problems by the (often unsuccessful) intensification of control in the factory (Chimoto 1986).

The state took a hands-off approach to labor law—formal guild control was abolished in 1872, establishing a formally free labor contract without outlining any specific rights or protections for employees (Chimoto 1986). As the Japanese state considered factory legislation during the 1880s, the managerial ideology of paternalism became the object of public controversy. The government viewed paternalism as an important tradition but was concerned about the difficulties implementing it given the absence of strong interpersonal relationships in large firms. Employers were repeatedly consulted and stalled the proposed laws on the grounds that factory legislation was a Western invention not suited to the unique moral traditions of Japan (Taira 1970). Factory legislation was not passed until 1911 and went into effect in 1916.

Paternalistic labor management found only small footholds in the late Meiji period. A growing number of managers had university educations and traveled to the West, gaining exposure to a greater variety of moral values and learning a bureaucratic view of management (Clark 1979, 37; Taira 1970). State-owned firms such as Yawata Steel, established in 1897, set important precedents in developing long-term and bureaucratic employment structures, as well as an ideology of total commitment to the firm (Dore 1973). Increasingly, managers adopted paternalistic labor policies: training programs, fringe benefits, improved working hours and conditions, moral education of workers, company newspapers, suggestion boxes, and others. At Mitsui, the house rules established in the new corporation explicitly abolished the master-servant relationship in the firm (Chimoto 1986). The moral image of the family guided many of these efforts.

Shifting Alliances among the State, Business, and Labor: 1911 to the 1930s. The growing movement for imperial democracy changed the power relations among the state, business, and organized labor. Growing size, bureaucratization, and technological sophistication of firms altered skills requirements. Companies instituted new training programs, sought to protect company secrets by reducing labor mobility, and shifted from the *oyakata* system of indirect craft control to direct employment, thereby co-opting the *oyakata* so that workers would become loyal members of the enterprise (Hazama 1997, 56; see also the Thelen and Kume chapter in this volume). As heavy industries grew, company policy also became increasingly aimed at the male as head of the household. Social insurance developed later than in Germany but had a similar effect of reinforcing company paternalism. The Health Insurance Act of 1926 required company welfare, and thus firms extended additional benefits to foster company loyalty (Daito 1979; Hazama 1997, 28). Unlike Germany, Japan lacked state unemployment insurance. Retirement and severance allowances became the targets of strikes and spread during the 1920s and 1930s in response to the layoffs of the Great Depression. Policies of "regular wage increases" by seniority spread—age-wage curves became steeper at many firms in the 1930s (Shirai and Shimada 1978). However, although some "decommodification" of labor occurred within large firms, the 1920s do not appear to have been decisive in the formation of "lifetime employment." Labor turnover remained high, and the diffusion of such practices remained uneven (see details in Dore 1973).

Taisho democracy—the political liberalization that occurred mainly in the Taisho period (1912–25)—established the rule of political parties and suffrage for property owners. But the state continued a repressive stance toward organized labor and developed a parallel strategy of substituting social rights. Interpretations of antiunion laws were loosened, police were able to promote enterprise-based associations, a labor representative was included in the International Labor Organization (ILO) delegation from Japan, and even a bill requiring mandatory works councils was drafted but later dropped because of business opposition (Garon 1987; Gordon 1992). The Factory Law in 1916 gave workers basic protections. Yet unionization rates remained lower than in Germany, peaking at only 7.5 percent in 1930 (Shirai and Shimada 1978).

Some firms experimented with works councils, both in response to strikes during the 1920s and as an expression of paternalism (Harada 1928). However, councils quickly became mere consulting bodies and their numbers declined as employees lost interest in them. Employers also tried to influence union development through closed-shop agreements and the establishment of company unions.

Hazama (1997) argues that an ideology of managerial "familism" guided these developments in labor relations. Managers increasingly abandoned the old benevolent paternalism of master-servant relations and moved toward paternalism as seen within families. The *zaibatsu* were significant in the development of familism due to the traditions of families within property rights. The debates over the Factory Law also led to the articulation and diffusion of such ideologies as employers attempted to prevent state intervention in labor relations. Furthermore, employers needed an ideological counterbalance to the rising labor movement, the extension of universal manhood suffrage in 1925, and growing unionization rates and worker discord in the late 1920s and 1930s. Management sought to institute paternalism within the enterprise while fighting the labor movement outside the company. As Hazama (1997, 29) explains, "In this way, enterprises which advocated managerial familism carried through the logic of capitalism by consolidating politically their collaboration with the 'nation as family' ideology which prevailed outside the firm, and by nurturing a 'my company feeling' (a sense of loyalty to the company) within the firm."

The Wartime Planned Economy: Coerced Integration of Labor. As in Germany, state intervention in the wartime economy ended the independent labor movement. The army intervened in 1936 to force arsenal workers to withdraw from labor unions. The Home Ministry also shifted from tolerating unions as a source of social order to viewing them as inappropriate. Beginning in 1938, the state bypassed existing organized labor and forced labor-management cooperation within the context of the Industrial Patriotic Society (Aoki 1988, 186; Okazaki 1994, 362–63). The Japanese reform was consciously modeled on Nazi labor laws and practices of the *Vertrauensrat* with common ideological and organizational features, such as replacing unions with plant advisory councils and promoting a "classless" national community based on mythic, primordialist identities of village, folk, or family (Gordon 1992, 321–22; Garon 1987, 212–18). Councils were based on the 1938 Industrial Relations Adjustment Measure (Roshi Kankei Chosei Hosaku) that recognized the firm as an organic organization of employers and employees. Firm-level branches of the Industrial Patriotic Society consisting of management and labor were established to address problems of efficiency and social concerns but in effect gave managers a free hand in running firms with military-like authority.

The status of owners was also reduced during wartime, and private interests were subordinated to national military goals. The position of workers in the firm was bolstered ideologically. Workers received a relatively high income and were involved in forms of profit-sharing under a resolution that instructed firms to pay bonuses for improved efficiency. But in fact, the authoritarian state absorbed or repressed all independent voices for organized labor.

Postwar Japan. Japanese labor was legally recognized for the first time in 1945 by the Allied occupation authorities. Japanese unions organized workers at a blinding rate, including 55.8 percent of the workforce by 1949, through a combination of favorable factors: the shortages of food and housing after war, the spread of Marxism, the promotion of labor unions by the Allied powers, and the weakened authority of war-tainted management within the workplace. Workers engaged in production control, locking out management and demanding the democratization of their enterprises. Unions made great inroads in the establishment of industrial citizenship and the basic features of enterprise community. In the words of Andrew Gordon:

In this early postwar surge of organizing and collective action blue-collar workers gained "citizenship" in the enterprise and a measure of control over it. Workers in companies as diverse as the nation's leading newspapers and steel mills demanded creation of powerful joint labor-management councils. Found in as many as two-thirds of all unionized firms by mid-1946, the councils gave organized workers partial control of the workplace, personnel management, and corporate strategy. Through council deliberations or collective bargaining, workers eliminated many petty and substantive status divisions between white-collar staff and blue-collar workers, which they had found pervasive and repugnant throughout the prewar era. Under union pressure managers did away with separate gates, dining halls, and toilets as well as distinctions in dress and terminology (some companies replaced the terms *worker* and *staff* with the single term *employee*). Workers also gained a new equality in wages and bonuses. Some enterprises replaced a distinction between workers, who were paid by the day, and staff, who were paid by the month, with a common calculation in terms of monthly wages and paid bonuses to all employees as multiples of this monthly amount. (Gordon 1993, 379)

"Democratization" was strongly linked to the norm of equality and was directed against the status-based discrimination of the prewar era as well as "insincere" paternalism (Gordon 1998, 20).

However, union demands were perceived as a potentially revolutionary attack on private property. In 1949 and 1950, Japanese management made a counterattack as the United States reversed policy and initiated a "red purge" of unions. This confrontation with management took place before labor had developed strong interfirm coordination and links to leftist political parties, as it had in Germany. Employers organized nationally through Nikkeiren, the Japan Federation of Employers' Associations, and achieved changes in labor laws such as eliminating the automatic renewal of labor contracts when no new agreements were reached. This allowed management to unilaterally refuse to renew existing agreements that granted employees a voice in decision making, which relegated the labor-management councils to advisory bodies.

As the market economy liberalized, competition increased, and hyperinflation was held in check by the Dodge Line, management was able to make inroads against union leadership during a wave of strikes, such as the drawn-out strikes in 1953 at Miike Coal Mines and Nissan Motors. The emerging "moderate" alliance between white- and blue-collar workers aimed at obtaining employment security in exchange for a cooperative politics of productivity in the firm. Companies agreed to negotiate with these "new" unions over wages and allowed some union influence in company reorganization, promising stable employment if the union would link its interests with those of the firm. How the resulting accommodation of labor within the firm led to industrial citizenship can be shown by three examples: a strong system of union consultation, the decommodification of wages, and institutionalized employment security.

Workers, rooted in the wartime experience with works councils and fused with a new impulse to democratize these structures, had come to demand participation in corporate governance. In 1948, Nikkeiren issued its "Appeal for Securing Managerial Prerogatives" (*Keieikon kakusho ni kansuru ikensho*) in an effort to regain control over the production process as well as discretion in hiring and firing. Production control by workers was outlawed, and the state sought to channel participation into a works council system after 1946. The new contracts were opposed by labor but often led to compromises in the collective bargaining agreements that established company-specified institutions of labor-management consultation and information rights on a variety of personnel and managerial issues (Kume 1998). Other national-level actors, such as the Ministry of Labor, supported these compromises. However, unlike Germany, Japan developed no legal provisions concerning the participation of workers (Hanami 1989), and unions usually possess codetermination rights on a narrower range of issues.

Employee voice is nonetheless significant in Japan compared to liberal countries such as the United States. Union power is rooted in the mutual dependency of labor and management in the context of firm-specific skills. Moreover, management feels that it must compromise with more conservative unions in order to forestall radicalism in splinter unions. Collective bargaining rights are anchored in the Japanese constitution and leave broad interpretation of the subjects open to bargaining—including all subjects that affect workers' economic situation, such as plant closings and relocations, automation, and subcontracting. Thus, the degree of worker participation depends to a greater degree than in Germany on the economic power relationship between the union and management.[33] Gradually, labor-management consultation was used to increase productivity on the condition that rationalization would not result in dismissals.

Another aspect of industrial citizenship related to union demands was coupling wages to "need"—for example, the wage pattern in the electric power industry tied wages to the cost of living (Gordon 1985; Kume 1998, 49–72). Union motives were based on food shortages and hyperinflation, but also on strong egalitarian principles aimed at eliminating status distinctions among employees reflected in pay scales and structures. Employers successfully opposed a pure need-based concept, linking wages with objective criteria such as age and seniority. In 1950, however, Nikkeiren issued its "Management's Attitude Toward Wages" (*Tōmen no chinginmondai ni taisuru keieisha no taido*) that advocated rationalizing the wage system based on productivity. Unions were able to combat job-based wages, leading to a compromise system of payments based on "merit" and seniority.

The postwar union demands for employment security aimed at zero dismissals and at the understanding that the corporation was primarily to serve the goal of providing employment. The postwar constitution contains a "right to employment" clause that commits government policy to full employment. Legal norms of lifetime employment arose through active courtroom struggles of unions and scholars against abusive dismissals of labor activists during the 1940s and 1950s. Japanese courts required employers to show "just cause" for the dismissal of regular employees, since dismissals were (and are) normally considered an "abuse of right" that shifts the bur-

33. By 1982, 59 percent of enterprise unions had established works councils through collective agreement: 52 percent at the enterprise level, 40 percent at the plant level, and 6 percent at the workplace level. While information and consultation rights are common, less than 10 percent of these councils had codetermination rights (see Hanami 1989, 287). Furthermore, no legal requirements exist for labor representation on corporate boards.

den of proof to employers. Thus, firms have had to exhaust alternative measures of reorganization and employment adjustment, thereby strengthening union involvement (Hanami 1989). Furthermore, employment security has been supported by effective cross-class alliances with business to make political demands for state support of jobs and employment adjustment in declining industries (Kume 1998). Microlevel union strength combined with the macrolevel incorporation of labor into politics shows that Japanese labor was not co-opted by management, but rather became a legitimate "citizen" within the firm.

Coevolution of Capital and Labor in Corporate Governance

The parallel evolution of financial commitment and industrial citizenship shows that nonliberal corporate governance in Germany and Japan did not arise from a single master process. Institutional change involved a complex series of continuities, discontinuities, reemergence of older institutions, and functional shifts of existing institutions. Different institutional elements emerged at different times and in response to different pressures. Financial commitment was shaped by corporate law, the financial system, competition policy, and pension provision. By contrast, industrial citizenship was shaped by the organization of the labor movement, managerial ideologies, and state policy. Yet, institutions undergo coevolution due to interdependence and complementarities across institutional spheres (Aoki 2001; Thelen 1999). In the remaining pages, the *coevolution* of financial commitment and industrial citizenship is explored.

How did financial commitment and industrial citizenship follow parallel developments, yet emerge as a relatively "coherent" institutional model able to produce durable competitive advantages in postwar Germany and Japan? This section presents two arguments. First, the coevolution of capital and labor was shaped by a broader sequence of institutional developments that separated Germany and Japan from the liberal pathways of the United States and Britain. The periodization of corporate governance shows remarkable parallels in the sequence of development in Germany and Japan. Sequence is particularly important to coevolution, since certain combinations of historical factors make certain subsequent events more likely because of their timing in relation to other processes. The ways in which organizations and their constituent actors respond to institutional constraints and opportunities depends on the sequence of their emergence. The interaction of multiple interdependent processes gives rise to critical junctures that shape institutions and the effects of these institutions on organizational behavior. Second, the institutional complementarities of nonliberal corporate governance at the organizational level largely resulted from an unintended fit of sector-specific institutional developments.

Historical Sequences and Critical Junctures in Institutional Development

In Germany and Japan, industrialization occurred during a period of economic liberalism without political liberalism. A "revolution from above" allied the state with industry under the auspices of authoritarian rule (Moore 1966). Centralized state bureaucracies emerged before corporations and promoted industrialization through conservative social reform (see the chapter by Gerhard Lehmbruch in this volume). Yasusuke Murakami (1982) describes this relative timing of industrialization with national political integration in terms of a nonliberal "late-comer conservatism." In Germany and Japan, institutional separation of state authority and private property rights and the dissolution of guild orders and modern systems of political and interest representation were comparatively late (Crouch 1986). This sequential interaction led to variation of policy networks across countries and, in particular, to attempts to reconcile "catch-up" industrial development with some features of the premodern social order. This developmentalist political program was pursued by seeking to either compensate for the failings of modern social organization (e.g., markets) or co-opt opposing forms of organization (e.g., unionism and socialism).

Germany and Japan inherited different "traditional" social structures, some features of which made positive contributions to early corporate organization. For example, German feudal traditions of authority, state bureaucratic and military traditions, and craft traditions of skill formation and self-administration all made important contributions to managerial ideologies and patterns of labor control (Dornseifer and Kocka 1993). In Japan, the tradition of the *ie* served as a positive organizational template for modern Japanese management (Murakami 1984). These "traditional" features were themselves dramatically transformed by the introduction of corporate law and the free labor contract, such that corporate governance in liberal and nonliberal contexts had important similarities: dominance of family owner-managers, laissez-faire financial systems, largely unregulated and union-free workplaces, as well as problems of capital mobilization, labor turnover and unrest, and skills shortages. Nonliberal corporate governance is not a direct outgrowth of traditionalism.

In the absence of liberal civil and political rights, liberal market institutions could not be developed through voluntaristic systems of contract alone. Nor could parliamentary democracy serve as a channel for the pursuit of universalistic welfare policies or redistribution. Characteristically, authoritative means were used to integrate private interests, either by co-opting opposition into political coalitions or subordinating private goals to the state. Although often unsuccessful, the strong interpenetration of state and society had consequences for corporate governance.

First, the corporation was not viewed as a purely private association but was subjected to a wide range of external social responsibilities. These oscillated between and often mixed two distinct elements. A strong public interest existed in the internal order of the corporation to protect shareholder confidence and to assure the social integration of the working class through the provision of social rights. A national interest also existed in the performance of the corporation during the "catching up" phase of industrialization, for wartime mobilization, or to consolidate the legitimacy of postwar capitalism through high growth and equality. The public and national interest elements were reinforced institutionally by the strong and centralized bureaucracies, the political dominance of state and military over industry, and the absence of political citizenship rights for workers. Economic crisis during the 1870s and 1930s and the two world wars proved to be catalysts for new institutions.

For capital, the promotion of public and national interests often involved directly curtailing shareholder rights, circumventing shareholders by promoting bank-led investment, "constitutionalizing" shareholder control, or organizing market competition by the state or business associations. For labor, state intervention or paternalism increased either participation rights and mandatory representation or the ideological status of labor within the corporation in the interest of "social peace," first as a substitute and later as a guarantee for democratic political representation. Thus, many of the similar characteristics of Germany and Japan were shaped before World War II, as were crucial differences between Germany and Japan due to their different political institutions, cultural legacies, and the different strength and impact of unions. Germany and Japan differed in the degree to which capital-labor linkages were created through horizontally organized corporatist institutions or through strong, vertically integrated ties between state bureaucracy and industry (see the chapter by Lehmbruch in this volume). The German version of industrial citizenship would later stress national social partnership within corporatist associations supported by law, while a vertically organized "microcorporatism" developed in Japan.

Through 1945, these nonliberal models remained very far from today's "stakeholder" patterns of governance. Labor participation was undemocratic, and interfirm networks had a strong monopolistic element or were used as instruments of state planning. Corporate governance was "organized" by political intervention and by the networks between large corporations. No one could foresee their inevitable development into postwar models. Yet on the one hand, the pre-1945 institutional legacies made positive contributions to the postwar institutional repertoire, and on the other served as a negative example that shaped future political contention over the nature of the corporation and the role of stakeholders within it.

The postwar period was crucial for the emergence of the "models" of nonliberal corporate governance characterized by both their efficiency and the parallel integration of capital and labor. Despite defeat and postwar democratization, neither country fully adopted Allied corporate governance institutions. Although both models incorporated liberal elements due to Allied influence, corporate governance further diverged in other dimensions. The experience of defeat and the policies of the victors in promoting democracy played a crucial role in reshaping the play of domestic social forces (Smith 1998, 204–8). Military defeat further weakened the legitimacy and position of capital owners within the enterprise and strengthened the political power of labor. Allied influence also helped close contested alternatives, such as socialism, while creating consensus to pursue class compromise within a framework of capitalist democracy. The Allies calmed much of the fractionalism from the unstable interwar democracies. Defeat also re-embedded Germany and Japan into a changed international environment that gave firms access to world markets without reliance on military conquest.

The concept of democratization involves an increasing degree of representation within an existing institutional structure. For corporate property rights, democratization was largely imposed by Allied powers through efforts of deconcentration and purges of Nazis or *zaibatsu* families. For reasons already noted, these efforts were less thorough in Germany than in Japan. Even where ownership was fragmented for a short period in Japan, individual ownership proved unstable and led to a renewed form of intercorporate networks. To be sure, interfirm cooperation now occurred within more liberal competition regimes that limited its monopolistic qualities.

Unlike the democratization of formal ownership, domestic social forces played a greater role in the democratization of enterprise authority relations. Allied policy gave footing to the labor movement yet did not directly make labor a legitimate stakeholder in corporate governance. This represents the major innovation of postwar corporate governance. Prior to and during the war, authority based on private property rights was fused with authoritarian political power. Enterprise hierarchies were widely conceived as authority relationships rather than free contracts between individuals. Initially, this related to the different political rights of property owners and workers; increasingly, however, it became related directly to the use of state power to enhance authority within enterprises. Large corporations were a focal point of contention not only over economic interests, but as a central institution mediating between the "lifeworld" of employees and modern institutions. Political democratization opened the path to the democratization of enterprise authority relations within the firm. As nonliberal institutions were democratized, employees came to be recognized as legitimate stakeholders within the corporation, which further increased their nonliberal character. Past cultural and institutional legacies provided organizational templates for integrating multiple groups within the firm, such as egalitarian membership combined with functional patterns of authority characteristic of the Japanese *ie* tradition, or corporatist notions of interest-group pluralism in Germany captured by the concept of *Parität*.

From Institutional Complementarities to Organizational Capacities: A "Societal Effect"

Although the politics of conservative social reform shaped the paths of corporate governance, politics does not guarantee beneficial economic effects from the resulting model. How did German and Japanese corporate governance come to "hang together" as a model of complementary institutions in the firm? Corporate governance is embedded within multiple institutional dynamics, each exerting separate pressures, but taken as a whole, such effects are cumulative and interdependent. Such interdependence does not guarantee a "fit" between institutions. However, as Masahiko Aoki has noted, given institutional complementarities, "one institution rather than another becomes viable in one domain, when a fitting institution is present in another domain" (Aoki 2001, 8). Embeddedness can be conceptualized as a "societal effect," where patterns of action in one domain have prerequisites and impacts in other domains (Maurice, Sellier, and Silvestre 1986; Sorge and Warner 1986).

An important insight of this chapter is that financial commitment emerged as a necessary condition for the maintenance and stabilization of industrial citizenship. Had ownership patterns in Germany and Japan been more fragmented and market-driven, industrial citizenship could have been undermined by shareholder pressures or hostile takeovers. To the degree that management was free from such constraints, management gained the opportunity to learn to utilize industrial citizenship as a productive asset promoting competitiveness.[34] Management accommodated industrial citizenship through company strategies that depended on lower levels of profitability, high rates of internal investment, and orientation toward

---

34. Contemporary studies of German codetermination also find that the "social order" of the firm has a decisive influence in explaining why some firms under codetermination law develop effective and cooperative labor representation, while others remain conflict-oriented (Kotthoff 1994).

growth—strategies not available under the strict capital constraints placed by a market for corporate control (De Jong 1996).[35] Long-term investments could be financed internally or through "patient" shareholders. As a result, capital was turned into a relatively stable "fixed cost" by providing very stable minimum returns in the form of dividends or "rents" based on relational financing. This supportive effect was particularly stable to the degree that capital had a limited capacity to exit from national systems of regulation that institutionalized industrial citizenship.

In this context, monitoring by shareholders remained "contingent" on gross managerial failure rather than continuous monitoring aimed at maximizing returns. Monitoring was largely delegated to banks and proved an important safeguard in the absence of other strong external controls. This pattern of contingent governance reinforced practices of internal managerial recruitment, slowed consensus-oriented decision-making styles, and put managerial functions such as personnel on a more even footing with finance.

Yet this type of "managerialism," in the sense of relative freedom from shareholder monitoring, remains distinct from Anglo-American varieties. Internal monitoring through employee voice complemented contingent governance by acting as a counterweight to managerial power, or sometimes concentrated ownership, to create a highly consensus-oriented management style. Constrained by employee power, management learned to use employee participation as a way to promote cooperation to increase labor productivity, raise quality, and thereby assure firm competitiveness in world markets. The democratization of the firm enhanced management's problem-solving capacity through the increased legitimacy of decision making and limited industrial conflict. Labor supported this because its institutional power did not rely solely on the economic value of labor as a "commodity," but derived from institutional sources. Nonliberal corporate governance should also not be confused with management in the one-sided interests of employees. Industrial citizenship involved channeling employee interests and binding them to the interests of the company—for example, the obligation of works councils to uphold the interests of the firm and maintain social peace or the high dependence of Japanese unions and workers on firm-specific skills.

Financial commitment and industrial citizenship thus developed economic complementarities through information and incentives (Aoki 1994; Jackson 1997). In the postwar era, the contingent governance by capital reinforced the development of organizational capacities involving high skills,

35. With higher capital liquidity, time horizons become shorter, profitability becomes more important, and a greater portion of value added must be paid out to the capital market rather than reinvested internally or consumed by labor (De Jong 1992; Ide 1998).

functional flexibility of labor, and long-term incentives that proved very successful for competition in world markets.[36] In this process, politically created institutions took on new economic functions, and these economic successes reinforced the legitimacy of new institutions.

In Germany, "constitutionalism" emerged in response to problems of shareholder control in nineteenth-century corporate law, although employee interests were only later constitutionalized by codetermination. Despite similarities to present-day institutions, the first attempts to integrate industrial citizenship in the Weimar Republic proved neither politically nor economically stable. Institutional stability was only possible after 1945 due to the shift in power after defeat and to economic changes leading to a sustained period of high growth. During this process, the institution of codetermination has undergone a remarkable series of transformations from its origins in revolution and class struggle, its institutionalization as a pillar of political democracy, its economic function in benevolent employment adjustment in the declining postwar steel and mining industries, and its present role as a form of comanagement and corporate governance promoting the international competitiveness of German industry. This change involved the continuous reconfiguration of codetermination through processes of organizational learning that were not foreseen at its inception. The beneficial economic impact of codetermination helped stabilize it as an institution but must nonetheless be viewed as an unintended institutional fit.

A similar pattern of unintended fit characterizes Japanese corporate governance (Aoki 1997). Wartime mobilization led to a variety of institutions designed for centralized government control over the economy by eliminating shareholder control over corporations. Shareholder rights were reduced and banks became concentrated and closely linked to industry. For labor, the Industrial Patriotic Society was formed to integrate employees into firms. However, despite structural similarities to contemporary institutions, wartime institutions did not provide effective and independent monitoring. Postwar democratization transformed these structures again. *Zaibatsu* firms were dissolved and share ownership "democratized," leading to cross-shareholdings that freed management from shareholder control. "Citizenship" was established in large enterprises in response to growing enterprise unionism. The institutional complementarities between the Jap-

---

36. See Streeck (1992) on "diversified quality production" in Germany. For Japan, Dore (1997) describes the "institutional interlock" between stable shareholding and other features of Japanese labor management: lifetime employment, seniority wages, low stratification of rewards, and the social perception of the firm as a community. Aoki (1988, 164) describes this interlock as a growth preference related to the weighted preferences of labor and capital as a coalition, wherein the Japanese firm diverts gains from shareholders to benefit incumbent employees by securing employment and promotion prospects.

anese "managerialism," contingent control by main banks, and enterprise unionism were unintended outcomes emerging in organizational practices only in the postwar period of growth.

These competitive advantages in corporate organization depended on binding constraints upon management. Constraints require actors to alter their strategic preferences, to "learn" methods of accommodation, and to transform their identities. Through organizational learning, constraints may also provide complementary opportunities that make them economically "beneficial" by limiting the pursuit of self-interest (Streeck 1997b). Short-term rationality can place shareholder and employee interests in a zero-sum relation that causes spirals of distrust, resulting in higher costs of capital or lower labor productivity. Such organizational learning processes were important to specifically nonliberal "politics of productivity."

Conclusion

This chapter views changes in corporate governance in Germany and Japan from the perspective of the complementarities, tensions, and coevolution among institutional spheres. The perspective presented on institutional change can inform analysis of the future development of German and Japanese corporate governance. In the first years of the twenty-first century, the internationalization of capital markets has been perceived as a major force in moving German and Japanese corporate governance in the direction of shareholder value.

The erosion of financial commitment places the viability of industrial citizenship into question. Significant pressures have arisen in Germany and Japan across all four dimensions of property rights examined in this chapter: international investors and mergers are changing ownership structures, financial systems are being reorganized, private pension provision is slowly making headway, and liberal elements are being introduced into corporate law, particularly regarding accounting standards. These pressures make corporate ownership more fragmented and increase the dominance of finance-oriented, rather than strategic shareholder, interests. Although new transnational interfirm networks are emerging among both internationalized production networks and institutional investors, it is unlikely that financial commitment will reemerge on an international scale. German and Japanese management now mediate between growing demands for shareholder value and relative continuity in the claims of labor. Will industrial citizenship adapt in a new form to the demands of financial markets, or will cooperative labor management become increasingly conflictual? A hybrid alternative may, of course, be the continued voice of labor alongside an "enlightened" shareholder-value orientation.

Neither financial commitment nor industrial citizenship alone is likely to produce the beneficial effects associated with past German and Japanese models. These growing institutional asymmetries may undermine past strengths but still fail to provide for new ones. This chapter should remind us that the economic effects of such changes will be dependent on the linkages between institutions, but the outcomes will also be shaped by politics.

The Origins of Bank-Based and Market-Based Financial Systems: Germany, Japan, and the United States

Sigurt Vitols

A crucial aspect of the industrialization process is the development of an autonomous financial system: that is, a set of specialized organizations and institutions dealing with the transfer of payments and mediating the flow of savings and investment.[1] Although all industrial societies have a specialized financial system, cross-national comparison of these systems indicates considerable structural diversity (Zysman 1983). One key difference is the degree to which financial systems are bank-based or market-based. In bank-based systems, the bulk of financial assets and liabilities consists of bank deposits and direct loans. In market-based systems, securities that are tradable in financial markets are the dominant form of financial asset. Bank-based systems appear to have an advantage in terms of providing a long-term stable financial framework for companies. Market-based systems, in contrast, tend to be more volatile but better able quickly to channel funds to new companies in growth industries (Vitols et al. 1997; see also the chapter by Gregory Jackson in this volume). A second key distinction between financial systems is the degree to which the state is involved in the allocation of credit. State involvement in credit allocation can turn the financial system into a powerful national resource for overcoming

This paper is much improved thanks to valuable comments and suggestions by John Cioffi, Douglas Forsyth, Gregory Jackson, Peter Katzenstein, Philip Manow, Wolfgang Streeck, Kozo Yamamura, and two anonymous reviewers.
1. With the increasing differentiation of the economy and the transformation of traditional arrangements such as serfdom, relationships between different sectors—the household, the sphere of production, the state, and the foreign sector—increasingly became mediated by the money nexus centered on this financial system.

market failure problems and achieving collective economic and social goals. However, financial targeting also runs the danger of resource misallocation due to inadequate reading of market trends or "clientelism" (Calder 1993).[2]

Although every country has a different mix of institutional arrangements, these two dimensions are useful for identifying broad distinctions between countries in capital-market dynamics. A quantitative comparison of Japan, Germany, and the United States in the mid-1990s along the first (banks versus markets) dimension indicates a major distinction between the first two countries on the one hand and the United States on the other (see Table 5.1). The banking systems in Japan and Germany account for the majority of financial-system assets (64 and 74 percent, respectively), whereas banks in the United States (with about one-quarter of total financial-system assets) are only one of a plurality of financial institutions. Altogether, over half of the combined assets of the nonfinancial sector (assets of the financial, household, company, government, and foreign sectors combined) in the United States are securitized versus only 23 percent in Japan and 32 percent in Germany. Particularly striking is the relatively small proportion of securitized company liabilities in Japan and Germany in comparison with the United States (15.4 percent and 21.1 percent versus 61.0 percent).

Comparison along the second dimension (the state's role in credit allocation), however, puts Germany closer to the United States than to Japan. Although public financial institutions in both Germany and Japan hold roughly the same proportion of financial assets (between 25 and 30 percent), there is little targeting of credits in Germany other than according to broad criteria, such as small firms. In contrast, the targeting of public credits in postwar Japan also influences private credit allocation through the signaling function played by public institutions (Calder 1993).

What explains these considerable differences in the financial systems of the three countries? The most widely accepted theory, the timing of industrialization (TOI) thesis, argues that key differences in national financial systems can be traced back to their respective industrialization phases (Gerschenkron 1962; Lazonick and O'Sullivan 1997). In countries where this process started early—the United Kingdom being the key example—firms were able to finance new investment gradually from internally generated funds or from securities issued in relatively developed financial markets. Firms in countries in which industrialization started later, however, faced a double disadvantage relative to their advanced competitors in early-industrializing countries. First, internally generated finance was inadequate (or,

2. Clientelism involves the allocation of resources on the basis of privileged relationships to the state rather than on competitive or developmental strategy.

Table 5.1 Structure of postwar financial systems, mid-1990s (percent)

	Japan	Germany	United States
Proportion of banking system assets in total financial system assets, 1996	63.6	74.3	24.6
Proportion of securitized assets in total financial assets, 1996	22.9	32.0	54.0
Proportion of securitized assets in total household sector assets, 1995	12.4	28.8	35.9
Proportion of securitized liabilities in total financial liabilities of nonfinancial enterprises, 1995	15.4	21.1	61.0
Outstanding financial liabilities of public sector accounted for by securities, 1995	71.2	56.7	89.6

Sources: Calculated from Flow of Funds Statistics, U.S. Federal Reserve Board; Deutsche Bundesbank; and Bank of Japan.

in the case of newly founded firms, nonexistent) relative to the large sums needed for investments in "catch-up" technologies and infrastructure. Second, market finance was difficult to raise because securities markets were underdeveloped and investors were more inclined to invest in safer assets such as government bonds. Thus, only banks could gather the large sums of capital required, take the risks involved in such pioneering ventures, and adequately monitor their investments. Once established, bank-based systems have a strong survival capacity. This interpretation of history provides support for the recommendation that developing countries follow the model of bank-based development (Aoki and Patrick 1994).

The timing of industrialization thesis draws on both the German and Japanese cases to back up its claim that bank-based systems were necessary for late industrializers to catch up with more developed countries. For TOI, Germany is the premier example of a developmental bank-based system. In the second half of the nineteenth century, particularly after 1870, joint-stock banks active in both lending and underwriting activities were established. These "mixed" banks enjoyed a close (*Hausbank*) relationship with many of their industrial customers. In addition to getting the lion's share of financial services business, these banks often held substantial stock in and appointed directors to the supervisory boards (*Aufsichtsräte*) of these companies. TOI claims that these mixed banks played an essential role in the rapid industrialization of Germany after 1870, not only by organizing large sums of capital unobtainable in nascent capital markets but also by providing entrepreneurial guidance (Gerschenkron 1962). The capacity of these banks for strategic planning was further demonstrated by the organization of rationalization cartels to deal with the overproduction crises in basic industry in the early twentieth century (Hilferding 1968). Finally, it is claimed that the three largest joint-stock banks (Deutsche Bank, Dresdner

Bank, and Commerzbank) continued to use their close links with large industrial companies to act as the locus of private industrial policy in the postwar period (Deeg 1992; Shonfield 1965; Zysman 1983). The role of German banks is most frequently contrasted with the U.K. clearing banks, which allegedly have been more interested in short-term commercial finance than long-term industrial finance (Ingham 1984).

The unparalleled rapid development of Japan from a primarily agriculturally based economy well into the second half of the nineteenth century to the world's second largest industrial power is also cited by TOI as an example of bank-based economic development (Allen 1946; Patrick 1967). More so than in Germany, however, the state played an important role in development after the Meiji Restoration (1868). In addition to establishing many factories, the state took the initiative in founding important financial institutions such as the postal savings system and the Industrial Bank of Japan. Banks played a developmental role not only in providing finance but also entrepreneurial advice for the nascent manufacturing sector. A typical line of analysis sees continuity in this developmental financial system from its early stages through the prewar *zaibatsu* holding companies to the current main-bank system.

On the basis of an empirical analysis of the development of financial systems in Germany, Japan, and the United States, this essay argues for a reexamination of the TOI thesis and a more nuanced analysis of the emergence of different types of financial regimes. Although sympathetic to historical-institutional approaches, I disagree with the timing of industrialization thesis on three points. First, TOI overstates both the significance of bank-based finance for the rapid industrialization of Germany and Japan and the extent to which the financial systems really were different. An important part of TOI is that banks in late industrializers are willing to take the large risks involved in investing the large sums of long-term capital needed to build industrial plant and infrastructure "from scratch." However, the order of development postulated by TOI—first banks, then industry in late industrializers—does not appear so clear-cut in the historical record. A number of large joint-stock banks were founded by industrialists, rather than the other way around. Furthermore, banks in fact had quite a conservative attitude toward risk and were careful in choosing the sectors and firms they would invest in. This cautious attitude toward lending has been characterized as "development assistance for the strong" (Tilly 1986).[3]

Second, TOI understates the importance of different patterns of state regulation, particularly starting in the 1930s, for explaining postwar differ-

---

3. For other literature supporting a reappraisal of TOI in the context of the German case, see Feldenkirchen (1991), Fohlin (1998), Wellhöner (1989), Wixforth (1995), and Wixforth and Ziegler (1995).

ences in the financial systems. Despite the significantly earlier industrialization of the United States, the three financial systems exhibited strong tendencies to convergence and, by World War I, were characterized by a model of largely laissez-faire domestic regulation, participation in the gold standard international regime, and increasing domination of the financial system by a small number of "mixed" banks (i.e., banks involved in both lending and underwriting activities). The 1930s and 1940s were the crucial "regulatory divide" (Forsyth and Notermans 1997) during which the United States became considerably more market-based and Germany and Japan more bank-based. The crucial actor in this process was the state, which departed from a more or less laissez-faire attitude toward financial regulation and took active steps to reshape the financial system. This activism was motivated by a number of factors, including the increasingly obvious tendencies of laissez-faire financial regimes toward instability—culminating in the Great Depression—and the shifting economic and social goals of the state.

Differences in the regulatory solutions developed by national states are attributable to the nature of state goals and national patterns of state intervention. The goals of the Japanese state regarding the rate of industrial buildup were much greater than was the case in Germany and the United States, and the state utilized financial targeting as one of the most efficient ways to achieve these goals. However, national patterns of state-economy relationships already established in other sectors—liberal regulation based on a contractual approach in the United States, corporatism in Germany, and administrative guidance in Japan—were also important factors influencing the financial regulatory structures that were developed. The U.S. liberal regime relies on sanctioned rules defining "fair play" in financial markets and restraining commercial banks from involvement in these markets. Although both the German and Japanese nonliberal financial regimes are much more bank-based, each has considerably different patterns of state involvement. In Germany, corporatist regulation has reinforced the dominant position of banks vis-à-vis markets but has removed the state from credit allocation decisions to a much greater extent than in Japan. Significantly, these differences persisted despite U.S. attempts to impose its liberal system of financial regulation in both countries after World War II.

The third problem with the timing of industrialization thesis is that differences in financial regimes are dependent not only on the narrow issue of financial regulation but also on the nature of the regulation of labor, including welfare regimes. Major trends in industrialization are the increasing proportion of national income accounted for by wages and salaries and a growing portion of household savings formally dedicated to retirement income. The way in which labor income and welfare is regulated thus influences whether savings will flow into the banking system (including public versus private institutions) or into marketable securities. The voluntarist system of capitalized pension funds established in the United States led to a higher demand for marketable securities than the solidaristic pension systems in Germany and Japan based on pay-as-you-go social security and non-capitalized company pensions (Jackson and Vitols 2000). In addition, the industrial relations systems established in Germany and Japan created a more equal distribution of income than the voluntarist system established in the United States. Since wealthier households tend to have a greater demand for marketable securities than low- and middle-income households, the more equal distribution of income for bank deposits in Germany and Japan supports greater demand for bank deposits (including nonliquid long-term deposits) than is the case in the United States. This elective affinity between solidaristic labor regimes and bank-based financial regimes is important in controlling the relative size of the market segment of the financial system.

The Emergence of Laissez-Faire Financial Regulatory Regimes

The major claim of the timing of industrialization thesis, as outlined above, is that key characteristics of national financial systems can be traced back to the industrialization period. However, a closer examination of the historical evidence—which is backed up by a good deal of recent scholarship on individual countries—supports a more nuanced interpretation than this simple TOI explanation. Although recognizing that there were important national peculiarities, this alternative interpretation stresses the degree of similarity in the structural development of financial systems—despite the timing of industrialization.

The first common feature of financial systems during industrialization is that, once traditional constraints on financial activity—as well as other constraints on "capitalistic" activity in general—had been removed and the joint-stock form of banking was authorized, there was relatively little state regulation of banking systems or securities markets.[4] The second common feature is that, under this laissez-faire regulatory regime, banks initially proliferated rapidly. After an initial period of numerical expansion, a concentration process set in and a small number of banks—typically based in one national financial center—accounted for an increasing proportion of banking-system assets. As stock markets grew in importance, these banks also expanded beyond traditional lending and deposit-taking activities into un-

---

4. Typical traditional constraints included usury laws, royal or parliamentary chartering requirements, granting of monopolies, and full financial liability for partners.

derwriting and brokerage activities. These "mixed" (commercial and investment) banks, which increasingly dominated financial systems, enjoyed a great deal of flexibility in providing finance: for example, in providing loans in anticipation of a securities emission and in carrying significant portions of these securities in their own portfolios. A third common feature is that banks in all countries—at least the banks that survived for longer periods—tended to seek out companies with established track records and limited risk. As the capital-labor ratio and the scale of companies increased in industries such as railroads, coal, and steel, the demand for external long-term finance grew. In order to reduce their long-term risk exposure, banks encouraged these companies to turn to stock markets for long-term finance.

These laissez-faire financial systems, however, were characterized by increasing tendencies to instability. The greater interdependence of financial institutions on regional and national levels (e.g., through greater interbank liabilities) rendered the banking systems vulnerable to systemic crises. Bank runs, for example, could be triggered by problems at one bank and spread throughout the region or even the country. The potential for systemic financial crises was increased through the speculative opportunities offered by the new securities markets (particularly futures markets) and through the increasing degree of "maturity mismatch" caused by reliance on short-term deposits to fund long-term investments.[5] These destabilizing tendencies led to increasingly severe financial panics and crises culminating in the Great Depression of the 1930s. The search for regulatory solutions to instability coincided temporally with the search to meet collective social and economic goals (such as economic development and mobilization for war) and to solve aspects of the "labor problem." One of the potential tools for achieving these goals was the financial system. In contrast to the laissez-faire regulatory regime, however, the new regulatory regimes differed greatly in accordance with national patterns of state intervention and with the nature of these collective social and economic goals.[6]

5. The increasing concentration of fixed capital (plant and equipment) posed a substantial challenge for a financial system basically organized around short-term financing techniques for trade and inventory. The loan evaluation techniques used by these systems were based on the value of assets used as security rather than on the expected increase in future income generated by the new investment. Relying on the current deposits of a group of local companies made the supply of long-term finance highly dependent upon the local and cyclical supply of savings. Furthermore, since the funding base of these banks was mainly short-term deposits, banks were exposed to increasing liquidity risk (the risk that adequate liquid funds are not on hand to cover a substantial withdrawal of deposits) as they increased their long-term investments.

6. Although it is beyond the scope of this essay to explain the causes of differences, the consistency of national regulatory patterns across issue areas appears to indicate dependence on fundamental factors such as the structure of government, the balance of power be-

Laissez-Faire Regulatory Regimes

Historical accounts of industrialization stress the low degree of regulation in the three countries once traditional constraints had been removed—both in banking and on the stock exchanges. In Germany, the crucial regulatory divide took place around 1870. Until then, the German financial system was dominated by a small number of private banks largely oriented toward government finance.[7] Financial functions in everyday business activities in an economy dominated by small owner-operated businesses were largely handled as ancillary activities by merchants, goldsmiths, etc. The stock exchanges that existed were small and geared toward commodities and government securities.

The takeoff period of the German financial system can be traced to the introduction of incorporation without prior special authorization of joint-stock banking in 1870.[8] This initiated the laissez-faire period of German financial-system regulation which lasted until 1931 (Büschgen 1983). Despite a number of banking crises, there were no successful attempts at imposing comprehensive legislation upon the banking system. Instead, specialized portions of the banking system were regulated, mainly the mortgage banks. Legislation on the provincial level also regulated municipal savings banks and cooperatives (Kluge 1991). Efforts to regulate the stock exchanges were ineffective. In the wake of the speculative crisis of the early 1890s, a national legal framework for the stock markets was created by the Stock Exchange Law of 1896 (H. Pohl 1992). However, this law contained few norms, delegated much rule-making to the regional exchanges themselves, and within a few years was amended to strip it of its most important restriction, the prohibition of futures trading.

In Japan, a laissez-faire financial regulatory regime also emerged in the decades after the Meiji Restoration in 1868. Following a number of experiments based in part on the Belgian central bank and the U.S. model of national banks, the central-bank monopoly over currency issue was introduced in 1882 and liberal entry to banking was established by 1890

---

tween different societal interests, and national traditions of policymaking (see the introduction to this volume for a discussion of this issue).

7. The term "private bank" is generally applied to banks owned by a single person or partnership. Joint-stock banks are also mostly privately owned, but distinguish themselves from private banks by the larger number of owners and the principle of limited liability (i.e., the financial liability of owners is limited to the amount of funds invested).

8. As an example of the difficulties of incorporation in financial services, Prussia (the largest German state) issued charters for only two joint-stock banks prior to this legislation: the Schaaffhausen'scher Bankverein in 1848 and the Deutsche Bank in 1870, only a few months before passage of the law. The reluctance of the Prussian authorities to authorize joint-stock banks (and companies in general) can be traced to their suspicion of "anonymous" ownership.

(Tamaki 1995). The uncertain attitude of the government toward stock exchanges also eventually gave way to a permissive regime. Initially, only one- to two-year licenses for brokers were issued, and trading in stocks was temporarily suspended a number of times. However, this policy changed and a more stable framework was created with the passage of the Exchange Law of 1893, which contained few substantive regulations. A revision of the Exchange Law in 1914 proved unsuccessful in curbing speculation-driven instability (Adams 1964, 57–59).

The first banks in the United States were founded after the American Revolution. Banks generally had to seek charters from legislatures. The ambiguity of the federal government toward banks can be seen in the ongoing debate on the necessity of a national banking system. The charter of the Bank of the United States, the only national bank, was granted only for a limited number of years and was not renewed by Andrew Jackson. With the withdrawal of the federal government from banking regulation in 1836, the era of "free banking," in which many states passed laws requiring only a minimum amount of capital for the establishment of a bank, was introduced (Dowd 1993). When federal regulation was reintroduced in the early 1860s during the Civil War, state-level regulation remained intact, resulting in a bifurcated system under which banks could choose a national or state-level charter. This dual regulatory system, which still exists, reinforced the laissez-faire tendency by allowing banks to choose the less restrictive regulatory regime. National and many state-level systems of bank regulation were characterized by infrequent bank examinations and ineffective enforcement of regulations. The major exception to this rule was branching restrictions on banks, including limits on the geographical area in which a bank could have branches or limits on the number of permissible branches.[9]

Early efforts on the national level to restrict bank involvement in securities activities were easily circumvented by banks, which obtained state charters for their investment-banking subsidiaries. Stock exchanges were basically self-regulated cartels, as there was no legislation regarding the issuance or trading of securities and no regulatory agency responsible for oversight of the stock exchanges (Seligman 1995).

Banking System Dynamics: From Proliferation to Concentration

The liberalization of joint-stock banking in 1870 led to the rapid transformation of the German financial system, which had previously been dom-

---

9. "Unit banking" states, in which banks were allowed to have only a central office and no branches, represented the limiting case.

inated by small private banks. Joint-stock banks were founded by manufacturers and merchants, and many private banks eventually chose incorporation in order to survive. The number of joint-stock banks peaked at 169 in
1890 (Deutsche Bundesbank 1976, 56). These banks were originally dis-
persed throughout the provinces. However, a dynamic of increasing concentration of both money-market activities and lending to larger industrial
companies emerged in Berlin. Cooperative arrangements (*Interessengemein-
schaften*) between the large Berlin banks and provincial banks were common up until World War I, but a pattern of outright acquisition of provincial banks by the Berlin banks became predominant thereafter (Feldman
1998). By 1928 the eight Berlin *Großbanken* (large banks) accounted for
about half of all banking-system assets. Through their underwriting and
price-stabilizing (*Kurspflege*) activities, these large joint-stock banks also replaced the associations of independent brokers (*Makler*) as the dominant
actors on the stock exchanges.

In Tokugawa Japan (1600–1868), banking functions were centered on
the money changers (*ryōgaeya*) located in the trading centers. The Meiji
government initially was quite cautious and provided special charters, in
some cases negotiated with the *ryōgaeya*, for a small number of banks. Between 1873 and 1876, the number of banks increased only from two to six.
Once liberal entry was established, the number of banks multiplied rapidly
and reached a peak of 2,358 in 1901 (Tamaki 1995, 223–24). After this
point, the first of a number of concentration waves started. The end result
was the emergence of a relatively small number of large banks, in many
cases linked with *zaibatsu* and for the most part based in Tokyo.

Japanese stock exchanges were also initially dominated by specialists involved in secondary trading (Adams 1964). New industrial securities were
offered directly by the issuer to the public. However, around the turn of the
century, the big banks came to play an increasing role on these exchanges
as underwriters. This seems to have been motivated by the growing size of
issues of industrial securities. Specialized securities dealers only gradually
expanded from secondary trading to securities underwriting. By the 1920s,
as Yamamura (1972) shows, the large Japanese banks had developed into
full-blown providers of industrial finance through both longer-term lending and investment-banking activities similar to the German mixed banks.

Mixed Banking and Finance for the Strong

An important part of the TOI theory is that banks in late industrializers
are willing to take the large risks involved in investing the large sums of
long-term capital needed to build industrial plant and infrastructure from
scratch. One would thus expect to find a different order of historical appearance of organizations as well as significantly different patterns of fi-

nance. Banks would clearly precede industry and provide more bank loans to heavy industry in late industrializers than in early industrializers.

However, careful studies on Germany question the extent to which German banks were really willing to take risks in developing new industries and to which bank involvement in company decision making was really welcomed by managers. One criticism is that the order of development postulated by the late industrializers—first banks, then industry—does not appear so clear-cut in the historical record. Second, the banks had quite a conservative attitude toward risk, for example in financing smaller firms and local government, which were arguably as important for industrialization as large firms (Tilly 1966). Third, companies were mainly internally financed, and most loans they received were short-term. Banks sought to minimize their lending risk (while at the same time maintaining their lucrative ties with industry) by encouraging customers to obtain long-term capital in capital markets. Although banks would hold a portion of the securities they underwrote, these holdings were generally seen as temporary, until buyers at an appropriate price could be found in the market (Edwards and Ogilvie 1996). Securities holdings of German banks at the beginning of the twentieth century were not significantly larger than U.K. bank holdings (Fohlin 1997). Industrial companies also generally appear to have disliked the controls banks wanted to place on them and sought to reduce their debt to (and thus increase their independence from) banks during periods of less rapid growth (Feldenkirchen 1982).

Similarly, Japanese banks and the state also played a more modest role in industrialization than is commonly claimed (Yamamura 1972). First—parallel to Tilly's "development assistance for the strong" argument in the German case—most of the nascent industrial companies were unable to get bank financing until they were well established (i.e., were better lending risks) and thus were self-financed during their early stages. Second, although the main source of external finance for industry in the earlier phases of industrialization was bank loans, most of the capital provided by banks was in the form of short-term loans rather than long-term finance. As the need for long-term capital grew, in the 1890s an increasing number of companies (particularly in the railroad, mining, shipping and shipbuilding, and cotton-spinning industries) started to raise long-term finance in stock markets. Although banks began to play a major role in underwriting after 1900, the banks themselves only retained a relatively modest proportion of these issues. Total equity holdings by all financial intermediaries fluctuated between 5 and 11 percent of all outstanding corporate stock from 1900 to 1905 (Ott 1961, 129). Finally, the link between the state's developmental activities and the new banks was more tenuous than is often claimed.

The activities of the large banks in Germany and Japan were thus similar to those of the large banks in the United States such as JP Morgan, which were extensively involved in both lending and securities underwriting activities. These banks engineered major sectoral reorganizations, including mergers in sectors such as railroads and steel through extensive shareholdings and board representation (Chernow 1990; White 1991). Since the United States lacked a central bank until World War I, the "House of Morgan" also played the role of informal "lender of last resort" a number of times (e.g., during the panic of 1907). A number of commercial banks, such as National City Bank, became increasingly active in underwriting operations during and after World War I.

Financial Instability and Social Costs

Whatever the long-run benefits of the laissez-faire regime might have been, the short-term social costs of maintaining it were often high. Under the gold standard, adjustment to short-term capital outflows required deflationary monetary policy, which often triggered sharp increases in unemployment and banking crises (Eichengreen 1995). Germany experienced severe banking crises in 1873 (one component of the Gründerkrise), the mid-1890s, 1907, and especially 1931. In Japan, there were systemic crises in the banking system in 1896, 1901, 1908, 1920, and 1922 (Yabushita and Inoue 1993). The worst banking crisis unfolded in the decade after the 1923 Great Kanto Earthquake in the Tokyo area. Festering problems with bad loans erupted in 1925 and again in the 1927 banking crisis. The United States also experienced a series of banking crises culminating in the banking-system collapse following the 1929 stock market crash.

As Eichengreen (1995) argues, the financial and social costs of these crises were increasingly unacceptable politically as their main victims (farmers and workers) gained political power and the links between monetary policy and these crises became better understood. At the same time, World War I and the ensuing reparations agreements had seriously weakened international monetary cooperation, which was also an essential part of the adjustment process to short-term capital flows. Thus, both the political and technical preconditions for sustaining the laissez-faire regime had seriously eroded by the 1930s.

Summing Up the Laissez-Faire Period

The main contribution of the state regarding financial-system development in the laissez-faire period was to enable the rapid proliferation of

Table 5.2 Financial aspects of Germany, Japan, and the United States, 1912 and 1925

	Germany	Japan	United States
Size of securities markets relative to GDP, 1912	1.21	0.97[a]	1.47
Banking system assets as a proportion of total financial system assets, 1925[b]	0.91	0.85	0.81

Sources: Deutsche Bundesbank 1976; Ott 1961; U.S. Department of Commerce 1975.
Notes: [a] Estimate based on share of new securities issues in total flow of funds 1909–14 (Ott 1961, 125–26); [b] Total financial system assets minus assets of central bank, insurance companies, and pension funds.

banks by reducing barriers to entry.[10] Although financial statistics before World War II should be treated with great caution, they suggest that differences between the countries were smaller than suggested by TOI (see Table 5.2). In all of these countries during this phase, banks dominated the financial system, accounting for over four-fifths of financial system assets. The links between these banks and growing firms can best be described as "development assistance for the strong," thus their contribution to industrial "takeoff" through entrepreneurship can most accurately be described as modest. The relative size of securities markets in the three countries (between 100 and 150 percent of GDP by the 1920s) also seems remarkably similar—despite considerable differences in the timing of industrialization. As one comparative study of Japan and the United States notes: "The striking thing . . . is that the broad contours of Japanese financial development were not radically different from—and in many respects quite similar to—those in the United States, over roughly comparable periods of economic development" (Ott 1961, 135). The same would appear to be the case for Germany (H. Pohl 1984).

Beyond Laissez-Faire: Liberal and Nonliberal Financial Regulatory Regimes

As noted, differences between financial systems in Germany, Japan, and the United States are extensive. When did these differences arise? If the timing of industrialization does not explain differences in the systems, what does? I argue that these differences mainly arose in the 1930s and 1940s with the construction of very different regulatory regimes by state actors.

One of the fundamental questions faced by the state during and after the Great Depression was how to reestablish and promote stability in financial

10. The other primary—and decidedly less-successful—contribution of early capitalist states in financial regulation was the attempt to provide an elastic but stable money supply.

markets. On this question, state elites were guided by their political ideology, in particular by their ideas about the proper role of markets within the economy and society. In both Japan and Germany, these elites were very critical of market capitalism and constructed a regulatory regime that gave clear preference to bank domination of the financial system. This critique was expressed in Germany in the choice of corporatist regulatory mechanisms and in Japan by a much more direct relationship between individual banks and the state through administrative guidance. Despite liberal rhetoric in postwar German politics under the guise of "ordo-liberalism" (see the chapter by Gerhard Lehmbruch in this volume), the basic philosophy of preference for banks persisted after the fall of the Nazi regime. Although Franklin D. Roosevelt's "New Deal" administration was also skeptical about the benefits of unfettered markets, the majority of his advisers and of New Deal supporters in Congress did not subscribe to a fundamental critique of capitalism. Instead, a liberal approach to regulating markets, which had already developed during the populist and progressive eras in areas such as antitrust and utilities, was applied to financial markets. This approach, which involved the definition by independent agencies of rules for "fair play" on markets, and recourse to the judiciary for the enforcement of these rules, had the effect of strengthening financial markets relative to the banking system.

A second important issue for the state was the extent to which the financial system was to be used as a "national resource" for the achievement of economic and social goals. The laissez-faire financial systems were poorly suited to support recovery from banking crises and depression, promotion of industries key to the war effort, and postwar reconstruction (including not only economic development but also the fulfillment of "social promises" made by postwar governments). State elites in Japan, which decided to actively use the financial system to steer war mobilization and postwar economic growth, created new financial institutions or upgraded existing institutions and constructed new mechanisms of control such as licensing and administrative guidance to achieve these goals. Due to Japan's relatively less-developed status, its economic goals regarding the rate of growth were of course much more ambitious than was the case in the other two countries.

In the liberal context of U.S. regulation, in contrast, the financial system was used mainly to support state goals indirectly through the purchase of government bonds or through the granting of tax preferences for classes of investments such as housing. Despite rhetoric among hardliners demanding the nationalization of banks, the Nazi regime supported the corporatist framework by also using a system of direct contracting rather than systematic targeting of credits to specific manufacturers. After World War II, the corporatist framework was sustained by channeling Marshall Plan funds for reconstruction through a special bank, the Kreditanstalt für Wiederaufbau (Bank for Reconstruction), rather than through the banking system as a whole.

Germany: Corporatist Regulation of Mixed Banking

The foundations of the current German financial regulatory regime were established in the wake of the banking crisis of 1931.[11] Similar to the pattern of state intervention established in other areas, the regulatory system established here was corporatist, in which self-regulation of the group in question—typically through collective representation through associations—is the regulatory mechanism. This approach generally relies on the "responsible" exercise of influence by group leaders. The difference between "voluntary" self-regulation and corporatism, however, is that regulations devised by the association are recognized as "binding" by the state. Although much of the influence of associations is of course informal in nature, these key regulations—and the need to have access to the resources the association can provide—give a "harder" quality to corporatist than to voluntary self-regulation (Schmitter and Streeck 1985).

The first comprehensive national banking regulation, which was imposed during the banking crisis of 1931, relied mainly on corporatist mechanisms (Born 1967). This regulation took the form of a number of emergency decrees. In order to put constraints on the destructive price competition that had characterized the 1920s, one decree authorized banking associations to determine binding interest rates on deposits and fees for standardized services. Another decree created a bank regulatory agency which, together with the central bank and in consultation with bank associations, was empowered to develop and enforce minimum capital and liquidity requirements and prudential regulations (insider credits, large credit limits, maturity matching requirements). Entry was more strictly regulated, particularly in the case of credit cooperatives which had to receive approval from the appropriate regional cooperative association.

Although some influential voices within the Nazi Party wished to nationalize or abolish the large banks as part of a campaign against capitalism, the banking community was able to successfully control the process for formulating the 1933 Banking Act, which for the most part retained the corporatist elements of the 1931 decrees (Kopper 1995). The department for

11. The banking crisis of 1931, which spread from the Austrian Credit Anstalt to Germany in June 1931, was exacerbated by imprudent banking practices such as over-reliance on foreign short-term capital and excessive long-term lending to one or a small group of customers. Many of the large banks became insolvent and had to be nationalized in order to keep the banking system from completely collapsing, and trading on securities markets was fully suspended.

banking regulation established at the Ministry of Finance was composed primarily of managers from the banking community. In contrast with the Japanese case, the Nazis largely preferred to bypass the banking system in the targeting of financial resources for military production. Although banks were instructed to purchase a large part of the national debt, the Nazi state usually prepaid military contracts rather than relying on bank credits.[12]

Although there was no major legislative reform of the Stock Exchange Law of 1896, a number of regulatory changes radically transformed the nature of capital markets, rendering stock markets unattractive sources of capital relative to bank loans. Stock markets were widely held by the Nazi government to have exacerbated the financial crisis through the investment of capital in "speculative" instead of "productive" purposes. When stock exchanges were reopened in early 1932, trading in futures on stocks and bonds, which was considered the most speculative part of securities markets, was completely prohibited. New stock emissions were subject to strict control, minimum information content for prospectuses for new securities issues was defined, and the statute of limitations for prospectus fraud was extended. Public (municipal and national) securities were given general priority over industrial securities in access to stock exchanges (Henning 1992; Merkt 1996).

Following World War II, the U.S. occupying authorities attempted to impose a U.S.-style financial system as part of a program of democratization (Horstmann 1991). The large banks were broken up into smaller units and regulatory authority delegated to the regions. Although the liberal rhetoric of the postwar government of Konrad Adenauer appeared to signal agreement with many of the reform goals of the United States—for example, in stressing the importance of efficient capital markets for reconstruction—many of the continuities with the 1930s are more striking than the changes. The core principles of regulation established in the 1931 emergency regulations and the Bank Act of 1933—such as corporatist interest-rate regulation—were quickly reimplemented. The experiment in financial federal-

---

12. This touches upon an important historical controversy, namely, the extent to which the institutional framework for the postwar "economic miracle" (*Wirtschaftswunder*) was established under the Nazi regime. One important point to note is that corporatism was established as the dominant mode of regulation in many spheres of economic and social activity well in advance of the 1930s. A second significant point is the fact that the initial organization of industry for military production under the authority of Göring was based on a hierarchical—and relatively inefficient—command form. One of the most significant achievements of Albert Speer, armaments minister after 1943, was to replace administrative control of production with more cooperative relations with industrial managers within a corporatist framework. This had the effect of significantly boosting armaments production (and in all likelihood extending the length of the war).

ism was terminated with the merger of the Bank deutscher Länder into the Deutsche Bundesbank and the remerger of the dismembered *Großbanken* (this time with headquarters in Frankfurt).

Government policy toward stock markets discouraged their development as a source of long-term capital for industry. The tax system, for example, favored public bonds (particularly for housing and infrastructure) over industrial bonds. Double taxation of equities (corporation tax plus individual income tax) stunted the development of equities markets. In addition to these measures, a corporatist bond committee composed of the leading securities issuers (joint-stock banks and the national banks for the credit cooperative and municipal savings-bank sector) was formed to control access to bond markets with priority for public and bank bonds.

As a result of these regulations, the pattern of industrial finance for large companies clearly shifted from the pre-1930s pattern of short-term loans from banks and long-term finance from securities markets (H. Pohl 1984). The number of companies listed on the stock exchanges declined throughout the postwar period until the late 1980s and new equity issues were rare. Company debt came almost completely through long-term bank loans instead of bonds. Postwar securities markets were almost entirely dominated by municipal and bank bonds (and, after the first oil crisis, federal bonds) (Vitols 1998).

Although long-term finance shifted from securities markets to banks, the degree of targeting through the banking system remained limited relative to the Japanese case. In the immediate postwar period, a limited quantity of funds (mainly European Recovery Program funds) were targeted through the Bank for Reconstruction to basic industry, transportation, and housing (M. Pohl 1973). The targeting of specific sectors within industry ended in the early 1950s, when long-term credit agencies shifted their main focus to the general support of small and medium-sized businesses. Significantly, these long-term credits were used to refinance these firms' *Hausbanken* (mainly credit cooperatives and savings banks), and thus to draw on the customer-specific relationships of the banks rather than to directly lend to the companies (Menzel 1960).

This regulatory system has supported one of the most stable banking systems among the industrialized countries. The German system, which is unique in the degree to which clear quantitative regulatory standards have been applied to the whole banking sector, has been remarkably free of the speculative bubbles and credit crunches experienced in other industrialized countries (Vitols 1998). The stock exchanges also have an exceptionally limited number of listed companies and a low degree of capitalization and turnover of shares—despite Germany's stature as a manufacturing power.

Japan: Administrative Guidance and Network Finance

Financial crisis, war mobilization, and postwar reconstruction triggered a quantum leap in the level of regulation of the financial system in Japan. As Kazuo Ueda notes:

> An interesting feature of the Japanese financial system until about the 1920s was that it was mostly free from government regulations. Financing through equities or bonds was as important as bank lending. There was no separation of banking and securities businesses. However, a series of financial panics and World War II had completely changed the character of the financial system. (Ueda 1994, 90)

The Banking Act of 1927, which was passed in response to the banking crisis of 1927, granted sweeping regulatory powers to the state. However, these powers were first utilized to a great extent in conjunction with military mobilization in the mid-1930s, when an effective system of close bank regulation under the Ministry of Finance was built up. Unlike the corporatist German system, however, the Ministry of Finance preferred the flexibility of administrative guidance in dealing with banks individually. The establishment of an extensive licensing system reinforced government influence by controlling entry to the financial system and by making existing institutions dependent upon government approval for many actions, such as the establishment of new branches (Sohn 1998).

Similar to the German case, a number of constraints imposed on stock markets rendered them unattractive sources of industrial finance relative to bank credits. Starting in the mid-1930s, public securities were prioritized over private securities. Controls on issuing new securities were imposed, including a requirement for collateral for industrial bonds and the requirement for permission from a bank-dominated Bond Committee. Eventually, only new securities issues for war-related industries were permitted (Adams 1964).

Another common aspect with Germany is that the U.S. occupation authorities unsuccessfully tried to export a U.S.-style financial system to Japan as part of a program of democratization of the economy after World War II (Tsutsui 1988). Although banking and brokerage activities were separated, these authorities did not achieve many other objectives. An independent securities regulatory commission created by the 1948 Securities and Exchange Law on the model of the U.S. Securities and Exchange Commission was abolished in 1952 and its functions taken over by the Ministry of Finance. A 5 percent maximum shareholding limit was rapidly raised to 10 percent. Although two-thirds of stocks were distributed to households after the war, stocks rapidly accumulated in the hands of "friendly" financial institutions and companies. By the 1960s, an estimated 60–65 percent of large-company stocks were held by "friendly" investors not terribly concerned with share price. Futures were also prohibited and an effective secondary market was hindered by the minimum transaction requirement of 1,000 shares (Baum, Hopt, and Rudolph 1996).

A final similarity with the German case is that the pattern of long-term finance for industry in Japan shifted away from securities markets to the banking system. The proportion of bank loans in external finance for industry increased from about half in the 1910s and 1920s to about four-fifths in the 1960s and 1970s. This seems to have strengthened the links between the main banks and industrial companies. Although the links between companies organized under the *zaibatsu* were dissolved by the U.S. occupying authorities after World War II, these companies were reconfigured into *keiretsu*, in which a trading company, manufacturing corporations, a main bank, and other financial institutions (e.g., insurance companies and trust banks) have considerable cross-shareholdings. The *keiretsu* appear to be more significant than the prewar *zaibatsu*: whereas almost all of the largest Japanese industrial companies now belong to a *keiretsu*, only a few of the largest Japanese manufacturing companies belonged to *zaibatsu* before the mid-1930s (see the chapter by Gregory Jackson in this volume).[13]

Unlike in Germany, however, the degree of targeting through the financial system was much higher (Zysman 1983). As previously discussed, military funding was channeled directly through the banking system to industry to a much greater extent in Japan than in Germany. Funds through the Fiscal Investment and Loan Program were targeted, and the Bank of Japan favored certain sectors throughout much of the postwar period (Suzuki 1987). These public funds also affect the allocation of private funds through their "signaling" of government support for these sectors and companies (Calder 1993).

United States: The Enforcement of Contract through a Liberal Regime

Although market systems are often associated with laissez-faire or non-regulation, the development of the U.S. financial system is a powerful illustration of how certain types of markets must be carefully regulated in order

---

13. The nonmarket elements of the *keiretsu* structure include: (1) the high proportion of external finance provided through bank loans rather than through securitized finance (bonds and equity); (2) the reciprocal obligations between the "main bank" and its primary clients (the main bank is obligated to "rescue" its clients in case of financial distress, while the clients are expected to turn to the main bank for financial services not necessarily at "market rates"); and (3) the high proportion of shareholdings in friendly hands not motivated by short-term dividend policy.

to avoid dysfunction.[14] As in the case of Germany and Japan, the U.S. financial system during its laissez-faire stage was characterized by increasing instability. The 1929 stock market crash was only the first stage of a multiyear financial crisis culminating in the banking crisis of 1933.

Upon taking office in 1933, President Roosevelt's "New Deal" approach to state-society relationships rejected the voluntarist attitude of Herbert Hoover's administration. However, despite calls from some advisers and members of Congress for a more radical approach (including nationalization of the large banks), the national regulatory system established for financial markets drew heavily on precedents from the populist and progressive eras. This approach, which was established in areas such as antitrust, railroad, and other utility regulation, involved congressional delegation of rule-making authority to independent agencies. These rules are intended to define fair play in markets where some actors are considerably stronger than others or enjoy significant information advantages. Rule making is guided by administrative law and the enforcement of these rules can be triggered by private actors through recourse to the judicial system. This mode of regulation has been aptly characterized as "adversarial legalism" (Kagan 1991).

The most significant pieces of legislation in the United States were the Securities Act of 1933 and the Securities Exchange Act of 1934. The first regulated the issuance of new securities by defining minimum information requirements for prospectuses and established a Securities and Exchange Commission (SEC) to oversee securities markets. The second authorized the SEC to develop rules for trading in secondary markets. In line with the adversarial legalistic pattern of state regulation, the SEC has developed an extensive set of rules and practices regarding conditions under which securities can be issued, minimum information requirements, fair determination of market prices, exercise of shareholder voting rights and communication with management, abuse of dominant market position, abuse of insider information, and takeover rules.

The weak system of national banking regulation was substantially strengthened under the New Deal, particularly under the 1933 and 1934 Banking Acts. A system of deposit insurance was established and an agency (the Federal Deposit Insurance Corporation) was created to administer this scheme. The Federal Reserve Board, the nation's central bank, was authorized under "Regulation Q" to establish maximum interest rates on de-

---

14. This shows that it is not necessarily correct to equate liberal regimes with laissez-faire regulation. As can be seen in the case of the financial system, it may in fact be necessary to have a strong regulatory state in order to create the conditions under which "free" and fair contracting is possible.

posits. Interestingly enough, attempts by bank regulators to encourage a limited form of corporatism in the guise of interest-rate cartels were struck down in the courts as a violation of competition law. Portions of the 1933 Banking Act (the "Glass-Steagall" provisions) effectively split the "mixed" banking system by forcing banks to choose between investment and commercial banking activities.

In contrast to Germany and Japan, this regulation led neither to the favoring of banks over securities markets nor to a significant increase in targeting of funds to specific sectors. Targeting was limited to some defense-related finance and, in the postwar period, favorable treatment of private residential housing finance. This type of regulation aimed more at separating the "speculative" securities markets from the commercial banking part of the financial system. Furthermore, speculative tendencies on securities markets were to be constrained by increasing transparency and imposing rules of fair play on more powerful market participants.

Unlike the German and Japanese cases, the importance of banks in the financial system as a whole and in the financing of industry decreased. Since the 1930s the relative importance of banks has shrunk from two-thirds to one-quarter of financial-system assets. With the exception of a brief comeback in the 1970s, bank loans have also decreased as a proportion of external liabilities of industrial companies since the 1920s.

Summing Up: Privileged Markets and Targeting

With the risk of some oversimplification, the primary characteristics of the financial regulatory systems in Germany, Japan, and the United States can be usefully diagramed according to two dimensions (see Figure 5.1). The vertical axis illustrates the degree to which banks were to be favored over securities markets in an attempt to encourage stability in the financial system. Germany and Japan both receive very high scores, with Germany somewhat higher. The U.S. regulatory system, in contrast, does little to privilege the banking system over securities markets. The second dimension illustrates the degree of targeting of funds through the financial system. Japan, however, has the highest degree of targeting, while both Germany and the United States have relatively low degrees of targeting.

The Regulation of Labor: Elective Affinities with Finance?

A topic of great importance to financial systems but almost completely neglected by the comparative literature on financial systems is the interre-

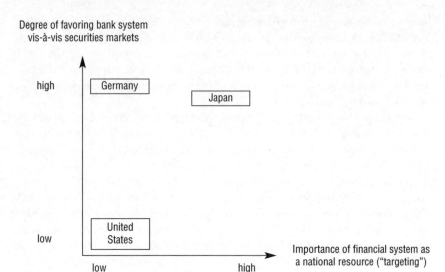

Figure 5.1 Classification of postwar financial regulatory systems: Predominant approach to stability

lationship between the regulation of finance and the regulation of labor.[15] Before and during the early phases of industrialization, income and financial assets were highly concentrated among the richest households. Early financial institutions catered to the savings of these households and were generally not interested in having small savers as their customers. With industrialization came an increase in the share of wage earners in the population and in their income, and thus a growing proportion of savings was accounted for by this group. These dependent employees came to be incorporated not only in an industrial relations regime but also in what might be termed a savings regime.

Since the household sector accounts for the bulk of savings in industrializing countries, one of the key problems for bank-based systems is to limit household investment in securities (i.e., to limit the flow of household savings into the market segment of the financial system). Conversely, market-based financial systems are dependent upon a sufficient flow of household savings into securities in order to insure adequate liquidity.

Two aspects of the incorporation of labor into a savings-and-investment regime have a major impact on the demand for different types of financial assets. First, since a growing proportion of household savings is accounted for by provision for retirement, the types of retirement savings programs es-

15. In this section what might be termed the technical relationship between finance and labor as defined by the flow and distribution of funds is emphasized. On the political culture or "political discourse" roots of cross-national regulatory differences, see the chapter by Lehmbruch in this volume.

tablished or promoted have an important influence on this demand.[16] In particular, private pension schemes organized on a fully funded (i.e., capitalized) basis have emerged in the postwar period as the largest purchasers of securities in market-based systems such as the United States and United Kingdom. The demand for securities is thus higher in "individualistic" systems emphasizing such capitalized private schemes. "Solidaristic" retirement systems, in contrast, are based more on the transfer of income between generations, defined either at the societal, company, or family level (in the case of social security, noncapitalized company pension plans, or family support). Solidaristic systems thus involve less demand for securities than capitalized systems.

Since different income groups have different preferences for various types of financial assets, the second important factor is the degree of inequality in the distribution of income (Vitols 1996). High-income households have the greatest demand for high-risk (but, on average, higher-yield) securitized assets such as stocks or corporate bonds. Middle-income households have a greater preference for less risky assets such as bank deposits. Low-income households have little ability to save, and what savings they do have is held mainly as cash or highly liquid bank deposits. The most important factors determining the distribution of income are the industrial relations regime and transfer programs (Mosher 1998). Bank-based systems are thus best supported by household sectors with low income inequality (and thus a high demand for bank deposits). Market-based financial systems, in contrast, are best supported by household sectors with high degrees of income inequality (and thus a high demand for securities with higher risk and return profiles).

The lower level of household-income inequality and greater emphasis on solidaristic retirement provision in Germany and Japan than in the United States are thus important factors supporting the bank-based systems in the former two countries.

Individualistic versus Solidaristic Retirement Systems

Of the three countries examined in this essay, the United States has by far the most significant capitalized pension system. The U.S. government has provided strong support for capitalized private pensions since 1942, mainly in the form of favorable tax provisions. The combined assets of private pension funds and insurance companies (which to a large part administer pension assets) were about four times greater as a percentage of GNP

---

16. An analysis of the relationship between different types of retirement systems and their impact on financial systems and corporate governance emerges from collaboration with Gregory Jackson. See Jackson and Vitols 2000.

Table 5.3 Pension fund and life insurance company assets, 1970 (percentage of GDP)

	Germany	Japan	United States
Pension fund	2	0	17
Life insurance companies	8	8	20
Total	10	8	37

Source: Calculated from Davis 1995, 55–56.

in the United States than in Germany and Japan in 1970 (see Table 5.3). The United States has the least solidaristic system of the three countries, with public payouts accounting for about two-thirds of pension payouts as opposed to about 80 percent for the other two countries. Although social security has a relatively high replacement rate for low-income earners, the replacement rate decreases steeply with increasing income. In 1986 social security accounted for 73 percent of the income of the lowest income quartile of retirees but only 13 percent of the income of the highest income quartile; in Germany the corresponding figures were 84 and 33 percent, respectively, for 1981.

Public pensions play the greatest role in Germany. In 1980, for example, public pension payout came to 10.6 percent of GDP (Table 5.4). Germany is known as a pioneer in social security policy, having established a statutory pension system in 1889 (see the chapter by Philip Manow in this volume). This system is organized on a pay-as-you-go basis and accumulates a reserve of only about one month's payout; thus it is not a major player in capital markets.

Germany is also distinguished by the degree to which noncapitalized company pensions have been encouraged. Postwar tax and pension policy encouraged companies to provide for future pension obligations through a system of book reserves rather than through establishing capitalized pension funds. Thus employees' future pensions were in effect re-lent to the company (and guaranteed by the efforts of future generations of employees) rather than invested in financial securities. The combination of generous pay-as-you-go public pensions and book reserve company pensions led to a low demand for securities.

Japan also has a considerably more solidaristic pension system than the United States. Japan first introduced a statutory pension system for private employees in 1941 (the Employees' Pension Insurance System) as part of a system of forced saving to finance the war. After the war, the public pension system evolved into a relatively generous system. However, actual payouts as a percentage of GDP were significantly lower than in the other two countries due to the much lower average age of the Japanese population after the war. Only larger companies (over 500 employees) were allowed to opt

Table 5.4 Public and private pension benefits, 1980 (percentage of GDP)

	Germany	Japan	United States
Public pensions	10.6	4.1	6.9
Private pensions	2.6	0.9	3.3
Total	13.2	5.0	10.2
Public/private mix	80/20	82/18	68/32

Source: Calculated from OECD 1988.

out of the public scheme on the condition that benefits provided were at least as generous as public pensions. Although statistics are not available to demonstrate this point, anecdotal evidence indicates that intergenerational transfers within the family (i.e., family solidarity) may play a greater role than in the other two countries.

Although the Japanese public pension system is partially funded and, over time, has accumulated substantial capital, much of it was channeled directly into the industrial policy apparatus rather than into open capital markets. Furthermore, as in the German case, companies were allowed to provide for a substantial portion of their pension liabilities through balance-sheet reserves rather than through capitalized pension funds. Thus, the demand for financial securities from Japan's pension system has been considerably lower than is the case in the United States.[17]

Distribution of Income

It is difficult to make precise comparisons regarding income inequality. The only major cross-national survey (the Luxembourg Income Study) started in the 1980s and excluded Japan, and national surveys vary somewhat in methodology and definition of variables. Nevertheless, the magnitude of many differences is large enough to allow for the following two conclusions: (1) all three countries experienced a major decrease in income inequality in the middle of the twentieth century, and (2) Germany and Japan became considerably more egalitarian than the United States.

Particularly striking are the differences between the highest and lowest income groups. The ratio between the income of the highest and lowest 10 percent of households in the 1980s was around 6 in the United States as compared to 3 in Germany and 3.5 in Japan (Atkinson, Rainwater, and Smeeding 1995, 40, 70). The poorest 20 percent of households in the

17. Although both Germany and Japan have more solidaristic systems than the United States, it is important to note that the focus of solidarity is quite different, with solidarity being defined much more at the firm level in Japan and at the societal level in Germany. This has important consequences (e.g., for the current politics of pension reform in both countries).

United States received about 5 percent of total household income during the postwar period versus about 9 percent for Japan and 10 percent in Germany (ibid., 44, 70; U.S. Department of Commerce 1975). The proportion of low-income households (those earning less than 50 percent of median income) in the United States in the 1980s was almost three times higher than in Germany (18.4 versus 6.5 percent).

These differences are to a large extent attributable to the industrial relations systems in the three countries (Mosher 1998). Germany developed in the 1920s and elaborated after World War II a corporatist collective bargaining system involving industry-wide unions and employers' associations.[18] In addition to narrowing the differences between different skill categories, wage dispersion within skill categories was also reduced. The rapidly expanding "middle income" group thus included not only the growing number of white-collar workers (*Angestellte*) but also skilled workers sharing in the fruits of productivity growth. Though a very different system of enterprise-based unionism was established in Japan, this system also involved relatively low wage dispersion due to low differentials between different skill levels and a system of coordinated wage bargaining between large companies (the so-called spring offensive). The United States, in contrast, retained quite large wage differentials between skill levels and between unionized and nonunionized companies.

These differences in income distribution have a major impact on the overall household sector pattern of demand for types of financial assets. In the United States in 1983, 78 percent of the financial wealth of the top 10 percent of households was accounted for by securities (equities and bank and municipal bonds) versus only 10 percent in bank-related assets (checking and savings deposits and certificates of deposit). The corresponding percentages for the bottom 90 percent of households were 29 for securities and 51 for bank-related assets (see Table 5.5). Other countries also display a similar large bias toward the accumulation of financial securities by wealthy households (Euler 1981, 1990; Willgerodt, Bartel, and Schillert 1971).

The Need for a Reexamination of the Timing of Industrialization Thesis

Although sympathetic to the historical institutionalist approach of explaining cross-national differences, this essay has argued for a reexamina-

---

18. Although postwar institutions of course shed the authoritarian principles of Nazi Germany, there were important institutional continuities between the two periods, including industrial unions, a high degree of "bindingness" in the employment relationship, and extra-company wage setting.

Table 5.5 Distribution of U.S. household financial assets by income group, 1983 (percent)

Type of Financial Asset	Bottom 90 percent	Top 10 percent	Top ½ percent
Checking accounts	7.6	2.4	1.3
Savings accounts	14.9	2.7	5.4
Certificates of deposit	28.3	6.2	2.9
Total bank-related assets	50.8	11.3	9.6
Money-market accounts	11.5	7.4	4.4
U.S. savings bonds	2.1	0.5	0.4
Notes owed to family	6.6	2.7	1.9
Other nonsecuritized assets	20.2	10.6	6.7
Municipal bonds	1.5	7.9	8.8
Corporate bonds	4.3	5.2	3.7
Corporate equities	14.6	38.6	36.1
Mutual funds	2.2	4.2	3.0
Trust accounts[a]	6.5	22.2	32.1
Total securitized assets	29.1	78.1	83.7
Total financial assets	100.0	100.0	100.0

Source: Calculated from Avery and Elliehausen 1986.
Note: [a] Trust accounts are included under securitized assets since these are almost entirely invested in securities.

tion of the timing of industrialization thesis—the orthodox explanation of differences in financial systems. A careful examination of the evidence indicates that TOI has overstated the contribution of banks to the late but rapid industrialization of Germany and Japan. Banks in both countries appear to have been relatively conservative in their lending policies and have favored companies that were already on a firm financial footing ("development assistance for the strong"). Furthermore, by the early twentieth century, the degree of differences in the financial systems of these two countries and of the United States, a country that industrialized considerably earlier, were smaller than suggested by TOI. All three countries had predominantly laissez-faire systems of regulation in the late nineteenth and early twentieth centuries. Financial systems in these countries were dominated by banks, which accounted for the bulk of financial assets and were involved in both lending and underwriting activities. These systems, however, were characterized by considerable instability culminating in the Great Depression.

I have argued that the differences in postwar systems are largely attributable to a major increase in regulatory intervention by the state in the 1930s and 1940s and to the different policy choices made in response to two questions: (1) How can financial instability be controlled; and (2) Should financial systems be used as a major tool for achieving collective economic and social goals? The diversity of regulatory solutions can be attributed to differences in the ideologies of state elites and in the nature of economic and social goals pursued. In the United States, where antimarket attitudes were weak, a liberal approach of defining and enforcing rules for fair play in markets supported the development of a market-based financial system with limited targeting. In Germany, the corporatist approach allowed banks to maintain a dominant position in the financial system but precluded major targeting of financial resources by the state. In Japan, an antimarket attitude combined with more ambitious public goals regarding war mobilization and reconstruction led to more extensive state micromanagement of the dominant banks through a system of licensing and administrative guidance.

The second major assertion of this chapter is that the establishment of stable regulatory regimes depended not only on the regulation of financial institutions in the narrow sense but also of labor. The sustainability of bank-based systems depends on limiting the flow of household savings into marketable securities instead of bank deposits. Furthermore, bank-based systems with high levels of targeting depend on a flow of household savings into the portions of the banking system over which the state has the most control. The social security and industrial relations systems have a crucial impact on the household sector's demand for different types of financial assets. The claim made here is that Germany and Japan have a constellation of factors in the regulation of labor, namely, high income equality and a lack of capitalized pensions, that limit the demand for marketable securities relative to bank deposits. These factors are considerably weaker in the United States, which has a higher degree of income inequality and a capitalized and significant private pension system.

This problem of the elective affinity of financial and labor regimes must be considered not only in the context of the construction of regulatory regimes in the mid-twentieth century but also in the current pressures for the transformation of these regimes. The potential for transformation of the U.S. market-based system into a more embedded system is clearly quite limited, because it would require the development of a comprehensive system of regulation not only for the financial system but also for labor markets. The more challenging question is the potential for transformation of the German and Japanese systems into more market-based systems. One question is: To what extent can the German and Japanese financial systems not only be deregulated but also reregulated, with the same types of constraints on capital markets as the United States has? A second question is: Do domestic labor markets also have to be transformed, or does foreign capital suffice for a transformation into a much more market-based variant?

A preliminary conclusion is that Germany would seem to have a greater potential for transformation toward a market system than Japan. The corporatist tradition in Germany is much more compatible with U.S.-style financial system constraints than the Japanese system of administrative guidance. The potential for some kind of "hybrid" system—which would mainly depend on foreign capital for more liquid finance but would also maintain more employment security and an equal distribution of income—would also appear to be greater in Germany than in Japan. First of all, a smaller number of companies accounting for a smaller proportion of employment are listed on stock exchanges in Germany; thus, a smaller proportion of the economy would be directly affected by the transformation of capital-market regulation. Second, the system of codetermination appears to have greater potential for adaptation to a more market-based system and "shareholder value" concepts than the Japanese system of lifelong employment. The codetermination system appears to have a higher capacity to maintain solidarity in the negotiation of changes such as an increase in performance demands, sale of noncore and underperforming subsidiaries, and transformation of payment systems.

The Rise of Nonliberal Training Regimes: Germany and Japan Compared

Kathleen Thelen and Ikuo Kume

A strong consensus has emerged in the literature on the political economy of advanced capitalism that the ability of firms to compete in contemporary world markets hinges crucially on the quantity and quality of skills their workers command (Boyer 1995; Finegold and Soskice 1988; Streeck 1988, 1992). However, it turns out that an abundance of skills is hard to create and maintain in liberal market economies, where collective action problems create strong disincentives for employers to invest in training. In the United States and Britain, for example, employers are reluctant to train because they cannot be sure that workers will stay in the firm long enough for them to recoup their investment.[1] The result is that economies such as these are characterized by a chronic underinvestment in skills, or as Finegold and Soskice (1988) put it, a "low skill equilibrium." However, other capitalist economies do in fact manage to generate an abundant supply of skills. Germany and Japan are typically cited as examples of

We thank Gerald Feldman, Andrew Gordon, Hal Hansen, Gary Herrigel, Takenori Inoki, Yukio Ito, Wolfgang Streeck, Peter Swenson, Kozo Yamamura, Jonathan Zeitlin, and the participants in the project "Germany and Japan: The Future of Nationally Embedded Capitalism in a Global Economy" for useful comments on this essay. In addition, Kume thanks the participants in the workshop "Japan in the 20th Century" (30 July 1997, Kyoto), and Thelen thanks Carl Lankowski and the American Institute for Contemporary German Studies in Washington. This article appeared in *The Journal of Japanese Studies* 25 (1999): 33–64.

1. Credible commitment problems also plague liberal training regimes. Where training is unregulated, firms often will be tempted to cut corners on training and use trainees as a source of cheap productive labor. Trainees, for their part, may prefer to abscond with their skills before the firm's investment in training has been paid off in the contribution of its newly trained skilled workers to production (see especially Hansen 1997, 277–87).

economies in which employers make a substantial investment in their workers' skills. The resulting "high skill equilibrium" in these countries rests on institutional arrangements that ameliorate costly competition among firms and mitigate the collective action problems associated with private-sector training.

But if both German and Japanese employers overcame their collective action problems in the area of training, they did so in radically different ways: in Germany through the construction of a national system that generates a relatively plentiful supply of workers with highly portable skills, and in Japan through plant-based training in the context of strong internal labor markets. Applying Peter Swenson's terminology, we can speak of a broad difference between skill formation regimes based on "solidarism" in the German case and "segmentalism" in the Japanese case (Swenson 1996, chap. 1).

In ideal typical terms, solidaristic strategies consist of measures to support the collective provision of a pool of skills on which all employers can draw. Such training could be accomplished either outside the firm (e.g., through public vocational schools), inside the firm (e.g., through coordinated and monitored apprenticeship), or a combination of the two. Such a system might (in a functionalist sense) avoid costly competition among firms for skilled labor through wage coordination, perhaps enforced by craft or industrial unions with whom all employers negotiate, or through other mechanisms (e.g., strong industry associations) for monitoring and punishing poaching. Germany's system of vocational training (with its strong "corporatist" oversight by broad-based employers' associations and unions) approaches the ideal-typical "collective" or "solidaristic" solution to skill formation.

The segmentalist strategy is the mirror image. Here employers combine firm-based (and company-specific) training with other measures to shield themselves from competition over skilled labor in the market. The solution to the problem of poaching in such a system is partly the company-specific nature of the skills; however, a segmentalist strategy in training might be associated with complementary personnel policies such as seniority wages and internal career ladders which reduce workers' incentives to leave. As Swenson (1996, 15) points out, segmentalist strategies will not necessarily succeed without some coordination among employers, at least among the segmentalists. Among other things, seniority-based wages only keep workers in place so long as other firms agree to hire each other's workers only at entry-level wages. The large-company sector in Japan comes close to the segmentalist ideal type.

Thus, in the two cases at hand we have stable systems for skill formation, but based on very different principles and sustained by quite different institutional arrangements. Both systems have generated a steady supply of skills and as such have contributed to the competitive success of these two countries in contemporary world markets. At the same time, the differences in institutional arrangements have important consequences for labor markets and the role of labor. Wolfgang Streeck has argued that where skills are nationally certified (as in Germany), they are also "portable" (because they are recognized not just in the firm's own internal labor market but in the national labor market). In this situation, the power (and voice) of skilled workers within the firm is enhanced by a credible exit option. Where skill formation is plant-based (as in Japan), labor is in a weaker position in terms of options in the national labor market. However, even in this situation, substantial investment by employers in skills makes the threat of a worker's exit costly (also because the skills that workers command are hard to replace), which can also enhance labor's voice in plant-level decision making (Kume 1998). The difference is that in Germany, skilled workers' exit options are what give them power on the shop floor, whereas in Japan union influence is based more on labor's indispensable cooperation in production in the context of the "stakeholder" position of enterprise unions in the firm.[2]

This chapter explores the origins of these two very different training regimes. The analysis involves answering two questions—first, how, in both countries, initial tendencies toward a liberal solution (freedom of trade in Germany and labor mobility in Japan) were suppressed, and second, what factors drove developments along *different* paths in these two countries. The answer to both lies in the specific opportunities and constraints faced by the state and organized interests in the early industrial period.

The defeat of the liberal alternative can be explained best through a comparison to Britain and the United States, both cases of the triumph of "liberal" training regimes, and both—not coincidentally—of the eventual emergence of a "low skill equilibrium." In the United States and Britain, industrialization occurred in a context in which traditional artisan organizations (the guilds) had either been destroyed (Britain) or never developed (United States) and where early labor organizations faced a less overtly repressive political regime.[3] In such a context, the traditional distinction between masters and journeymen faded and the more permissive political climate encouraged skilled workers to band together to defend their interests by attempting to control the market in their skills. As it turns out, the consolidation of stable craft-labor markets was rarely successful, but the important point is that the emergence of craft unions in the early industrial pe-

---

2. See Streeck 1996, esp. 144–51, for an extended analysis.
3. For a very insightful discussion of Germany with reference to the contrasting British experience, see Kocka 1984, esp. 108. For other useful comparisons between the two, see Mommsen and Husung 1985.

riod led to a situation in which skill formation was *contested across the class divide*, as unions sought to set limits on apprenticeship (to maintain the value of their scarce skills) and employers sought to defeat union attempts to control training (to get the upper hand in labor conflicts). In particular, where unions of skilled workers sought to manipulate the supply of skills by imposing restrictions on apprenticeship training, employers fought tenaciously (also generally successfully) against these measures, and the conflicts between unions and employers over skills resulted in an overall deterioration of apprenticeship and training.

In Germany and Japan, by contrast, industrialization occurred under authoritarian auspices, and the traditional artisan sectors survived as important corporate actors in apprenticeship training. In such cases, unions emerged later and in a context in which strategies based on controlling craft-labor markets were not an option, this "space" being already filled by the traditional artisan sector, or artisanate (cf. Herrigel 1993). Here, skill formation was not contested between labor and capital, but rather, between the artisan sector and the modern industrial sector. This competition proved constructive rather than destructive to the preservation of skills and training. What is important here is that the defeat of "liberal" training regimes goes back in both cases to the fate of the artisanate and, above all, to the fact that in both cases, unions were unable to organize their strategies around the attempt to control the market in skills.

The second question is why Japan and Germany embarked on such different trajectories. The divergent institutional and political outcomes in these two countries go back to differences in the treatment by the state of the artisan sector in the early industrial period, which in turn affected the strategies of firms that depended heavily on skills and also powerfully shaped company relations with emerging unions. As late industrializers, both Germany and Japan had states that took a more direct role in attempting to promote development. However, when it came to skill formation these two states were confronted with rather different sets of opportunities and constraints. To put it bluntly, the Japanese state had less of an indigenous model to work with in terms of organized, corporate control of skill formation and—because of the relative weakness of unions—fewer political motives to promote an independent artisanate as a counterweight to labor.

In the German case, artisans were better organized, and there existed (specifically in the southwestern states) models of organized skill formation that could be used to push the handicraft sector in a direction that supported the production of "modern" skills (Hansen 1997, chaps. 4 and 5). Facing a stronger labor movement, the German state had an interest in shoring up a strong independent handicraft sector as a political counterweight to the Social Democrats. In the late nineteenth century, the German government responded to these opportunities and constraints by instituting policies that actively *organized and modernized* the artisan (*Handwerk*) sector, in the process also endowing it with "parapublic"[4] authority in the area of skill formation. In this context, industries that relied heavily on skills were pushed toward a more solidaristic or coordinated approach to skill formation through their competition with the artisan sector, whose power to certify skills they coveted. And, after their full political incorporation in 1919, German unions—whose greatest organizational strength was concentrated among skilled workers in these sectors—emerged as potential allies in support of a solidaristic skill formation regime for industry.

The handicraft sector in Japan was less organized than in Germany and more completely backward-looking (lacking the progressive element found in Germany in the southwestern states), which contributed to more intense skilled-labor shortages in the early industrial period. Given the weakness of the labor movement in the late nineteenth century, the political motives for shoring up the artisan sector were weak, and, given its developmental aspirations, the Japanese state in fact viewed the artisanate as an impediment to modernization. Thus, whereas in Germany government policy promoted the corporate organization and modernization of handicraft organizations, state policy in Japan if anything disorganized the artisan sector. Here the state took a more direct hand in promoting skill formation, importing foreign engineers and establishing training programs in state-owned enterprises. Private firms followed the lead of public-sector companies in embarking on a more segmentalist path, dealing with the problem of skill formation by incorporating traditional craftsmen into a system of direct employment and company-based training. As in Germany, there were contests between artisans and industry over the content and character of apprenticeship training, but in Japan these were played out at the company (rather than at the national political) level. Early labor unions reinforced segmentalist tendencies in the 1920s to the extent that they defined their goals and strategies within the context of these internal labor markets.

Our analysis of developments in both countries ends in the late 1920s, with only a glance forward. This is not meant to imply that either the German or the Japanese system was fully developed at that point—far from it. However, already by the late 1920s the divergence between a more solidaristic versus a more segmentalist approach to skills that is the subject of this chapter was quite evident. In the long run, the protection of the artisan economy and of handicraft organizations in Germany preserved the option of a corporatist training regime that, however, would only emerge in its present form later. In Japan, by contrast, state policy contributed to the demise

4. This term is from Katzenstein 1987.

of such an alternative while promoting the development of a more seg-mentalist, enterprise-based training regime.

The next two sections sketch out developments in Germany and Japan, respectively, in both cases focusing heavily on the metalworking sector. Met-alworking firms have always been especially dependent on a highly skilled workforce, and as an early and heavy user of skills, this sector was a key actor in promoting skill formation and in pushing developments along two very different trajectories in Germany and Japan in the early industrial pe-riod. The final section summarizes the empirical argument and draws out some of the theoretical implications of our analysis.

The Evolution of Skill Formation in Germany

The crucial starting point in Germany is the survival of an independent, *organized* artisan sector which was formally endowed by the state with para-public authority to regulate training and to certify skills. This was an out-come that was actively promoted by the state as part of the imperial govern-ment's effort in the 1880s and 1890s to shore up a healthy, conservative small-business sector (*Mittelstand*) as a bulwark against political polarization and working-class radicalism (see, for example, Volkov 1978, esp. 276). But although the political motives were conservative, the economic impact was quite progressive, for, as Hal Hansen (1997, chap. 5) has emphasized, the decisive legislation—the so-called Handicraft Protection Law of 1897—was strongly influenced by indigenous models (especially in the southwestern states) that—in contrast to the more backward-looking aspirations of the tra-ditional artisanate—were strongly progressive and market conforming. The result was legislation that was specifically designed "to encourage and force handicraft producers to embrace the market, not [as the law's name sug-gests and as commonly asserted] to protect them from it" (ibid., 315).[5]

The 1897 law created a network of handicraft chambers (*Handwerkskam-mern*) endowed with extensive powers to regulate the content and quality of craft apprenticeship, including the right to administer apprenticeship ex-aminations for the purpose of certifying skills and the power to revoke the right of a firm to train apprentices if its training was not up to their stan-dards (Hoffmann 1962, 11–12; Muth 1985, 21; Abel 1963, 35–36; Schriewer 1986, 83; Winkler 1971, 164; Wolsing 1977, 400–2). To accomplish their en-hanced regulatory responsibilities, the chambers were authorized to send

5. For an analysis of the politics behind this legislation, and especially of the role played by Germany's dynamic southwestern regions in influencing its contents, see Hansen 1997, chap. 5.

representatives to artisan firms to evaluate their training arrangements, set limits on the number of apprentices they could take, and establish the required length of training (Hoffmann 1962, 12; see also Wolsing 1977, 69). The existence of a chamber system endowed with parapublic authority to certify skills and to monitor in-plant training had very profound implications for both organized labor and industry.

For labor, the most important consequence was effectively to rule out organizational strategies premised on attempts to control the supply of skills in the economy. We now know that the German labor movement was not "born" centralized, and, in fact, at the turn of the century unions hung in the balance between two more or less equally plausible alternatives—craft-based (or at least skill-based) organization versus industrial organization. Most analyses of the triumph of industrial unionism emphasize late industrialization or socialist ideology. However, one of the factors that undoubtedly discouraged skilled workers from organizing around crafts (and associated strategies based on controlling skilled labor markets) was the fact that union expansion occurred in a context in which the "space" for regulating skills was already rather decisively occupied—by the handicraft chambers. In this situation, skilled workers held on to their occupational *identities* even as they abandoned craft-based *strategies* and threw their lot in with industrial unions.[6]

In the longer run, this meant that (like in Britain) labor's strength could be premised substantially on skill, but (unlike in Britain) without skill formation itself being contested across the class divide (e.g., with unions trying to limit apprenticeship in order to control the supply of skills). Thus, when unions in Germany enter the picture in terms of skill formation (during the Weimar years in a limited way, later as full participants in the vocational education system), they frame their goals in terms of maintaining the quality rather than regulating the quantity of skills in the economy. This is what made Germany's industrial unions powerful potential *allies* of industries that were heavily dependent on skills in the pursuit of a solidaristic skill-formation regime.

For industry, the consolidation of a system for skill formation in the organized artisan sector had equally important implications. For one thing, the existence of a recognized, parapublic system for certifying skills and for monitoring apprenticeship meant that training would actually take place in these firms (see esp. Hansen 1997, 380–85). This stands in sharp contrast to other countries, such as Britain, where—in the absence of reliable mon-

6. This is a topic unto itself, and one that cannot be dealt with exhaustively here. Germany's industrial unions frequently grew by absorbing preexisting craft-based organizations, and unions like the metalworkers continued to accommodate skilled workers and their distinctive identities (see especially Domanski-Davidsohn 1981, chap. 1).

itoring capacities (and indeed, in the context of ongoing conflicts with unions over skill formation)—apprenticeship deteriorated at the turn of the century into cheap "boy labour" (Childs 1990, esp. 788–89; Knox 1980; 1986, 172–73).

German industry benefited in many ways from this system of *Handwerk*-based skill formation. Unlike in Japan (where, as we will see, apprenticeship was unregulated), German industry could rely on a relatively steady stream of certified skilled workers from the artisan sector. German industry's dependence on *Handwerk*-based skills was virtually absolute until at least the 1880s (von Behr 1981, 44–45; Tollkühn 1926, 4–5), and diminished only very slowly in subsequent decades.[7]

Handwerk firms provided a crucial collective good but they too benefited since apprentices acquired their skills while they worked, and artisan firms depended heavily on apprentices as a source of cheap productive labor (Muth 1985, 18; Tollkühn 1926, 9–12; Volkov 1978, 73).[8] Traditionally, firms received a fee from the apprentice; and although industry began paying its apprentices around the turn of the century, as late as 1927 seven percent of *Handwerk* apprentices still received no wage at all (Schütte 1992, 137). Because of an apprentice's contribution to production in *Handwerk* firms, and because the training itself could be accomplished during lulls in production, *Handwerk* firms could generally recoup their investment in apprentice training.[9] Moreover, they may also have been perfectly happy to see their freshly trained apprentices disappear (as journeymen) into large industrial firms; better this than that they set up shop independently and in more direct competition with their erstwhile masters.

Virtually the only complaints against this system before the turn of the century came from Germany's large machine firms—companies such as Maschinenfabrik Augsburg-Nürnberg (M.A.N.), Ludwig Loewe and Com-

---

7. In 1907, 46.5 percent of all youth in training were still in the smallest artisan workshops (up to five workers) (Muth 1985, 36). As late as 1925, training in industry was still concentrated in the small-firm sector; a national business census in that year showed that 55 percent of all apprentices were being trained in *Handwerk* firms as against 45 percent in industry (Schütte 1992, 65). In fact, to this day, *Handwerk* is still a major training sector (see Wagner 1997, 23).

8. Tollkühn (1926) provides evidence pointing to widespread exploitation of apprentices in the late nineteenth century, a problem to which the law of 1897—with its provisions against such practices—was one response.

9. Figures on the net costs of training for the period under analysis are not available. However, a recent study shows that even today (when apprenticeship wages are negotiated by unions) the net costs of taking apprentices (gross cost of training minus productive output of the trainee) is much smaller for *Handwerk* firms (where training takes place in the context of production) than for industrial firms (where training is more likely to take place in workshops). Moreover, the net variable cost (variable cost minus fixed costs) was in fact negative for 30 percent of the *Handwerk* firms in the study, which is to say that apprentices' contribution to production outweighed the cost of training them (Wagner 1997, 9–11).

pany, Borsig, and Koenig and Bauer. Like everyone else, these firms benefited from the skills generated by the artisan sector; indeed, they drew on
this source for most of their skill needs well into the twentieth century.
However, beginning in the 1890s, these large firms began to complain that
they were pushing up against the limits of the skills provided by the *Handwerk* sector. First, *Handwerk* could not produce skilled workers fast enough
to keep pace with the needs of this industry, which was expanding expo-
nentially at the turn of the century and around 1900 surged to first place as
the single biggest employer of post-school-age males.[10] Second, these large
firms complained that workers trained in the artisan sector did not arrive
in the factory fully competent in the new technologies that were being introduced at an accelerated pace in this period (von Behr 1981, 60–61;
Muth 1985, 30; Tollkühn 1926, 14–16).

Strategies of the Metalworking Sector: The Importance of Certification

Responding to the perceived inadequacies of craft training, large machine firms embarked on segmentalist policies that were not so different
from those of their Japanese counterparts: internalizing skill formation
and incorporating training into complementary plant-based social policies
and internal labor markets. In contrast to the traditional "Meisterlehre"
model (on-the-job training by working alongside a master craftsman), these
firms sought to "rationalize" training by instituting firm-based apprenticeship workshops where apprentices would be trained in somewhat larger
groups and, initially at least, separate from the production process (see von
Behr 1981 for case studies; also Eichberg 1965). M.A.N. established its
training workshop in the 1890s, a move that was accompanied by a steep increase in the number of apprentices at the firm. Siemens and other large
firms in the machine and electro-mechanical industries followed suit
around the same time (von Behr 1981, 41, 69–167).

As in Japan, plant-based training programs in these companies were
linked to other measures designed to retain and co-opt their workers. Heidrun Homburg's studies show that employer-dominated company unions
were established in key machine firms including Siemens, Eckert, Loewe,
and M.A.N., all of which were also leaders in plant-based training (Homburg 1982, 226–28). Plant-based social policies were meant to build a stable
core of skilled workers; companies such as M.A.N. provided worker housing, established firm-based sickness insurance, improved working conditions, and also pursued a policy of recruiting apprentices from among the

---

10. Together with metal processing, the machine industry accounted for almost 40 percent of employment of 14–16 year-old-factory workers by 1912 (Linton 1991, 28).

families of current workers (von Behr 1981, 93–94; Rupieper 1982, 85). As Anton von Rieppel, the head of M.A.N., put it, in-house training created a "connection between the workers and the plant management . . . so that the workers did not want to leave" (quoted in Ebert 1984, 221; see also 166).

However, these firms were hobbled by their inability to *certify* the skills their training conferred.[11] After 1897 the only way to become certified as a "skilled worker" in Germany was through the *Handwerk* chambers. There existed no similar authority or officially recognized framework to certify *industrial* training, and this created special problems for those firms (mostly in the machine industry) that were engaged in training. First, the lack of a regulatory framework for certifying skills increased the costs of training to these firms by exposing them to poaching by other firms. In *Handwerk*, apprentices had to stay on long enough at least to earn their certificate, but no such incentives existed in industry. Since the big machine companies were really the only industrial firms engaged in systematic industrial training, they were especially vulnerable to poaching by other firms. And because their training programs were more expensive to begin with (accomplished in workshops, where—unlike in *Handwerk*—apprentices were not contributing to production), they were especially interested in finding a solution to these problems. The *Handwerk* model of regulation and certification provided just such a solution, but again, this model only covered training in the handicraft sector (Hansen 1997, 283, 511).

Second, industrial firms were at a disadvantage in recruiting the most ambitious and desirable apprentices because they could not offer their trainees the same kind of certification that *Handwerk* firms could. Despite the much higher quality of training provided by large industrial firms—apprentices (but especially their parents) frequently preferred a *Handwerk* apprenticeship, because certification itself held value, opening up avenues that uncertified industrial training did not. Certification was a prerequisite for advancement in certain public-sector occupations (Hoffmann 1962, 46); it was also necessary for attaining independent master status (which in turn conferred the right to take on apprentices). More generally, *Handwerk*-trained craftsmen—with certificates in hand—could easily move into industrial work, but the reverse was not true, as industry-based training was not recognized in the artisan sector. In short, large machine firms such as M.A.N. and Loewe could offer prospective apprentices all manner of privileges and benefits, but what they could not do was confer the status and rights that accompanied skill certification through the *Handwerk* chambers (Hansen 1997, 512; Schütte 1992, 84).

Contemporary accounts make it very clear that these firms understood

11. See especially Hansen 1997, 380–91, on the importance of certification.

the advantages of testing and certification, and perceived their inability to certify skills as a great disadvantage (see, for example, DATSCH 1919, 5, 7; *Technische Erziehung*, November 1926, 1; Gesamtverband Deutscher Metallindustrieller 1934, 18–19). And for precisely the reasons elaborated above, firms such as M.A.N. and Siemens made arrangements with their local craft chambers to examine and certify their apprentices (Hansen 1997, 273–74). Such ad hoc arrangements, however, were not always stable, and indeed they frequently led to conflicts, for example, over the composition of the examination boards and the types of skills to be tested (see, for example, Fürer 1927, 30–36; and Botsch 1933, 7–8).

As a consequence, and in stark contrast to Japan, modern industrial firms that depended heavily on skills did not retreat into the splendid isolation of segmentalism and internal labor markets. Instead, they organized among themselves to demand the creation of a *parallel* system for industrial training under the collective control of the industry and trade chambers (and endowed with powers equal to those of the handicraft chambers). Thus, in 1908, Germany's large machine firms took the lead in founding the German Committee for Technical Education (Deutscher Ausschuß für Technisches Schulwesen, or DATSCH), whose goal was to "heighten interest in the promotion of a well-educated, skilled labor force" (Tollkühn 1926, 38–39; Abel 1963, 41; also DATSCH 1910, 2–5 on the founding of the organization).

The precipitating factors that pushed these firms toward a more coordinated approach to skill formation were widespread skill shortages in 1907 and 1908, but the backdrop to the machine industry's initiatives was tensions between *Handwerk* and industry over apprenticeship training and certification, tensions that the 1897 law and subsequent events had, if anything, exacerbated. For example, artisans had long sought legislation that would require a master's examination of anyone engaged in training, in industry as well as *Handwerk*, and in small and large firms alike (Volkov 1978, 143). In addition, the handicraft chambers had demanded that all firms that used artisan-trained apprentices also be required to make contributions to maintaining the *Handwerk* chambers (Muth 1985, 35–36; Schütte 1992, 20).

Firms like M.A.N. found it preposterous that their own training—more systematic by far than that of the *Handwerk* sector—was not recognized and that they were being asked to contribute to *Handwerk*'s inferior training to boot. Already in 1902, the association of Berlin Metal Industrialists had sought, unsuccessfully, official recognition and certification for industrial apprenticeship in Berlin and accreditation for the training workshops of that city's premier industrial training firms—AEG, Borsig, Loewe, and others (Hansen 1997, 510–11). Early publications by DATSCH denounced *Handwerk*'s demands for an industry contribution, pointed out that *Hand-*

werk training was in fact inadequate to the needs of industry, and documented industry's increasing self-reliance when it came to training (see for example, the contribution by von Rieppel in DATSCH 1912, 1–10).

Political Coalitions and the Evolution of the System

The machine industry's calls for reform fell on deaf ears among other segments of industry, however.[12] In particular, heavy industry relied more on semiskilled labor, and firms in these sectors—frequently huge, integrated producers that dominated the regional economy—were better able to sustain segmentalist strategies with regard to skill (Herrigel 1996, chap. 3). Heavy industry occupied a very strong position in the Congress of German Industry and Commerce (Deutscher Industrie und Handelstag, or DIHT). So, in 1911 and 1914 when—at DATSCH's urging—the Social Policy Commission of the DIHT took up the issue of industrial training, the response was lukewarm. The commission concluded that "opinions within industry are still so far apart on the advisability of separate examinations for apprentices . . . in industry, that the DIHT cannot yet take a position on the issue" (Hoffmann 1962, 43). This was the kiss of death, because the local Chambers of Commerce were the ones who would have been administering apprenticeship certification for industry in the machine industry's plan (Hansen 1997, 588).

The machine industry did not give up its cause, however, and the early years of the Weimar Republic provided an important political opening. The reform of apprenticeship training was very much on the agenda in this period, a consequence of skill shortages due to war casualties and the deterioration of *Handwerk* apprenticeship during the war. The Social Democratic government was extremely receptive to the idea of reform, and initially an agreement between industry and labor on this issue appeared within reach. The corporatist (labor-business) "alliance" that was formed just after the war (*Zentralarbeitsgemeinschaft*, or ZAG; Central Working Group), took up the issue of vocational education reform, and by 1921 its social policy committee had produced a set of guidelines for future anticipated legislation in this area. The direction of these proposals was to create a uniform framework for the regulation of training (i.e., covering both industry and *Handwerk*).[13] What unions would have gotten out of this was equal representation on the oversight boards, in exchange for which they

12. The authors are grateful to Hal Hansen for emphasizing the importance of this to us.
13. The guidelines called for the creation of oversight committees composed of equal numbers of representatives of employers and workers and endowed with the power to regulate firm-based training (including granting and revoking training privileges) as well as to oversee and administer the examination and certification process for skilled industrial workers.

were prepared to define the apprenticeship contract as involving an educational rather than an employment relationship (and therefore not a subject for collective bargaining). Industry, for its part, would have achieved the independent certification authority that at least some industries had long sought (Ebert 1984, 276; Vereinigung der Deutschen Arbeitgeberverbände, *Geschäftsbericht* 1922, 142–43).

Although reforms along these lines did not materialize in the Weimar years, a good deal of the foundation on which Germany's future system of industrial training would ultimately be built was constructed during this period. Simplifying greatly, we might characterize the politics of skills during the Weimar Republic in terms of the early failure of a coalition for the reform of apprenticeship training (including separate industrial certification and with union participation) premised on a core alliance between the machine industry and newly incorporated unions (and with the support of key ministries),[14] and the growing strength of an alternative coalition in defense of employer self-regulation and *against* union participation (with heavy industry and the *Handwerk* sector at the center).

The most important new voice in the debate on apprenticeship training in the post-World-War-I period was that of Germany's newly incorporated unions. Already in 1919 the unions called for reforms that involved stripping the artisan sector of its monopoly and introducing a more democratic structure, including full union participation in overseeing and administering plant-based skill formation.[15] As Heinrich Abel (1963, 48) notes, what is most interesting here is that German unions had no trouble with the idea of firm-based training; in fact they called for more firms to do more of it. This stands in contrast to the position of socialist unions in other countries, such as Sweden, who preferred school-based vocational education and were skeptical of firm-based training as inherently biased toward employer interests.

The machine industry was labor's natural ally on the employer side when it came to reforming apprenticeship. As we have seen, large firms in the machine industry had their own reasons for wanting to break the artisan chambers' monopoly on skill certification. In 1918, DATSCH (under the leadership of the director of M.A.N., G. Lippart) had set out an eight-point reform program "to overcome *Handwerk*'s hegemony" in this area through targeted cooperation with the unions (Schütte 1992, 29). Although *Handwerk* actively opposed the ZAG guidelines for apprenticeship reform out-

---

14. Although there were differences of opinion regarding the scope of reforms and the precise institutional arrangements that should prevail. See, for example, DATSCH 1920, 7–34.

15. These proposals, though not uncontroversial, carried the day at the 1919 congress of the central trade union confederation in Nuremberg (see Hoffmann 1962, 95–97; also Schütte 1992, 31–33).

lined above, and other segments of industry ranged from indifferent to hostile, some DATSCH members endorsed the proposals as a "worthwhile framework" for legislation. The willingness of some firms in the metalworking industry to collaborate across the class divide was also evident on a regional level. In Chemnitz, for example, the regional employers' association and the local union reached an agreement in 1919 on the regulation of apprenticeship (DATSCH 1921; Ebert 1984, 270, 276; Muth 1985, 448).

The trade association for the machine building industry (VDMA) was at the forefront of reform efforts in the early Weimar years (Schütte 1992, 28). Once dominated by the large machine firms, the VDMA drew in increasing numbers of smaller producers, the so-called *industrielle Mittelstand*, in the early postwar years. In fact, by 1923 the VDMA had organized fully 90 percent of all machine construction firms in Germany (Feldman and Nocken 1975, 422). The changing composition of the VDMA advanced the cause of solidarism, for these small metalworking firms had already developed the capacity for coordination, in some cases by virtue of their participation in regional production networks (Herrigel 1996, chap. 2), but also because union strength within such firms had encouraged relatively stable collective bargaining (and thus wage coordination) in this sector. In the 1920s, these firms found themselves in intensified competition with *Handwerk* over youth apprenticeship. Lacking the resources that would have been needed to internalize skill formation, these firms had a strong interest in a collective solution to skill formation that would both increase industrial training and render it more systematic and uniform.

The 1920s in fact mark the high point of DATSCH's most intensive efforts at developing a framework for standardized, uniform training in industry (Muth 1985, 348–52). DATSCH's pioneering efforts to systematize and rationalize industry-based training earned it considerable prestige and established the organization as a widely recognized authority in this area. In the 1920s, DATSCH produced a standardized inventory of skilled trades for the metalworking industries (including a number of new, specifically industrial trades), with profiles of the content of skills required for each. The organization also generated and disseminated standardized training materials, including very detailed training courses (*Lehrgänge*) for the various trades, beginning with the most common—machine builders, fitters, toolmakers, patternmakers, molders, smiths, and precision mechanics.

Although much progress was made on a voluntary basis (supported by exhortations but not sanctions by trade associations such as VDMA, and in some cases apparently by a degree of union regulation through collective bargaining), separate and reliable certification for industrial apprenticeship and firmly institutionalized union rights in this area remained distant goals. In this, the continuing opposition of the Chambers of Commerce and important segments of industry were decisive. Although the Ministry of Trade favored reforms for unifying training, heavy industry grew even less accommodating during the Weimar years. Of course, the leading firms had supported some accommodation with labor early on, but by the late 1920s many reverted to their previous paternalistic-authoritarian *Herr-im-Hause* stance, at which point they also began espousing a segmentalist alternative to DATSCH's solidaristic approach to skills. Thus, in 1925 a number of Ruhr industrialists founded the Deutsches Institut für Technische Arbeitsschulung (German Institute for Technical Training), which was devoted to the cultivation of a special kind of worker—trained by and for individual firms and instilled with deep loyalty to the company (see especially Nolan 1994, chap. 9).

Handwerk, for its part, opposed all reforms from the start, both to preserve its monopoly on skill certification and to keep unions out of the picture. *Handwerk*'s opposition to the reforms that were being proposed goes back to the heavy reliance of artisan firms on the productive labor of apprentices (see Nolan 1994; Abel 1963, 45; Hansen 1997). Without a monopoly on certification, these firms would have a very hard time competing with industry (which offered higher wages and—often—better training). But the biggest threat to *Handwerk* was labor, since union participation in regulating apprenticeship would undermine *Handwerk*'s ability to use apprentices as a source of cheap labor.[16]

Events in the late 1920s promoted more intense interindustry coordination on skills, even as they completely undermined any possibility of reform based on union participation. Key government ministries seemed willing to sponsor legislation to reform apprenticeship training, but the political and economic context had shifted considerably. Unions by this time were on the defensive, and in the economic turbulence that followed the hyperinflation of the early 1920s, arbitration was increasingly filling in where free collective bargaining failed. Thus not only was organized labor much weaker, but also those sectors that once had been most willing to contemplate some form of joint (union-employer) regulation balked, as it increasingly looked as if "union regulation" in the end meant "state regulation," which was the one thing that all segments of German business—for all their differences—could agree to try to avoid (Feldman 1970). Combined with the continuing opposition of *Handwerk* and growing antiunionism among big business as a whole, this constellation formed the basis of a coalition against reform, or more specifically, in support of employer-dominated

16. Despite union efforts (mostly through attempts to have collective bargains declared "generally applicable"), *Handwerk* managed through most of the Weimar period to shield itself from union influence in this area. Thus, one study covering over 3,000 collective bargains from 1922–23 revealed that while the union was able to conclude contracts that dealt with apprenticeship matters covering 37 percent of all industrial apprentices, it could only influence conditions for 3 percent of *Handwerk* apprentices (Schütte 1992, 131).

"self-regulation" premised on voluntarism and a commitment to greater co-operation between *Handwerk* and industry (see especially Ebert 1984, 318–20; also Hoffmann 1962, 101; Schütte 1992, 84–87).

In the end, the certification that the machine industry had long sought was finally granted by the National Socialists, who presided over a massive increase in vocational education and also the inauguration of a standardized system for industrial training, with Industry and Trade Chambers—with prerogatives now comparable to the handicraft chambers—in charge of the administration and certification of training of skilled industrial workers (*Facharbeiter*). Based on the state's interests in standardized skills (to allocate labor flexibly as necessary for the war effort), the state converted DATSCH into the Imperial Institute for Vocational Training and explicitly charged it with creating a unified system of skill profiles and training, not just for skilled but also for semiskilled occupations (Wolsing 1977, 278–79). The state obligated firms to adopt and employ DATSCH guidelines and methods, thus ensuring that they would be diffused widely throughout the economy (Abel 1963, 59). In sum, the National Socialists implemented a system for apprenticeship training in industry that was explicitly patterned after the *Handwerk* model of plant-based training and that substantially incorporated and applied the technical/organizational innovations that had been developed on a voluntary basis by industry, and above all, as we have seen, the machine industry.

The final piece of the puzzle, full labor participation in the administration and oversight of in-plant training, was achieved only much later, in the post-World-War-II period. But here again, important developments were strongly foreshadowed in the Weimar years. Thus, for example, the demands of German unions after 1945 (with respect to apprenticeship training) were virtually the same as those they had made after World War I: not a dismantling of in-firm training, nor even of the core principle of industrial "self-regulation," but rather an equal role with employers in administering and overseeing training. The accomplishments of the subsequent periods in fact represent a return to many of the important elements of the proposals of the early Weimar years.

The Evolution of Skill Formation in Japan

In Germany, as we have seen, the legislation that became the cornerstone of the German system of skill formation—the Handicraft Protection Law of 1897—was constructed around indigenous institutions and models. In passing this law, the state embraced a policy that nurtured existing artisan organizations as a political bulwark against the radical labor movement, while at the same time transforming them into a stable source of skills for emerging industry. In Japan, both the labor movement and the artisan sector were less organized in the early industrial period. The political motives that inspired government policy in Germany toward the artisan sector were absent and, if anything, the Japanese government saw the guilds as impediments to industrial development. Traditional artisans remained important actors in the skill formation regime that emerged, but the very different interaction between the state, artisans, industry, and labor pushed Japan toward a segmentalist rather than solidaristic approach to skill formation.

As in Germany, state policy played a key role in determining the trajectory that the skill formation regime would take. However, the character of government policy in this area was quite different from that in Germany. In Japan, the artisanate was less organized, and the more progressive (southwestern) model on which German policymakers were able to build was completely absent. Thus, after the Meiji Restoration of 1868, the Japanese government—believing that destroying various feudal institutions was necessary for Japan's industrial development and eager to abolish all previous barriers to labor mobility—embarked on a broad liberalization policy that undermined the traditional privileges of the artisan sector (Sumiya 1955, 33–36). Traditional craftsmen continued to take apprentices, but unlike in Germany, apprenticeship training was largely unregulated.[17]

In addition, the government itself took an active role in supporting skill development in the early industrial period. In comparison with Germany, the gap in Meiji Japan between the skill levels that existed in the endogenous artisan sectors and those required in emerging metal industries was much wider. The traditional sector was not able to provide the skills needed for the emerging metal industry, and the dearth of skilled labor was a greater problem for industry. The Meiji government took a direct hand in redressing skill shortages by sending students to foreign countries to study industrial technology and by employing foreign engineers and craftsmen in government-owned factories as a means of raising the skill level among Japanese officials and workers. The state firms thus were meant to become a source of skills that could be diffused throughout the economy. Traditional artisans fit into this picture as intermediaries; they were expected to learn the skills necessary for the metalworking industries and gradually to take over the role played by the foreign craftsmen.

The Yokosuka Shipyard is an example (Yokosuka Kaigun Kōshō 1983, vol. 1, 6). When it was constructed in 1865 by the Tokugawa shogunate, the

---

17. Although the government issued a decree to regulate apprenticeship in 1872, it simply declared that only master craftsmen could take apprentices for a maximum seven-year term and prohibited human traffic. In some traditional industries, such as brewing and construction, the artisan organizations still played an important role in skill formation, but they did not have any legal privileges.

shipyard employed forty-five French engineers and craftsmen, and over the next twenty years the number decreased to almost zero, as the skills and technology were acquired by Japanese engineers and workers (Saegusa et al. 1960, 61). The core artisans and regular workers employed at the shipyard were recruited mainly from the pool of traditional craftsmen.

Private-sector employers could draw on government-run firms as a source of skills, but in the early industrial period most private firms were likely to rely on traditional apprenticeship based on "continuous skill" teaching (i.e., adapting traditional skills to new tasks) (cf. Sawai 1996, 302; A. Suzuki 1992). In this pattern, skilled craftsmen—either from the traditional artisan sector or from government firms—came to work in the factory, bringing their journeymen. They worked as a unit and, in addition to his contribution to production, the master craftsman (*oyakata*) was in charge of training his journeymen.

The government sector—as the most technologically advanced in Japan—depended more on "modern" skills, and state firms pioneered the establishment of factory-based technical schools that included in-class instruction. These schools were not themselves intended to train ordinary workers; rather, the graduates of the technical schools were meant to preside over on-the-job training of others, in effect playing a similar role to the *oyakata* in training these workers.[18]

Government factories that invested in this kind of training also frequently introduced policies designed to retain a core group of skilled craftsmen who could preside over the training of others. Thus, already in 1868, management at the Yokosuka Shipyard granted sixty-five core artisans (*kakae shokkō*) "life-time" employment privileges.[19] By 1873, the shipyard had introduced several further inducements to retain key skilled craftsmen. In that year, the shipyard selected 110 skilled craftsmen for "salaried" status, which guaranteed these workers a fixed monthly salary even if they were absent due to sickness. The company also added a retirement bonus to keep skilled craftsmen on the job (Hazama 1964, 421).

In both the private and the public sectors, training was based on the traditional *oyakata-kokata* (master-apprentice) relationship (Sumiya 1970, vol. 1, 100), and *oyakata* craft masters came to play an important role and to exert wide discretion on the shop floor (Gordon 1985, 38–45). In the case of private firms, companies often delegated extensive managerial functions (e.g., hiring, firing, evaluation) to the *oyakata*. Some firms even subcontracted work

18. Again, the Yokosuka Shipyard is a good example. The shipyard had two schools, one for engineers and one for technicians. In 1883, the number of students admitted to these two schools was 37 and about 50, respectively, as against a total of 1,505 employees (in 1887) in the factory as a whole (Sumiya 1970, vol. 1, 17).

19. At this time, the Yokosuka Shipyard employed 113 regular workers (*jōyatoi*), 397 helpers, and 54 common laborers (Hazama 1964, 403; Taira 1978, 176).

to the master craftsmen, who each led a team of workers—a practice that had the advantage of spreading risk in the context of very unstable markets.[20] In general, private companies lacked the extensive training resources of the government sector, and thus preferred to rely on master craftsmen as suppliers of skilled labor (themselves skilled but also responsible for apprentice training).

In the public sector as well, the *oyakata* craft masters were very powerful. Here the *oyakata*'s power derived less from the structure of production and more from the feudal organization of companies in this period. In most government factories, ex-samurai (warrior class in the feudal status system) assumed management positions. Given their own lack of managerial skills, and in light of the cultural and behavioral gap that separated them from the traditional artisans and ordinary laborers who worked for them, these samurai-managers delegated important managerial powers to the *oyakata*.

Strategies of the Metalworking Industry: The Problem of Labor Mobility

The *oyakata* system fulfilled the minimum need to provide skilled labor in the metal industry in the early industrial period. Although this system was premised on plant-based training, the practice in and of itself did not produce stable segmentalism, at least in the sense of stable internal labor markets. In fact, labor mobility was very high. Since an *oyakata* master regulated the supply of labor—managing craftsmen by controlling well-paid jobs and assigning the jobs to members of his group—there were some incentives for craftsmen to stay with the *oyakata*. But there were no formal controls, and, in fact, an *oyakata*'s workers could and did leave the factory at their own will (Ministry of Agriculture and Commerce 1903, vol. 2, 10).

If anything, and in light of prevailing severe shortages of skilled labor, the *oyakata* system of training may itself have promoted labor mobility. This system of skill formation, though plant-based, in fact produced rather portable (because still quite general) skills. In the early industrial period, this was not perceived as a problem but as an asset for industry. Apprentices trained in one factory could easily move to another, and changing jobs helped workers to develop their skills by experiencing various types of work (Sumiya 1970, vol. 1, 162–67). The *oyakata* were themselves important intermediaries, helping craftsmen who became redundant in one factory to find jobs elsewhere (Yamamoto 1994, 167–68).

---

20. However, it is not certain to what extent this indirect management system prevailed in a pure form in the machine and metal industries. Even craftsmen who belonged to an *oyakata* had formal employment relations with the factory. Therefore, when *oyakata* could not complete the subcontracted work within the budget assigned, individual workers could demand their normal wages from the factory management (Ministry of Agriculture and Commerce 1903, vol. 3, 271). In this sense, the employment relationship was not as indirect.

Although the resulting labor mobility accommodated fluctuating demand in the metal industries in the closing decades of the nineteenth century, over time it created a number of problems. Many producers complained of high turnover among apprentices as well as ordinary workers.
Unlike in Germany, Japanese apprentices had few incentives to complete
their apprenticeships (which in some parts of Japan lasted eight years!)
(Ministry of Labor 1961, 22). German apprentices had good reasons to stay
to the end of their training period in order to collect the skill certification
that was the ticket to many opportunities in the labor market. By contrast, in
Japan apprentices could abscond and take better-paying jobs once they had
learned the necessary skills. This they did in larger and larger numbers as
the demand for skills grew, making business very unstable and training extremely costly for firms.[21] This situation gradually posed a serious problem
not just for the *oyakata* craftsmen but for industry. The result was chronic
skill shortages and intense competition among firms for skilled workers.

Thus, at the same historical juncture in which machine and metalworking firms in Germany were becoming adamant about achieving rights to
certify skills, their Japanese counterparts were becoming obsessed with controlling *labor mobility*. We find in the early 1900s in Japan a number of attempts to impose restrictions on labor mobility—both through efforts at
collective self-restraint by employers to reduce poaching and through attempts to impose restrictions directly on workers themselves.[22] In some industries such as spinning, silk, and coal, the efforts of trade associations to
reduce poaching enjoyed some limited success.[23] However, these arrangements were unstable everywhere, and in the metalworking industry they
were even less successful than elsewhere.[24]

In general, such attempts foundered due to a number of problems. One

21. In 1902, the median length of employment was less than one year in private machine
companies in Aichi Prefecture (Odaka 1990, 320).

22. The attempts at collective self-restraint occurred in the context of a proliferation of
trade associations in the early twentieth century (Morita 1926, 31–33). Around the same
time, business groups also began demanding government regulation of labor mobility (Ministry of Labor 1961, 22, 36).

23. For instance, in the spinning industry, in which skilled workers are necessary but on a
seasonal basis, employers competed fiercely for skilled workers, resulting in high labor costs.
As a solution, the employers organized their local trade association (*kōjō dōmei*) and introduced a worker-registration system. In this system, once a worker was hired by one employer,
other employers could not hire that worker (Morita 1926, 107–14). In this industry, the cartel practice worked well in some regions. In the silk industry, the national confederation of
Silk Associations announced in 1920 that workers who were hired by a particular employer
in that year were reserved for the same employer in 1921. A similar practice could be found
in the coal-mining industry in Hokkaido in the 1920s. However, even in these successful
cases, the practice broke down from time to time (see, e.g., *Jiji shinpo*, 22 March 1926).

24. In the Tokyo area, the Tōkyō Kikai Tekkō Dōgyō Kumiai (Association of Machine and
Iron Works) was organized and tried to control labor mobility, but it did not work as well as
in other sectors (Tekkō Kikai Kyōkai 1974).

was the resistance of the state, which—though more supportive of cartel practices for regulating *product* markets—looked less favorably on restrictions on *labor* market mobility (such as cartelized wage capping and restrictions on the ability of craftsmen to change jobs) (see, e.g., the Decree of the Vice Minister of Agriculture and Commerce, 29 June 1916, cited in Morita 1926, 115). But collective self-restraint also failed because of conflicts of interest among firms themselves. Although the traditional sectors wanted greater labor-market regulation, emerging industries wanted more "liberated" labor (Furusho 1969). In addition, within the metal industry, private companies were less eager to introduce such regulation because they continued to recruit skilled workers from the government-run factories, a practice that—as we have seen—had the blessing of the government (Yamamura 1977). In 1904, when naval arsenals established a voluntary rule that no arsenals should hire craftsmen who quit their jobs at another arsenal, the private sector stayed out of the arrangement, not least because private companies relied rather heavily on poaching from the government-owned factories as a source of skilled labor (Hazama 1964, 454–55).

Finally, it did not help matters that apprenticeship training was itself unregulated—a situation that did nothing to discourage labor mobility among trainees, which in turn contributed to shortages by making training very expensive for firms. Japanese trade associations in the late nineteenth century—historically concentrated on merchant interests and institutionally separate from traditional guild structures (Mataji Miyamoto 1938)—attacked the problem from the demand side, while the supply side of skills remained in the hands of the *oyakata* craftsmen whose traditional organizations, as noted above, had been destroyed. Attempts by employers to reduce poaching were hobbled by the lack of any collective institutional framework that would have eased their collective action problems by directly generating a steady supply of skilled labor. Thus, time and again their attempts to negotiate collective solutions to the problem of labor mobility broke down in the face of intense competition over scarce skilled workers.

This competition redounded to the benefit of *oyakata* craftsmen, whose power derived not (as in Germany) from their institutionalized privileges as an organized social and political group, but rather from the scarcity of their skills. Whereas in Germany, tensions between the artisan sector and industry were played out at the national political level, in Japan these tensions were played out at the plant level, as individual employers sought to control labor mobility and to create for themselves a more stable source of skills.

As in Germany, the rapid growth of the metal industry around the end of the nineteenth century generated demands for more and more sophisticated skills (Hazama 1964, 436).[25] The number of workers in military arse-

---

25. See also Yamamoto 1994, 188, and Inoki 1996 on the need for more differentiated and specialized skills.

nals rose from about 25,000 in 1899 to just over 75,000 by 1912. Employment in private metal factories rose from just under 21,000 to almost
70,000 in the same period. The result was even more intense competition
for skilled workers and rampant poaching, both among private companies
and, especially, with private companies recruiting workers from government-owned firms. According to a 1901 survey, in the ten major private
metalworking factories, more than 50 percent of workers had been employed for less than one year. Although firms such as the Mitsubishi Nagasaki Shipyard had attempted to achieve stability by hiring craftsmen on a
fixed term (three-year) basis, neither employers nor workers took this seriously (Hazama 1964, 452). Moreover, as private manufacturing as a whole
grew in size, it became difficult for individual companies to recruit a sufficient number of skilled workers from the government-owned firms. In addition, the modernization of production technology within the private sector came to require a larger number of workers with higher skill levels than
the traditional *oyakata* system was generating.

In this context, private firms in metalworking embraced the strategy previously pioneered in the government sector by instituting their own company-based training schools for trainee workers (*minaraiko*). The first company training school in the private sector was the Mitsubishi Kōgyō Yobi
Gakkō (Mitsubishi Preliminary School for Industry), established in 1900.
According to a survey by the Tokyo Advanced School for Industry, more
than ten large companies had established such schools by 1911. These
schools combined on-the-job training with classroom instruction. The
training term was at least three years, and any worker who completed the
training was expected to become a core skilled craftsman and to commit
himself to stay in the factory (after completing the training) for at least as
many years as the training term had been (Sumiya 1970, vol. 2, 37).

However, the more skills the workers acquired, the more likely it was that
they would be recruited by other companies, and nothing prevented these
workers from reneging on the requirement to stay in the company. Therefore, the development of intracompany training prompted management to
make parallel efforts to encourage long-term employment. Some of the
measures that figured most prominently in firm strategies in this regard
were seniority-based wages, company welfare provisions, and loyalty indoc-
trination for core skilled workers. For instance, in 1900 the management of
the private Nagasaki Shipyard introduced a system of regular workers with
long-term employment guarantees and created a temporary worker status
without secure employment. In that year, there were 5,247 regular workers
and 440 temporary workers in the shipyard; this regular worker system re-
sembled the regular craftsmen system of the government-owned Yokosuka
Shipyard. Management introduced various inducements, such as a retirement bonus, to maintain regular workers for a longer period. Labor
turnover among regular workers in the Nagasaki Shipyard was very high

until 1901, but decreased gradually thereafter, an indication that management inducements seemed to be working (Hazama 1964, 454; Odaka 1984, 208).[26] Here we can find a prototype of the management system that proliferated in postwar Japan, one of the characteristics of which is company-based skill formation and internal labor markets.

The Evolution of the Japanese Management System

As we have seen, in Germany political realignments in the 1920s were crucial in shaping the fate of vocational training in the Weimar years. There, an increasingly well-organized machine industry (by then representing a growing number of small and medium-sized firms) led efforts to collectivize and standardize vocational training in industry, even though the possibility for reform based on a cross-class coalition with labor foundered due to political and economic obstacles. Likewise in Japan, industrial and political realignments during and after World War I were decisive in the evolution of the Japanese training system. As in Germany, labor would play a supportive though not constitutive role, but unlike in Germany, the cross-class coalitions that were forged with labor in Japan were at the plant level and not the national political level. Developments in the interwar years thus pushed the Japanese training regime further along a segmentalist trajectory.

As emphasized above, Japanese firms in the early industrial period had to contend first and foremost with a high degree of workforce instability. However, the 1920s brought economic conditions that eased the problem of labor mobility considerably. As Solomon B. Levine and Hisashi Kawada (1980, 118) note, an economic downturn in the 1920s rendered skills relatively more abundant and, combined with increased urbanization and education (including more government support for vocational education), "one reasonably might have expected segmentation to break down and a more open labor market to reemerge." As the context shifted from one of labor shortage to labor surplus, Japanese employers might have abandoned in-plant training and the accompanying generous policies they had instituted to stabilize internal labor markets. But this did not happen.

One important factor in shoring up the system was the emergence following World War I of a strongly dualistic industrial structure consisting of large firms (which were *zaibatsu*-connected) on the one hand, and small and medium-sized firms on the other. Whereas in Germany, small and medium-sized machine firms were becoming more and more organized

---

26. After the company introduced the regular worker system in 1910, the mobility rate (calculated by dividing the number of hired and fired workers in a given year by the total number of workers at the end of that year) dropped substantially, from an average (between 1898 and 1909) of 115 percent to an average (between 1910 and 1913) of 57 percent.

and adapting to market changes with the aid of the dynamic VDMA, in Japan the small-firm sector was falling behind. Meanwhile, the more dynamic large firms grew rapidly in this period and underwent significant modernization premised on technology borrowed from the West (Yamamura 1986). These large firms thus became even more dependent on skills—and on highly advanced skills not easily acquired in the labor market—but at the same time, their considerable market power made it possible for them to absorb rather large fixed costs, including permanent employment, to protect their investment in training.

Another factor—pushing in the same direction—was the rise of the trade union movement. It is true that the labor movement in the prewar period was extremely weak, fragmented along ideological lines and organizing less than 10 percent of all workers. However, during the 1910s the labor movement had gradually gained some power, and since Japanese managers were not accustomed to dealing with any organized labor movement and relatively vulnerable to any labor offensive, from time to time trade unions succeeded in achieving their demands against management.

An examination of the political dynamics within these conflicts reveals interesting changes in the configuration of actors and alliances. As described above, the *oyakata* craftsmen were in charge of managing as well as training workers. Although the skill shortages in some ways enhanced their power within the plant, their skills were becoming outdated as new (imported, advanced) technology was introduced in factory production. At the same time, young skilled workers who had graduated from the company training schools began playing an important role on the shop floor. This new situation threatened the shop-floor regime which had been dominated by the traditional *oyakata* craftsmen. In some cases, union activists organized and mobilized semiskilled workers against the *oyakata* regime, and in such conflicts management frequently sided *with the union*. Gradually, in the large firms in the metal industry, the *oyakata* lost their power, and management began directly exerting managerial control (Sumiya 1970, vol. 2, 56).

In these labor conflicts, management made concessions to the union in order to incorporate newly skilled workers into the factory regime. In fact, many union demands—such as for the introduction of an annual bonus and a retirement bonus system for regular workers—had the effect of further institutionalizing internal labor markets (Gordon 1985, 163–206). These demands were met in a number of cases, including at Shibaura Manufacturing (1916), Nagasaki Shipyard (1917), and Nippon Steel Hiroshima Factory (1919) (Odaka 1995, 153). In addition, in 1919 workers at the Yahata Steel Mill (the largest mill at the time) went on strike demanding not just an improvement of working conditions but also equal treatment of regular blue-collar workers and white-collar officials. The young skilled workers also demanded that career paths for managerial positions should be open to skilled workers. These claims were met after a long labor conflict

(Sumiya 1970, vol. 2, 86). All these claims had the effect of promoting long-term employment and internal labor markets.

However, perhaps even more important than the overt conflicts were the extensive efforts by management in this period to *preempt* labor conflict—and forestall union organizing in the first place—by developing Japanese management practices (Gordon 1985, 207–35). An official of the Ministry of Interior argued that "it is critically important to establish collaborative labor-management relations within the company before class conflict appears. For that purpose, it is urgent to introduce intracompany labor-management consultation mechanisms" (Ikeda 1982, 9). In the 1920s a number of factory committees were in fact established in order to facilitate labor-management communication. This preference on the part of management for intracompany arrangements was very much consistent with management practices that had begun prevailing in the large companies in response to labor conflicts. These political dynamics played an important role in founding Japanese company-based managerial practices.

Initiatives under the Japanese government of the 1930s and 1940s pushed further in the direction of segmentalism.[27] In response to a dramatic four-fold increase in strike activity in 1937 (measured in the number of striking workers), the government instituted the Sangyō Hōkokukai (Industrial Patriotic Council, or IPC) (Okazaki 1993). The IPC consisted of management and labor and was designed to improve communication between the two, as well as provide workers with company welfare privileges as part of a war mobilization program (Saguchi 1991, 168). By the end of 1940, the coverage rate increased to 70 percent (Sakurabayashi 1985). Although the IPC fell short of its formal purpose (Garon 1987, chap. 6; Gordon 1985, 299–326), it did promote a "managerial revolution" and encouraged deep changes in Japanese corporate governance (see, e.g., Okazaki 1993). Although a full-fledged transformation of Japanese corporate governance structure, in which employees' interests have become prioritized over those of shareholders, did not occur until after the labor offensive in the post-World-War-II period (Kume 1998), we can find the roots of such a transformation in this effort (Noguchi 1995).

Conclusion

In both Germany and Japan, employers invest substantial resources in training their workers. The existence in both countries of a relatively stable

---

27. By contrast, the attempt by the military government to introduce a nationwide system of skill formation (through the so-called youth schools) failed, largely because the two goals that animated the initiative—skill formation and infantry training—were frequently in conflict and the latter very often overrode the former (Sumiya 1970, vol. 2, 272).

and enduring system of skill development distinguishes them from other political economies—such as the United States and Britain—that are characterized by much lower levels of private-sector investment in training. This chapter has sought to explain the origins of Germany's and Japan's different systems of skill formation, which—employing Peter Swenson's terms—we have characterized as a difference between "solidaristic" and "segmentalist" strategies for skill formation. We traced these divergent outcomes to differences in the relationship between the artisan sector and industry in the early industrial period, and particularly to the way in which the interaction between these two in turn influenced relations between industry and the emerging labor movement. The argument can be summarized in three steps.

First, we found that *state policy* toward the artisan sector was crucial to the subsequent development of the two systems. In Germany, the state actively organized the artisan sector and granted it monopoly rights to certify skills, but in Japan state policy did nothing to regulate traditional apprenticeship training. This difference had a profound impact on the quality and supply of skills available to industry in the two countries. Hal Hansen has analyzed the problems that plague traditional apprenticeship everywhere: while masters are tempted to underinvest in training and to exploit apprentices as a source of cheap labor, apprentices are tempted to abscond with their skills before masters have been able to recoup their investment in the apprentice's training (Hansen 1997, 277–82). As Hansen has argued, skill certification through the *Handwerk* chambers in Germany ameliorated these problems, since masters had to train their apprentices well (or else lose their training privileges and, with those, the contribution of low-pay apprentices to production), and apprentices had to stay with the firm long enough to collect their certificates. With no similar mechanisms in place in Japan, masters could shirk their training responsibilities and apprentices could abandon their masters—and did so in large numbers. Thus the first big difference between the two cases is the overall supply of skills available to industry and the fate of the artisanate. Simplifying greatly, Japanese managers faced more severe and chronic shortages of skilled labor and became obsessed with *controlling labor mobility*, while in Germany the large firms most dependent on skill became obsessed with *securing the right to certify skills*, a right that the *Handwerk* sector monopolized and that large industrial firms coveted.

This, in turn, had important consequences for the *political relationship* between the artisanate and industry. In both countries, the emerging metal industries tapped into the traditional artisanate to cover their skill needs, and in both cases frictions and tensions emerged as a result. The difference lay in the level at which such tensions (between the artisanate and skill-dependent industries) were played out—at the plant level in Japan, at the national-political level in Germany. In Japan, where the *oyakata* craftsmen were not organized, emerging large firms could address their skill needs by contracting with individual *oyakata* to both recruit and train skilled workers. This strategy solved some problems but it also created others, as independent and mobile *oyakata* could use competition *among* industrial firms over scarce skilled labor to enhance their own power *within* the firm. After repeated attempts on the part of industry to find a solution through "collective self control" failed, private firms followed the lead of public-sector firms that had internalized skill formation, setting Japanese firms on a very different trajectory favoring plant-based training.[28]

In Germany, by contrast, industry drew heavily on *Handwerk*-generated skills in the early industrial period, but the artisanate there was well organized and thus could not be absorbed and subordinated to industry in the same way. Here, tensions between the artisanate and industry (more specifically, the machine industry) were played out at the national-political rather than the plant level. The large industrial firms that relied most heavily on skills organized among themselves to contest the *Handwerk* sector's monopoly on skill certification, creating institutions (such as DATSCH) that would lead the way in charting a more solidaristic approach to skill formation in industry.

However, it is important to note that the actual *skills* possessed by skilled workers in Japan and Germany after the turn of the century were probably not so different. In Japan, training was plant-based and internal to large firms, but high levels of labor mobility suggest that the skills themselves were very portable. Conversely, in Germany, the existence of skill certificates should not imply that skills were particularly standardized—that development came only later, in the machine and metalworking industries in the 1920s and other industries in the 1930s and 1940s under the National Socialists.

Finally, then, the *consolidation* of segmentalist and solidaristic strategies has to be understood in terms of the way in which these previous developments mediated *industry's relationship with the emerging labor unions*. In both cases, alignments and realignments among the artisanate, industry, and unions in the 1920s appear to be crucial. In both countries, economic trends in the early 1920s called the existing system into question, and critical realignments (in Japan between the managers of large industrial firms and emerging labor unions at the plant level; in Germany between some segments of industry and labor unions at the industry level) reinforced previous trajectories.

---

28. In addition, in Germany, the ongoing modernization of "traditional" skills was built into the market-conforming character of the 1897 law, which, as pointed out above, facilitated *Handwerk*'s adaptation to the market (including technological change). This was quite different from Japan, where if traditional skills were upgraded at all, it was in the context of the internal labor markets of the industrial sector.

In Japan, segmentalist strategies before World War I were a response to intense skilled labor shortages, and so the slack labor markets of the 1920s might have undermined the strong internal labor markets that had been developing. What prevented this was the growing complexity of firms' skill needs combined with the increasing threat of trade union influence at the plant level, which produced a critical realignment (management with union against the *oyakata*) that consolidated and deepened segmentalism. In Germany, where skills were more plentiful before World War I, the crisis of the 1920s was different and stemmed from *Handwerk*'s own economic crisis, which severely tested *Handwerk*'s capacity for "collective self-regulation" and sparked concerns about impending skill shortages. Newly incorporated labor unions emerged as potential allies for industry against the *Handwerk* monopoly and in support of a solidaristic system of skill formation for industry. In both cases, in other words, there was a critical realignment that brought segments of industry into alliance with labor and against the artisanate, with the difference that in Japan this occurred at the plant level and in Germany at the industry level.

In each case, labor was not the driving force toward more segmentalist versus more solidaristic skill development, but unions formulated their goals within the different logics of the two systems, and in so doing helped to push developments further along these divergent tracks. In Japan, for example, unions defined their goals within the context of strong internal labor markets in ways that helped to consolidate segmentalism and indeed to drive skill formation down an increasingly organization-specific path. Similarly, in Germany, the fact that unions "grew up" in a context in which skill formation was already regulated (by *Handwerk*) discouraged craft-based control strategies and made unions potential allies of industry in the latter's struggles for separate certification, though labor's relative weakness (especially in Germany's large-firm sector) contributed to the problems of consolidating solidarism in the Weimar years.

References

Abel, Heinrich. 1963. *Das Berufsproblem im gewerblichen Ausbildungs- und Schulwesen Deutschlands (BRD)*. Braunschweig: Georg Westermann Verlag.

Abelshauser, Werner. 1980. "Staat, Infrastruktur und interregionaler Wohlstandsausgleich im Preußen der Hochindustrialisierung." In *Staatliche Umverteilungspolitik in historischer Perspektive. Beiträge zur Entwicklung des Staatsinterventionismus in Deutschland und Österreich*, edited by Fritz Blaich, 9–58. Berlin: Duncker & Humblot.

——. 1983. *Wirtschaftsgeschichte der Bundesrepublik Deutschland 1945–1980*. Frankfurt am Main: Suhrkamp.

——. 1984. "The First Post-Liberal Nation: Stages in the Development of Modern Corporatism in Germany." *European History Quarterly* 14:285–348.

——. 1987. "Freiheitlicher Korporatismus im Kaiserreich und in der Weimarer Republik." In *Die Weimarer Republik als Wohlfahrtsstaat. Zum Verhältnis von Wirtschafts- und Sozialpolitik in der Industriegesellschaft*, edited by Werner Abelshauser, 147–70. Stuttgart: Steiner.

——. 1990. "Neuer Most in alten Schläuchen? Vorindustrielle Traditionen deutscher Wirtschaftsordnung im Vergleich mit England." In *Bevölkerung, Wirtschaft, Gesellschaft seit der Industrialisierung. Festschrift für Wolfgang Köllmann*, edited by Dietmar Petzina and Jürgen Reulecke, 117–32. Dortmund: Gesellschaft für Westfälische Wirtschaftsgeschichte.

——. 1991. "Die ordnungspolitische Epochenbedeutung der Weltwirtschaftskrise in Deutschland: Ein Beitrag zur Entstehungsgeschichte der Sozialen Marktwirtschaft." In *Ordnungspolitische Weichenstellungen nach dem Zweiten Weltkrieg*, edited by Dietmar Petzina, 11–29. Berlin: Duncker & Humblot.

——. 1999. "Vom wirtschaftlichen Wert der Mitbestimmung: Neue Perspektiven ihrer Geschichte in Deutschland." In *Mitbestimmung in Deutschland: Tradition und Effizienz*, edited by Wolfgang Streeck and Norbert Kluge, 224–38. Frankfurt am Main: Campus Verlag.

Adams, T. F. M. 1964. *A Financial History of Modern Japan*. Tokyo: RESEARCH (Japan) Ltd.

Aktiengesetz. Textausgabe des Aktiengesetzes vom 6.9.1965. 1965. Düsseldorf: Verlagsbuchhandlung des Instituts der Wirtschaftsprüfer.

Alber, Jens. 1982. *Vom Armenhaus zum Wohlfahrtsstaat: Analysen zur Entwicklung der Sozialversicherung in Westeuropa.* Frankfurt am Main: Campus Verlag.

Albert, Michel. 1991. *Capitalisme contre capitalisme.* Paris: Éditions du Seuil.

——. 1993. *Capitalism vs. Capitalism: How America's Obsession with Individual Achievement and Short-Term Profit Has Led It to the Brink of Collapse.* New York: Four Walls Eight Windows.

Allen, C. G. 1946. *A Short Economic History of Modern Japan.* London: G. Allen & Unwin Ltd.

Ambrosius, Gerold. 1977. *Die Durchsetzung der sozialen Marktwirtschaft in Westdeutschland: 1945–1949.* Stuttgart: Deutsche Verlags-Anstalt.

Anderson, Stephen J. 1990. "The Political Economy of Japanese Saving: How Postal Savings and Public Pensions Support High Rates of Household Saving in Japan." *Journal of Japanese Studies* 16 (1):61–92.

——. 1993. *Welfare Policy and Politics in Japan: Beyond the Developmental State.* New York: Paragon.

Aoki, Masahiko. 1988. *Information, Incentives, and Bargaining in the Japanese Economy.* Cambridge: Cambridge University Press.

——. 1990. "Towards an Economic Model of the Japanese Firm." *Journal of Economic Literature* 28 (1):1–27.

——. 1994. "The Japanese Firm as a System of Attributes." In *The Japanese Firm: Sources of Competitive Strength,* edited by Masahiko Aoki and Ronald Dore, 11–40. Oxford: Oxford University Press.

——. 1997. "Unintended Fit: Organizational Evolution and Government Design of Institutions in Japan." In *The Role of Government in East Asian Economic Development: Comparative Institutional Analysis,* edited by Masahiko Aoki, Hyung-Ki Kim, and Masahiro Okuno-Fujiwara, 233–53. Oxford: Clarendon Press.

——. 2001. *Towards a Comparative Institutional Analysis.* Cambridge, Mass.: MIT Press.

Aoki, Masahiko, and Hugh Patrick. 1994. *The Japanese Main Bank System: Its Relevance for Developing and Transforming Economies.* Oxford: Oxford University Press.

Atkinson, Anthony, Lee Rainwater, and Timothy Smeeding. 1995. *Income Distribution in OECD Countries.* Paris: OECD.

Avery, Robert, and Gregory Elliehausen. 1986. "Financial Characteristics of High-Income Households." *Federal Reserve Bulletin* 72 (3):163–77.

Avineri, Shlomo. 1972. *Hegel's Theory of the Modern State.* Cambridge: Cambridge University Press.

Bähr, Johannes. 1989. *Staatliche Schlichtung in der Weimarer Republik: Tarifpolitik, Korporatismus und industrieller Konflikt zwischen Inflation und Deflation, 1919–1932.* Berlin: Colloquium Verlag.

Barkai, Avraham. 1977. *Das Wirtschaftssystem des Nationalsozialismus: der historische und ideologische Hintergrund 1933–1936.* Köln: Nottbeck.

——. 1990. *Nazi Economics: Ideology, Theory, and Policy.* Oxford: Berg.

Baum, Harald, K. J. Hopt, and B. Rudolph. 1996. "Börsenreform. Eine ökonomische, rechtsvergleichende und rechtspolitische Untersuchung." Gutachten im Auftrag des Bundesministeriums der Finanzen. Hamburg: Max-Planck-Institut für ausländisches und internationales Privatrecht.

Baumgartner, Frank R., and Bryan D. Jones. 1991. "Agenda Dynamics and Policy Subsystems." *Journal of Politics* 53:1044–73.

Baums, Theodor, and Christian Fraune. 1995. "Institutionelle Anleger und Publikumsgesellschaft: eine empirische Untersuchung." *Die Aktiengesellschaft* 40:97–112.

Beasley, William Gerald. 1990. *The Rise of Modern Japan.* London: Weidenfeld and Nicolson.

Beck, Hermann. 1995. *The Origins of the Authoritarian Welfare State in Prussia: Conserva-*

tives, Bureaucracy, and the Social Question, 1815–70. Ann Arbor: University of Michigan Press.

Behr, Marhild von. 1981. *Die Entstehung der industriellen Lehrwerkstatt: Materialien und Analysen zur beruflichen Bildung im 19. Jahrhundert.* München: Campus.

Bendix, Reinhard. 1956. *Work and Authority in Industry.* Berkeley: University of California Press.

——. 1964. *Nation Building and Citizenship.* New York: John Wiley and Sons.

Berghahn, Volker R. 1986. *The Americanisation of West German Industry: 1945–1973*, ext. and rev. English version. Leamington Spa: Berg.

Berghoff, Hartmut. 1997. "Unternehmenskultur und Herrschaftstechnik. Industrieller Paternalismum: Hohner von 1871 bis 1918." *Geschichte und Gesellschaft* 23:167–204.

Bergmann, Joachim, Otto Jacobi, and Walter Müller-Jentsch. 1975. *Gewerkschaften in der Bundesrepublik: gewerkschaftliche Lohnpolitik zwischen Mitgliederinteressen und ökonomischen Systemzwängen.* Frankfurt am Main: Europäische Verlagsanstalt.

Berle, Adolf, and Gardiner Means. 1933. *The Modern Corporation and Private Property.* New York: Macmillan.

Bertelsmann Stiftung and Hans-Böckler-Stiftung, eds. 1998. *Mitbestimmung und neue Unternehmenskulturen: Bilanz und Perspektiven. Bericht der Kommission Mitbestimmung.* Gütersloh: Verlag Bertelsmann Stiftung.

Biernacki, Richard. 1995. *The Fabrication of Labor: Germany and Britain, 1640–1914.* Berkeley: University of California Press.

Bisson, T. A. 1954. *Zaibatsu Dissolution in Japan.* Berkeley: University of California Press.

Blackbourn, David, and Geoff Eley. 1984. *The Peculiarities of German History: Bourgeois Society and Politics in Nineteenth-Century Germany.* Oxford: Oxford University Press.

Blasius, Dirk, and Eckart Pankoke, eds. 1977. *Lorenz von Stein: geschichts- und gesellschaftswissenschaftliche Perspektiven.* Darmstadt: Wissenschaftliche Buchgesellschaft.

Blumenberg-Lampe, Christine. 1973. *Das wirtschaftspolitische Programm der "Freiburger Kreise": Entwurf einer freiheitlich-sozialen Nachkriegswirtschaft, Nationalökonomen gegen den Nationalsozialismus.* Berlin: Duncker & Humblot.

——, ed. 1986. *Der Weg in die soziale Marktwirtschaft: Referate, Protokolle, Gutachten der Arbeitsgemeinschaft Erwin von Beckerath 1943–1947.* Stuttgart: Klett-Cotta.

Böckenförde, Ernst-Wolfgang. 1976. "Lorenz vom Stein als Theoretiker der Bewegung von Staat und Gesellschaft zum Sozialstaat." In *Staat und Gesellschaft*, edited by Ernst-Wolfgang Böckenförde, 131–71. Darmstadt: Wissenschaftliche Buchgesellschaft.

Boelcke, Willi A. 1983. *Die deutsche Wirtschaft 1930–1945: Interna des Reichswirtschaftsministeriums.* Düsseldorf: Droste Verlag.

Böhm, Franz. 1937. *Die Ordnung der Wirtschaft als geschichtliche Aufgabe und rechtsschöpferische Leistung.* Stuttgart: Kohlhammer Verlag.

Bombach, Gottfried, Hans-Jürgen Ramser, Manfred Timmermann, and Walter Wittmann. 1976. *Der Keynesianismus. II: Die beschäftigungspolitische Diskussion vor Keynes in Deutschland: Dokumente u. Kommentare.* Berlin: Springer.

Born, Karl Erich. 1967. *Die deutsche Bankenkrise 1931. Finanzen und Politik.* München: Piper.

Botsch, R. 1933. *Lehrlingsausbildung und Gesellenprüfung in der metallverarbeitenden Industrie.* Berlin: Verlag von Julius Beltz.

Bowen, Ralph H. 1947. *German Theories of the Corporative State: With Special Reference to the Period 1870–1919.* New York: Whittlesey House.

Boyer, Robert. 1995. "Wage Austerity and/or an Educational Push: The French Dilemma." *Labour* (special issue):S19–S65.

Brackmann, Michael. 1993. *Vom totalen Krieg zum Wirtschaftswunder: die Vorgeschichte der westdeutschen Währungsreform 1948.* Essen: Klartext Verlag.

Brandes, Stuart D. 1976. *American Welfare Capitalism, 1880–1940*. Chicago: University of Chicago Press.

Braun, S., W. Eberwein, and J. Tholen. 1992. *Belegschaft und Unternehmen. Zur Geschichte und Soziologie der deutschen Betriebsverfassung und Belegschaftsmitbestimmung.* Frankfurt am Main: Campus Verlag.

Brauneder, Wilhelm, and Kaname Nishiyama, eds. 1992. *Lorenz von Steins "Bemerkungen über Verfassung und Verwaltung" von 1889 zu den Verfassungsarbeiten in Japan.* Frankfurt am Main: Peter Lang.

Brinton, Mary C. 1994. *Women and the Economic Miracle: Gender and Work in Postwar Japan.* Berkeley: University of California Press.

Brockstedt, Jürgen. 1984. "Family Enterprise and the Rise of Large-Scale Enterprise in Germany, 1871–1914—Ownership and Management." In *Family Business in the Era of Industrial Growth. Its Ownership and Management. Proceedings of the Fuji Conference,* edited by Akio Okochi and Shigeaki Yasuoka, 237–67. Tokyo: University of Tokyo Press.

Brose, Eric Dorn. 1993. *The Politics of Technological Change in Prussia: Out of the Shadow of Antiquity, 1809–1848.* Princeton: Princeton University Press.

Broszat, Martin. 1969. *Der Staat Hitlers: Grundlegung und Entwicklung seiner inneren Verfassung.* München: dtv.

———. 1981. *The Hitler State: The Foundation and Development of the Internal Structure of the Third Reich.* London: Longman.

Brunner, Otto. 1980. *Neue Wege der Verfassungs- und Sozialgeschichte.* Göttingen: Vandenhoeck & Ruprecht.

Burnham, James. 1942. *The Managerial Revolution, or, What is Happening in the World Now.* London: Putnam.

Büschgen, Hans E. 1983. "Zeitgeschichtliche Problemfelder des Bankenwesens der Bundesrepublik Deutschland." In *Deutsche Bankengeschichte,* edited by I. f. B. F. e.V., 349–409. Frankfurt am Main: Fritz Knapp Verlag.

Calder, Kent E. 1990. "Linking Welfare and the Developmental State: Postal Savings in Japan." *Journal of Japanese Studies* 16 (1):31–59.

———. 1993. *Strategic Capitalism: Private Business and Public Purpose in Japanese Industrial Finance.* Princeton: Princeton University Press.

Campbell, John Creighton. 1992. *How Policies Change: The Japanese Government and the Aging Society.* Princeton: Princeton University Press.

Campbell, John L., J. Rogers Hollingsworth, and Leon Lindberg, eds. 1991. *Governance of the American Economy.* Cambridge: Cambridge University Press.

Castles, Francis G. 1986. *The Working Class and Welfare: Reflections of the Political Development and the Welfare State in Australia and New Zealand, 1890–1980.* Wellington: Allen & Unwin.

Chandler, Alfred D. 1990. *Scale and Scope. The Dynamics of Industrial Capitalism.* Cambridge, Mass.: Harvard University Press.

Chernow, Ron. 1990. *The House of Morgan: An American Banking Dynasty and the Rise of Modern Finance.* New York: Simon & Schuster.

Childs, Michael J. 1990. "Boy Labour in Late Victorian and Edwardian England and the Remaking of the Working Class." *Journal of Social History* 23 (4).

Chimoto, Akiko. 1986. "Employment in the Meiji Period: From 'Tradition' to 'Modernity.' " *Japanese Yearbook of Business History* 3:135–59.

Cho, Lee-Jay, and Yoon Hyung Kim, eds. 1998. *Ten Paradigms of Market Economies and Land Systems.* Seoul: Korea Research Institute for Human Settlements.

Cho, Young-Hoo. 1994. "Enterprise Unionism and the Emergence of the Japanese Welfare State." Ph.D. dissertation, University of Michigan.

Clark, Rodney. 1979. *The Japanese Company.* New Haven: Yale University Press.

Cohen, Stephen S. 1969. *Modern Capitalist Planning: The French Model.* Berkeley: University of California Press.

Collick, Martin. 1988. "Social Policy: Pressures and Responses." In *Dynamic and Immobilist Politics in Japan,* edited by J. A. A. Stockwin et al., 205–36. Honolulu: University of Hawaii Press.

Converse, Philip E. 1964. "The Nature of Belief Systems in Mass Publics." In *Ideology and Discontent,* edited by David E. Apter, 206–61. New York: Free Press.

Coulmas, Florian. 1993. *Das Land der rituellen Harmonie: Japan: Gesellschaft mit beschränkter Haftung.* Frankfurt am Main: Campus Verlag.

Crouch, Colin. 1986. "Sharing Public Space: States and Organized Interests in Western Europe." In *States in History,* edited by John A. Hall, 177–210. Oxford: Blackwell.

——. 1993. *Industrial Relations and European State Traditions.* Oxford: Clarendon Press.

Crouch, Colin, and Wolfgang Streeck, eds. 1996. *Les capitalismes en Europe.* Paris: Éditions La Découverte.

——. 1997. *The Political Economy of Modern Capitalism: Mapping Convergence and Diversity.* London: Sage.

Daito, Eisuke. 1979. "Management and Labor: The Evolution of Employer-Employee Relations in the Course of Industrial Development." In *Labor and Management. Proceedings of the Fourth Fuji Conference,* edited by Keiichiro Nakagawa, 1–25. Tokyo: University of Tokyo Press.

DATSCH. Various years. *Abhandlungen und Berichte über Technisches Schulwesen* (Band I-XIII). Leipzig: Verlag von B. G. Teubner.

David, Paul A. 1985. "Clio and the Economics of QWERTY." In *American Economic Review: Papers and Proceedings* 75:332–37.

——. 1997. "Path Dependence and the Quest for Historical Economics: One More Chorus of the Ballad of QWERTY." Discussion Papers in Economic and Social History. Oxford: University of Oxford.

Davis, E. Philip. 1995. *Pension Funds. Retirement-Income Security and Capital Markets: An International Perspective.* Oxford: Clarendon Press.

Decker, Franz. 1965. *Die betriebliche Sozialordnung der Dürner Industrie im 19. Jahrhundert.* Köln: Rheinisch-Westfälischen Wirtschaftsarchiv zu Köln.

Deeg, Richard. 1992. "Banks and the State in Germany: The Critical Role of Subnational Institutions in Economic Governance." Ph.D. dissertation, Massachusetts Institute of Technology.

De Jong, Henk W. 1992. "Der Markt für Unternehmenskontrollen. Eine historische, theoretische und empirische Analyse." In *Der Markt für Unternehmenskontrollen,* edited by Helmut Gröner. Berlin: Duncker und Humblot.

——. 1996. "European Capitalism Between Freedom and Social Justice." In *International Regulatory Competition and Coordination: Perspectives on Economic Regulation in Europe and the United States,* edited by William Bratton, Joseph McCahery, Sol Picciotto, and Colin Scott, 185–206. Oxford: Clarendon Press.

Delbrück, Rudolph von. 1905. *Lebenserinnerungen.* Leipzig: Duncker & Humblot.

Deutsche Bundesbank, ed. 1976. *Währung und Wirtschaft in Deutschland, 1876–1975.* Frankfurt am Main: Fritz Knapp Verlag.

Dickey, Laurence. 1987. *Hegel: Religion, Economics, and the Politics of Spirit 1770–1807.* Cambridge: Cambridge University Press.

DiMaggio, Paul, and Walter Powell. 1983. "The Iron Cage Revisited: Institutional Isomorphism and Collective Rationality." *American Sociological Review* 48:147–60.

Domanski-Davidsohn, Elisabeth. 1981. "Arbeitskämpfe und Arbeitskampfstrategien des Deutschen Metallarbeiter-Verbandes, 1891–1914." Ph.D. dissertation, Ruhr-University, Bochum.

Dore, Ronald P. 1969. "The Modernizer as a Special Case: Japanese Factory Legislation 1882–1911." *Comparative Studies in Society and History* 11:433–50.

——. 1973. *British Factory, Japanese Factory: The Origins of National Diversity in Industrial Relations.* Berkeley: University of California Press.

——. 1979. "More about Late Development." *Journal of Japanese Studies* 5 (1):137–51.

——. 1987. *Taking Japan Seriously: A Confucian Perspective on Leading Economic Issues.* Stanford: Stanford University Press.

——. 1997. "The Distinctiveness of Japan." In *Political Economy of Modern Capitalism: Mapping Convergence and Diversity,* edited by Colin Crouch and Wolfgang Streeck, 19–32. London: Sage.

Dornseifer, Bernd, and Jürgen Kocka. 1993. "The Impact of Preindustrial Heritage: Reconsiderations on the German Pattern of Corporate Development in the Late Nineteenth and Early Twentieth Centuries." *Industrial and Corporate Change* 2 (2):233–48.

Dowd, Kevin. 1993. *Laissez-Faire Banking.* London: Routledge.

Dudley, Geoffrey, and Jeremy Richardson. 1996. "Why Does Policy Change over Time? Adversarial Policy Communities, Alternative Policy Arenas, and British Trunk Roads Policy, 1945–1995." *Journal of European Public Policy* 3:63–83.

Ebbinghaus, Bernhard and Philip Manow, eds. 2001. *Comparing Welfare Capitalism: Social Policy and Political Economy in Europe, Japan, and the USA.* London: Routledge.

Ebert, Roland. 1984. *Zur Entstehung der Kategorie Facharbeiter als Problem der Erziehungswissenschaft* (Historische Studie zur Berufspädagogik; Wissenschaftliche Reihe, Band 26). Bielefeld: Kleine Verlag.

Economic Planning Agency (EPA). 1993. *Economic Survey of Japan 1993–1994.* Government of Japan.

Edwards, Jeremy, and Sheilagh Ogilvie. 1996. "Universal Banks and German Industrialization." *Economic History Review* 49:1–29.

Eichberg, Ekkehard. 1965. *Die Lehrwerkstatt im Industriebetrieb.* Pädagogische Studien Herausbegeben von Georg Geissler, Band 11. Weinheim/Bergstr.: Verlag Julius Beltz.

Eichengreen, Barry. 1995. *Golden Fetters. The Gold Standard and the Great Depression, 1919–1939.* New York: Oxford University Press.

Esping-Andersen, Gøsta. 1985. *Politics against Markets: The Social Democratic Road to Power.* Princeton: Princeton University Press.

——. 1990. *The Three Worlds of Welfare Capitalism.* Cambridge: Polity Press.

——. 1994. "The Emerging Realignment between Labor Movements and Welfare States." In *The Future of Labor Movements,* edited by Marino Regini, 133–49. London: Sage.

——. 1997. "Hybrid or Unique? The Japanese Welfare State between Europe and America." *Journal of European Social Policy* 7 (3):179–89.

——. 1999. *Social Foundations of Postindustrial Economies.* Oxford: Oxford University Press.

Estevez-Abe, Margarita. 1996. "The Welfare-Growth Nexus in the Japanese Political Economy." Paper presented at the Annual Meeting of the American Political Science Association, 29 August-1 September 1996, San Francisco.

——. 2001. "Welfare-Finance Nexus as a Forgotten Link: The Role of Pension Mix in the Japanese Model of Capitalism." In *Comparing Welfare Capitalism,* edited by Bernhard Ebbinghaus and Philip Manow. London: Routledge.

Estevez-Abe, Margarita, David W. Soskice, and Torben Iversen. 1999. "Social Protection and the Formation of Skills: A Reinterpretation of the Welfare State." Paper presented to the American Political Science Association, 2–5 September 1999, Atlanta.

Eulenburg, Franz. 1906. "Die Aufsichtsräte der deutschen Aktiengesellschaften." *Jahrbücher für Nationalökonomie und Statistik* 87:92–109.

Euler, Manfred. 1981. "Probleme der Erfassung von Vermögensbeständen in privaten

Haushalten im Rahmen der Einkommens- und Verbrauchsstichproben." *Wirtschaft und Statistik* 1990 (4):252–62.

———. 1990. "Geldvermoegen und Schulden privater Haushalte Ende 1988." *Wirtschaft und Statistik* 1990 (11):798–808.

Evans, Robert, Jr. 1970. "Evolution of the Japanese System of Employer-Employee Relations, 1868–1945." *Business History Review* 44 (1):110–25.

Feldenkirchen, W. 1982. *Die Eisen- und Stahlindustrie des Ruhrgebietes 1879–1914: Wachstum, Finanzierung, und Struktur iherer Grossunternehmen.* Berlin: Duncker & Humblot.

———. 1991. "Banking and Economic Growth: Banks and Industry in Germany in the Nineteenth Century and Their Changing Relationship during Industrialisation." In *German Industry and German Industrialisation: Essays in German Economic and Business History in the Nineteenth and Twentieth Centuries,* edited by W. R. Lee, 116–47. London: Routledge.

Feldman, Gerald. 1966. *Army, Industry, and Labor in Germany, 1914–1918.* Princeton: Princeton University Press. Reprint: Providence: Berg Publishers, 1992.

———. 1970. "German Business Between War and Revolution: The Origins of the Stinnes-Legien Agreement." In *Entstehung und Wandel der modernen Gesellschaft: Festschrift für Hans Rosenberg zum 65. Geburtstag,* edited by Gerhard A. Ritter. Berlin: Walter de Gruyter & Co.

———. 1981. "German Interest Group Alliances in War and Inflation, 1914–1923." In *Organizing Interests in Western Europe: Pluralism, Corporatism, and the Transformation of Politics,* edited by Suzanne Berger, 159–84. Cambridge: Cambridge University Press.

———. 1998. "Responses to Banking Concentration in Germany, 1900–1933." Unpublished paper.

Feldman, Gerald, and Ulrich Nocken. 1975. "Trade Associations and Economic Power: Interest Group Development in the German Iron and Steel and Machine Building Industries, 1900–1933." *Business History Review* 49 (4).

Feldman, Gerald, and Irmgard Steinisch. 1985. *Industrie und Gewerkschaften 1914–1924: die überforderte Zentralarbeitsgemeinschaft.* Stuttgart: Deutsche Verlags-Anstalt.

Finegold, David, and David Soskice. 1988. "The Failure of Training in Britain: Analysis and Prescription." *Oxford Review of Economic Policy* 4 (3).

Fischer, Wolfram. 1978. "Die Pionierrolle der betrieblichen Sozialpolitik im 19. und beginnenden 20. Jahrhundert." In *Zeitschrift für Unternehmensgeschichte,* edited by Wilhelm Treu and Hans Pohl, 34–50. Betriebliche Sozialpolitik deutscher Unternehmen seit dem 19. Jahrhundert. Beiheft 12.

———. 1979. "Labor-Management and Industrial Relations in Germany, 1870–1930." In *Labor and Management: Proceedings of the Fourth Fuji Conference,* edited by Keiichiro Nakagawa, 99–123. Tokyo: University of Tokyo Press.

Fligstein, Neil. 1990. *The Transformation of Corporate Control.* Cambridge, Mass.: Harvard University Press.

Flora, Peter, and Jens Alber. 1981. "Modernization, Democratization, and the Development of Welfare States in Western Europe." In *The Development of Welfare States in Europe and America,* edited by Peter Flora and Arnold Heidenheimer, 37–79. New Brunswick: Transaction Books.

Fohlin, Caroline M. 1997. *Bank Structure and Growth: Insights from British and German Bank Balance Sheets before World War I.* Pasadena: California Institute of Technology.

———. 1998. "Relationship Banking, Liquidity, and Investment in the German Industrialization." *Journal of Finance* 53 (October):1737–58.

Forsyth, Douglas, and Ton Notermans, eds. 1997. *Financial Institutions and Regulatory Regimes in Europe from the 1930s to the 1990s.* Providence, R. I.: Berghan Books.

Fruin, W. Mark. 1994. *The Japanese Enterprise System: Competitive Strategies and Cooperative Structures.* Rev. ed. Oxford: Clarendon Press.

Fukuzawa, Hiroomi. 1988. "Zur Rezeption des europäischen Wissenschaftsvokabulars in der Meiji-Zeit." *Nachrichten der Gesellschaft für Natur- und Völkerkunde Ostasiens* 143:9–18.

Fürer, Dr. 1927. "Förderung der Facharbeiter-Ausbildung durch Industrieverbände." In *Der Arbeitgeber: Zeitschrift der Vereinigung der Deutschen Arbeitgeberverbände*, 2:30–36.

Fürstenberg, Friedrich. 1958. "Der Betriebsrat–Strukturanalyse einer Grenzinstitution." *Kölner Zeitschrift für Soziologie und Sozialpsychologie* 10:418–29.

Furusho, Tadashi. 1969. "Shoki rōdōrippō no tenkai to keizai dantai." *Komazawa Daigaku keizaigaku ronshu* 1 (1–2).

Gall, Lothar. 2000. *Krupp. Der Aufstieg eines Industrieimperiums.* München: Siedler Verlag.

Gamble, Andrew, Gregory Jackson, John Parkinson, and Shawn Donnelly. 2000. *The Public Interest and the Company in Britain and Germany.* London: Anglo-German Foundation.

Gao, Bai. 1994. "Arisawa Hiromi and His Theory for a Managed Economy." *Journal of Japanese Studies* 20:115–53.

———. 1997. *Economic Ideology and Japanese Industrial Policy: Developmentalism from 1931 to 1965.* Cambridge: Cambridge University Press.

Garon, Sheldon. 1987. *The State and Labor in Modern Japan.* Berkeley: University of California Press.

———. 1997. *Molding Japanese Minds: The State in Everyday Life.* Princeton: Princeton University Press.

Geary, Dick. 1991. "The Industrial Bourgeoisie and Labour Relations in Germany, 1871–1933." In *The German Bourgeoisie: Essays on the Social History of the German Middle Class from the Late Eighteenth to the Early Twentieth Century*, edited by David Blackbourn and Richard J. Evans, 140–61. London: Routledge.

Georg, Stefan O. 1996. *Die Leistungsfähigkeit japanischer Banken.* Berlin: Sigma.

Gerlach, Michael. 1992. *Alliance Capitalism: The Social Organization of Japanese Business.* Berkeley: University of California Press.

Gerschenkron, Alexander. 1962. *Economic Backwardness in Historical Perspective: A Book of Essays.* Cambridge, Mass.: Harvard University Press.

Gesamtverband Deutscher Metallindustrieller. 1934. *Planmäßige Lehrlingsausbildung in der Metallindustrie.* Berlin: GDM.

Giersch, Herbert. 1977. *Konjunktur- und Wachstumspolitik in der offenen Wirtschaft.* Wiesbaden: Gabler.

Gitter, Wolfgang. 1985. "Der Weg zur Unfallversicherung aus rechtswissenschaftlicher Sicht." In *100 Jahre gesetzliche Unfallversicherung*, edited by Vom Hauptverband der gewerblichen Berufsgenossenschaften, 22–31. Wiesbaden: Universum.

Goodman, Roger, and Ito Peng. 1996. "The East Asian Welfare States: Peripatetic Learning, Adaptive Change, and Nation-Building." In *Welfare States in Transition*, edited by Gøsta Esping-Andersen, 192–224. London: Sage.

Goodman, Roger, Gordon White, and Huck-Ju Kwon. 1998. *In Search of an East Asian Welfare State.* London: Routledge.

Gordon, Andrew. 1985. *The Evolution of Labor Relations in Japan: Heavy Industry, 1853–1955.* Cambridge, Mass.: Harvard University Press.

———. 1992. *Labor and Imperial Democracy in Prewar Japan.* Berkeley: University of California Press.

———. 1993. "Contests for the Workplace." In *Postwar Japan as History*, edited by Andrew Gordon, 373–94. Berkeley: University of California Press.

———. 1998. *The Wages of Affluence: Labor and Management in Postwar Japan.* Cambridge, Mass.: Harvard University Press.

Granovetter, Mark. 1985. "Economic Action and Social Structure: The Problem of Embeddedness." *American Journal of Sociology* 91:481–510.

Groebner, Valentin. 1995. "Außer Haus: Otto Brunner und die 'alteuropäische Ökonomik.'" *Geschichte in Wissenschaft und Unterricht* 46:69–80.

Guillen, Mauro F. 1994. *Models of Management: Work, Authority and Organization in Comparative Perspective.* Chicago: University of Chicago Press.

Haas, P. A. 1992. "Introduction: Epistemic Communities and International Policy Coordination." *International Organization* 46:12–35.

Hackett, Roger F. 1971. *Yamagata Aritomo in the Rise of Modern Japan, 1838–1922.* Cambridge, Mass.: Harvard University Press.

Hall, John Whitney. 1985. "Reflections on Murakami Yasusuke's '*Ie* Society as a Pattern of Civilization.'" *Journal of Japanese Studies* 11:47–55.

Hall, Peter A. 1986. *Governing the Economy: The Politics of State Intervention in Britain and France.* New York: Oxford University Press.

———. 1997. "The Role of Interests, Institutions, and Ideas in the Comparative Political Economy of the Industrialized Nations." In *Comparative Politics: Rationality, Culture, and Structure,* edited by Mark I. Lichbach and Alan S. Zuckerman, 174–207. Cambridge: Cambridge University Press.

———, ed. 1989. *The Political Power of Economic Ideas: Keynesianism across Nations.* Princeton: Princeton University Press.

Hanami, Tadashi. 1989. "Industrial Democracy." In *Democracy in Japan,* edited by Takeshi Ishida and Ellis S. Krauss, 281–98. Pittsburgh: University of Pittsburgh Press.

Hansen, Hal. 1997. "Caps and Gowns: Historical Reflections on the Institutions that Shaped Learning for and at Work in Germany and the United States, 1800–1945." Ph.D. dissertation, University of Wisconsin, Madison.

Harada, Shuichi. 1928. *Labor Conditions in Japan.* New York: Cornell University Press.

Hasek, Carl William. 1925. *The Introduction of Adam Smith's Doctrines into Germany.* New York: Longmans, Green & Co.

Haselbach, Dieter. 1991. *Autoritärer Liberalismus und Soziale Marktwirtschaft. Gesellschaft und Politik im Ordoliberalismus.* Baden-Baden: Nomos Verlag.

Hashimoto, Jurō. 1996. "How and When Japanese Economic and Enterprise Systems Were Formed." *Japanese Yearbook on Business History* 13:5–26.

Hatch, Walter, and Kozo Yamamura. 1996. *Asia in Japan's Embrace: Building a Regional Production Alliance.* Cambridge: Cambridge University Press.

Haußherr, Hans. 1953. *Verwaltungseinheit und Ressorttrennung vom Ende des 17. bis zum Beginn des 19. Jahrhunderts.* Berlin: Akademie-Verlag.

Hazama, Hiroshi. 1964. *Nihon romukanri-shi kenkyū.* Tokyo: Daiyamondosha.

———. 1992. "Management Philosophy in the Early Years of Industrialization in Japan: In Search of the Theoretical Framework for International Comparison." *Japanese Yearbook on Business History* 9:87–123.

———. 1997. *The History of Labour Management in Japan.* New York: St. Martin's Press.

Heclo, Hugh. 1974. *Modern Social Politics in Britain and Sweden: From Relief to Income Maintenance.* New Haven: Yale University Press.

———. 1978. "Issue Networks and the Executive Establishment." In *The New American Political System,* edited by Anthony King, 87–124. Washington: American Enterprise Institute.

Hegel, Georg Wilhelm Friedrich. 1833. *Grundlinien der Philosophie des Rechts, oder Naturrecht und Staatswissenschaften im Grundrisse,* edited by Eduart Gans (Werke. Achter Band). Berlin: Duncker & Humblot.

Heidenheimer, Arnold J. 1980. "Unions and Welfare State Development in Britain and Germany: An Interpretation of Metamorphoses in the Period 1910–1950." Science Center Berlin, Discussion Paper IIVG 80–209, Berlin.

Heiman, G. 1971. "The Sources and Significance of Hegel's Corporate Doctrine." In

Hegel's Political Philosophy—Problems and Perspectives; A Collection of New Essays, edited by Z. A. Pelczynski, 111–35. Cambridge: Cambridge University Press.

Henning, Friederich-Henning. 1992. "Börsenkrise und Börsengesetzgebung in 1914 bis 1945 in Deutschland." In *Deutsche Börsengeschichte*, edited by Hans Pohl, 211–90. Frankfurt am Main: Fritz Knapp Verlag.

Hentschel, Volker. 1996. *Ludwig Erhard: ein Politikerleben*. München: Olzog.

Herbst, Ludolf. 1982. *Der Totale Krieg und die Ordnung der Wirtschaft: die Kriegswirtschaft im Spannungsfeld von Politik, Ideologie und Propaganda, 1939–1945*. Stuttgart: Deutsche Verlags-Anstalt.

———. 1996. *Das nationalsozialistische Deutschland, 1933–1945. Die Entfesselung der Gewalt: Rassismus und Krieg*. Frankfurt am Main: Suhrkamp Verlag.

Herrigel, Gary. 1993. "Identity and Institutions: The Social Construction of Trade Unions in the United States and Germany in the Nineteenth Century." *Studies in American Political Development* 7:371–94.

———. 1996. *Industrial Constructions: The Sources of German Industrial Power*. Cambridge: Cambridge University Press.

Hilferding, R. 1968. *Das Finanzkapital*. Frankfurt: Europäische Verlags-Anstalt.

Hirata, Mitsuhiro. 1996. "Die japanische torishimariyaku-kai." *Zeitschrift für Betriebswirtschaft*, Ergänzungsheft 3:1–27.

Hirschmann, Albert. 1970. *Exit, Voice, and Loyalty*. Cambridge, Mass.: Harvard University Press.

Hirschmeier, Johannes. 1964. *The Origins of Entrepreneurship in Meiji Japan*. Cambridge, Mass.: Harvard University Press.

———. 1976. "Ideologie des japanischen Managements 1945–1972." In *Gesellschaft Japans: Soziale Gruppen und sozialer Prozeß*, edited by Ikutarō Shimizu and Yoshirō Tamanoi, 141–67. Opladen: Westdeutscher Verlag.

———. 1986. *Die japanische Unternehmung. Schriften aus dem Nachlaß*, edited by Willy Kraus and Erhard Louven. Hamburg: Institut für Asienkunde.

Hirschmeier, Johannes, and Tsunehiko Yui. 1981. *The Development of Japanese Business, 1600–1980*, 2d ed. London: Allen & Unwin.

Hoffmann, Ernst. 1962. *Zur Geschichte der Berufsausbildung in Deutschland*. Bielefeld: W. Bertelsmann Verlag.

Hollingsworth, J. Rogers. 1997. "Continuities and Changes in Social Systems of Production: The Cases of Japan, Germany, and the United States." In *Contemporary Capitalism: The Embeddedness of Institutions*, edited by J. Rogers Hollingsworth and Robert Boyer, 265–310. Cambridge: Cambridge University Press.

Hollingsworth, J. Rogers, and Robert Boyer, eds. 1997. *Contemporary Capitalism: The Embeddedness of Institutions*. Cambridge: Cambridge University Press.

Hollingsworth, J. Rogers, Philippe C. Schmitter, and Wolfgang Streeck, eds. 1994. *Governing Capitalist Economies: Performance and Control of Economic Sectors*. New York: Oxford University Press.

Homburg, Heidrun. 1982. "Externer und interner Arbeitsmarkt: Zur Entstehung und Funktion des Siemens-Werkvereins, 1906–1918." In *Historische Arbeitsmarktforschung: Entstehung, Entwicklung, und Probleme der Vermarktung von Arbeitskraft*, edited by Toni Pierenkemper and Richard Tilly. Göttingen: Vandenhoeck & Ruprecht.

Hommelhoff, Peter. 1985. "Eigenkontrolle statt Stattkontrolle-rechtsdogmatischer Überblick zur Aktienrechtreform 1884." In *Hundert Jahre modernes Aktienrecht. Eine Sammlung von Texten und Quellen zur Aktienrechtsreform 1884*, edited by Werner Schubert and Peter Hommelhoff, 53–106. Berlin: Walter de Gruyter.

Hopt, Klaus. 1979. "Zur Funtion des Aufsichtsrats im Verhältnis von Industrie und

Bankensystem." In *Recht und Entwicklung der Großunternehmen im 19. und frühen 20. Jahrhundert*, edited by Nobert Horn and Jürgen Kocka, 227–38. Göttingen: Vandenhoeck und Ruprecht.

Horn, Nobert. 1979. "Aktienrechtliche Unternehmensorganisation in der Hochindustrialisierung (1860–1920)." In *Recht und Entwicklung der Großunternehmen im 19. und frühen 20. Jahrhundert*, edited by Nobert Horn and Jürgen Kocka, 123–81. Göttingen: Vandenhoeck und Ruprecht.

Horstmann, Theo. 1991. *Die Alliierten und die deutschen Großbanken. Bankenpolitik nach dem Zweiten Weltkrieg in Westdeutschland.* Bonn: Bouvier Verlag.

Hoston, Germaine A. 1986. *Marxism and the Crisis of Development in Prewar Japan.* Princeton: Princeton University Press.

Huber, Ernst Rudolf. 1988. *Deutsche Verfassungsgeschichte seit 1789*, Band 3: *Bismarck und das Reich*, 3d ed. Stuttgart: Kohlhammer.

Huber, Evelyne, and John D. Stephens. 2000. "Welfare State and Production Regimes in the Era of Retrenchment." In *The New Politics of the Welfare State*, edited by Paul Pierson. New York: Oxford University Press.

Iber, Bernhard. 1985. "Zur Entwicklung der Aktionärsstruktur in der Bundesrepublic Deutschland." *Zeitschrift für Betriebswirtschaft* 55:1101–19.

Ide, Masasuke. 1998. *Japanese Corporate Finance and International Competition: Japanese Capitalism versus American Capitalism.* London: Macmillan.

Ikeda, Makoto. 1982. *Nihonteki kyōchōshugi no seiritsu.* Tokyo: Keibunsha.

Ikegami, Naoki. 1996. "Overview: Health Care in Japan." In *Containing Health Care Costs in Japan*, edited by Naoki Ikegami and John C. Campbell. Ann Arbor: University of Michigan Press.

Ingham, Geoffrey K. 1984. *Capitalism Divided? The City and Industry in British Social Development.* Basingstoke, Hampshire: Macmillan.

Inoki, Takenori. 1996. *Gakkō to kōjō.* Tokyo: Yomiuri Shinbunsha.

Ishida, Takeshi. 1968. "The Development of Interest Groups and the Pattern of Political Modernization in Japan." In *Political Development in Modern Japan*, edited by Robert E. Ward. Princeton: Princeton University Press.

Iwata, Ryushi. 1992. "The Japanese Enterprise as a Unified Body of Employees: Origins and Development." In *The Political Economy of Japan.* Vol. 3: *Cultural and Social Dynamics*, edited by Shumpei Kumon and Henry Rosovsky, 170–97. Stanford: Stanford University Press.

Jackson, Gregory. 1997. "Corporate Governance in Germany and Japan: Development within National and International Contexts." Manuscript, www.mpi-fg-koeln.mpg.de/~gj.

Jackson, Gregory, and Sigurt Vitols. 2000. "Pension Regimes and Financial Systems: Between Social Security, Market Liquidity and Corporate Governance." In *Varieties of Welfare Capitalism*, edited by Bernhard Ebbinghaus and Philip Manow. London: Routledge.

Jacobs, Didier. 1998. "Social Welfare Systems in East Asia: A Comparative Analysis Including Private Welfare." Center for Analysis of Social Exclusion, CASE/10, London School of Economics, London.

Jacoby, Sanford. 1993. "Pacific Ties: Employment Systems in Japan and the United States." In *Industrial Democracy in America: The Ambiguous Promise*, edited by Nelson Lichtenstein and Howell John Harris, 206–48. Cambridge: Cambridge University Press.

——. 1996. "From Welfare Capitalism to the Welfare State: Marion B. Folsom and the Social Security Act of 1935." In *The Privatization of Social Policy? Occupational Welfare and the Welfare State in America, Scandinavia, and Japan*, edited by Michael Shalev, 44–72. London: Macmillan.

Jobert, Bruno. 1994. "Introduction: Le retour du politique." In *Le tournant néo-libéral en*

Europe. Idées et récettes dans les pratiques gouvernementales, edited by Bruno Jobert, 9–20. Paris: L'Harmattan.

——. 1995. "Rhétorique politique, controverses scientifiques et construction des normes intellectuelles: esquisse d'un parcours de recherche." In *La construction du sens dans les politiques publiques: débats autour de la notion de référentiel*, edited by Alain Faure, Gilles Pollet, and Philippe Warin, 13–24. Paris: L'Harmattan.

Jobert, Bruno, and Pierre Muller. 1987. *L'état en action: politiques publiques et corporatismes*. Paris: Presses Universitaires de France.

Johnson, Chalmers. 1982. *MITI and the Japanese Miracle: The Growth of Industrial Policy, 1925–1975*. Stanford: Stanford University Press.

Jünger, Ernst. 1931. *Die totale Mobilmachung*. Berlin: Verlag für Zeitkritik.

Kaelble, Hartmut. 1986. "The Rise of Managerial Enterprise in Germany, c. 1870 to c. 1930." In *The Development of Managerial Enterprise*, edited by Kesaji Kobayashi and Hidemasa Morikawa, 71–97. Tokyo: University of Tokyo Press.

Kagan, Robert. 1991. "Adversarial Legalism and American Government." *Journal of Policy Analysis and Management* 10 (3):369–406.

Katzenstein, Peter J. 1987. *Policy and Politics in West Germany: The Growth of a Semisovereign State*. Philadelphia: Temple University Press.

Kelly, George Armstrong. 1978. *Hegel's Retreat from Eleusis: Studies in Political Thought*. Princeton: Princeton University Press.

Kester, W. Carl. 1996. "American and Japanese Corporate Governance: Convergence to Best Practice?" In *National Diversity and Global Capitalism*, edited by Suzanne Berger and Ronald Dore, 107–37. Ithaca, N.Y.: Cornell University Press.

Kikkawa, Takeo. 1995. "Kiygo Shudan: The Formation and Functions of Enterprise Groups." *Business History* 1:44–53.

Kingdon, J. 1984. *Agendas, Alternatives, and Public Policy*. Boston: Little, Brown.

Kinzley, W. Dean. 1991. *Industrial Harmony in Modern Japan: The Invention of a Tradition*. London: Routledge.

Kitschelt, Herbert, Peter Lange, Gary Marks, and John D. Stephens. 1999. *Continuity and Change in Contemporary Capitalism*. Cambridge: Cambridge University Press.

Kluge, Arnd. 1991. *Geschichte der deutschen Bankgenossenschaften. Zur Entwicklung mitgliederorientierter Unternehmen*. Frankfurt am Main: Fritz Knapp Verlag.

Knox, William. 1980. "British Apprenticeship, 1800–1914." Ph.D. dissertation, Edinburgh University.

——. 1986. "Apprenticeship and De-Skilling in Britain, 1850–1914." *International Review of Social History* 31 (2).

Kocka, Jürgen. 1975. *Unternehmer in der deutschen Industrialisierung*. Göttingen: Vandenhoeck und Ruprecht.

——. 1979. "Familie, Unternehmer und Kapitalismus. An Beispielen aus der frühen deutschen Industrialisierung." *Zeitschrift für Unternehmensgeschichte* 24 (3):99–135.

——. 1981. "Class-Formation, Interest Articulation, and Public Policy: The Origins of the German White-Collar Class in the Late Nineteenth and Early Twentieth Centuries." In *Organizing Interest in Western Europe: Pluralism, Corporatism, and the Transformation of Politics*, edited by Suzanne Berger. Cambridge: Cambridge University Press.

——. 1984. "Craft Traditions and the Labour Movement in Nineteenth-Century Germany." In *The Power of the Past: Essays for Eric Hobsbawm*, edited by Pat Thane, Geoffrey Crossick, and Roderick Floud. Cambridge: Cambridge University Press.

Kocka, Jürgen, and H. Siegrist. 1979. "Die hundert größten deutschen Industrieunternehmen im späten 19. und frühen 20. Jahrhundert: Expansion, Diversifikation und Integration im internationalen Vergleich." In *Recht und Entwicklung der Großun-*

ternehmen im 19. und frühen 20. Jahrhundert, edited by Norbert Horn and Jürgen Kocka, 55–117. Göttingen: Vandenhoeck und Ruprecht.

Kohli, Martin, Martin Rein, Anne-Marie Guillemard, and Herman van Gunsteren. 1991. *Time for Retirement: Comparative Studies of the Decreasing Age of Exit from the Labour Force.* Cambridge: Cambridge University Press.

Kommission Mitbestimmung. 1998. *Mitbestimmung und neue Unternehmenskulturen Bilanz und Perspektiven.* Gütersloh: Verlag Bertelsmann Stiftung.

Kopper, Christopher. 1995. *Zwischen Marktwirtschaft und Dirigismus. Bankenpolitik im "Dritten Reich," 1933–1939.* Bonn: Bouvier Verlag.

Korpi, Walter. 1983. *The Democratic Class Struggle.* London: Routledge.

Kosai, Yutaka. 1988. "The Reconstruction Period." In *Industrial Policy of Japan*, edited by Ryutaro Komiya, Masahiro Okuno, and Kotaro Suzumura, 25–48. Tokyo: Academic Press.

Koselleck, Reinhart. 1975. *Preußen zwischen Reform und Revolution: allgemeines Landrecht, Verwaltung und soziale Bewegung von 1791 und 1848.* Stuttgart: Klett.

Kotthoff, Hermann. 1994. *Betriebsräte und Bürgerstatus. Wandel und Kontinuität betrieblicher Mitbestimmung.* München: Rainer Hampp Verlag.

Krohn, Claus-Dieter. 1981. *Wirtschaftstheorien als politische Interessen: Die akademische Nationalökonomie in Deutschland, 1918–1933.* Frankfurt am Main: Campus Verlag.

Kume, Ikuo. 1997a. "Co-optation or New Possibility? Japanese Labor Politics in the Era of Neo-Conservatism." In *State and Administration in Japan and Germany: A Comparative Perspective on Continuity and Change*, edited by Michio Muramatsu and Frieder Naschold, 221–45. Berlin: Walter de Gruyter.

——. 1997b. "Institutionalizing Postwar Japanese Political Economy: Industrial Policy Revisited." Unpublished paper. Kobe University.

——. 1998. *Disparaged Success: Labor Politics in Postwar Japan.* Ithaca, N.Y.: Cornell University Press.

Lange-von Kulessa, Jürgen, and Andreas Renner. 1998. "Die soziale Marktwirtschaft Alfred Müller-Armacks und der Ordoliberalismus der Freiburger Schule—Zur Unvereinbarkeit zweier Staatsauffassungen." *Ordo-Jahrbuch für die Ordnung von Wirtschaft und Gesellschaft* 49:79–104.

Lazonick, William. 1995. "Cooperative Employment Relations and Japanese Economic Growth." In *Capital, the State, and Labour: A Global Perspective*, edited by Juliet Schor and Jong-Il You, 70–110. Aldershot, United Kingdom: United Nations University Press.

Lazonick, William, and Mary O'Sullivan. 1996. "Organization, Finance, and International Competition." *Industrial and Corporate Change* 5 (1):1–49.

Lebra, Takie Sugiyama. 1985. "Is Japan an *Ie* Society, and *Ie* Society a Civilization?" *Journal of Japanese Studies* 11:57–64.

Lehmbruch, Gerhard. 1976. *Parteienwettbewerb im Bundesstaat.* Stuttgart: Kohlhammer.

——. 1996. "Die korporative Verhandlungsdemokratie in Westmitteleuropa." *Schweizerische Zeitschrift für Politische Wissenschaft* 2:19–41.

——. 1997. "From State of Authority to Network State: The German State in Developmental Perspective." In *State and Administration in Japan and Germany: A Comparative Perspective on Continuity and Change*, edited by Michio Muramatsu and Frieder Naschold, 39–62. Berlin: de Gruyter.

——. 1999. "The Intermediation of Interests in Agricultural Policy: Organized Interests and Policy Networks." In *The Significance of Politics and Institutions for the Design and Formation of Agricultural Policies*, edited by Klaus Frohberg and Peter Weingarten, 92–104. Kiel: Wissenschaftsverlag Vauk.

Leibenstein, Harvey. 1976. *Beyond Economic Man: A New Foundation for Microeconomics.* Cambridge, Mass.: Harvard University Press.

Levine, Solomon B., and Hisashi Kawada. 1980. *Human Resources in Japanese Industrial Development*. Princeton: Princeton University Press.

Lewis, Paul Martin. 1981. "Family, Economy, and Polity: A Case Study of Japan's Public Pension Policy." Ph.D. dissertation, University of California, Berkeley.

Lincoln, James, Michael Gerlach, and Christina Ahmadjian. 1994. "Changing Patterns of Keiretsu Organization in Japan." Unpublished paper.

Linton, Derek S. 1991. *"Who Has the Youth, Has the Future": The Campaign to Save Young Workers in Imperial Germany*. New York: Columbia University Press.

Lockwood, William M. 1968. *The Economic Development of Japan: Growth and Structural Change*. Expanded ed. Princeton: Princeton University Press.

Ludendorff, Erich. 1935. *Der totale Krieg*. München: Ludendorff.

Maier, Charles S. 1987. *In Search of Stability: Explorations in Historical Political Economy*. Cambridge: Cambridge University Press.

Maier, Hans. 1980. *Die ältere deutsche Staats- und Verwaltungslehre*. München: C. H. Beck.

Manow, Philip. 1997. "Social Insurance and the German Political Economy." MPIfG Discussion Paper 97/2. Max-Planck-Institute für Gesellschaftsforschung, Köln.

——. 2000. "Wage Coordination and the Welfare State: Germany and Japan Compared." MPIfG Working Paper 00/06, Max-Planck-Institut für Gesellschaftsforschung, Köln.

Marcuse, Herbert. 1941. *Reason and Revolution: Hegel and the Rise of Social Theory*. New York: Oxford University Press.

Mares, Isabela. 1998. "Negotiated Risks: Employers and Social Policy Development." Ph.D. dissertation, Harvard University.

Markovits, Andrei S. 1982. "Introduction: Model Germany—A Cursory Overview of a Complex Construct." In *The Political Economy of West Germany: Modell Deutschland*, edited by Andrei S. Markovits, 1–11. New York: Praeger.

Marks, Gary. 1989. *Unions in Politics*. Princeton: Princeton University Press.

Marshall, Byron K. 1967. *Capitalism and Nationalism in Prewar Japan: The Ideology of the Business Elite, 1868–1941*. Stanford: Stanford University Press.

Marshall, T. H. 1964. *Class, Citizenship, and Social Development*. Garden City, New York: Doubleday & Company.

Martin, Bernd. 1995. *Japan and Germany in the Modern World*. Providence, R.I.: Berghahn Books.

Mason, Timothy W. 1977. *Sozialpolitik im Dritten Reich: Arbeiterklasse und Volksgemeinschaft*. Opladen: Westdeutscher Verlag.

Maurice, Marc, Francios Sellier, and Jean-Jacques Silvestre. 1986. *The Social Foundations of Industrial Power: A Comparison of France and Germany*. Cambridge, Mass.: MIT Press.

McKenzie, Colin. 1992. "Stable Shareholdings and the Role of Japanese Life Insurance Companies." In *International Adjustment and the Japanese Firm*, edited by Paul Sheard, 83–98. St. Leonards: Allen & Unwin.

Menzel, H. 1960. *Die Mitwirkung der Hausbanken bei der Vergebung und Verwaltung öffentlicher Kredite*. Berlin: Dunker & Humblot.

Merkt, Hanno. 1996. "Zur Entwicklung des deutschen Börsenrechts von den Anfängen bis zum Zweiten Finanzmarktförderungsgesetz." In *Börsenreform. Eine ökonomische, rechtsvergleichende und rechtspolitische Untersuchung*, edited by H. Baum, K. J. Hopt, and B. Rudolph, 1–130. Gutachten im Auftrag des Bundesministeriums der Finanzen. Hamburg: Max-Planck-Institut für ausländisches und internationales Privatrecht.

Mieck, Ilja. 1965. *Preußische Gewerbepolitik in Berlin, 1806–1844. Staatshilfe und Privatinitiative zwischen Merkantilismus und Liberalismus*. Berlin: Walter de Gruyter.

Ministry of Agriculture and Commerce. 1903. *Shokkō jijō*.

Ministry of Labor. 1961. *Rōdō gyōsei-shi* 1. Tokyo: Rōdōhōrei Kyōkai.

Miyamoto, Mataji. 1938. *Kabunakama no kenkyū*. Tokyo: Yūhikaku.

Miyamoto, Matao. 1984. "The Position and Role of Family Business in the Development of the Japanese Company System." In *Family Business in the Era of Industrial Growth: Its Ownership and Management: Proceedings of the Fuji Conference*, edited by Akio Okochi and Shigeaki Yasuoka, 39–91. Tokyo: University of Tokyo Press.

Mjøset, Lars, et al. 1997. *Metholodogical Issues in Comparative Social Science*. Greenwich, Conn.: JAI Press.

Moellendorff, Wichard von. 1916. *Deutsche Gemeinwirtschaft*. Berlin: Siegismund.

Mommsen, Wolfgang J., and Hans-Gerhard Husung, eds. 1985. *The Development of Trade Unionism in Great Britain and Germany, 1880–1914*. London: Allen and Unwin.

Moore, Barrington. 1966. *The Social Origins of Dictatorship and Democracy*. Boston: Beacon Press.

Morikawa, Hidemasa. 1986. "Prerequisites for the Development of Managerial Capitalism: Cases in Prewar Japan." In *The Development of Managerial Enterprise*, edited by Kesaji Kobayashi and Hidemasa Morikawa, 1–27. Tokyo: University of Tokyo Press.

——. 1992. *Zaibatsu: The Rise and Fall of Family Enterprise Groups in Japan*. Tokyo: University of Tokyo Press.

——. 1993. "Japanese Top Management." *Japanese Yearbook on Business History* 10:1–26.

Morita, Yoshio. 1926. *Wagakuni no shihonkadantai*. Tokyo: Tōyō Keizai Shinpōsha.

Morris-Suzuki, Tessa. 1989. *A History of Japanese Economic Thought*. London: Routledge.

Morsey, Rudolf. 1957. *Die oberste Reichsverwaltung unter Bismarck, 1867–1890*. Münster: Aschendorffsche Verlagsbuchhandlung.

Mosher, Jim. 1998. "Supply-Side Equity: Labor Markets and Welfare." Unpublished paper.

Müller, Elmar. 1988. *Widerstand und Wirtschaftsordnung: Die wirtschaftspolitischen Konzepte der Widerstandsbewegung gegen das NS-Regime und ihr Einfluß auf die Soziale Marktwirtschaft*. Frankfurt am Main: Peter Lang.

Müller, Gloria. 1987. *Mitbestimmung in der Nachkriegszeit: Britische Besatzungsmacht, Unternehmen, Gewerkschaften*. Düsseldorf: Schwan Verlag.

Muller, Pierre. 1984. *Le technocrate et le paysan: essai sur la politique française de modernisation de l'agriculture, de 1945 à nos jours*. Paris: Éditions Ouvrières.

——. 1995. "Les politiques publiques comme construction d'un rapport au monde." In *La construction du sens dans les politiques publiques: débats autour de la notion de référentiel*, edited by Alain Faure, Gilles Pollet, and Philippe Warin, 153–79. Paris: L'Harmattan.

Müller-Armack, Alfred. 1933. *Staatsidee und Wirtschaftsordnung im neuen Reich*. Berlin: Junker u. Dünnhaupt.

——. 1956. "Soziale Marktwirtschaft." *Handwörterbuch der Sozialwissenschaften* 9. Stuttgart: Fischer.

——. 1976. *Wirtschaftsordnung und Wirtschaftspolitik*. Bern: Paul Haupt.

Murakami, Yasusuke. 1982. "The Age of New Middle Mass Politics: The Case of Japan." *Journal of Japanese Studies* 8 (1):29–72.

——. 1984. "*Ie* Society as a Pattern of Civilization." *Journal of Japanese Studies* 10 (2):281–363.

Muth, Wolfgang. 1985. *Berufsausbildung in der Weimarer Republik*. Stuttgart: Franz Steiner Verlag.

Najita, Tetsuo. 1974. *The Intellectual Foundations of Modern Japanese Politics*. Chicago: University of Chicago Press.

Nakamura, Takafusa. 1995. *The Postwar Japanese Economy: Its Development and Structure, 1937–1994*. Tokyo: University of Tokyo Press.

Nakane, Chie. 1970. *Japanese Society*. London: Weidenfeld and Nicolson.

Naphtali, Fritz. 1928. *Wirtschaftsdemokratie: ihr Wesen, Weg und Ziel*. Berlin: Verlags-Gesellschaft des Allgemeinen Deutschen Gewerkschaftsbundes.

Nawrocki, Johann. 1992. *Der japanische Nachlass Lorenz von Steins (1815–1890).* Kiel: Schleswig-Holsteinische Landesbibliothek.

Neumann, Franz L. 1942. *Behemoth: The Structure and Practice of National Socialism.* London: Gollancz.

———. 1944. *Behemoth: The Structure and Practice of National Socialism, 1933–1944.* New York: Harper Torchbooks.

Nicholls, A.J. 1994. *Freedom with Responsibility: The Social Market Economy in Germany, 1918–1963.* Oxford: Clarendon Press.

Nishiyama, Kaname. 1992. "Lorenz von Stein's Influence on Japan's Meiji Constitution of 1889." In *Lorenz von Steins "Bemerkungen über Verfassung und Verwaltung" von 1889 zu den Verfassungsarbeiten in Japan,* edited by Wilhelm Brauneder and Kaname Nishiyama, 39–59. Frankfurt am Main: Peter Lang.

Noguchi, Yukio. 1995. *1940–nen taisei.* Tokyo: Tōyō Keizai Shinpōsha.

Nolan, Mary. 1994. *Visions of Modernity: American Business and the Modernization of Germany.* New York: Oxford University Press.

Nörr, Knut Wolfgang. 1995. "Law and Market Organization: The Historical Experience in Germany from 1900 to the Law against Restraints of Competition (1957)." *Journal of Institutional and Theoretical Economics* 151 (1):5–20.

North, Douglass C. 1990. *Institutions, Institutional Change, and Economic Performance.* Cambridge: Cambridge University Press.

Odaka, Konosuke. 1984. *Rōdōshijō bunseki.* Tokyo: Iwanami Shoten.

———. 1990. "Sangyō no ninaite." In *Nihon keizaishi* 4, edited by Shunsaku Nishikawa and Takeshi Abe. Tokyo: Iwanami Shoten.

———. 1995. *Shokunin no sekai, kōjō no sekai.* Tokyo: Libro.

OECD. 1988. *Reforming Public Pensions.* Paris: OECD.

———. 1993. *Employment Outlook.* Paris: OECD.

———. 1997. *Employment Outlook.* Paris: OECD.

Oexle, Otto Gerhard. 1984. "Sozialgeschichte-Begriffsgeschichte-Wissenschafts-geschichte: Anmerkungen zum Werk Otto Brunners." *Vierteljahrschrift für Sozial- und Wirtschaftsgeschichte* 71:305–41.

Offe, Claus. 1981. "The Attribution of Public Status to Interest Groups: Observations of the West German Case." In *Organizing Interests in Western Europe: Pluralism, Corporatism and the Transformation of Politics,* edited by Suzanne D. Berger, 123–58. Cambridge: Cambridge University Press.

Okazaki, Tetsuji. 1993. "Kigyō shisutemu." In *Gendai Nihon keizai shisutemu no genryū,* edited by Tetsuji Okazaki and Masahiro Okuno. Tokyo: Nihon Keizai Shinbunsha.

———. 1994. "The Japanese Firm under the Wartime Planned Economy." In *The Japanese Firm: The Sources of Competitive Strength,* edited by Masahiko Aoki and Ronald Dore, 350–75. Oxford: Oxford University Press.

———. 1997. "The Wartime Institutional Reforms and Transformation of the Economic System." In *The Political Economy of Japanese Society.* Vol. 1: *The State or the Market?* edited by Junji Banno, 277–302. Oxford: Oxford University Press.

Osano, Hiroshi, and Toshio Serita. 1994. " 'Main' Bank System, Implicit Contracts, and Trust in Deferred Payment Arrangements." In *Labour Market and Economic Performance: Europe, Japan, and the U.S.A.,* edited by Toshiaki Tachibanaki, 312–46. Houndsmills, Basingstoke: Macmillan.

Otake, Hideo. 1987. "The Zaikai under the Occupation: The Formation and Transformation of Managerial Councils." In *Democratizing Japan: The Allied Occupation,* edited by Robert Ward and Yoshikazu Sakamoto, 366–91. Honolulu: University of Hawaii Press.

Ott, David J. 1961. "The Financial Development of Japan." *Journal of Political Economy* 69 (2):122–41.

Paqué, Karl Heinz. 1998. "Zur Zumutbarkeit von Arbeitsplätzen: Bestandsaufnahme und Reformvorschlag." In *Ökonomische Theorie der Sozialpolitik*, edited by Eckhard Knappe and Norbert Berthold, 71–89. Heidelberg: Physica.

Passow, Richard. 1922. *Die Aktiengesellschaft—Eine wirtschaftswissenschaftliche Studie.* Jena: Fischer.

Patrick, Hugh T. 1967. "Japan, 1868–1914." In *Banking in the Early Stages of Industrialization*, edited by Rondo Cameron, 239–89. London: Oxford University Press.

Pelczynski, Z. A. 1984. "Political Community and Individual Freedom in Hegel's Philosophy of the State." In *The State and Civil Society: Studies in Hegel's Political Philosophy*, edited by Z. A. Pelczynski, 55–76. Cambridge: Cambridge University Press.

Pempel, T. J. 1987. "The Tar Baby Target: 'Reform' of the Japanese Bureaucracy." In *Democratizing Japan: The Allied Occupation*, edited by Robert Ward and Yoshikazu Sakamoto, 157–87. Honolulu: University of Hawaii Press.

Pempel, T. J., and Keiichi Tsunekawa. 1979. "Corporatism without Labor? The Japanese Anomaly." In *Trends toward Corporatist Intermediation*, edited by Philippe Schmitter and Gerhard Lehmbruch, 231–70. Beverly Hills, Calif.: Sage.

Pittau, Joseph. 1967. *Political Thought in Early Meiji Japan, 1868–1889.* Cambridge, Mass.: Harvard University Press.

Plumpe, Gottfried. 1990. *Die I.G. Farbenindustrie AG. Wirtschaft, Technik und Politik 1904–1945.* Berlin: Duncker & Humblot.

Plumpe, Werner. 1992. "Die Betriebsräte in der Weimarer Republik: Eine Skizze zu ihrer Verbreitung, Zusammensetzung und Akzeptanz." In *Unternehmen zwischen Markt und Macht: Aspekte deutscher Unternehmens-und Industriegeschichte im 20. Jahrhundert*, edited by Werner Plumpe and Christian Kleinschmidt, 42–60. Essen: Klartext Verlag.

Pohl, Hans. 1982. "Zur Geschichte von Organisation und Leitung deutscher Grossunternehmen seit dem 19. Jahrhundert." *Zeitschrift für Unternehmensgeschichte* 28:143–78.

———. 1984. "Forms and Phases of Industry Finance up to the Second World War." In *German Yearbook on Business History*, edited by W. Engels and H. Pohl, 75–94. Berlin: Springer Verlag.

———, ed. 1992. *Deutsche Börsengeschichte.* Frankfurt am Main: Fritz Knapp Verlag.

Pohl, Hans, Stephanie Habeth, and Beate Brüninghaus. 1986. *Die Daimler-Benz AG in der Jahren 1933 bis 1945.* Stuttgart: Franz Steiner Verlag.

Pohl, Manfred. 1973. *Wiederaufbau: Kunst und Technik der Finanzierung 1947–1953. Die ersten Jahre der Kreditanstalt für Wiederaufbau.* Frankfurt am Main: Fritz Knapp Verlag.

———. 1986. *Entstehung und Entwicklung des Universalbankensystems.* Frankfurt am Main: Knapp Verlag.

Polanyi, Karl. 1944. *The Great Transformation.* Boston: Beacon Press.

Potthoff, Erich. 1957. *Der Kampf um die Montan-Mitbestimmung.* Köln: Bund Verlag.

Powell, Walter W. 1991. "Expanding the Scope of Institutional Analysis." In *The New Institutionalism in Organizational Analysis*, edited by Walter W. Powell and Paul J. DiMaggio, 183–203. Chicago: University of Chicago Press.

Preller, Ludwig. 1978. *Sozialpolitik in der Weimarer Republik.* Kronberg/Ts.: Athenaeum.

Pross, Helge. 1965. *Manager und Aktionäre in Deutschland: Untersuchungen zum Verhältnis von Eigentum und Verfügungsmacht.* Frankfurt am Main: Europäische Verlagsanstalt.

Pyle, Kenneth B. 1974. "Advantages of Followership: German Economics and Japanese Bureaucrats, 1890–1925." *Journal of Japanese Studies* 1 (1):127–64.

———. 1978. *The Making of Modern Japan.* Lexington, Mass.: Heath.

Rabenschlag-Kräusslich, Jutta. 1983. *Parität statt Klassenkampf? Zur Organisation des Arbeitsmarktes und Domestizierung des Arbeitskampfes in Deutschland und England 1900–1918.* Frankfurt am Main: Peter Lang.

Raeff, Marc. 1983. *The Well-Ordered Police State: Social and Institutional Change through Law in the Germanies and Russia, 1600–1800.* New Haven: Yale University Press.

Reich, Norbert. 1979. "Auswirkung der deutschen Aktienrechtsreform von 1884 auf die Konzentration der deutschen Wirtschaft." In *Recht und Entwicklung der Großunternehmen im 19. und frühen 20. Jahrhundert,* edited by Nobert Horn and Jürgen Kocka, 255–71. Göttingen: Vandenhoeck und Ruprecht.

Riedel, Manfred. 1969. *Studien zu Hegels Rechtsphilosophie.* Frankfurt am Main: Suhrkamp.

Riesser, J. 1910. *Die deutschen Grossbanken und ihre Konzentration.* Jena: Fischer.

Ritter, Gerhard A. 1983. *Sozialversicherung in Deutschland und England: Entstehung und Grundzuege im Vergleich.* München: Beck.

——. 1991. *Der Sozialstaat: Entstehung und Entwicklung im internationalen Vergleich.* München: Oldenbourg.

——. 1998. *Über Deutschland: die Bundesrepublik in der deutschen Geschichte.* München: C. H. Beck.

Ritter, Gerhard A., and Jürgen Kocka. 1974. *Deutsche Sozialgeschichte: Dokumente und Skizzen,* Band II: *1870–1914.* München: C. H. Beck.

Ritter, Joachim. 1957. *Hegel und die französische Revolution.* Köln: Westdeutscher Verlag.

Roe, Mark J. 1994. *Strong Managers, Weak Owners: The Political Roots of American Corporate Finance.* Princeton: Princeton University Press.

Rohlen, Thomas. 1985. "Why Evolution Isn't Progressive." *Journal of Japanese Studies* 11:65–69.

Röpke, Wilhelm. 1942. *Die Gesellschaftskrisis der Gegenwart.* Erlenbach-Zürich: Rentsch.

Rosenberg, Hans. 1967. *Grosse Depression und Bismarckzeit. Wirtschaftsablauf, Gesellschaft und Politik in Mitteleuropa.* Berlin: Walter de Gruyter.

Rothfels, Hans. 1927. *Theodor Lohmann und die Kampfjahre der staatlichen Sozialpolitik (1871–1905).* Berlin: E. S. Mittler & Sohn.

Rothstein, Bo. 1992. "Labor-Market Institutions and Working-Class Strength." In *Structuring Politics: Historical Institutionalism and Comparative Analysis,* edited by Sven Steinmo, Kathleen Thelen, and Frank Longstreth, 33–46. Cambridge: Cambridge University Press.

Rupieper, Hermann-Josef. 1982. *Arbeiter und Angestellte im Zeitalter der Industrialisierung.* Frankfurt am Main: Campus.

Rüther, Martin. 1988. "Zur Sozialpolitik bei Klöckner-Humboldt-Deutz während des Nationalsozialismus: 'Die Masse der Arbeiterschaft muss aufgespalten werden.'" *Zeitschrift für Unternehmensgeschichte* 2:81–117.

Sabatier, Paul A., ed. 1993. *Policy Change and Learning: An Advocacy Coalition Approach.* Boulder, Colo.: Westview Press.

Sachße, Christoph, and Florian Tennstedt. 1988. *Geschichte der Armenfürsorge in Deutschland,* Band 2: *Fürsorge und Wohlfahrtspflege 1871–1929.* Stuttgart: Kohlhammer.

Saegusa, Hirone, et al. 1960. *Kindai Nihon sangyō gijutsu no seiōka.* Tokyo: Tōyō Keizai Shinpōsha.

Saguchi, Kazuo. 1991. *Nihon ni okeru sangyō minshushugi no zentei.* Tokyo: University of Tokyo Press.

Saile, Wolfgang. 1958. *Hermann Wagener und sein Verhältnis zu Bismarck: ein Beitrag zur Geschichte des konservativen Sozialismus.* Tübingen: Mohr-Siebeck.

Sakurabayashi, Makoto. 1985. *Sangyō hōkokukai no soshiki to kinō.* Tokyo: Ochanomizu Shobō.

Samuels, Richard. 1987. *The Business of the Japanese State: Energy Markets in Comparative and Historical Perspective.* Ithaca, N.Y.: Cornell University Press.

Sawai, Minoru. 1996. "Kikai kōgyō." In *Nihon keizai no 200 nen,* edited by Shunsaku Nishikawa et al. Tokyo: Nihon Hyōronsha.

Scalapino, Robert A. 1964. "Ideology and Modernization: The Japanese Case." In *Ideology and Discontent*, edited by David E. Apter, 92–127. New York: Free Press.

Schenck, Paul-Christian. 1997. *Der deutsche Anteil an der Gestaltung des modernen japanischen Rechts- und Verfassungswesens: deutsche Rechtsberater im Japan der Meiji-Zeit*. Stuttgart: Steiner.

Schmidt, Hartmut, et al. 1997. *Corporate Governance in Germany*. Baden-Baden: Nomos Verlag.

Schmitter, Philippe C. 1974. "Still the Century of Corporatism?" *Review of Politics* 36:85–131.

Schmitter, Philippe C., and Wolfgang Streeck. 1981. "The Organization of Business Interests: A Research Design to Study the Associative Action of Business in the Advanced Industrial Societies of Western Europe." WZB discussion paper IIM/LMP 81–13. Social Science Center Berlin.

——. 1985. "Community, Market, State—and Associations? The Prospective Contribution of Interest Governance to Social Order." In *Private Interest Government: Beyond Market and State*, edited by Wolfgang Streeck, 119–38. London: Sage Publications.

Schmoller, Gustav. 1911. "Volkswirtschaft, Volkswirtschaftslehre und -methode." In *Handwörterbuch der Staatswissenschaft* 9:426–46. Jena: S. Fischer. 3rd ed.

Schneider, Michael. 1975. *Das Arbeitsbeschaffungsprogramm des ADGB: zur gewerkschaftlichen Politik in der Endphase der Weimarer Republik*. Bonn-Bad Godesberg: Verlag Neue Gesellschaft.

Schriewer, Jürgen. 1986. "Intermediäre Instanzen, Selbstverwaltung und berufliche Ausbildungsstrukturen im historischen Vergleich." *Zeitschrift für Pädagogik* 32 (1):69–90.

Schröder, Ernst. 1964. *Otto Wiedfeldt. Eine Biographie*. Essen: Fredebeul & Koenen.

Schulz, Günther. 1985. "Die Entflechtungsmaßnahmen und ihre wirtschaftliche Bedeutung." In *Kartelle und Kartellgesetzgebung in Praxis und Rechtsprechung vom 19. Jahrhundert bis zur Gegenwart*, edited by Hans Pohl, 210–28. Stuttgart: Franz Steiner Verlag.

——. 1991. "Betriebliche Sozialpolitik in Deutschland seit 1850." In *Staatliche, städtische, betriebliche und kirchliche Sozialpolitik vom Mittelalter bis zur Gegenwart*, edited by Hans Pohl, 136–76. Stuttgart: Steiner.

Schütte, Friedhelm. 1992. *Berufserziehung zwischen Revolution und National-Sozialismus: Ein Beitrag zur Bildungs-und Sozialgeschichte der Weimarer Republik*. Weinheim: Deutscher Studien Verlag.

Seligman, Joel. 1995. *The Transformation of Wall Street. A History of the Securities and Exchange Commission and Modern Corporate Finance*. Boston: Northeastern University Press.

Shalev, Michael. 1983. "The Social Democratic Model and beyond: Two Generations of Comparative Research on the Welfare State." *Comparative Social Research* 6:315–51.

Sheard, Paul. 1994. "Interlocking Shareholdings and Corporate Governance." In *The Japanese Firm: The Sources of Competitive Strength*, edited by Masahiko Aoki and Ronald Dore, 310–49. Oxford: Oxford University Press.

Shimizu, Shin. 1939. *Itō Hirobumi no kenpō shirabe to Nihon kenpō*. Tokyo.

Shinkawa, Toshimitsu, and T. J. Pempel. 1996. "Occupational Welfare and the Japanese Experience." In *The Privatization of Social Policy? Occupational Welfare and the Welfare State in America, Scandinavia, and Japan*, edited by Michael Shalev, 280–326. Houndsmills, Basingstoke: Macmillan.

Shinkawa, Toshimitsu, and Haruo Shimada. 1978. "Japan." In *Labor in the Twentieth Century*, edited by John T. Dunlop and Walter Galenson, 241–322. London: Academic Press.

Shirai, Taishiro, and Haruo Shimada. 1978. "Japan." In *Labor in the Twentieth Century*, edited by John T. Dunlop and Walter Galenson, 241–322. London: Academic Press.

Shishido, Zenichi. 1994. "Institutional Investors and Corporate Governance in Japan."

In *Institutional Investors and Corporate Governance*, edited by Theodor Baums, Richard M. Buxbaum, and Klaus Hopt, 665–87. Berlin: Walter de Gruyter.

——. 2000. "Reform in Japanese Corporate Law and Corporate Governance: Current Changes in Historical Perspective." Unpublished paper.

Shonfield, Andrew. 1965. *Modern Capitalism: The Changing Balance of Public and Private Power*. Oxford: Oxford University Press.

Siegrist, Hannes. 1980. "Deutsche Großunternehmen von späten 19. Jahrhundert bis zur Weimarer Republik." *Geschichte und Gesellschaft* 6:60–102.

Siemes, Johannes. 1968. *Hermann Roesler and the Making of the Meiji State: An Examination of His Background and His Influence on the Founders of Modern Japan and the Complete Text of the Meiji Constitution Accompanied by His Personal Commentaries and Notes*. Tokyo: Sophia University in cooperation with Charles E. Tuttle.

——. 1975. *Die Gründung des modernen japanischen Staates und das deutsche Staatsrecht: der Beitrag Hermann Roeslers*. Berlin: Duncker & Humblot.

Singer, Otto. 1990. "Policy Communities and Discourse Coalitions: The Role of Policy Analysis in Economic Policy Making." *Knowledge: Creation, Diffusion, Utilization* 11:428–58.

Skocpol, Theda. 1992. *Protecting Soldiers and Mothers: The Political Origins of Social Policy in the United States*. Cambridge, Mass.: The Belknap Press of Harvard University Press.

Smith, Tony. 1998. "The International Origins of Democracy: The American Occupation of Japan and Germany." In *Democracy, Revolution, and History*, edited by Theda Skocpol, George Ross, Tony Smith, and Judith Eisenberg Vichniac, 191–209. Ithaca, N.Y.: Cornell University Press.

Sohn, Yul. 1998. "The Rise and Development of the Japanese Licensing System." In *Is Japan Really Changing Its Ways? Regulatory Reform and the Japanese Economy*, edited by Lonny E. Carlile and Mark C. Tilton, 16–32. Washington, D.C.: Brookings Institution Press.

Sorge, Arndt, and Malcom Warner. 1986. *Comparative Factory Organization: An Anglo-German Comparison of Manufacturing, Management, and Manpower*. Aldershot: Gower.

Soskice, David W. 1990. "Reinterpreting Corporatism and Explaining Unemployment: Coordinated and Non-Coordinated Market Economies." In *Labor Relations and Economic Performance*, edited by Renato Brunetta and C. Dell'Aringa, 170–211. London: Macmillan.

——. 1995. "Finer Varieties of Advanced Capitalism: Industry-versus Group-based Coordination in Germany and Japan." Unpublished paper.

——. 1999. "Divergent Production Regimes: Coordinated and Uncoordinated Market Economies in the 1980s and 1990s." In *Continuity and Change in Contemporary Capitalism*, edited by Herbert Kitschelt, Peter Lange, and Gary Marks, 101–34. Cambridge: Cambridge University Press.

Spaulding, Robert M., Jr. 1967. *Imperial Japan's Higher Civil Service Examinations*. Princeton: Princeton University Press.

——. 1970. "Japan's 'New Bureaucrats,' 1932–45." In *Crisis Politics in Prewar Japan*, edited by George M. Wilson, 51–70. Tokyo: Sophia University.

Speer, Albert. 1969. *Erinnerungen*. Berlin: Propyläen Verlag.

Staubitz, Richard Louis. 1973. *The Establishment of the System of Local Self-Government (1888–1890) in Meiji Japan: Yamagata Aritomo and the Meaning of "Jichi" (Self-Government)*. Ann Arbor: University Microfilms.

Stein, Lorenz. 1850. *Geschichte der socialen Bewegung in Frankreich von 1789 bis auf unsere Tage*. Leipzig: Wigand.

Stein, Lorenz von. 1887. "Studie zur Reichs- und Rechtsgeschichte Japans." *Österreichische Monatsschrift für den Orient* 1–9.

——. 1964. *The History of the Social Movement in France, 1789–1850.* Totowa, N.J.: Bedminster Press.

Steinmetz, George. 1991. "Workers and the Welfare State in Germany." *International Labor and Working-Class History* 40:18–46.

——. 1993. *Regulating the Social: The Welfare State and Local Politics in Imperial Germany.* Princeton: Princeton University Press.

Stephens, John D. 1979. *The Transition from Capitalism to Socialism.* London: Macmillan.

Stolleis, Michael. 1979. "Die Sozialversicherung Bismarcks. Politisch-institutionelle Bedingungen ihrer Entstehung." In *Bedingungen für die Entstehung und Entwicklung von Sozialversicherung,* edited by Hans F. Zacher, 387–420. Berlin: Duncker & Humblot.

Streeck, Wolfgang. 1988. "Skills and the Limits of Neo-Liberalism: The Enterprise of the Future as a Place of Learning." Discussion Paper FS I 88–16. Wissenschaftszentrum Berlin für Sozialforschung, Berlin.

——. 1991. "On the Institutional Conditions of Diversified Quality Production." In *Beyond Keynesianism: The Socio-Economics of Production and Full Employment,* edited by Egon Matzner and Wolfgang Streeck, 21–61. Brookfield, Vt.: Elgar.

——. 1992. *Social Institutions and Economic Performance: Studies of Industrial Relations in Advanced Capitalist Economies.* London: Sage Publications.

——. 1993. "Klasse, Beruf, Unternehmen, Distrikt: Organisationsgrundlagen industrieller Beziehungen im europäischen Binnenmarkt." In *Innovation und Beharrung in der Arbeitspolitik,* edited by Burkhard Strümpel and Meinolf Dierkes, 39–68. Stuttgart: Schäffer-Poeschel.

——. 1996. "Lean Production in the German Automobile Industry: A Test Case for Convergence Theory." In *National Diversity and Global Capitalism,* edited by Suzanne Berger and Ronald Dore. Ithaca, N.Y.: Cornell University Press.

——. 1997a. "Citizenship under Regime Competition: The Case of the 'European Work Councils.'" *Jean Monnet Chair Papers* 42. European University Institute, Robert Schuman Centre, Florence.

——. 1997b. "Beneficial Constraints: On the Economic Limits of Rational Voluntarism." In *Contemporary Capitalism: The Embeddedness of Institutions,* edited by J. Rogers Hollingsworth and Robert Boyer, 197–219. Cambridge: Cambridge University Press.

Streeck, Wolfgang, and Norbert Kluge. 1999. *Mitbestimmung in Deutschland: Tradition und Effizienz.* Frankfurt am Main: Campus.

Streeck, Wolfgang, and Kozo Yamamura, eds. Forthcoming. *The Future of Nationally Embedded Capitalism in a Global Economy.*

Sumiya, Mikio. 1955. *Nihon chin-rōdō shiron.* Tokyo: University of Tokyo Press.

——. 1970. *Nihon shokugyō kunren hattenshi.* Tokyo: Nihon Rōdō Kyōkai.

Suzuki, Atsushi. 1992. "Teppōkaji kara kikaikō e." *Nenpō kindai Nihon kenkyū* 14.

Suzuki, Yoshio. 1987. *The Japanese Financial System.* Oxford: Clarendon Press.

Swenson, Peter. 1996. "Employers Unite: Labor Market Control and the Welfare State in Sweden and the U.S." Unpublished paper.

Tabata, Hirokuni. 1997. "Industrial Relations and the Union Movement." In *The Political Economy of Japanese Society.* Vol. 1: *The State or the Market?* edited by Junji Banno, 85–108. Oxford: Oxford University Press.

——. 1998. "Community and Efficiency in the Japanese Firm." *Social Science Japan Journal* 1 (2):199–216.

Taira, Koji. 1970. "Factory Legislation and Management Modernization during Japan's Industrialization, 1886–1916." *Business History Review* 44 (1):84–109.

——. 1978. "Factory Labour and the Industrial Revolution in Japan." In *The Cambridge History of Europe* VII, edited by Peter Mathias and M.M. Postan. Cambridge: Cambridge University Press.

——. 1997. "Factory Labor and the Industrial Revolution in Japan." In *The Economic Emergence of Modern Japan,* edited by Kozo Yamamura, 239–93. Cambridge: Cambridge University Press.

Takahashi, Takeshi. 1974. "Social Security for Workers." In *Workers and Employers in Japan: The Japanese Employment Relations System,* edited by Kazuo Okochi, Bernard Karsh, and Solomon B. Levine, 441–84. Princeton: Princeton University Press.

Tamaki, Norio. 1995. *Japanese Banking: A History, 1859–1959.* Cambridge: Cambridge University Press.

Tekkō Kikai Kyōkai. 1974. *Tōkyō Kikai Tekkō Dōgyō Kumiai-shi.* Tokyo: Tekkō Kikai Kyōkai.

Tennstedt, Florian. 1976. "Sozialgeschichte der Sozialversicherung." In *Handbuch der Sozialmedizin,* Bd. III: *Sozialmedizin in der Praxis,* 383–492. Stuttgart: Enke.

——. 1983. *Vom Proleten zum Industriearbeiter. Arbeiterbewegung und Sozialpolitik in Deutschland 1800 bis 1914.* Köln: Bund Verlag.

Teranishi, Juro. 1994. "Loan Syndication in Wartime Japan and the Origins of the Main Bank System." In *The Japanese Main Bank System,* edited by Masahiko Aoki and Hugh Patrick, 51–88. Oxford: Oxford University Press.

Teuteberg, Hans-Jürgen. 1961. *Geschichte der industriellen Mitbestimmung in Deutschland: Ursprung und Entwicklung ihrer Vorläufer im Denken und in der Wirklichkeit des 19. Jahrhunderts.* Tübingen: Mohr/Siebeck.

——. 1981. "Ursprünge und Entwicklung der Mitbestimmung in Deutschland." In *Mitbestimmung: Ursprünge und Entwicklung,* edited by Hans Pohl, 7–73. Wiesbaden: Franz Steiner Verlag.

Thelen, Kathleen A. 1991. *Union of Parts: Labor Politics in Postwar Germany.* Ithaca, N.Y.: Cornell University Press.

——. 1999. "Historical Institutionalism in Comparative Politics." *The Annual Review of Political Science* 2:369–404.

Tilly, Richard H. 1966. *Financial Institutions and Industrialization of the Rhineland, 1815–1870.* Madison: University of Wisconsin Press.

——. 1980. *Kapital, Staat und sozialer Protest in der deutschen Industrialisierung.* Göttingen: Vandenhoeck & Ruprecht.

——. 1986. "German Banking, 1850–1914: Development Assistance for the Strong." *Journal of European Economic History* 15 (1):113–49.

Titmuss, Richard M. 1974. *Social Policy: An Introduction.* London: Allen & Unwin.

Tollkühn, Gertrud. 1926. *Die Planmäßige Ausbildung des gewerblichen Fabriklehrlings in den Metall- und Holzverarbeitenden Industrien.* Jena: Fischer.

Totten, George Oakley, III. 1977. "The Adoption of the Prussian Model for Municipal Government in Meiji Japan: Principles and Compromise." *Developing Economies* 15:487–510.

Treue, Wilhelm. 1951. "Adam Smith in Deutschland: zum Problem des 'politischen Professors' zwischen 1776 und 1810." In *Deutschland und Europa: historische Studien zur Völker- und Staatenordnung des Abendlandes. Festschrift für Hans Rothfels,* edited by Werner Conze. Düsseldorf: Droste Verlag.

——. 1981. "Preußische Wirtschafts- und Technikgeschichte im 19. Jahrhundert." In *Moderne Preußische Geschichte 1648–1947: eine Anthologie,* edited by Otto Büsch and Wolfgang Neugebauer, 1112–40. Berlin: Walter de Gruyter.

Tribe, Keith. 1988. *Governing Economy: The Reformation of German Economic Discourse, 1750–1840.* Cambridge: Cambridge University Press.

——. 1995. *Strategies of Economic Order: German Economic Discourse, 1750–1950.* Cambridge: Cambridge University Press.

Tschierschky, Siegfried. 1913. "Neumerkantilismus und wirtschaftliche Interessenorganisation." *Schmollers Jahrbuch für Gesetzgebung, Verwaltung und Volkswirtschaft im Deutschen Reich* 37:15–47.

Tsutsui, William. 1988. *Banking Policy in Japan: American Efforts at Reform during the Occupation.* London: Routledge.

Turner, Henry Ashby, Jr. 1985. *German Big Business and the Rise of Hitler.* Oxford: Oxford University Press.

Ueda, Kazuo. 1994. "Institutional and Regulatory Frameworks for the Main Bank System." In *The Japanese Main Bank System: Its Relevance for Developing and Transforming Economies,* edited by Masahiko Aoki and Hugh Patrick, 89–108. Oxford: Oxford University Press.

U.S. Department of Commerce, Bureau of the Census. 1975. *Historical Statistics of the U.S.: Colonial Times to 1970.* Washington: U.S. Government Printing Office.

Veblen, Thorstein B. 1915. *Imperial Germany and the Industrial Revolution.* New York: Macmillan.

Vereinigung der Deutschen Arbeitgeberverbände. 1922. *Geschäftsbericht über das Jahr 1921.* Berlin: VDA.

Vitols, Sigurt. 1996. "Modernizing Capital: Financial Regulation and Long-Term Finance in the Postwar U.S. and Germany." Ph.D. dissertation, University of Wisconsin, Madison.

——. 1998. "Are German Banks Different?" *Small Business Economics* 10 (2):79–91.

Vitols, Sigurt, Steven Casper, David Soskice, and Stephen Woolcock. 1997. *Corporate Governance in Large British and German Companies: Comparative Institutional Advantage or Competing for Best Practice.* London: Anglo German Foundation.

Vogel, Barbara. 1983a. *Allgemeine Gewerbefreiheit: die Reformpolitik des preußischen Staatskanzlers Hardenberg (1810–1820).* Göttingen: Vandenhoeck & Ruprecht.

——. 1983b. "Beamtenkonservatismus. Sozial- und verfassungsgeschichtliche Voraussetzungen der Parteien in Preußen im frühen 19. Jahrhundert." In *Deutscher Konservatismus im 19. und 20. Jahrhundert: Festschrift für Fritz Fischer zum 75. Geburtstag und zum 50. Doktorjubiläum,* edited by Dirk Stegmann, B.J. Wendt, and Peter-Christian Witt, 1–31. Bonn: Verlag Neue Gesellschaft.

——. 1988. "Beamtenliberalismus in der Napoleonischen Ära." In *Liberalismus in 19. Jahrhundert: Deutschland im europäischen Vergleich,* edited by Dieter Langewiesche. Göttingen: Vandenhoeck & Ruprecht.

Volkov, Shulamit. 1978. *The Rise of Popular Antimodernism in Germany: The Urban Master Artisans, 1873–1896.* Princeton: Princeton University Press.

Wagner, Karin. 1997. "Costs and Other Challenges on the German Apprenticeship System." Paper presented at the workshop, "Skills for the 21st Century," Institute for Contemporary German Studies, Johns Hopkins University, 10 January 1997, Washington, D. C.

Waszek, Norbert. 1988. *The Scottish Enlightenment and Hegel's Account of "Civil Society."* Dordrecht: Kluwer.

Weber, Hajo. 1991. "Political Design and Systems of Interest Intermediation: Germany between the 1930s and the 1950s." In *Organizing Business for War: Corporatist Economic Organization during the Second World War,* edited by Wyn Grant, Jan Nekkers, and Frans van Waarden, 107–34. New York: Berg.

Wehler, Hans-Ulrich. 1987. *Deutsche Gesellschaftsgeschichte.* Band 1: *Vom Feudalismus des Alten Reiches bis zur defensiven Modernisierung der Reformära: 1700–1815.* München: C. H. Beck.

——. 1995. *Deutsche Gesellschaftsgeschichte.* Band 3: *Von der "Deutschen Doppelrevolution" bis zum Beginn des Ersten Weltkrieges: 1849–1914.* München: C. H. Beck.

Weil, Eric. 1950. *Hegel et l'état. Cinq conférences.* Paris: Vrin.

Weisbrod, Bernd. 1978. *Schwerindustrie in der Weimarer Republic: Interessenpolitik zwischen Stabilisierung und Krise.* Wuppertal: Hammer.

Weiss, Linda. 1998. *The Myth of the Powerless State.* Ithaca, N.Y.: Cornell University Press.

Wellhöner, Volker. 1989. *Großbanken und Großindustrie im Kaiserreich.* Göttingen: Van-denhoecht und Ruprecht.

Westney, D. Eleanor. 1987. *Imitation and Innovation: The Transfer of Western Organizational Patterns to Meiji Japan.* Cambridge, Mass.: Harvard University Press.

White, Eugene N. 1991. "Before the Glass-Steagall Act: An Analysis of Investment Banking Activities of National Banks." *Explorations in Economic History* 23 (1):33–55.

Wickenhagen, Ernst. 1980. *Geschichte der gewerblichen Unfallversicherung. Wesen und Wirken der gewerblichen Berufsgenossenschaften.* München: Oldenbourg.

Willgerodt, Hans, Karl Bartel, and Ullrich Schillert. 1971. *Vermögen fuer Alle: Probleme der Bildung, Verteilung und Werterhaltung des Vermögens in der Marktwirtschaft. Eine Studie der Ludwig-Erhard-Stiftung.* Düsseldorf: Econ Verlag.

Williams, David. 1994. *Japan: Beyond the End of History.* London: Routledge.

Windolf, Paul. 1994. "Die neuen Eigentümer. Eine Analyse des Marktes für Unternehmenskontrolle." *Zeitschrift für Soziologie* 23 (2):79–92.

Winkler, Heinrich August. 1971. "Der rückversicherte Mittelstand: Die Interessenverbände von Handwerk und Kleinhandel im deutschen Kaiserreich." In *Zur soziologischen Theorie und Analyse des 19. Jahrhunderts,* edited by Walter Rüegg and Otto Neuloh, 163–79. Göttingen: Vandenhoeck & Ruprecht.

———. 1972. *Pluralismus oder Protektionismus? Verfassungspolitische Probleme des Verbandswesens im deutschen Kaiserreich.* Wiesbaden: Franz Steiner Verlag.

Wittrock, Björn, Peter Wagner, and Hellmut Wollmann. 1991. "Social Science and the Modern State: Knowledge, Institutions, and Societal Transformations." In *Social Sciences and Modern States: National Experiences and Theoretical Crossroads,* edited by Peter Wagner, Carol Hirschon Weiss, Björn Wittrock, and Hellmut Wollmann, 28–85. Cambridge: Cambridge University Press.

Wixforth, Harald. 1995. *Banken und Schwerindustrie in der Weimarer Republik.* Köln: Böhlau Verlag.

Wixforth, Harald, and D. Ziegler. 1995. "Bankenmacht: Universal Banking and German Industry in Historical Perspective." In *The Evolution of Financial Institutions and Markets in Twentieth-Century Europe,* edited by Youssef Cassis, Gerald Feldmann, and U. Olsson, 249–72. Aldershot: Scholar Press.

Wolsing, Theo. 1977. *Untersuchungen zur Berufsausbildung im Dritten Reich.* Kastellaun: A. Henn.

Yabushita, Shiro, and Atsushi Inoue. 1993. "The Stability of the Japanese Banking System: A Historical Perspective." *Journal of the Japanese and International Economies* 7:387–407.

Yamamoto, Kiyoshi. 1994. *Nihon ni okeru shokuba no gijutsu to rōdōshi.* Tokyo: University of Tokyo Press.

Yamamura, Kozo. 1972. "Japan 1868–1930: A Revised View." In *Banking and Economic Development: Some Lessons of History,* edited by R. Cameron, 168–98. London: Oxford University Press.

———. 1977. "Success Illgotten: The Role of Meiji Militarism in Japan's Technological Progress." *Journal of Economic History* 37 (1).

———. 1986. "Japan's Deus ex Machina: Western Technology in the 1920s." *Journal of Japanese Studies* 12 (1).

———. 1997. "Entrepreneurship, Ownership, and Management in Japan." In *The Economic Emergence of Modern Japan,* edited by Kozo Yamamura, 294–352. Cambridge: Cambridge University Press.

Yasuoka, Shigeaki. 1984. "Capital Ownership in Family Companies: Japanese Firms Compared with Those in Other Countries." In *Family Business in the Era of Industrial Growth: Its Ownership and Management. Proceedings of the Fuji Conference,* edited by Akio Okochi and Shigeaki Yasuoka, 1–32. Tokyo: University of Tokyo Press.

Yokosuka Kaigun Kōshō, ed. 1983. *Yokosuka kaigun senshō-shi* 1. Tokyo: Hara Shobō.

Zöllner, Reinhard. 1990. " 'Appreciating Critic': Lorenz von Steins Japan-Korrespondenz. Auswahl und Kommentar." *NOAG* 147/148:9–74.

——. 1992. "Lorenz von Stein und Japan." In *Lorenz von Stein 1890–1990: akademischer Festakt zum 100. Todestag,* edited by Albert von Mutius, 29–40. Heidelberg: R. v. Decker.

Zysman, John. 1983. *Governments, Markets and Growth: Financial Systems and the Politics of Industrial Change.* Ithaca, N.Y.: Cornell University Press.

Index

Cornell Studies in Political Economy

A series edited by

PETER J. KATZENSTEIN